D0301613

OFFICIAL (ISC)²® GUIDE TO THE ISSAP® CBK®

OTHER BOOKS IN THE (ISC)²® PRESS SERIES

Official (ISC)²® Guide to the ISSAP® CBK®
Harold F. Tipton, Editor
ISBN: 978-1-4398-0093-5

Official (ISC)²® Guide to the ISSMP® CBK®
Harold F. Tipton, Editor
ISBN: 978-1-4200-9443-5

Official (ISC)²® Guide to the CISSP® CBK®, Second Edition
Harold F. Tipton, Editor
ISBN: 978-1-4398-0959-3

CISO Leadership: Essential Principles for Success
Todd Fitzgerald and Micki Krause, Editors
ISBN: 978-0-8493-7943-X

Official (ISC)²® Guide to the SSCP® CBK®
Diana-Lynn Contesti, Douglas Andre, Eric Waxvik,
Paul A. Henry, and Bonnie A. Goins
ISBN: 978-0-8493-2774-1

*Building and Implementing a Security Certification and Accreditation
Program: Official (ISC)²® Guide to the CAP® CBK®*
Patrick D. Howard
ISBN: 978-0-8493-2062-3

Official (ISC)²® Guide to the CISSP®-ISSEP® CBK®
Susan Hansche
ISBN: 978-0-8493-2341-X

OFFICIAL (ISC)²®
GUIDE TO THE
ISSAP® CBK®

Edited by
Harold F. Tipton, CISSP-ISSAP, ISSMP

(ISC)²®

SECURITY TRANSCENDS TECHNOLOGY®

CRC Press
Taylor & Francis Group
Boca Raton   London   New York

CRC Press is an imprint of the
Taylor & Francis Group, an **informa** business

AN AUERBACH BOOK

Auerbach Publications
Taylor & Francis Group
6000 Broken Sound Parkway NW, Suite 300
Boca Raton, FL 33487-2742

© 2011 by Taylor and Francis Group, LLC
Auerbach Publications is an imprint of Taylor & Francis Group, an Informa business

No claim to original U.S. Government works

Printed in the United States of America on acid-free paper
10 9 8 7 6 5 4 3 2 1

International Standard Book Number: 978-1-4398-0093-5 (Hardback)

Library of Congress Cataloging-in-Publication Data

Official (ISC)2 guide to the ISSAP CBK / editor, Harold F. Tipton.
    p. cm. -- ((ISC)2 press series)
  Includes bibliographical references and index.
  ISBN 978-1-4398-0093-5 (hardcover : alk. paper)
  1. Electronic data processing personnel--Certification. 2. Computer
security--Examinations--Study guides. 3. Computer architecture--Examinations--Study
guides. 4. Computer networks--Examinations--Study guides. I. Tipton, Harold F.

  QA76.3.O384 2010
  004--dc22   2010009661

Visit the Taylor & Francis Web site at
http://www.taylorandfrancis.com

and the Auerbach Web site at
http://www.auerbach-publications.com

Contents

Foreword

As the information security industry continues to grow in size, complexity, and specialization, employers are increasingly in search of qualified individuals who possess the knowledge, skills, and abilities that demonstrate proven capabilities and subject-matter expertise beyond that required for the CISSP® credential. Just as those pursuing academic degrees in broad subject areas often choose to narrow their focus with specialized study, so too are information security professionals.

Those who specialize in security architecture play a key role with responsibilities that fit between the C-suite/upper management levels and the implementation of the security program. Responsible for developing, designing, or analyzing the overall security plan, they not only need an understanding of multiple aspects of IT from a technical, developmental, and implementation perspective, they must also understand how the proper application of security protocols can help an organization safely meet its goals, improve productivity, profitability, and efficiency.

Security architecture requires a firm grasp of the organization's business strategy and an ability to assess the value of security investments in terms of the returns they bring and the opportunities they enable. Delivered successfully, effective security architecture allows both business and IT strategies to drive each other and can be one of the key means to achieving competitive advantage.

As the only credential designed for the advanced security architecture professional that focuses on high-level security for enterprise-wide systems and infrastructure, the CISSP-ISSAP® is appropriate for Chief Security Architects, analysts, and others who often work as independent consultants or in similar capacities within an enterprise.

(ISC)² is pleased to offer the first *Official (ISC)²® Guide to the ISSAP® CBK®*. This book will review and deepen your knowledge of security architecture, covering each of the six domains contained in the CISSP-ISSAP CBK. We believe you will find this book helpful in your pursuit of the CISSP-ISSAP certification and as a reference guide throughout your career.

W. Hord Tipton, CISSP-ISSAP, CAP, CISA
Executive Director (ISC)²

ISSAP® Introduction

Security architecture can be defined as the process of creating and maintaining the information security structure of an enterprise to ensure the confidentiality, integrity, and availability of critical and/or sensitive business systems. It follows, then, that the security architect is the individual that is responsible and qualified to perform the functions necessary to accomplish security architecture goals. To be considered a professional security architect, it is necessary to delve much deeper into the elements that must be understood and employed to perform that role. ISSAP® certification is intended to measure and evaluate the ability of an individual to be accredited as a professional in this demanding field.

Some believe that the concept of security architecture is relatively new. Actually, however, it had its genesis with the development of the Open System Interconnection (OSI) by NIST, which started in 1978 and continued into the early 1990s. It became an ISO/IEC standard (7498) in 1984 and is defined as a seven-layered model of network architecture. It also identified the security types and mechanisms that were intended to be implemented at each layer(s). While it failed to overtake the lead obtained by the DoD model (TCP/IP) and actually become the worldwide standard, some of its protocols (e.g., X.400 Message Handling and X.500 Directory Services) have survived.

It is interesting to note that during the early 1980s when organizations asked their information security function to identify the security architecture, many simply mapped the installed security mechanisms to the existing network structure and called that the security architecture. While this did show where specific security mechanisms were employed throughout the organization, they merely reflected what evolved over time rather than describing the results of a well thought out and thoroughly planned security structure that could be explained and justified. To accomplish the latter, the security architect must begin with a comprehensive requirements analysis; obviously, it is not possible to construct a valid architecture without identifying what needs to be protected and at what level of protection. Then, the architect must understand the currently available architectures to enable the selection of a structure that best fits the culture and risk appetite of the organization. A thorough understanding of the several architectural views is then necessary to ensure that the final product is complete. These include the enterprise security architecture and its subsets: physical security architecture, network security architecture, application security architecture, and system security architecture.

CISSP®-ISSAP® CBK has been developed to encompass all of the knowledge elements needed to create security architecture. It consists of six domains: Requirements Analysis, Access Control, Cryptography, Physical Security, BCP/DRP, and Telecommunications and Network Security.

The topics included in the Requirements Analysis domain include

- Risk analysis, data valuation, business requirements (legal and regulatory)
- Current architectures
- Architectural solutions
- System engineering methodologies
- Design validation

The Access Control domain covers topics related to

- Access control concepts
- Access control architecture
- Access control administration
- Design validation

The topics contained in the Cryptography domain involve

- Cryptographic principles (applications and methodologies)
- Key management
- Public key infrastructure
- Design validation

In the Physical Security domain, the topics addressed are

- Unauthorized access and facility protection
- Physical security plans
- Design validation

The BCP/DRP domain consists of topics related to

- Business impact analysis
- Recovery strategy
- Plan validation

The Network and Security Architecture domain includes the topics of

- Voice and facsimile communications
- Network architecture
- Network security
- Network security design considerations
- Security configuration development
- Design validation

The candidate for CISSP-ISSAP professional certification will demonstrate a thorough understanding of these topics and the ability to apply them to develop a detailed security architecture for an enterprise that meets all requirements. Although most of the topics included in the CISSP-ISSAP CBK are also found in the CISSP CBK, the ISSAP must be able to translate an in-depth knowledge into a comprehensive, well-structured architecture.

The security architecture profession is relatively new and is rapidly growing. It should prove to be not only challenging but very rewarding as well.

Hal Tipton

About the Authors

Alex Golod, CISSP, is a senior security consultant with 29 years of experience for one of the Fortune 100 IT firms. He has focused the last 12 years of his career on information security. Alex's many responsibilities include architecture, engineering, and operations of security solutions. His broad area of expertise covers application, network and data security, as well as risk analysis and mitigation.

Dr. Paul Baker, CPP, is a security manager with more than 30 years of extensive experience in all phases of law enforcement and industrial security. He holds a Doctorate in strategic leadership from Regent University, along with a Master of Science in criminal justice from Troy University, and is a Certified Protection Professional (CPP). Dr. Baker spent 6 years in the U.S. Marine Corps and has retired from the Maryland State Police. Dr. Baker is currently employed as a senior security manager for one of the top ten banks in the Washington, D.C. area. Dr. Baker is also an adjunct professor, teaching homeland security parttime for the University of Maryland University College and security management for Southwestern College.

Robert B. Batie, Jr., CISSP-ISSEP, ISSAP, ISSMP, CISM, CAP, has over 20 years of experience in communication security and information assurance. He is a senior principal systems engineer at Raytheon NCS, in St. Petersburg, FL. He is a Raytheon Author, Inventor and Technical Honoree, as well as a contributing author for the *Official Guide to the CISSP-ISSEP CBK*. He has published articles in the *CSI Journal, Alert Newsletter* and presented at Raytheon symposiums, the CSI Conferences, and the International Biometric Conference. He is an active member of (ISC)².

Bob has a Master of Science in computer systems management from the University of Maryland and is currently working on a Ph.D. at Nova Southeastern University.

Gilbert Held graduated from Pennsylvania Military College with a B.S. in electrical engineering; he also has earned an MSEE degree from New York University and an MSTM and M.B.A. from The American University. He spent 27 years in the U.S. Army and retired as a Lieutenant Colonel. Gil was the Chief of Data Communications for the U.S. Post Office of Personnel Management for 20 years. He also designed, acquired, and constructed the OPM's Web presence and received the Directors Award for his efforts.

Gil has written over 100 technical books that have exceeded over a million copies, over 500 technical articles on personal computing and data communications and business, and taught 14 different graduate level courses. He has also served as the editor-in-chief of the Wiley *International Journal of Network Management* and was selected by the Vice President of the United States to represent the United States at the Jerusalem Conference on Information Technology.

Mark J. Makowski, CISSP-ISSAP, is a security architect who has worked in IT for more than 29 years. A graduate of Lawrence Technological University, Mark began his career as a field engineer at Burrough's Corporation in the early 1980s. In the mid-1990s, Mark began engineering tools to help secure UNIX servers for EDS customers. Since then, Mark has been responsible for developing security architectures across a broad range of technologies and industries. Currently, he is helping engineer enterprise services security offerings at a technology company operating in more than 170 countries around the globe. Mark is a member of the Motor City Chapter of ISSA.

Kelley Okolita is a principal consultant and director of business continuity and disaster recovery for Hanover Insurance in Rhode Island. She built a new contingency program that costs less than industry peers. Within the first year she also renegotiated a hostile vendor contract saving the firm $500,000 annually and reducing the recovery timeline by 80% for time-sensitive applications and added business recovery capabilities.

Kelley has also held key roles in Fidelity Investments as director of risk management, where she was responsible for the recovery and business contingency efforts for roughly one third of the business operations and previously as director of corporate contingency planning. While in this role, Kelley spent 9 weeks in New Jersey supporting the recovery efforts of Fidelity's New York operations from the events of September 11th.

She joined Fidelity in 1976 and has more than 20 years of experience in disaster recovery and business contingency planning from both a data center perspective and business perspective. Through the years she has supported a number of business recoveries, both large and small. Kelley is an MBCP (Master Business Continuity Planner) and is a member of the board of directors for Disaster Recovery Institute International.

Sean M. Price, CISA, CISSP, is an independent security consultant and researcher in northern Virginia. Over the last 15 years he has specialized in designing and evaluating organizational information assurance programs and system security architectures. His research interests include access control, insider threat, information flows, and applications of artificial intelligence to information assurance problems. Sean's prior publications include book chapters for the *Information Security Management Handbook* series and the *Official (ISC)² Guide to the CISSP CBK*. A number of his articles and papers have appeared in peer-reviewed journals and conference proceedings. Industry publications include the *IEEE Computer Magazine, ISSA Journal, IA newsletter*, and *ISACA J-Online*. You can reach him at sean.price@sentinel-consulting.com.

Chapter 1

Access Control Systems and Methodology

Sean Price

Contents

The Access Control Systems and Methodology domain details the critical requirements to establish adequate and effective access control restrictions for an organization. Access control protects systems, data, physical infrastructure, and personnel in order to maintain their integrity, availability, and confidentiality.

Failure to design, develop, maintain, and enforce access control will leave an organization vulnerable to security breaches. This applies to all types of breaches, whether they are locally or remotely initiated. It is imperative that you, as a security professional, understand the types of controls available, current technologies, and the principles of access control.

The security professional is also expected to apply both the hard and the soft aspects of access control, including controls provided through physical controls, policy, organizational structure, and technical means. You should also be able to demonstrate an awareness of the principles of best practices in designing access controls. Key areas of knowledge include the following:

- Control access to systems and data through understanding and applying access control concepts, methodology, and techniques
- Control techniques and policies
- Access control administration
- Identification and authentication techniques
- Credentialing architecture
- Design validation

Introduction

In the very early days of DOS, users did not have the benefit of logical access controls. Large mainframe systems had some form of access control, but users of the personal computer (PC) did not. Information was stored on floppy disks because most people could not afford the newfangled 10 MB hard drive. Besides, who would ever need that much space anyway? As long as a user could boot the computer and manage to cram the applications and data into the 600 or so kilobytes of memory space, all was well. Individuals made decisions about who could use their data by physically restricting access to the floppy disk. People did not necessarily trust everyone borrowing their stuff so, occasionally, copies were created or that little notch in the disk was covered to make it read-only. This allowed for some discretion on how someone else accessed the precious files. If the file was returned corrupted, then blame could easily be fixed. This was good enough for most users. Organizational members sharing the same PC did not concern themselves about the activities of the person who last used the PC.

Eventually, some creative programmers, later referred to as hackers, began to make software that would play pranks on users. Some of their antics involved moving characters around on the screen, displaying strange messages, or worse, attaching little programs to every executable file until the system abruptly halted. During this same period, the concept of distributed computing began to emerge and compete with mainframes and minicomputers. Soon, users were able to share and access files over a local area network. People began to rely on network storage, and it quickly became apparent that some rudimentary security was needed. Vendors began implementing logical access control in the networked operating systems as a way to secure data from mischievous programmers and their annoying creations. It also helped organizational members protect their data from other insiders with malicious intent. The integration of logical access control appeared to be a great way to control access to data. Certainly, it was superior to managing floppy disks because it was automated.

The implementation of access control in most environments has not changed much over the years. Access decisions are often left to the discretion of the information owner. Instead of covering the notches on floppies, access control lists are used. The availability of files stored on the network is ensured through backups. This represents the last line of defense against maliciously altered or deleted files, much the same as creating an extra floppy disk before passing it along to a co-worker. Automation of these previously manual controls does not entirely protect data from tampering or loss. Access controls must be properly set, otherwise information may be inappropriately copied or removed. Backups must be periodically checked to make sure that all target files were archived. Human interactions with these and other elements of a system can result in losses when activities are not conducted properly.

Automation of access control is also a double-edged sword. It does have benefits such as allowing a single individual to control access to a multitude of resources. However, the access and control an individual has can also be misused. Malicious code executing in the context of users can seriously impact the confidentiality, availability, and integrity of their resources. The design and implementation of access controls within a system must consider that the controls ultimately must be useable by humans, but also provide additional measure to detect, prevent, and correct undesirable resource access.

Access Control Concepts

Security architects are interested in access control because it has desirable attributes that can preserve our critical information. Similar to how individuals jealously guarded floppy disks, systems with logical access controls watch over important information. These desirable attributes of logical access controls can

- Protect resources from loss or exposure
- Provide accountability for those accessing the information or system

Arguably, the primary purpose of access control is to protect information from losses and exposure. This is accomplished through techniques that merge the attributes of actions between users and the information within a system. Access control occurs when rules are used to control the type of access a person has to a given resource. Essentially, access control is a way to discover

- *Who* is accessing the information?
- *What* is being accessed?
- *How* might the access occur?

Knowing the answers to these questions are prerequisites for basic access control functionality. These questions are associated with a particular security policy governing actions within a system. This aids in the identification of subject's actions on objects with respect to the permissions and rights granted according to a particular security policy. Some definitions follow:

- *Subject*—The person, entity, or process in question. It is the *who* in access control.
- *Objects*—A resource such as a file, device, or service. This is the *what*.
- *Permissions*—The type of access a subject is given. Common permissions include read, write, modify, delete, and execute. This describes *how* a *who* is permitted to interact with *what*.
- *Rights*—Special abilities granted to a subject. For example, an administrator has the right to create accounts, while ordinary users do not. This has policy influences over the interactive *who*, *what*, and *how* questions of the access control mechanism.

The combined usage of subjects, objects, permissions, and rights forms the foundation of a system's access control. A security architect must strive to implement access control that conforms to the security policy of a system. Figure 1.1 illustrates access control flow for subjects requesting specific objects. In the diagram, the access control system first determines if the subject has the appropriate rights to access the object. If the subject possesses the correct rights, then a subsequent check determines if the subject has sufficient permissions to view or manipulate the object.

Access control coupled with auditing establishes the basis for accountability. Auditing is the process of recording access control actions and is the principal method used to achieve accountability. Reviewing the actions of subjects on

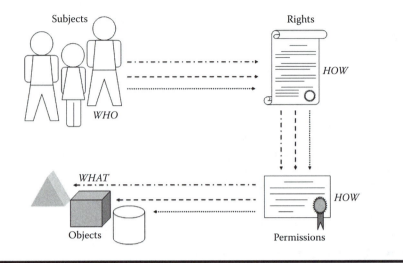

Figure 1.1   Interaction between subjects, rights, permissions, and objects.

particular objects helps managers to determine if inappropriate activity occurred. Figure 1.2 shows how an access control mechanism is used to audit successful and failed access. In the diagram, Alice makes a request, noted by ①, to read Doc_A. The Access Control mechanism compares the request ② from Alice with the Access Control List (ACL) for Doc_A. The ACL indicates that Alice has the permission to read the document. The Access Control mechanism creates an entry in the Audit Log ③ and allows Alice access to the document ④. Bob also requests access to Doc_A ❶. The Access Control mechanism determines through the Doc_A ACL ❷ that Bob

Figure 1.2   Access control support for auditing.

has no permission to the document. The Access Control mechanism creates an audit log entry ❸ of Bob's failed request and informs him that access is denied ❹.

Access control is the fundamental mechanism that provides for the confidentiality, integrity, and availability of information within an information technology (IT) system. Confidentiality is supported by only allowing access to a particular object for those entities that are explicitly authorized. Granular-level stipulations on how an entity can interact with a particular object can be used to ensure the object's integrity. The combined services of confidentiality and integrity help ensure that an object is available to those who are authorized access. Access control enables

- *Confidentiality*: Through measures that protect objects from unauthorized disclosure
- *Integrity*: By preventing unauthorized modifications when properly implemented
- *Availability*: When integrity is properly enabled

The ability of an access control mechanism to provide the desired security services is predicated upon the correct implementation of a security policy. A system should be governed by a written standard that specifies the rules applicable to the system. These rules are derived from

- Laws
- Regulations
- Industry standards
- Organizational policy

The compilation of rules applicable to a particular IT system forms the security policy. Ideally, the security policy addresses managerial, operational, and technical security requirements for a system. A system security policy can be viewed as a structure, such as the one depicted in Figure 1.3. Confidentiality, integrity, and availability establish the foundation of a security policy. Rules formed by laws, regulations, standards, and policy are the primary pillars supporting the policy. It is interesting to note that most rules exist for the purpose of establishing accountability for entry and activity within the system. The rules impart managerial, organizational, and technical controls that make up the foundation of the system security policy. More often than not, access control in an IT system represents the bulk of the technical security within the security policy. The interpretation of the correct access control implementation of the security policy is the responsibility of the security architect, based on the direction of the data owner.

Interpreting security policy is not a trivial matter. If the policy is written in terms that are too general, it might have multiple interpretations or at least give rise to implementation issues. Suppose a security policy contains the statement "Users are not allowed to access information for which they are not authorized." Does this mean

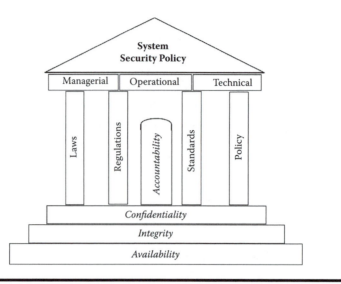

Figure 1.3   System security policy structure.

if someone shares sensitive information with them that they are now authorized? The sharing might contradict some other part of the policy. If the sharing violates another part of the policy, does this mean that the system is flawed? What if someone saves sensitive information into a directory accessible by users not authorized to view the information? If some of these users view the sensitive information, does this mean they violated the policy or that the system failed to properly enforce the policy? Indeed, these issues arise on a daily basis and are not easily defined or enforced.

At first glance, it might seem that access control is more of an art than a science. This is true to some extent, but considerable science underlies access control. Much of the science is based on mathematical theories and formulas. Computer scientists continually dwell on the intricacies of access controls and strive to improve these techniques. The main issue with access control implementation is the art of interpreting security policy. A security architect needs to understand some of the science behind access control in order to integrate it with the world of abstract thought representative of security requirements. The art of implementing access controls involves the merging of a logical system, which is rigid in structure, with that of an organization, which is dynamic, amorphous, and not likely to have policies that are discrete to the point of being mathematically sound. Security architects must anticipate these issues and make interpretations based on their understanding of the organization, intent of the security policy, and the capabilities of the IT in which the access control is considered.

The art of interpreting security policy is at its core an attempt to balance requirements against available controls. Consider Figure 1.4, which shows the balancing task that a security architect faces to achieve the ideal security policy. The correct balance between requirements and controls is neither too weak nor restrictive. On the one side, interpretation of requirements must consider the intent of policy. An

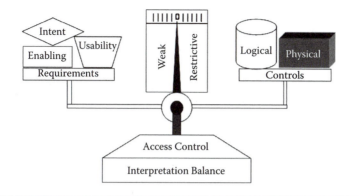

Figure 1.4 Balancing access control.

absolute interpretation of policy could be insufficient to provide sufficient coverage or so pervasive as to be prohibitively expensive. The controls selected should not prevent the organization from accomplishing its mission. Rather, controls selected based on the requirements should enable the organization to continue routine operations. Finally, controls should be usable, otherwise they will likely be circumvented by system users.

The mechanisms of access control can be found in a variety of products and at multiple levels within an IT system. The more common products implementing access control include

- *Network devices*—Routers, switches, and firewalls
- *Operating systems*—Linux, Unix, and Windows
- *Database management systems*—Oracle, MySQL, and SQL Server
- *Applications*—Certificate authorities, encryption software, and single sign-on products

Do certification authorities implement access control? Well, sort of. It is more correct to say that certification authorities *support* access control. What about encryption software? Actually, when an object is encrypted, unauthorized users are denied access to the cleartext information. This has the same effect as not being allowed permission to read an object. In reality, single sign-on products do not implement access control either. However, they do *facilitate* the integration of disjoint access control systems. This reduces the user and management headaches often experienced when switching between systems or components with different access control mechanisms.

Access control at the network level tends to be more connection oriented, such as allowing or disallowing ports and protocols associated with given IP addresses. Typically, an access control mechanism is limited to the box itself. Most commodity operating systems provide some form of access control by default. At this level, an access control mechanism is sometimes shared among workstations and servers in a network. However, this is not always the case for every commercial operating system. Many databases provide capabilities to control access to the data they contain. In some cases, a database management system might also be able to distribute access control functionality among distributed systems, in much the same way as some operating systems.

Some applications contain their own access control mechanisms, which might be as simple as allowing or denying access based on presenting acceptable credentials or a robust access control mechanism similar to those found in an operating system or database. Unfortunately, these various access control mechanisms, more often than not, are proprietary and do not integrate easily with one another. This situation complicates the job of the security architect. Furthermore, the variety of access control mechanisms also compounds the problem of trying to determine at which layer or level in the network to enforce the security policy. For instance, if a security policy prohibits the use of unauthorized protocols, should this be enforced at the operating system only or should it also include all routers and switches? The security architect will need to make judgments about the depth and breadth of access control implementations to meet the security policy. Figure 1.5 illustrates many different access control methods and techniques that can be applied to the various layers of the Open System Interconnectivity (OSI) model.

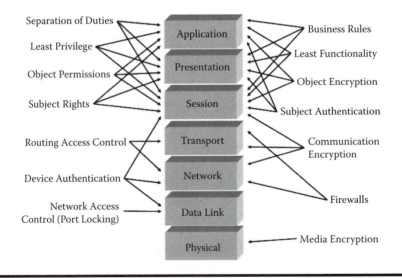

Figure 1.5 Access control within the OSI model.

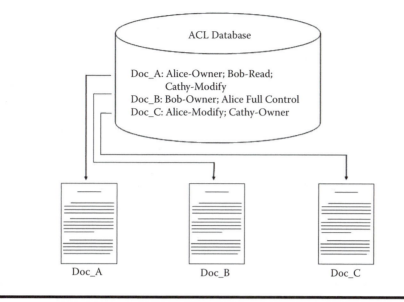

Figure 1.6   ACL database.

A variety of access control techniques and policy mechanisms exist. It is interesting to note that many of the access control techniques are designed to implement a particular type of policy. This means that a particular access control technique might not be the best choice in a given circumstance. Unfortunately, commercial-off-the-shelf (COTS) products do not typically provide a method of selecting an access control technique ideal for a particular paradigm. This requires the security architect to make a particular type of access control mechanism fit as best it can when a more desirable mechanism is not available.

Two important features of access control mechanisms are the access control list (ACL) and the ACL repository. The ACL identifies the security attributes of a particular system object. Typically, this will include information about the object owner and other entities having authorized access associated with the rights granted to each entity. Each subject identified in an ACL is known as an access control entry (ACE). The ACL repository is used to manage each ACL in the system. Figure 1.6 illustrates these access control features.

Discretionary Access Control

Discretionary access control (DAC) is the predominant access control technique in use today. Most commodity systems implement some form of DAC. The underlying concept of DAC is to give an object owner the discretion to decide who is authorized access to an object and to what extent. In this regard, the policy is set or controlled by the owner of a particular object. At its most basic level, DAC implementations include the specific rights to read, append, modify, delete, and execute. The read permission allows a designated entity the ability to load the contents of an object into memory. The permission to append allows an entity to attach new information to the end of an object. Permission to modify an object means an entity can change any and all of the contents of an object. Entities with the permission to delete can destroy an object and cause it to be removed from volatile or nonvolatile memory. The execute permission gives an entity the ability to cause the system to create a new process or thread of execution based on the binary nature of the object.

Implementing DAC can give rise to security problems if the mechanism is not well understood or if it is used contrary to its design. There are three important aspects of DAC that must be understood and questioned by the security architect:

■ *Read*—What does it mean?
■ *Write*—What are the implications?
■ *Execute*—What is running on the box?

Although these aspects are essential elements of DAC, they can reveal apparent flaws in the access control mechanism.

It is essential to understand that the read permission does not mean read-only. It really means read-and-copy. Any subject with the permission to read a file can also make a copy of the same file. This frequently occurs during the reading process. When an application reads a data file, it makes a copy of the contents in memory. Because the user of the application owns the memory space where it is copied, the application user essentially creates a new copy of the data file. Thus, the entity provided with the permission to read a particular data file is now the owner of a copy of the same file. This functionality of DAC potentially empowers an attacker bent on information theft. Thus, read permission may complicate insider threat mitigation efforts.

The difficulty of limiting access to information is shown in Figure 1.7. In this illustration, Bob has permission to read Doc_A. Bob's ACE only allows him to read the document from the disk device that is owned by the system. When Bob reads the document, a copy of it is created on his local system in an area of memory over which he has full control. Bob is now the owner of the new document copy. At this point Bob can do what he wants with any portion of document. He could make copies of any section and send it to an output where he has the appropriate permission.

The next important aspect that must be considered is permission to write. Giving an entity the ability to write to a file object allows it to write anything to that object. "Anything" could include a virus, appended to the end. Another problem with this permission is that an entity could also replace all of the data in a file with one byte of information. Suppose a document file includes charts, graphs, and over a megabyte of text. The malicious entity could simply perform an overwrite, causing a multimegabyte file to shrink to one byte in a microsecond. This is similar to having the ability to delete a file. The implication of the permission to write is

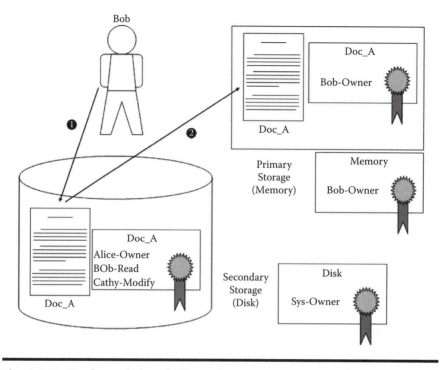

Figure 1.7   Read permission challenge.

that object integrity can be affected. Inappropriate granting of the write permission has far-reaching and potentially devastating consequences.

Yet another troubling issue with the ability to write is when the object in question is a directory. Writing to a directory essentially means a subject is allowed to create a new object. In this case, entities with the ability to write to a directory can create any type of object in that directory, with ownership permissions on the newly created object. Consider the situation in Figure 1.8. In this example, Bob can create an exact copy of Doc_A in the same directory by using a new unique name, in this case Doc_D. As the new owner of the object, Bob could grant others access to the document, which may violate organizational policy.

A malicious entity may choose to write objects that are binary executables to any permitted directory, according to the subject's write permission. Even though an entity might not be given execute permissions for the directory object, this is not a hindrance because the object owner can change any inherited permissions on the new object from the directory to anything he or she likes.

The third significant DAC consideration is the execution permission. More specifically, it is essential to understand the concept of the context of an executing process. When an entity executes a process, that process typically has access to all objects available to the entity. A program executed by the user has access

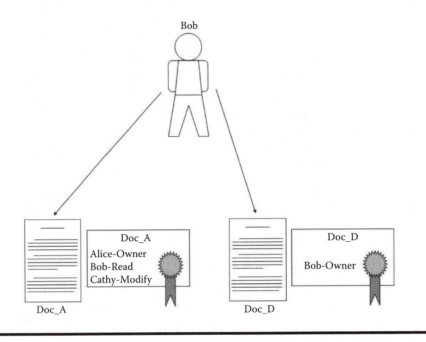

Figure 1.8   Write permission problem.

to all files, interfaces, and other programs running in their context. Typically, an operating system does provide some memory separation between running processes. However, interprocess communications as well as graphical interfaces open avenues for one process to affect the execution of another. This feature of DAC is what gives a Trojan horse the ability to steal information or damage a system. This problem with DAC is well known and studied. Although researchers have proposed a variety of solutions to this problem, their solutions have not seen widespread commercial adoption.

Although the aforementioned problems seem to be flaws in the design of DAC, they are more essentially issues that arise due to implementation errors of the mechanism. The security architect should take proactive measures to overcome the shortcomings of DAC, which will reduce any risk that might be present. Some strategies for implementing DAC follow.

DAC Implementation Strategies

Overcoming the challenges of the read permission is a difficult task, but mitigations are possible. The efforts of a security architect will require technical and nontechnical techniques. The following points identify some approaches to consider:

■ *Limit access to essential objects only.* Ensure user access to resources is restricted to only that which they need for the performance of their duties. Giving more

user access than users need will make it more difficult to re
ized movement of information.

- *Label sensitive data.* Use file- and folder-naming conventions, a
  and footers within documents that provide users with visual
  sensitivity of the information. Extended attributes of a file might also provide an
  area to include label information of a file. For instance, the Summary Properties
  of a file within Windows include editable values such as Title, Subject, Category,
  Keywords, and Comments that can be used to store label information.
- *Filter information where possible.* Use filters on e-mail or other mechanisms to
  detect inappropriate transfers of sensitive information.
- *Promulgate guidance that prohibits unauthorized duplication of information.*
  Policies and procedures should inform users about the types of information
  that require protection, limited distribution, or replication. Provide users
  with periodic training and guidance reminders.
- *Conduct monitoring for noncompliance.* Use tools to quickly search files containing sensitive information or labels in repositories where they should not
  exist. The Windows Explorer Search tool and the grep utility in Unix are
  useful for finding particular words or phrases within a file.

Controlling write actions is essential to protect information and system integrity. Preventing unauthorized modification of resources is the primary means of
controlling system integrity. Why do viruses have such a field day with a system?
Excessive permissions on configuration settings and files allow the virus to write to
or delete critical files. Implementing the most restrictive permissions, such as read
or no access, would prevent a virus from writing to important objects. Consider the
access control list displayed in Figure 1.9 for explorer.exe.

This is a common security setting in many Windows systems. In fact, it is a
recommended setting found in various security configuration publications. Is there
a problem with it? Unfortunately, the answer is yes. The trouble with this ACL is
that the integrity of the file is not protected in the context of the System or any
user in the Administrators group. Malicious processes executing in either context
could either attach a virus to explorer.exe or associate a backdoor with the program.
Furthermore, the file could also be deleted altogether. So much for availability as
well! The ACL should specify the Read permission for System and Administrators
as well. So why would many publications recommend an ACL such as this? It is
believed that the reason for this ACL recommendation is because it allows updates
to binaries to be made on the fly. It supports the Windows Update process and
simplifies life for administrators too. The weak ACL eases file level administration. This is a prime example of a trade-off between security and simplicity. It is
challenging to meet both these goals simultaneously because there are thousands
of executables in a given Windows box. Does an alternative exist? Instead of living
with the weak ACL, it is desirable that an automated process be instituted as a sup-
portive measure. Assume that a file system is initially configured with a strong ACL

Figure 1.9 Commonly recommended permissions for explorer.exe.

(read permission for all subjects). Fortunately, the means to alter the restrictive setting to a more relaxed ACL before and after a file update exists. Microsoft provides the cacls.exe tool, which can be scripted to handle ACL and ACE changes for any file. Here is a quick way to solve this problem.

Just before conducting a system update, run the following from the command line:

```
C:\cacls *.exe /t /e /p administrators:f system:f
```

This command instructs cacls.exe to edit the ACL for each executable in the C:\ drive, including subdirectories, and change the ACE for the Administrators group and the System account to full control. This will allow changes to any executable file on the C:\ drive. When the system update is complete, execute the following at the command line:

```
C:\cacls *.exe /t /e /p administrators:r system:r
```

This edits the ACL for each program on the drive and reduces the Administrators group and the System account to read, which restores the most appropriate settings.

Consider using these commands on other important binary files such as ActiveX controls, libraries, drivers, screensavers, and applets. The primary caveat is that ACL changes must be coordinated with updates, whether via Microsoft Update or some other tool. It is important to note that this example of cacls.exe use disregards inheritable directory permissions. However, this tool does give the capability to accommodate those permission settings too. As with any new security management technique, it is important that testing be conducted first to ensure that the most appropriate configuration is achieved.

> Encouraging users to make use of access control mechanisms can help limit loss of data due to malicious code. Owners of shared files, such as word processing documents, should be set to the ACE for all other subjects to read-only. Applying this philosophy will prevent other users from accidentally (or unwittingly, when compromised by malware) deleting a document shared by someone else. Promoting the least privilege would serve the user community well by avoiding the restoration of accidentally (or maliciously) deleted files.

Although the discussion has centered on securing binary files, the importance of securing other objects should not be dismissed. Appropriate access control settings should be established for all resources within a system. The following are a few more objects for which write permission is advised to be restricted:

- *Configuration files*—Any file used to store configuration information should be set to read-only where updates are not routine actions.
- *Windows registry*—Lock down system registry keys to read-only. This is especially important for the Run keys, which designate software to execute at boot. Run keys are a primary target for malware.
- *Services*—If a service is not needed, it should be disabled. If particular users do not need a service, then they should be prevented through the ACL from interacting with it.
- *Data*—Follow the concepts of least privilege and separation of duties when assigning permissions to data files.

Solving the execute problem with DAC is by far the most important measure. The execution of unauthorized processes can threaten the integrity of user context, or worse, that of the entire system when the context is that of an administrator or the system itself. The best approach to this problem is to apply restrictive access controls to existing executables and monitor for unauthorized access instances. The following is a list of recommended approaches:

■ *Set access control entries for all executable binary files to read-only.* This helps to protect their integrity. Examples of Windows-based executables, libraries, and other specialized binaries that should be set to read-only include those with the following extensions: com, exe, scr, dll, tlb, ocx, drv, sys, vxd, cpl, hlp, and msc.

■ *Prevent execution from removable media.* Prevent applications from automatically running from removable media. Where possible, implement tools and other settings that can prevent programs running from removable media.

■ *Use host-based firewalls.* Set the policy to explicitly identify which programs are allowed to connect to the network. Ensure that the associated policy file or registry entries are set to read-only using DAC.

■ *Conduct software integrity inventories.* Use tools such as Tripwire to identify unauthorized changes in programs, and validate the integrity of those that are authorized.

■ *Monitor executions.* Consider implementing specialized tools that can keep an audit of software running on a machine. This can be used to identify users violating policy or malware not detected by antivirus monitoring.

Nondiscretionary Access Control

Access control mechanisms that are neither DAC nor mandatory access control (MAC) are referred to as forms of nondiscretionary access control. These types of access control still rely on the fundamental concept of subjects, objects, and permissions. However, the association or specifications of these elements are different from DAC and MAC. It is interesting to note that nondiscretionary access control mechanisms are more similar to DAC than to MAC.

■ *Role-based access control* (RBAC)—It is desirable to limit individuals to only those resources that are needed to support their duties. Ideally, an access control mechanism would be able to ensure that the assignment of privileges to a particular resource does not introduce a conflict of interest or issue with separation of duties. This can be achieved when user access is controlled according to assigned job function or role. RBAC is a specialized access control mechanism providing this capability. The unique quality of RBAC is that rights and permissions are ordered in a hierarchal manner. In a business world implementation, RBAC allocation of rights and permissions will descend from an office head through subordinate job functions. Privileges on resources are mapped to job functions. This prevents an object from being shared with those not authorized, which might violate separation of duties.

■ *Originator controlled* (ORCON)—An information owner may desire to control the life cycle of certain types of information. Some of the desired control might concern how long the information remains available or who is allowed to view it. The United States military makes use of ORCON designations in paper documents that direct readers not to disseminate the information without the express consent of the originator (McCollum, Messing, Notargiacomo, 1990). Recently, researchers have begun to consider electronic methods to implement this type of control.

■ *Digital rights management* (DRM)—Controlling access to intellectual content is an emerging issue. Intellectual content such as music, movies, and books need methods to control who is authorized to access these types of content. Clearly, DAC is of no use in controlling the unauthorized distribution of these types of information. Additionally, DRM must have portability features because a user might want to access the protected content from different systems or platforms. DRM relies on cryptographic techniques to preserve the authenticity and access to protected information. Researchers are also investigating the use of multilevel security policies to improve DRM resistance to attackers (Popescu, Crispo, and Tanenbaum, 2004).

■ *Usage controlled* (UCON)—Another problem associated with protecting intellectual content involves frequency of access. Suppose a video store desires to rent access to its movies, but wants to limit the ability of consumers to only view each rental a maximum of three times. DRM techniques provide measures that attempt to control who can access the content, but they do not control how often. Addressing the "how often" issue will establish the ability to license the frequency of access to protected content. UCON is one technique currently being investigated by researchers to control the frequency of access to protected content (Park and Sandhu, 2004).

■ *Rule-based access control*—A number of different devices and applications provide their own type of access control mechanism in which decisions are made based on some predetermined criteria. These mechanisms use rules to decide if an action is permitted or denied. Rule-based access control tends to be extensively used, but it is not scaleable. Firewalls, routers, virtual private network (VPN) devices, and switches are examples of products using rule-based access control.

Authentication is an important aspect of rule-based mechanisms. Subjects of a rule-based mechanism are usually identified as human users or system activity. People authenticated with rule-based access control often use passwords or cryptographic proofs such as a digital certificate. Authentication of system activity relies on operational aspects such as media and network addresses as well as cryptographic proofs. For example, a firewall enforces authentication decisions based on network addresses.

Rules developed for this type of access control can be complex. DAC makes determinations based on access control lists as opposed to rule-based access control, which evaluates activity. For example, a firewall may evaluate a network connection based on the address, port, and protocol used. This is a much more complicated evaluation than evaluating a subject's access to a particular object in DAC.

Permissions in rule-based access control are simplistic binary decisions. Either access is allowed or it is not. If the rule is met, then the action is allowed. This is in contrast to DAC, where a degree of access can be permitted, for example, read, write, or modify.

It is important to note that MAC is sometimes referred to as a rule-based access control (Bishop, 2003). It is differentiated within this text because the implementation and functionality of MAC contrasts significantly with other devices and applications that employ rule-based mechanisms.

Mandatory Access Control (MAC)

An organization may have many different types of information that need to be protected from disclosure. The United States government has identified three particular classes of information that require integrity and unauthorized disclosure countermeasures due to the level of harm that their exposure might cause to the country. These classes in ascending hierarchal *sensitivity* are Confidential, Secret, and Top Secret. All other types of information are considered unclassified and must be protected according to other policies. Suppose an individual is granted a *clearance* to access Secret information. Such a person could view any Secret information, as well as Confidential information, when he has an appropriate need to know. However, he would not be allowed to access Top Secret information, because his clearance is lower than the sensitivity designation of the classified information. MAC was devised to support the concept of access based on a subject's clearance and the sensitivity of the information. The fundamental principles of MAC prevent a subject from reading up and writing down between classifications (Bertino and Sandhu, 2005).

MAC functions by associating a subject's clearance level with the sensitivity level of the target object. It is important to note that systems supporting MAC implement DAC as well. The key to the proper functioning of MAC is the use of specialized labels on each system object. The label specifies the highest classification for the particular object. The system protects the labels from alteration. A subject must have a clearance equal to or greater than the sensitivity of the target object. Furthermore, the system relies on DAC methods to determine if the subject has been granted the permission to interact with the object. Figure 1.10 illustrates the association between clearance, sensitivity levels, and the use of DAC. In the figure, Alice interacts with the system at the Secret level. Although she is the owner of a document within each sensitivity level, MAC prevents reading to higher levels and writing to lower. This aspect of MAC prevents the flow of information from a higher classification to one that is lower.

The important feature of MAC is its ability to control information flows. Subjects with higher clearances are permitted to read information at a lower classification level. Thus, a subject with a Secret clearance is permitted to access information at the Confidential level. However, MAC prevents a subject with a Secret clearance from writing information to an object at the Confidential level.

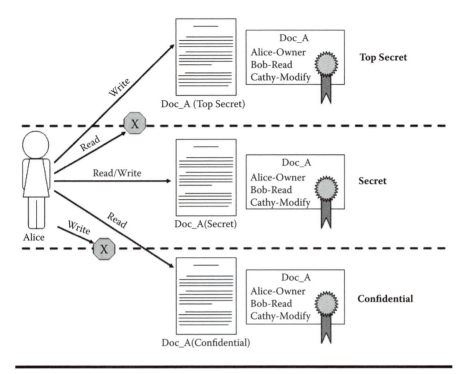

Figure 1.10 Classifications and sensitivity levels in MAC.

This restriction of writing to a lower classification level prevents the accidental or intentional flow of information from a higher classification to a lower classification. This helps protect against policy violations or unauthorized exposures of the information to those without a need to know. Obviously, a subject with a lower clearance cannot read objects with a higher classification, but they are permitted to write information to a higher classification. This has the somewhat interesting consequence that a user can write information up, but will have no way to reread what was written. One might humorously consider this a type of access-controlled amnesia. Figure 1.11 is another way to view the read and write properties of MAC regarding clearance and sensitivity.

Suppose a manufacturing organization desires to use MAC as a way to protect its proprietary products. Manufacturing of proprietary products involves many people along the way, but not everyone needs to be aware of every step. Separate classifications are established based on the life cycle of a product based on materials used, fabrication techniques, and experimental improvements. Given these scenarios, three classifications for our hypothetical manufacturing company are proposed:

- *Development*—Those involved in research and development of new products
- *Processing*—Individuals involved in the proprietary assembly of the components
- *Components*—Ordering and storage of the base components

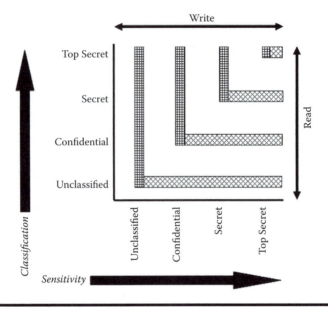

Figure 1.11   Sensitivity, classification, reading, and writing matrix of MAC.

Figure 1.12 describes the interaction between the classification levels and product life-cycle activity. In this example, subjects who order the base components have no idea about quantities used to create a particular product, because they write the quantity from their components classification to the processing classification. Similarly, they have no comprehension of the processing and development activities the components are involved in. Those involved in processing consume select components to create different products depending on the particular process used. Processing is prevented from reading the quantities used for development. The output from processing is not accessible by those with a components clearance, but it is available to those with the development clearance. Workers in the development arena create experimental processes and consume various components to devise new products. The experimental output in the development classification is not accessible by those with a processing or components clearance.

Least Privilege

Generally, individuals are opposed to people probing their personal information. Most individuals prefer to keep their compensation and medical information private. Many think of this type of information as personal and thus sensitive. Consider an organization that does not restrict access to personnel records. Given a lack of access control, anyone browsing through the records could obtain privacy-protected information or information on compensation. This may be an

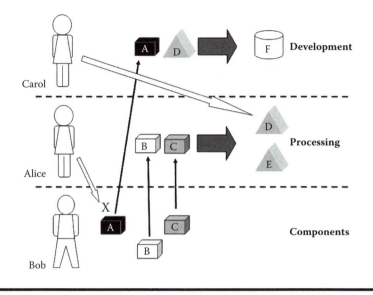

Figure 1.12 Use of MAC in a business environment.

extreme case, but what if compensation information is limited to only the people in the finance department? This is better, but is insufficient. Should the people who receive payments, also known as accounts receivable, from customers also have access to an individual's salary information? This is obviously unnecessary as the job function of people working in accounts receivable has nothing to do with payroll. As such, one would expect an appropriate use of the concept of least privilege to be implemented, preventing accounts receivable personnel from browsing payroll information. Limiting access to sensitive information is the crux of information security.

Implementing least privilege implies that an individual has access to only those resources that are absolutely necessary for the performance of his duties. This is, of course, an elegant statement, but in practice, implementation is fraught with difficulties. More commonly, the access granted is typical of what is seen in Figure 1.13. It is evident from the figure that the user is granted rights and permissions beyond what is needed to conduct his tasks. Why does this occur? Some of the reasons for this could be

- *Lack of explicit definition of duties*—Neither the user nor manager has a clear grasp or definition of the duties assigned to the individual.
- *Weak internal controls*—Where explicit duties are known, changes in duties or access controls on the system may not be periodically reviewed for conflicts.
- *Complexities in administration*—In very large, distributed organizations, it is difficult to know the access limitations that should be imposed when access control is centralized.

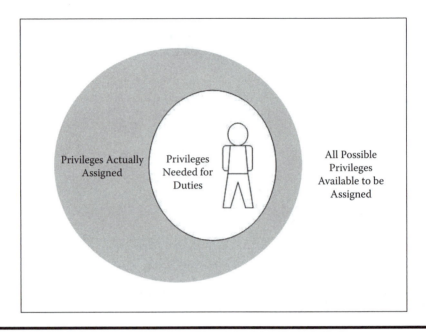

Figure 1.13 Common misallocation of privileges.

Thus far, the complexities of least privilege, from the aspect of information access, have been considered, but are there considerations that extend beyond information? Assume that an organization has a centralized database containing sensitive information. Does it seem reasonable that each database user is allowed to have database administrator rights? This scenario would most likely violate least privilege because users would have the ability to easily access information outside of the scope of their duties. If the duty of a database user does not include administration functions, then following the concept of least privilege, a user would not be provided database administrative rights.

Another factor to be considered is access to system resources. Should a user be given access to all network resources? Suppose the sales team, as shown in Figure 1.14, has wireless access into the network. Assume that they require wireless access because they rely heavily on their laptops as their primary computing platform. The finance department is contemplating whether to connect its new laptops to the network using wired or wireless access. Does it seem reasonable that users in the finance department should also be allowed the ability to connect to the wireless access point? It is doubtful that the individuals in the finance department have a business need to connect to the wireless access point. Given this perspective, preventing their ability to connect to the wireless access point and reverting to wired access would follow the concept of least privilege.

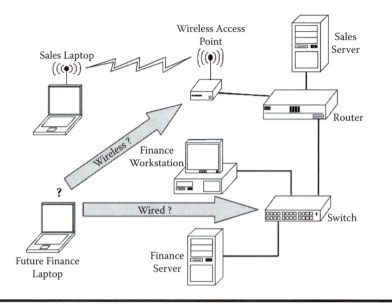

Figure 1.14   Least privilege dilemma in network resources.

Least Functionality: A Cousin of Least Privilege

Limiting access to resources is fairly straightforward. If an individual needs to run a tool, then access to the tool should be allowed. However, some tools contain *functionality* that can be damaging. In some cases, an acceptance of risk is necessary given the need to use the tool. When possible, the functionality of a tool should be reduced to mitigate actual or potential risk.

Consider the issue of phishing. A user receives an e-mail from what appears to be his or her personal banking institution. The message claims that the account password must be updated or access to the account will be lost. The "phishy" part is a hyperlink to the individual's bank. Some uneducated users will click, while wise ones will not. Protecting unsuspecting or uninitiated users from these types of attacks can be accomplished through simplistic measures. Many e-mail clients provide the capability to display plaintext information, excluding the rich or hypertext content. Configuring the e-mail client to display only plaintext exemplifies the application of least functionality. The sacrifice is a loss of aesthetically pleasing e-mails, but the gains in preventing individuals from unwittingly facilitating own identify theft are substantial.

A security architect must consider design issues related to least privilege. Ideally, a system will provide technical methods for enforcing least privilege. The use of access control mechanisms will be the architect's primary method to design in the ability to implement least privilege. Consider the following techniques to implement least privilege:

- *Access control lists*—Use network- and system-based access controls to allow or deny access to network resources.
- *Encryption*—Using cryptographic measures for network traffic prevents surreptitious gathering of information that a user is not authorized to access.

Nontechnical measures should also be implemented to support least privilege. Although an architect may not be responsible for these aspects, they should be promoted and considered nonetheless:

- *Define data and associated roles*—Sensitive data requiring least privilege implementations should be identified. Data owners should explicitly identify the individuals or roles that are authorized access to the information.
- *Sensitive data-handling procedures*—Rules on the use of data exiting the system should be explicitly identified. Data is commonly moved from systems through removable media, electronic sharing, and printing. Policies should establish acceptable circumstances and methods of transferring sensitive data. Ideally, procedures will also explicitly identify the best methods to securely transfer information.
- *User education*—All users handling sensitive media should be made aware of the proper methods used to handle the information. They should be instructed on how to identify transfers of information that might violate least privilege. Obviously, the necessary tools used to facilitate secure transfer should be available for their use.

A security architect following the concept of least privilege designs a system that limits resources to only those subjects who require access in the performance of their duties. Resources of concern include files, devices, and services. Access control and encryption are two techniques that can be used to enforce least privilege. User role identification, data sensitivity, and user education are important factors supporting least privilege implementations.

Separation of Duties

One way to enforce accountability is through techniques that prevent a single individual from circumventing internal controls. Suppose Mr. Alexander is allowed to make purchases for Glasnost Enterprises. He orders 153 ACME widgets. We assume Mr. Alexander is allowed to sign for the receipt of the products. Upon receipt, he modifies the paperwork to reflect an order and receipt of 100 ACME widgets. Glasnost is none the wiser about the 53 widgets pocketed by Mr. Alexander. This situation occurred due to a lack of separation of duty. Conceptually, separations of duties preclude an individual from perpetrating a fraud. With sufficient separation, a single person should not have the ability to violate policy undetected. From a system security standpoint, separation of duty is necessary to ensure accountability for actions taken in the system. Weaknesses in separation of duties are identifiable by the excessive assignment of system privileges, which could allow an individual to perpetrate fraud and avoid detection.

Every person within an organization has at least one role. Ideally, all roles within an organization are discrete, which means that every role is unique. It is also desirable for every individual to be assigned to only one role. However, this is seldom the case, especially when there are staffing shortages. It is also common to see multiple people in the same role. The goal of separation of duties is to prevent the perpetration of fraud. To meet the goal of separation of duties requires confidence that the rights and permissions assigned to subjects are correct, without conflicting overlaps between roles.

A role is nothing more than a job function within the organization. The duties assigned to individuals define their role. Ideally, they are assigned tasks that do not involve a separation of duties issue. An individual's role fits into the patterns of activity supporting the mission of the organization. Some of the patterns will involve workflows consisting of tasks that link together. An example of workflow is the assembly line seen in Figure 1.15. Each station on the line adds components or makes modifications until a final product emerges at the end. The tasks and duties of each worker are naturally segregated by the workflow process of the assembly

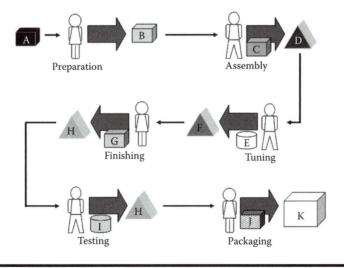

Figure 1.15 Assembly line work.

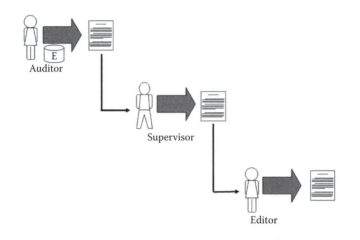

Figure 1.16   Document workflow.

line. Thinking in these terms regarding security in information systems, the security architect can find ways to build in segregation of duties into organizations as well.

Does the assembly line paradigm of the Industrial Age apply to the Information Age? It does, if we consider workflows within an organization that generate information as the output. Consider the work of an information systems auditor. A high-level overview of the job role entails

- Enumeration of system requirements
- System assessment against requirements
- Report of findings and recommendations

Think about what the reporting aspect of the role might involve. After assessing a system, auditors must compile a document for perusal by the management staff. A conjectural document workflow of this process is presented in Figure 1.16. Some organizations use tools that facilitate or even define the type of process seen in the figure.

The diagram depicts the auditor generating a report that is intended for review by a supervisor. The document is sent to a technical editor, who makes final adjustments for style and grammar. The final document is then delivered to the customer. This simplistic workflow involves three people with a single document. There are three very different roles—that of an auditor, supervisor, and technical editor—involved in the workflow. All three persons have access to the same data, but their duties are quite different. From this perspective, it is evident in what respect document management is similar to assembly line work. Therefore, following the paradigm of workflows in a system is helpful when defining individual user roles.

A system does not define the role of a person. Even when workflow tools are used, it is important to realize that people often have other tasks outside of a system. So how can job duties or roles be used to identify separation of duties within a system? This can be

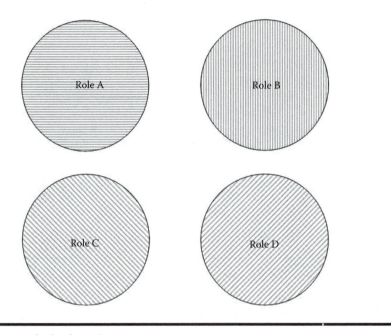

Figure 1.17   Ideal role assignments.

accomplished by establishing the necessary separation between the combined rights and permissions granted to subjects. In this regard, a role is composed of the following:

- *Rights*—The type of actions an individual is permitted to make in the system
- *Permissions*—Access granted to information shared or used in job-related workflows

The discussion thus far suggests that a role is the aggregate of a subject's rights and permissions. Figure 1.17 presents an ideal situation, in which subject roles work together, but do not overlap. This example epitomizes the perfect separation of duties situation.

Reality is less than ideal. In fact, it can be quite challenging to match reality to the ideal implementation. In practice, it can be difficult to determine the exact rights and permissions an individual needs for the job. Ensuring separation of duties becomes a more difficult issue when people are assigned multiple roles, when there is greater potential for conflict. Figure 1.18 shows us the unfortunate reality of separation of duties. The overlap between roles indicates that one role has excessive rights or permissions compared to those of another.

A broad observation can be made regarding the relation between rights and permissions. Those assigned elevated rights in a system should have less permission to data involved in workflows. This is necessary because those with elevated rights can potentially compromise confidentiality, integrity, and availability of workflows. Having

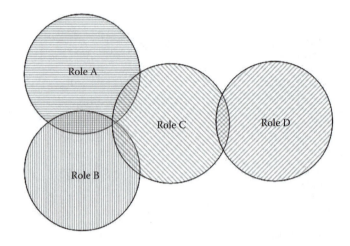

Figure 1.18   The challenge of role assignments in reality.

this ability could enable an individual to perpetrate a fraud. Consider a scenario with the following roles which, incidentally, are common within many organizations:

- *Developer*—Individuals within this role are responsible for developing or maintaining applications for organizational users. Their creativity enhances the usefulness of an information system. They should not have access to the production system.
- *Administrator*—This role ensures the system is available for organizational use. Administrators are commonly tasked with managing user accounts and resources. Their duties do not ordinarily require access to or manipulation of sensitive organizational information. However, their powers of access into the system are such that they can be fairly characterized as minor deities.
- *Security Officer*—Monitors system for misuse. Individuals in this role commonly review audit logs and the output from security tools such as those used for intrusion detection and vulnerability assessments. They are the information assurance sentinels tasked with protecting a system's security services.
- *Ordinary User*—It is most likely that this role will span a plethora of subordinate roles where one type of user is separated from another. Users are the primary consumers and manipulators of organizational data. An information system exists primarily to connect ordinary users with the data they need to perform their assigned duties.

Assume that these roles are mutually exclusive; that is, a user in one role should not have the ability to perform the functions of another role. This represents an ideal implementation of separation of duties. Now, suppose that weaknesses in the assignment of separation of duties occur, as shown in the following tables.

Table 1.1   Inappropriate Roles Assigned to a Developer

Conflicting Role	*Potential Violation*
Administrator	Can circumvent most, if not all, security controls through software changes such as the deployment of a malicious driver acting as a root kit.
Security Officer	Security events generated by malicious software deployed would be ignored. Developers in this capacity would be checking their own work and could easily cover up a fraud.
Ordinary User	With this level of access, a developer could create a covert channel allowing access to unauthorized information.

As a general rule, developers should not have access to a production system. When this rule is followed, separation of duties is not an issue. However, when the conflicting roles shown in Table 1.1 are coupled with a disregard of the aforementioned rule, problems can occur. If a developer is assigned conflicting roles, a situation is created in which data theft or system disruption becomes possible, and it will be difficult to track violations.

By default, an administrator has the ability to access the most sensitive information within a system. A corrupt administrator has the potential to cause significant damage or expose a substantial amount of data. The substantial degree of access associated with this role necessitates a commensurate degree of monitoring. However, when this role is inappropriately merged with other roles seen in Table 1.2, it becomes possible for administrators to avoid critical monitoring.

Security officers are primarily concerned with monitoring and enforcement of a system security policy. In this regard, there should be little or no interaction with data workflows in the system outside the scope of their duties. Providing a security officer with additional abilities shown in Table 1.3 would make it difficult to detect

Table 1.2   Inappropriate Roles Assigned to an Administrator

Conflicting Role	*Potential Violation*
Developer	This has the same effect as a developer given administrator rights. It is absolutely the worst possible violation of the principle of separation of duties.
Security Officer	Administrators with this role would be checking their own work and could easily cover up security violations generated through monitoring activity.
Ordinary User	If granted ordinary user access, administrators might be able to bypass monitoring activity specifically designed to identify administrator abuse.

Table 1.3 Inappropriate Roles Assigned to the Security Officer

Conflicting Role	Potential Violation
Developer	Access violations due to malicious software developed by the security officer would be covered up.
Administrator	Changes in accounts or system policies might go unnoticed, and most likely unreported.
Ordinary User	Attempts to access unauthorized information would not be reported.

Table 1.4 Inappropriate Roles Assigned to an Ordinary User

Conflicting Role	Potential Violation
Developer	A user could craft specialized code allowing backdoor access into the context of other system users.
Administrator	User could change workflow data with this level of privileged access.
Security Officer	Violations made by the user could be covered up or disregarded.

their fraudulent activity. Corrupt security officers given excessive privileges would most likely be able to hide their activity.

The focus of the role of an ordinary user is to facilitate a job function as a workflow. The primary tasks involve the creation, manipulation, and consumption of system data. The assignment of conflicting roles as seen in Table 1.4 would enable ordinary users to either perpetrate a fraud or prevent their malicious activities from being detected.

The previous scenario suggests an intuitive method of separating duties for individuals accessing a system. An initial separation determination based on the job function of an individual is possible with respect to the system. An individual with management or operational influence on the system should have reduced interaction with system data. In this regard, there are two broad categories that can be used as the initial basis for separation of duties:

- *Individuals responsible for operational aspects of the system*—Within this area, duties are further decomposed according to their functions which might enable circumvention of accountability.
- *Those primarily interacting with system data and information workflows*—Users are separated according to the type of data they interact with.

Security design efforts should consider various aspects that could affect separation of duties. At a minimum, it should be possible to enforce separation of duties

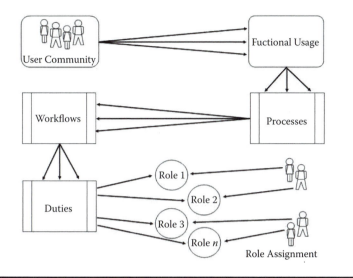

Figure 1.19   Decomposition of user community into roles.

through the user access control mechanisms whether the designation is manual or automated. A system should have sufficient administrative flexibility to accommodate the following aspects:

■ *Identify each explicit role*—Decompose all system use and management functions using a process similar to that shown in Figure 1.19. From there, examine each function and consider if further decomposition is needed to ensure appropriate separations to support workflow processes. Collect users into groups or roles according to the access control supported by the system. Attention should be given to disjoint access control. This occurs when multiple access control systems exist that do not share information. It is necessary that tracking of user grouping between the various access control systems be coordinated to avoid separation of duty issues. Document the process used to arrive at the segregations for repeatability purposes. The results of the segregations should also be documented.

■ *Assign appropriate permissions*—Be aware of ways in which a role may violate segregation of duties (SoD). For each grouping, consider the rights necessary for users to accomplish their tasks. Within a system, rights may be cumulative. A user assigned multiple roles may end up with excessive rights. One way to counteract this scenario is to assign a user a specific account with properly separated rights.

■ *Avoid unnecessary rights*—When privileges are cumulative, ensure excessive access is not inadvertently granted.

■ *Mitigate workflow violation potentials*—Consider situations in which an identified role might be able to affect a workflow outside.

Organizations with constrained resources will find it difficult to fully achieve separation of duties. This is especially true in organizations with a small staff. In these cases, it is common to find that an individual is assigned to multiple roles. This situation makes separation of duties difficult to achieve. However, the following techniques can be of some assistance to help identify potential fraud:

- *Assign accounts on a per-role basis*—An individual should have a separate account for each role used. The rights corresponding to separate roles should be separated to the greatest extent possible.
- *Prevent those with multiple roles from reading and writing to the same storage area*—Where possible, prevent an individual with multiple roles from writing information with one role into an area that could be read by another role. Ideally, the permissions for the roles should be mutually exclusive.
- *Auditing is vital*—Consider implementing object-level auditing for individuals with multiple roles. Identify key areas where abuse might occur, and implement multiple methods to monitor for violations.
- *Conduct more frequent evaluations*—Use external system auditors and more frequent internal audits of the system to ensure that all controls are functioning properly. Audit workflows to assess any improper activity.

As stated earlier, the primary purpose of separation of duties is to ensure that an individual is unable to perpetrate a fraud and simultaneously avoid accountability. However, separation of duties can also be a tool used to identify omitted job functions. Various system-related duties and organizational workflows require particular elements that must be filled by an individual to ensure a particular task is completed in its entirety. When a key element of a task is missing, it might cause a critical process to fail at an inopportune time. Missing task elements create a gap in separation of duties. Consider the following scenario depicted in Figure 1.20. In this situation, suppose one administrator is assigned to manage operating systems, and another administrator is tasked with managing networking equipment. The system contains a Linux box running a firewall application at one of the network borders. The operating system administrator views the firewall as a network device because it is functioning as a network device. In contrast, the network administrator views the firewall as an operating system because it is built with commodity hardware and software. Neither has taken management responsibility of the firewall. This represents a gap in separation of duties.

Evaluating separation of duties involves identification of inappropriate and insufficient assignment of rights and permissions related to subject roles in a system. A security architect must consider all of the possible duties within a system and ensure that appropriate separations are identified and that capabilities exist for proper enforcement. An evaluation of separation of duties will look for

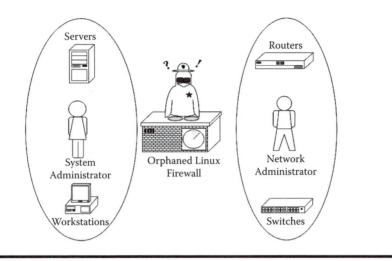

Figure 1.20   The orphaned Linux firewall.

■ *Overlaps*—The assignment of roles that conflict with one another. Overlaps can be identified by considering the rights and permissions assigned to any given account with that of another, where the two accounts should have distinct roles. Where it is possible for a fraud to be perpetrated, another role should exist that can detect abuse.

■ *Gaps*—Roles should be designed to accommodate all operational aspects of the system and organizational workflows processed. Aspects of system management and workflows that orphan critical tasks represent gaps in separation of duties. Unassigned or abandoned tasks can potentially jeopardize the security services of a system.

It is interesting to note the complementary nature of least privilege and separation of duties. Much like the components of the bridge shown in Figure 1.21, the functional aspects of these security principles influence one another. Least privilege is necessary for the proper functioning of separation of duties. Without least privilege, it is not possible to provide separation of duties. Excessive assignment of rights or permissions violates the concept of least privilege and can provide an avenue to exploit a weakness in separation of duties. The misalignment of duties, in the case of an overlap, suggests that one role is in possession of too many privileges. Overlaps in duties violate least privilege. Thus, harmony between least privilege and separation of duties is achieved when rights and permissions are properly balanced in support of the system security services.

Ideally, the design of a system allows easy implementation of separation of duties. However, this is often not the case, and the security architect must consider design aspects that will provide the necessary assignment of rights and permissions

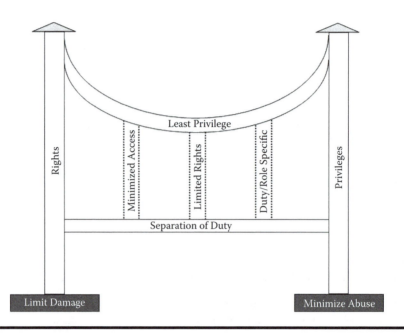

Figure 1.21   The mutual influence of least privilege and separation of duties.

while preventing a role or individual from concealing a fraud. Assigning individuals to multiple roles is a common practice fraught with the possibility of inadvertent violation of separation of duties. The totality of a subject's access should be compared with all other subjects to identify overlaps and gaps. Overlaps violate separation of duties, while gaps represent orphaned aspects of critical tasks that may result in a security control weakness.

Architectures

The design of the security functions for a system should support its security policy. A well-designed system will be capable of making the necessary access decisions. Ideally, the system will fully support a defined security policy. In reality, access control systems are often capable of supporting a subset of the security policy. Nontechnical methods such as procedures and other operational aspects must be relied on to ensure that a security policy is met. To the greatest extent possible, the technical functions in a system should be designed to automate support for the security policy.

An architect must consider in what manner a subject should be allowed to access which objects in the system. A security kernel and the security reference monitor act as the electronic gatekeepers for the system by mediating a subject's access to authorized objects. The security monitor mediates object requests from the subject. Each request is provided to the reference monitor, which determines if the request

Figure 1.22 The trusted computing base.

is allowed and what degree of access should be permitted. Joint operations of the security kernel and reference monitor should be established to support the system security policy. In this way, a subject will be allowed or denied access according to the security policy enforced by the security kernel and reference monitor.

The security of an entire system depends on the joint properties of the controls implemented; that is, the security of a system is the sum of its collective security mechanisms. All of the technical security controls in a system are collectively referred to as the trusted computing base (TCB). In this regard, the overall security of a system is no stronger than the most vulnerable components of the TCB. Figure 1.22 provides an illustration of common components that comprise the TCB of most enterprise systems.

A security kernel is the collection of components of a TCB that mediate all access within a system. It is important to note that a security kernel may be centralized or of a distributed nature. For instance, a router with access control capabilities has a self-contained security kernel. In contrast, a distributed system that implements a domain security model relies on the proper operation of different devices and operating systems. It is collectively recognized as a security kernel. Because it is responsible for mediating access requests, it is a choke point in the system. Any failure in the security kernel will affect the supported system. Ideally, components of a security kernel are not complicated and made up of a small amount of code. This allows for easier analysis to identify any flaws that might be present. The integrity of the security kernel's components is absolutely critical. The architect should make

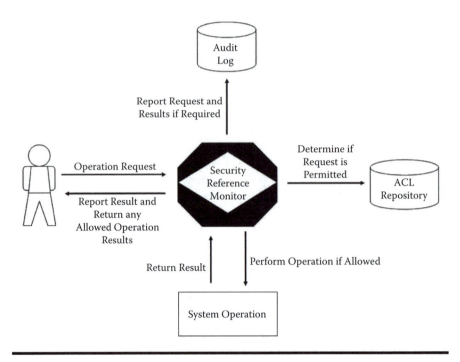

Figure 1.23 Functional aspects of a security reference monitor.

every effort possible to prevent unauthorized modifications to the kernel as well as provide mechanisms to monitor for any malicious changes.

The most common functions of the security kernel include authentication, auditing, and access control. The operational aspect of the security functions is referred to as the security reference monitor. Generally, the security reference monitor compares an access request against a listing that describes the allowed actions. Figure 1.23 provides a brief overview of a security reference monitor.

Authentication, Authorization, and Accounting (AAA)

One might recognize the acronym AAA as an organization to call upon within the United States if your automobile becomes disabled. However, AAA has an entirely different meaning in the world of cyber security. The acronym refers to Authentication, Authorization, and Accounting. In fact, it is supported by RFC 2904, which specifies an authorization framework for using AAA. The term is heavily used to discuss the access control mechanisms built into networking equipment and repeated to a large extent within many IETF RFC documents.

The design of access control within a security architecture is driven by system usage and requirements. In some cases, it is necessary to retain tight centralized management of the access control mechanisms. In other cases, a distributed or decentralized technique is best employed to meet organizational needs. Enabling access control between systems from collaborating organizations requires yet another approach, which is considered a type of federated access control. The differentiating factor among the potential architectures is the point where an access control decision is made.

Centralized Access Control

An access control system that is centralized relies on a single device as the security reference monitor. Authorization and access control decisions are made from the centralized device, which is referred to here as the access control server (ACS). This means that login as well as resource access requests are handled in one place. Figure 1.24 describes the fundamental processes and decisions that centralized access control systems follow. There are three architectural approaches to achieving centralized access control. Each method conforms to the generic concept of centralized access control as seen in Figure 1.24. However, the approaches are differentiated in the way each handles client resource requests.

One approach to centralized access control is for the ACS to proxy client resource requests. In this case, the ACS accesses resources on behalf of the client.

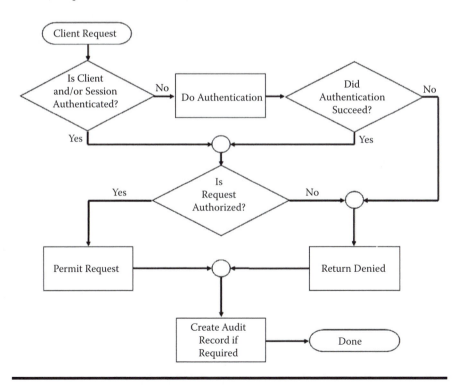

Figure 1.24 Flowchart of centralized access control.

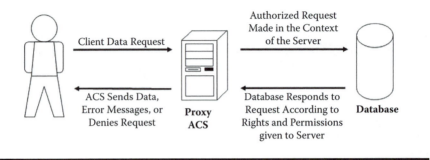

Figure 1.25 Proxy access control system.

Figure 1.25 depicts centralized access control using a proxy methodology. This approach is commonly used in Web portals and database management systems (DBMSs). The front end to the portal or DBMS evaluates requests according to the permissions and rights of the subject and manipulates data based on the request. This approach tightly couples permissions on particular objects, but does not scale well. Permitting access via other protocols or to resources outside of the scope of the authentication server may involve substantial development effort.

The approach illustrated in Figure 1.26 shows client resource requests by way of a gatekeeper mechanism. Conceptually, the ACS allows or disallows client access to

Figure 1.26 Centralized access control using a gatekeeper.

Figure 1.27 Centralized access control with credentials.

network resources. Similar to a guard working a perimeter gate, it allows or denies traffic according to the rights and permissions allocated to the subject. A firewall with an integrated authentication mechanism is an example of a centralized access control device using the gatekeeper approach. This type of approach is primarily used to control access to resources and services at particular locations within the protected network. Generally, it lacks the ability to control granular-level access to resources. This is frequently the case when different proprietary solutions are used for access control and resource availability within the system. For instance, a firewall may allow externally authenticated individual access to a particular file server, but it might not be able to limit which directories are accessed.

The previous approaches to centralized access control exert communication dominance over the client. The ACS by proxy or traffic direction prevents the client from attempting to communicate with resources outside of the bounds established by its rule sets and permissions. A different concept is to allow clients to roam freely in a network, but requests for resources are validated with the ACS before access is allowed. An authenticated subject is given a temporary credential that is used to identify him or her within the network. This approach, shown in Figure 1.27, has a scalability quality greater than that for the approaches previously mentioned. Subjects requesting a resource from a server submit their credential as a proof of who they are. The server with the requested resource verifies the requested access with the ACS. If the credential is authentic and the subjects have the appropriate permissions, then access to the resource is allowed.

Advantages of ACS include the following:

■ *Single point of management*—Accounts, permissions, and rights are centrally managed. Having all of the security attributes in the same device simplifies access control management.

■ *Audit log access*—A centralized access control mechanism also places the heart of the audit logging process in one location. This makes it easier for security and administrative personnel to access and manage the logs.

■ *Physical security*—A device centralizing access control provides the opportunity to incorporate additional physical security measures promoting confidentiality and integrity. The access control device can be placed in a physically segregated area restricted to only those who are granted administrative access to the device.

Disadvantages of ACS to consider are the following:

■ *Single point of failure*—The unavailability of a centralized access control mechanism would prevent access to authorized resources. Localized network and power disruptions may prevent geographically dispersed users from accessing resources. Software or hardware failures in the device itself could also disrupt operations.

■ *Single point of compromise*—An attacker successfully compromising the device may be able to grant themselves access to all protected resources. Alternatively, an attacker might be able to compromise the authentication information and subsequently masquerade as the authorized users, thus hiding the nefarious activity.

■ *Capacity*—The device itself can be a limiting factor in centralized access control. It might not have sufficient capacity to concurrently handle a large number of requests or connections, given the type of implementation. Locating the device in an area of the network with heavy traffic or bandwidth constraints may impede or disrupt user access to resources.

Common Implementations

A number of protocols exist that support centralized access control. TACACS, TACACS+, RADIUS, and EAP are just a few of the most common access control protocols that a security architect should be familiar with.

■ *TACACS*—This older protocol was originally used for authenticating dial-up users. RFC 1492, "An Access Control Protocol, Sometimes Called TACASC" (Finseth, 1993), describes the protocol and suggests that the acronym is short for "Terminal Access Controller Access Control System." TACACS functions over UDP on port 49 or TCP on any locally defined port. This older protocol lacks many important features found in others that were more recently developed. A critical shortcoming in TACACS is the lack of encryption. All communication from a TACACS client to the server is in cleartext. Using this protocol through an untrusted or public network exposes the session and endpoints to a potential compromise.

■ *TACACS+*—This proprietary protocol by Cisco is based on and meant to displace TACACS. It is primarily used with TCP on port 49. This protocol overcomes the security weaknesses of its predecessor by providing encryption for the packet payload. Authentication, Authorization, and Accounting (AAA) capabilities are built into the protocol, whereas it is missing from TACACS. However, the use of AAA capabilities is implementation specific. Therefore, a security architect must ensure that each TACACS+ implementation is consistent with the policy of the organization. An Internet-Draft memorandum describing TACACS+ is available through the IETF.

■ *RADIUS*—The Remote Authentication Dial In Service (RADIUS) also has AAA capabilities built into the protocol. RADIUS is a centralized access control protocol commonly used in the telecommunications industry as well as by Internet service providers. A network access server (NAS) acting as the gateway to a network passes client access requests to the RADIUS server. This enables RADIUS to be used in a variety of environments, such as dial-up or wireless. Callback and challenge response attributes are built into the protocol, supporting dial-up and other implementations that require additional security measures. According to the Internet Assigned Numbers Authority (IANA), which controls numbers for protocols, UDP is used to encapsulate RADIUS on ports 1812 for authentication and 1813 for accounting. However, some devices still implement RADIUS over ports 1645 and 1646, which were in use prior to the IANA decision. The user password is protected with MD5 and some additional XOR techniques when transmitted. No other aspects of the protocol implement cryptographic measures. As of this writing, RFC 2865 is the latest Internet Engineering Task Force (IETF) memo describing RADIUS. However, there are a multitude of other RFCs that describe other implementations and attributes of RADIUS.

■ *EAP*—The Extensible Authentication Protocol (EAP) is a protocol supporting multiple authentication methods. It operates above the data link layer and therefore does not rely on IP. This enables its use in a variety of wired and wireless implementations. EAP, defined in RFC 3748 (Aboda, Blunk, Vollbrecht, Carlson, and Levkowetz, 2004), is essentially a peer-to-peer protocol. The protocol relies on the lower layer to ensure packet ordering, but retransmissions are the responsibility of EAP. Its design as an authentication protocol prohibits its use for data transport, which would be inefficient.

Request, response, success, and failure are the four main types of messages or codes in the protocol. EAP can pass through other authentication methods and protocols as long as they conform to the four types of codes. Both WPA and WPA2 require EAP as the supporting authentication methods. A number of methods of implementing EAP exist. For instance, EAP-TLS defined in RFC 5216 is one method that employs Public Key Infrastructure (PKI) to secure RADIUS in wireless environments.

Design Considerations

Protection of the device used for centralized access control is vital. Designs for this type of access control should include countermeasures that preserve the confidentiality, integrity, and availability of the implementation.

- *Reduce attack surface*—Remove unnecessary services from the device. Prevent the device from communicating on unauthorized ports. Consider the use of firewalls or packet-filtering routers between the device and the rest of the network. Only allow inbound and outbound connections according to those ports allocated to support management, authentication, and access control functionality.
- *Active monitoring*—Monitor network activity with the device. Dedicate an intrusion detection node at each physical network interface. Configure the intrusion detection node to monitor for known attacks as well as any activity outside the scope of the device. Enable internal auditing of the device. Each administrator provided access to the device should have their own unique credentials for access. Regularly review the audit logs for unauthorized changes or activity within the device.
- *Device backup*—The database of users and authorized resources can be very large. Regular backups are needed for disaster recovery and contingency operations. The confidentiality and integrity of the backups must be preserved. Ideally, backups should be encrypted. In cases where encryption is not practical or possible, strong physical controls will be needed. Passwords or other secret keys would be retained on the backups; thus the confidentiality of the data contained within the backups must be protected from unauthorized disclosure or exposure. Integrity may be affected when a loss of physical control of backups is exploited by an attacker, who may allow for unauthorized access that could be subsequently granted during a restore process.
- *Redundancy*—Ensure that sufficient redundancy is contained within the design to ensure continued availability when failures occur. External aspects to the device such as communications and power are normally addressed for other components of the system. However, these items become more important when distributed systems or remote clients depend on the centralized

device to access resources unaffected by these types of disruptions. Where possible, implement a secondary access control device that can take over for failures in the primary.

Decentralized Access Control

A collection of nodes that individually make access control decisions through a replicated database characterizes a decentralized access control mechanism. The Microsoft Windows Domain model is a prime example of decentralized access control. Figure 1.28 provides a view of decentralized access control. Note that while authentication information is distributed, access control is applies only to the local resource. This type of access control mechanism has the following qualities:

- *Distributed*—Access control decisions are made from different nodes. Each node makes decisions independent of the others.
- *Shared database*—Distributed nodes share the same database used to authenticate subjects. Changes to the database are communicated among the participating nodes. Ideally, the security policy is shared between nodes as well.
- *Robust*—The access control mechanism continues to operate when an access control node fails or communications are severed.

Figure 1.28   Decentralized access control.

■ *Scalable*—Access control nodes can be added or removed from the architecture with little impact on the rest of the architecture or the access control mechanism as a whole.

Although decentralized access control has some nice features, it is not perfect. Some of the issues that need to be considered when implementing decentralized access control include

■ *Continuous synchronization considerations*—The access control mechanism is only as current as the last synchronization. Excessive gaps in the time between synchronizations may allow inappropriate access to the system or objects.

■ *Bandwidth usage*—Synchronization events might consume a lot of bandwidth. Nodes joined through low-bandwidth connections may consume a disproportionate amount of bandwidth when synchronizing.

■ *Physical and logical protection of each access control node*—A compromise of one access control node could propagate a compromise to all. Successful attacks against the centralized database in one location could provide the attacker with the ability to attack any node participating in the architecture.

Design Considerations

Inconsistencies in security countermeasures are a common issue with systems using decentralized access control. Servers providing access control services could be located in different facilities in the same region or in different parts of the world. Ensuring that the intended design is consistently applied for each instance can be quite challenging.

■ *Physical security*—The integrity of the access control system can be globally impacted by a weakness in the physical security at just one site. Every site hosting a decentralized access control server must have sufficient physical security. Physical security is affected not only by the facility itself, but also by the individuals granted access to the areas housing the system. Physical security controls should be explicitly defined and periodically validated. Every site containing a decentralized access control server must adhere to a minimum baseline of controls.

■ *Management coordination*—A decentralized access control system that is geographically distributed may have a multitude of individuals from various offices involved with system development, maintenance, and administration. The activities and duties of these individuals should be considered when assigning rights and privileges to their accounts. Furthermore, actions affecting the baseline of the system should only be permitted through appropriate change control processes. Ideally, the access control system is designed to facilitate separation of duties and least privilege. However, applying these concepts can make management coordination difficult. The design of the access controls should consider organizational structure, such as human resources, that will need to participate in the management of the decentralized access controls and the system in general.

■ *Remote maintenance*—Organizations with decentralized access control often use remote management methods to maintain the distributed aspects of the system. Administrators conducting remote maintenance may iterate through a number of commands that could allow an attacker to compromise the access control system. The activities of the administrators must be protected with encryption during the communication session. Some devices might not directly support sufficient encryption of the entire session. In these cases, alternative devices, such as a VPN, should be used to ensure that administrator actions captured on the network could not be used to exploit the access control device. Where possible, connect the VPN device directly to an unused physical interface on the decentralized access control device. When this is not possible, use secondary network filtering such as a firewall or router to prevent propagation of the output from the VPN to other nodes in the subnet. Refer to Figure 1.29 for an example.

■ *Exclude from demilitarized zone (DMZ)*—Decentralized access control devices share a common database allowing distributed AAA. An exploited

Figure 1.29 Remote maintenance with a VPN.

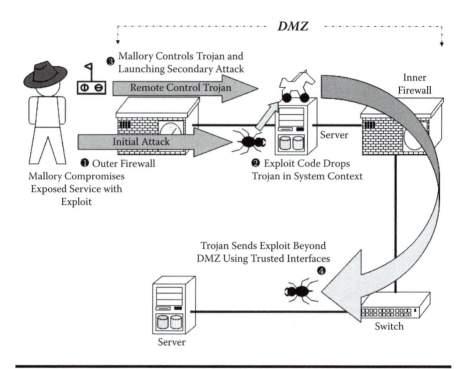

Figure 1.30   Problems with decentralized access control servers in a DMZ.

vulnerability in one device, such as that seen in Figure 1.30, can result in compromise of resources dependent on the access control system. Given this situation, it is best to avoid placing a decentralized access control device within a DMZ. Servers and devices within a DMZ should not contain sensitive information. Rather, access to sensitive information by those outside of the trusted aspects of the organizational network should be handled by proxy servers that do not have rights or permissions outside of the DMZ. Figure 1.31 illustrates this point. This design philosophy assumes that servers within the DMZ are at greater risk of exploitation than those that are inside the trusted area of the network. Decentralized access control servers require a high degree of protection and as such should not be placed directly inside the DMZ.

Federated Access Control

Authentication is an essential part of any access control system. Each subject having access to organizational resources must be appropriately authenticated prior to being allowed access. This becomes problematic when an organization extends resource access to business partners and customers. Organizations with a large customer or partner population could potentially need to manage more accounts

Figure 1.31 Using proxy servers in a DMZ to counter attacks.

for external subjects than for those of its own employees. Recent efforts in the areas of Services Oriented Architecture (SOA) using Web 2.0 enable organizational sharing of resources for individual subjects that are authenticated by an external organization. This is made possible through the establishment of a federation of organizations.

A federation consists of two or more organizational entities with access control systems that do not interoperate or functionally trust each other. At least one of the federation members has authenticated users that desire access to resources from another of the participating organizations. Members of the federation agree to recognize the claimed identity of a subject that has been fully authenticated by one of the members. Rather than require an individual to have a separate account in each organization, only one is required. This is the power of federated access, which is closely related to identity management and single sign-on, but crosses organizational boundaries.

Federated access control occurs when an organization controlling access to a particular resource allows a subject access based on his or her identity, which is affirmed by the partner organization. The proof provided by a subject typically consists of a token or piece of information digitally signed by the authenticating organization, affirming the identity of the individual. Once the proof is verified,

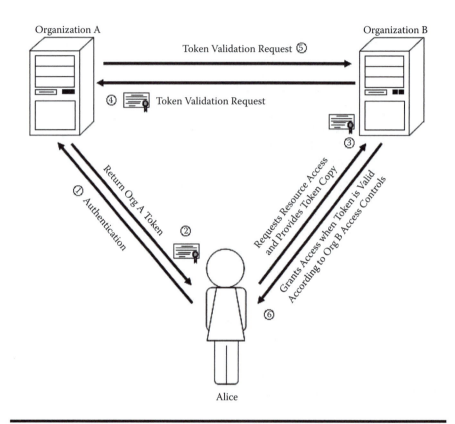

Figure 1.32   Federated access control.

access is permitted to the subject. Access to resources can further be mediated using DAC, RBAC, or any other access control technique deemed appropriate by the organization. Figure 1.32 illustrates an example of how a federated access control could be implemented.

Design Considerations

There are a number of issues that must be carefully considered when implementing federated access control. Given that an organization allows access to protected resources, great care must be given when providing access. This is a prudent precaution because the federation member providing access to a subject of another organization is required to extend a substantial amount of trust.

- *Cooperative effort*—The federation is a joint effort that derives its ability to function based on the agreements of the participants. A written agreement should detail how individuals are authenticated and the handling of proofs used to confirm a subject's identity. This is minimally needed to ensure interoperability, but more importantly, an agreement should establish a set of security requirements that must be met by the participants.

■ *Mutual risk*—Compromised subject accounts in one organization can impact other federation members. A security architect should consider this likelihood when designing controls to support participation in the federation. Nefarious activity could cause damage to both organizations and can even strain the trust of the participating members of the federation. In this regard, abuses and attacks must be considered ahead of time to ensure that appropriate countermeasures and responses are in place prior to accepting subject identities of external organizations within the federation.

■ *Utilize a DMZ*—Externally authenticated subjects from a participating federation member should not be allowed direct access to internal resources. Just as in e-commerce, it is best to contain the activities of these types of customers and partners within a DMZ as well. Use proxy servers within the DMZ to retrieve information that is needed. Avoid storing sensitive information in the DMZ.

■ *Exclude access control integration*—From the standpoint of a federation member, a previously authenticated subject from another organization should not be considered a subject in the primary access control system of the organization. In this regard, it is better to establish a centralized access control system dedicated to the support of a federated access control rather than mix outsiders with those on the inside. Keeping this type of barrier will prevent accidental or malicious escalation of privilege due to a weakness in the main access control system.

Directories and Access Control

In modern operating systems, information is stored and retrieved from directory structures. Data elements comprising information may be kept in a giant file, but generally, access to the information is in a hierarchal format that is managed either by the operating system or an application. Many commodity software products make use of proprietary formats to store information. This can inhibit the ability to share information between products of different vendors. Furthermore, proprietary formats might not have granular access control capabilities, do not interoperate with host-based access controls, or fail to function with those of other hosts.

The challenges of sharing information were recognized early on in the development of IT systems. The International Telecommunications Union–Telecommunications Standardization Sector (ITU-T) recognized this problem and developed X.500 Directory Specifications. This specification was subsequently adopted by the International Organization for Standardization (ISO) and International Electrotechnical Commission (IEC) as the ISO/IEC 9594 multipart standard.

The X.500 Directory Specification provides the framework to specify the attributes used to create a directory as well as the methods used to access its objects. An entry in the directory has its own Directory Information Tree comprising different types of objects. A directory schema describes how information is organized in a directory, while object classes indicate how each entry is to be structured. Access and management of X.500 information is conducted using the Directory Access Protocol (DAP), which requires an OSI-compliant protocol stack. In this regard, DAP is the X.500 standard.

Protecting the confidentiality of information transferred using DAP is not defined in X.500. However, protection of authentication factors, such as passwords, used to connect or *bind* to an X.500 directory are specified in the X.509 subset standard. This subset establishes the basis for Public Key Infrastructure (PKI) certificates. It also defines hashing techniques and the use of public-key encryption as methods to protect the confidentiality of bind requests.

The IETF has subsequently defined an alternative method to access an X.500-based directory over IP that is known as Lightweight Directory Access Protocol (LDAP). RFC 4510 (Zeilenga, 2006) provides a general overview of the specifications of LDAP and lists other applicable RFCs. Version 3 of the protocol (LDAPv3) is described in RFC 4511 and supports a limited number of DAP operations over TCP port 389. LDAPv3 also supports the use of TLS to secure directory access over TCP port 636. LDAP supports authenticated and unauthenticated access during the bind process. When authentication is desired, the credentials could be sent in plaintext using simple authentication or secured with Simple Authentication and Security Layer (SASL). Refer to RFC 4422 for a detailed explanation of SASL.

The concept of using directory access protocols is quite powerful. Vendors of network operating systems have embraced the concept and integrated directory access protocols into their products. For instance, the latest Microsoft servers rely extensively on their proprietary DAP implementation known as Active Directory (AD). The initial release of AD had limited support for LDAP. However, AD can now be extensively accessed using LDAP. This enables cross-domain and vendor product access to Windows resources. Security architects are advised to learn the intricacies of LDAP as it is likely to increase in relevance and importance in the future.

Design Considerations

Directory specifications such as X.500 enable an organization to publish information in a way that supports hierarchical access to structured information. However, attention to security must be given when deploying a directory solution.

- ◾ *Access security*—Some directories may contain sensitive information. Ensure that directory access is protected with cryptographic measures in instances where an exposure of the information transitting a network would be unacceptable.
- ◾ *Protect authentication information*—A Simple Bind operation passes authentication information in cleartext over the network. This could be a default behavior in some implementations where a server accepts anonymous or

unauthenticated bind operations. Verification of the correct functioning of the authentication mechanism should be conducted. Consider storing authentication information for publicly accessible servers within a DMZ in another location within the private network.

▪ *Leverage existing access control mechanisms*—According to RFC 2820, LDAP does not currently specify an access control model. Therefore, it is important that existing access control mechanisms on the host server be employed to protect directory access. In cases where anonymous or unauthenticated access to a directory is permitted, access to other files in the system should not be accessible by the service or daemon running the directory service. This is a prudent measure that can protect the rest of the system in the event a vulnerability in the service is exploited.

Identity Management

Identification is a token representation of a particular subject. In the physical realm, official documents such as a driver's license or a passport are representative of different token forms identifying the same person. Both types of identification have different levels of trust. For instance, a passport is a trusted form of identification when traveling internationally, while a driver's license is not normally given this level of trust. In contrast, within the United States, a passport is insufficient proof of an individual's ability to operate a motor vehicle. In this regard, one type of identification is not compatible with the purpose or trust of another even though they refer to the same person.

In the cyber realm, individuals frequently use multiple identities to access different services within the same system. Similar to Figure 1.33, an individual may have one account for network login and another for accessing a database. The most common form of identity is an account name, which is frequently nothing more than a string of characters. An account name, or identification, is the logical representation of a subject in most access control systems.

Individuals join and depart organizations. Assigned duties will also change, which might require extended or reduced access to system resources and services. In these situations, it is necessary to equate the identity of an individual with the totality of access needed to conduct their duties. Multiple identities and changes in access exemplify the need for identity management.

As previously mentioned, it is not uncommon for an individual to have multiple identities within an organizational system. Identities exist for a variety of IT products within any given system. Some of the more common instances include

▪ *Operating systems*—Microsoft, Unix, Linux, and mainframes are the most prevalent.
▪ *Directory services*—LDAP-enabled operating systems and applications may integrate with other products or deploy their own identity schemes.

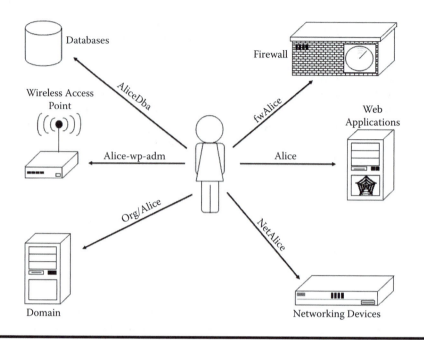

Figure 1.33 **Identity management challenges.**

- *Public Key Infrastructure (PKI)*—Each individual issued a public key certificate essentially has an identity within the PKI.
- *Network authentication*—Authentication of network devices makes use of a variety of protocols such as Kerberos, SSH, RADIUS, and TACACS. Each may have its own account identifier or integrate with an operating system.
- *Network management*—Simple Network Management Protocol (SNMP).
- *Database management systems*—Many popular databases have their own internal accounts for user access. Some integrate with the operating system for authentication purposes, but an account is still maintained in the database.
- *E-mail*—Most e-mail servers are integrated with the host operating system for identification purposes, but some are not. Access to an e-mail server from outside the organizational boundary will require a separate account in most cases.
- *Smartcards*—These tokens represent the identification of the authorized holder. A separate list must be maintained matching a token to a particular user. Some smartcards contain multiple identities that can be used to accommodate multiple users.
- *Biometrics*—The identifier comprises features of an individual. Devices supporting biometrics collect the minutia according to a particular template.

■ *Network equipment*—Routers, switches, encryption devices, and printers commonly have console or remote management interfaces. These types of devices frequently have only one type of administrative account that is shared by those responsible for maintenance.

■ *Networked applications*—Specialized software and services, such as financial accounting packages, may implement their own access control mechanism.

■ *Web applications*—Many Web-based applications relay a user's account and password to a back-end database. However, some specialized Web applications have their own access control mechanism, which is separate from the underlying operating system or back-end database.

■ *Encryption products*—Media encryption products such as those used for hard drive or file encryption may rely on the combined use of an identifier and authenticator. Other forms of identification, such as smartcards, might also be used.

An account identification is the fundamental identity for a system user. Within an access control mechanism, a subject is frequently equivalent to an account identifier. However, a user may have multiple accounts within a system. The identity of an individual user is therefore considered to encompass the totality of his or her access within a system.

Should standardized account-naming conventions be used within a system? The argument for standardization is that it simplifies account management. Using the same naming convention for system and application accounts expedites an administrator's ability to associate account actions, permissions, as well as manipulate account attributes for a given user. The counterargument is that a guessable naming convention gives attackers an advantage against a system. This may allow them to target particular users for phishing and spyware attacks or conduct focused attacks against system accounts. However, the ease of administration need not give rise to a weakness in the system. Consider the following:

■ *E-mail filtering*—Malicious attachments and messages with mismatched header information should be discarded at the e-mail server.

■ *Malware scanning*—Discovering and eliminating malware mitigates the threat.

■ *Account lockouts*—Establishing low thresholds on the number of failed attempts mitigates guessing attacks.

- *User awareness*—Training is essential in any security program.
- *Process validation*—Knowing what is allowed to execute in the environment will enable countermeasures against and discovery of unauthorized software.
- *Intrusion detection*—Tune the network IDS to detect attacks against accounts. Use host-based IDS to identify malicious or abnormal activity.
- *Audit log review*—Look for attempts to access an account from an unusual location. For instance, attempts to log on with service accounts from a workstation strongly indicate system misuse when it is contrary to a system policy.

So it seems that a standard naming convention, when accompanied by other controls, will simplify account management without sacrificing the system's security posture.

The assignment of account identifications should be tightly coupled with the concepts of separation of duties and least privilege. This means if an individual does not require access to a particular database for his or her duties, then an associated account should not be given. The security design of a system should accommodate this type of granular access. Furthermore, manual or automated methods should be used to associate, track, and validate an individual with the rights and permissions granted. Manual methods could entail the use of spreadsheets or small databases. Automated management typically requires the use of specialized tools for single sign-on.

Some IT products have only one administrative account for management purposes. Linux, Unix, and many networking devices rely on a root or superuser account for management. It is quite common for IT departments to share the passwords associated with accounts among a group of individuals responsible for administrative support. Accountability is difficult to achieve when accounts are shared. Considerations for achieving some level of accountability for shared accounts include

- *Use of specialized protocols*—Consider the use of TACACS+ or RADIUS to manage access to network devices.
- *Manual tracking of account usage*—Implement a log to track the time and date of an individual's use of the privileged account. Change the password at short intervals where practical.
- *Verification of audit events*—Compare audit records for the device against those of manual logs or from specialized protocols.

There exist some organizations that have sufficient resources to implement specialized software packages to manage shared accounts. Yet, there are many less well-

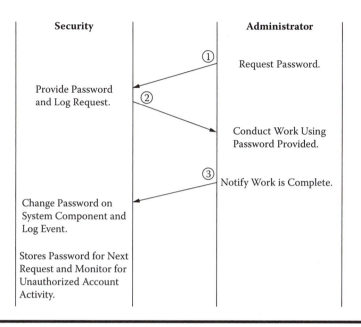

Figure 1.34 Simple method to control a shared account.

funded organizations that must rely on manual techniques to control these shared accounts. A well-defined procedure or process implementing steps in a particular order is essentially a protocol. In Figure 1.34, a manual protocol that can be used to control access to a shared account is demonstrated.

The manual protocol described in Figure 1.34 is very simplistic, and has a significant drawback. The security person has access to the password as well as the audit records. This might enable persons in that capacity to conceal any nefarious activity they might pursue. Simply put, this simple method may not have sufficient separation of duties implemented in the protocol for some organizations. The situation could be improved if someone else is introduced who is involved with the audit records or manages the password. Figure 1.35 describes an improvement where part of the password is split with a third party identified as a helper. This improved manual protocol also has a built-in feature that enables the security officer to evaluate the strength of the password while establishing better separation of duties as well.

Most devices have physical and logical addresses. The physical, or media access control address, should be unique for every device within a system. Unfortunately, this may not always be the case. In the early days, physical addresses were hardwired into network interfaces from the manufacturer and could not be easily changed. Nowadays, some devices, and even operating systems, provide the ability to change the physical address. The most prevalent logical address is the Internet Protocol (IP) address. It is either manually assigned to a device or acquired through the Dynamic Host Configuration Protocol (DHCP). These attributes should be used to help

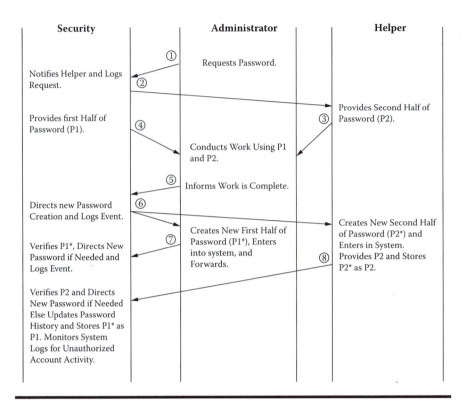

Figure 1.35   Password splitting to achieve greater accountability for a shared account.

uniquely identify each host connected to an organizational network. Due to the nonpersistent nature of a device identity, it should not be relied upon exclusively as a means of authentication. Rather, device identity is a starting point that is useful to discover unauthorized devices connected to a system. Knowing what is connected to a network is an essential element in protecting a system. Use a scanning tool, such as Nmap, to discover unauthorized devices on a network.

Some devices, such as those used for encryption, have the ability to participate in a PKI. Each device participating in the PKI has its own private key and public key certificate loaded on the system. This provides an enhanced means to identify participating devices. However, the integrity of those participating in the PKI is predicated on the physical security of the device. Any breakdown in the physical security affecting a device calls into question the authenticity of those affected by the weak controls. Use of a PKI to manage device identity is powerful, but it must be moderated with the appropriate physical controls as well.

The security architect should design systems to aid in the management of the complete identity of each subject. Properly designed identification management will help support the concepts of least privilege and separation of duties. Shared accounts present special challenges, and that must be accommodated. Device identification should also be a factor in a system's design.

Accounting

The initial concept of system accounting had a dual meaning. The term *accounting* evolved from the mainframe world. In the early days, computing time was very expensive. To recoup resources, system users or their departments were billed or charged back according to the amount of processing time consumed. In this respect, accounting literally meant financial accountability. However, it was also used in the traditional sense of security as in accounting for user actions.

Today, accounting is predominately used to established individual accountability. The term accounting goes by different names such as event logging, system logging, and auditing. Accounting records provide security personnel with the means to identify and investigate system misuse or anomalies. Ideally, all instances where accounts are used as means to identify subjects for access control purposes will have an auditing capability. The purpose of accounting is to minimally establish *who* accessed *what*. Recall that the *who* is the subject and *what* is the resource. *What* should also include administrative activity such as policy changes and account management. To be more precise, it is also helpful to know from *where* and *when* the access occurred as well as the *effect* of the event. So accounting or auditing records should minimally include

- *Who*—The subject (device or user) conducting the action
- *What*—Resources affected and administrative activity conducted
- *Where*—Location of the subject and resource
- *When*—Time and date of the attempt
- *Effect*—Whether the action succeeded

Audit records are frequently used to identify anomalous or malicious activity. Investigators piece together information from audit logs into a time line of action to determine what happened. This effort can be more tedious when there is a difference between system clocks. The problem is best resolved by synchronizing the clocks of each device. Manual and automated methods can be used to synchronize system clocks. Regardless of the approach, a central clock must be chosen as the reference by which all other device clocks will be set. It is best to select a clock that is highly accurate and not affected by system activity. Manual methods are often necessary for those devices that lack automated means to update their time. Manual synchronization should be conducted at regular intervals. However, the best approach is to use automated techniques such as the Network Time Protocol (NTP). The protocol enables device clock synchronization from one host that acquires a time-base from another. Figure 1.36 illustrates the use of NTP in a system.

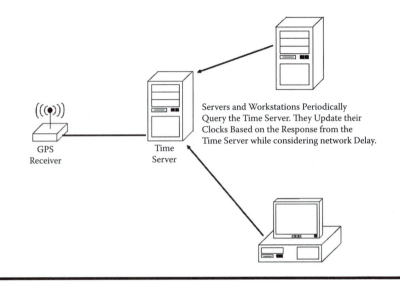

Figure 1.36   Clock synchronization in a system.

Log diversity abounds as vendors are free to proliferate their proprietary formats. Many systems have logs from numerous points and in a variety of formats. Fortunately, most vendors have settled on either syslog or integration with Microsoft Windows Event log as the audit recording method. The locations and types of services generating logs are substantial. Figure 1.37 identifies just a few technologies that can be used to generate security events and information.

Audit records are most useful when they are analyzed. The most efficient way to analyze audit records and security events is when they are consolidated. Relevant audit records should be regularly collected into a centralized repository that enables their examination. Figure 1.38 shows several methods commonly used to collect security logs and events. Further explanation of these popular methods used to collect audit and security information follows:

- *Listen*—Use a service that receives events as they are transmitted from network nodes. A syslog server is an example of this.
- *Polling*—A centralized server can be used to query other services to collect events periodically. It might also be used to copy log files from a shared directory.
- *Agents*—Autonomous process running on a node collects events as they are generated and sends them to a centralized collection point. Agents can be used to filter log messages and only transmit those that are the most important.

Some security-related logs can become quite large, so the period used to collect them is important. File transfers of large logs can consume a substantial amount of network bandwidth. Similarly, an audit log source that automatically transmits events in near real time can affect bandwidth as well. Consideration for the timing

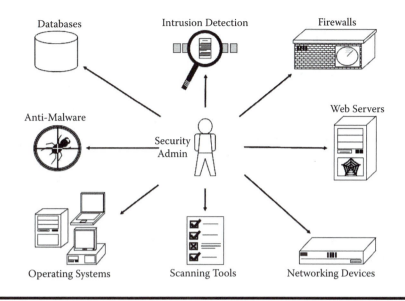

Figure 1.37 Sources of security events, information, and logs.

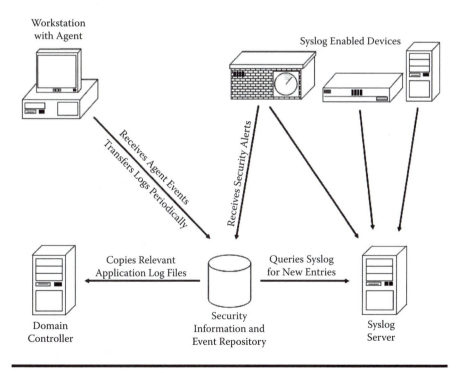

Figure 1.38 Methods of collecting security logs and events.

of audit log collection should be weighed against operational needs of system users versus security requirements.

Two important considerations regarding audit log collection involve analysis and forensic value. Analysis requires logs to be consolidated in such a way that patterns of activity across multiple logs can be analyzed to detect violations and misuse. Inserting logs into a database is the most ideal way to accomplish this. Log records are decomposed into common elements and inserted into the database for query analysis. Unimportant records are commonly filtered out as they do not add value to the investigation. The decomposition and filtering helps an analyst discover security issues. It may also be necessary for the audit records to be preserved in their original state if they are to be presented as evidence in a court of law. In this case, unmodified logs are kept in a special archive where their integrity is assured. Cryptographic hashes of the logs should also be retained and protected to serve as evidence of the log's integrity. Accordingly, some logs are parsed for use, while others are retained as potential evidence.

A security architect must consider all of the possible locations where audit logs can be collected. Numerous devices, services, and applications produce a variety of useful logging information. At a minimum, audit logs should be collected from those devices where access control decisions are made. The collection process should be planned to consolidate the necessary logs in a timely manner, avoiding operational conflicts, providing the ability for detailed analysis, while guaranteeing their forensic value.

Access Control Administration and Management Concepts

Access Control Administration

Each type of access control architecture presents its own challenges for managing the fundamental aspects of subjects, objects, permissions, and rights. The security architect should consider the mechanisms that must be implemented to enable access control administration.

There are two principal entity types that are the subjects of access control. Ultimately, a subject is either a human or an automated feature of the system. The architect should ensure processes exist such that accounts assigned to each entity type are

- *Authorized*—Each account is approved and documented. This establishes its authenticity.
- *Monitored*—Accounts should be assessed for inactivity and abuse. Unused and unnecessary accounts are promptly removed. Employ specialized tools to identify abnormal use of accounts.

- *Validated*—The continued need for each account is reviewed on a periodic basis as established by the organization. This affirms the authenticity of each account.

Each person requiring access to a system should be individually identified. This enables accountability as well as the application of granular access controls. Limit the number of accounts assigned to each individual. Avoid the use of shared accounts as this will make accountability much more difficult.

Processes executing on a system do so within a security context; that is, every process has certain rights and permissions. An operating system that relies on an access control model, such as DAC, must regard human interactions and running processes within an appropriate security context. Human interaction occurs through an associated process. This might be a single process or more than one hundred processes. Regardless of the number, the actions taken by the process are forced to conform to the security context of the user. In this respect, processes are not permitted to take any actions beyond what the user is allowed. Processes not executing in the context of a user may have a security context of the system or their own unique context.

Some system processes have the special ability (right) to impersonate a user. When applied correctly, this technique allows the service to execute with the permissions and rights of the client. Processes with the ability to impersonate must be closely monitored. Vulnerabilities associated with impersonating processes may allow privilege escalation and system compromise.

Although permissions are commonly associated with objects within a system, a security architect must think in a broader perspective. A system is a collection of resources that may or may not be considered objects within a given access control mechanism. Each resource may contain many objects that can be managed by one or more access control techniques. Resources provide utility to the end user and may be consumable or enable system functionality. Diversity in resource types complicates the application of access control. Consider the following shortlist of resources common to many systems:

- *Web server*—Traditional Web servers enable access to Web-based content. Vendors are more frequently embedding Web servers into hardware products. In some cases, the access control mechanisms of embedded Web servers do not integrate with other security mechanisms, creating isolated islands that require security maintenance and configuration.
- *E-mail server*—This ubiquitous communication platform may be accessible inside as well as outside of an organization's security boundary. This resource is commonly abused by those peddling spam and launching phishing attacks.
- *Networked printer*—This device is loosely coupled to the access control mechanisms of a system. A printer is normally dependent on other security measures to protect it from abuse.

■ *Network devices*—Switches, routers, and firewalls are resources that enable system functionality. Many have console or remote management ports that enable device configuration. The internal configuration features may not easily integrate with other access control mechanisms within a system. The loss of availability of one of these resources will likely impact the ability of users to access other resources.

■ *Applications*—The most common applications are those installed locally on a system. However, advances in mobile code and the emergence of Web 2.0 demand a broader perspective on what is considered an application and how it should be secured.

■ *Removable media*—Removable-media devices such as USB, CD-ROM, tape, and disk drives provide users with access to resources beyond local or networked system storage. These resources enable sharing, backup, and transport of information.

■ *Internet access*—Many organizations depend on Internet access as a core business resource. System users depend on the Internet for research, collaboration, and e-commerce. Internet use is similar to human use of fire. If used inappropriately, it can consume organizational resources in time and money. When used effectively, the Internet can be used to forge a wealth of opportunities to transact business and advance organizational objectives.

■ *File server*—This type of repository contains the bulk of an organization's information. A variety of networked storage is available for system consumption. Simple file servers functioning with commodity operating systems are the principal remote storage devices in any given system. Dedicated devices such as storage area networks and network attached storage are gaining in popularity as a means to enable massive storage capabilities for organizations of any size. Integrating these devices within an access control methodology for a system requires attention to detail on the part of a security architect.

■ *Databases*—Much of the business intelligence of an organization is kept in database repositories. Access to databases is often routed through a Web tier. But direct access through specialized tools or other databases is also a common practice. Database management systems often have their own access control mechanisms that are stand-alone, or, in some instances, integrate with those of other vendor products. As with file servers, a security architect should give special attention to database access control planning and implementation.

A system user is the principal subject of interest within an access control mechanism. Resource permissions are granted to users individually or collectively. The access control mechanism constrains user interaction with a resource object according to the permission granted. The possible exception to this statement is when a subject is identified as an object owner, such as within a DAC mechanism. In this case, the subject has full control over the permissions on the object. For instance, suppose an object owner only has read access to the object. This would prevent casual or unintentional modification of the object. However, as the object owner, a subject could readjust his or her permissions on the object to perform any action desired. It is important to note that object owners have the ability to grant any permission to themselves or to others at their discretion when operating within the context of DAC.

Ideally, every object of a resource will be subject to an access control mechanism. This affords the ability to granularly control access to all aspects of a given resource. Unfortunately, this is not always the case. There are many technological resources that are not fully subject to an access control mechanism. For instance, network printers are commonly accessible to any device attached to a network. As long as the appropriate protocols are used, most printers will service any request received. Similarly, file permissions are not present on removable media. Aside from backups, most removable media are formatted using a file allocation table (FAT) or ISO 9660 for DVD and CD-ROM. This is understandable, considering that file-level access controls would not be useable from one access control system to another where a database of subjects is not held in common. Where granular access control is not possible, other methods are employed to control access to the entire resource. Although the all-or-nothing approach is less desirable, it is nevertheless a valid access control technique given security requirements and associated risk.

An effective access control mechanism is not easily bypassed. The mechanism should tightly couple permissions with protected objects. For any object protected, the permissions should be enforced; that is, a subject should not be able to circumvent a permission by manipulating the object or permissions when not authorized. Any situation that allows a subject to exceed permissions represents a flaw in the access control mechanism. Vulnerabilities such as these are regularly discovered in commercial products. A security architect must be acutely aware of this situation when an organization develops proprietary applications with access control mechanisms. Testing of any homegrown security solution for access control weaknesses is critical.

The Power to Circumvent Security

Most systems do not encrypt stored data by default. When a system is powered down intentionally or not, the access control mechanism ceases operation. Data is vulnerable to physical attack when the system is without power. This could allow anyone with physical access to bypass access control and auditing mechanisms. To protect against this situation, a system should be designed with

■ Auditing of system restart, power on, and power off events

- Sufficient physical security measures to prevent or detect unauthorized access to system hardware
- Redundant or backup power

All unscheduled power-down or system restart events should be followed up with an investigation to determine the reason for the interruption and to detect if any malicious activity occurred.

File sharing occurs outside and within access control mechanisms. Transmitted e-mail attachments and files transported with removable media are examples of file sharing outside of an access control mechanism. Within a system's access control mechanism, it is common practice to make a file available to multiple users. A file is considered shared when it is accessible by more than one subject.

Assigning the appropriate permissions to a shared file is critical. A file with more than read access is subject to unintentional modification. Note that this is not to say that modification of the file is necessarily unauthorized. For instance, it is often necessary for people to make modifications to a file during collaboration activity. Modification of files used for collaboration is often expected. But this does not mean that every modification is intentional. Allowing modification of a collaboration file essentially authorizes changes to those who have access. Although this may not be an intended action, it is nonetheless authorized if not explicitly prohibited by policy. In contrast, it is almost never acceptable for ordinary users to modify binary files such as libraries and executables. Providing ordinary users with more than read access to a binary file is a risky proposition. Suppose a system policy prohibits users from modifying program files. In this case, it is reasonable to set permissions that prohibit a user from changing aspects of the file. Given the aforementioned policy, a system that does not restrict a user from making modifications to binary files is said to be noncompliant. Establishing the appropriate permission for shared files is an important consideration for any system.

Peer-to-Peer (P2P): An Unintended Backdoor

Programs with the capability to allow file sharing represent a potential backdoor into an organization's system. A P2P program running in the context of the user has potential access to all the files that the user does. Normally, the program is configured to allow access to only specific file types or directories. When the program runs, it makes itself available to other systems outside of the protected network. Any flaw in the software or misconfiguration of the program parameters could allow

- Compromise of the workstation in the context of the user
- Access to sensitive information available to the user
- Propagation of malicious software such as spyware, Trojans, viruses, and worms

Although P2P software is an interesting collaboration technology, it is fraught with substantial risk. Users who are not security experts may make poor judgments regarding the installation and configuration of this type of software. Security architects must carefully consider access control implementations to guard against misuse or flaws arising from authorized use of P2P applications.

Files such as word processing and spreadsheet documents are commonly shared during collaboration activities. It is not uncommon to find large directory structures with thousands of subdirectories and documents shared among users of certain groups. Typically, users are free to modify many of the documents within these directories. This is facilitated when permissions at the directory level are propagated to all its child objects. Each new object created in a directory inherits the permissions established for the parent. This situation is a disaster waiting to happen. Because users have read, write, and delete permissions in this scenario, the following situations may occur:

- User deletes files or whole directories by accident.
- Files or directories are accidentally moved.
- A user maliciously modifies, moves, or deletes files or directories.
- Malicious code is allowed to modify, move, or delete files or directories.

Each of these situations demonstrates an impact on information integrity and availability. Giving users the ability to modify file attributes, such as content and location, is not a best business practice. Users can make mistakes. Access controls on file shares should be established to prevent mistakes and malicious actions. Restricting users to only read access to resources is an effective method to control accidental or intentional modification to files used for collaboration (Price, 2007).

Database Access

Many organizations use a database management system (DBMS) as a centralized information repository. Databases are ideal tools used to manage and share structured data. Some of the functional attributes of a DBMS can be used as mechanisms to support access control. Functionality such as views, triggers, and stored procedures can be leveraged to enhance access control within a DBMS.

- *Views*—These virtual tables are named queries derived from a single or multiple tables. Although a view is virtual, it can be queried like a normal database table. A common use of views is to provide read-only data to the end user, which prevents the user from changing the data in the originating table. A well-constructed view enables granular access control over the database tables. Rather than giving database users the rights to a sensitive table, a view can be used to explicitly identify the attributes need for their duties. As such, users can be restricted to interact with specific columns, rows, or elements based on the attributes of the view's query.
- *Triggers*—Database events can be preceded or followed by a set of procedures. Triggers can be used to take an action according to database statements issued by the user or actions to interact with individual rows. This is useful to validate inputs from users or take actions based on the parameters or values in the SQL statement.
- *Stored procedures*—These subroutines enable performance of complex data manipulation tasks. Stored procedures enable programming languages, such as C or Java, to be used to conduct intricate actions on data that go beyond the capability of generic SQL. For instance, standard SQL returns an aggregate value based on a given query. Using stored procedures, it is possible to perform multiple unrelated queries and report the result individually or aggregately. Stored procedures are often used in conjunction with triggers to perform data validation or filtering actions.

Views, triggers, and stored procedures permit enforcement of business logic on data elements within a DBMS. These capabilities essentially allow the coding of business rules into database applications, which enables a level of access control that is more granular that the mechanism native to the DBMS. Using the power of these database extensions enables enhancements to security goals, such as separation of duties and least privilege, by restricting user access to only those data elements necessary for the performance of their assigned duties or tasks.

Access to information within a DBMS is enabled through a variety of authentication techniques. Users are identified individually or as a group. Permissions should be applied according to the method of access as well as business rules and the risk associated with the affected data. The various methods of access can be generally categorized as proxied anonymous, proxied access, direct access, and integrated authentication. Each category requires the security architect to consider the implications of the access type for potential data exposures that may occur.

The first category of access involves a logical grouping of all database requests. As seen in Figure 1.39, users are not individually identified, but rather, grouped together. Individual accountability is difficult if no other authentication methods are used to associated connection events with actions in the database. In the figure, user requests for access to database items are proxied through a middle tier such as a Web server. This is a common scenario for public Web sites that provide search-

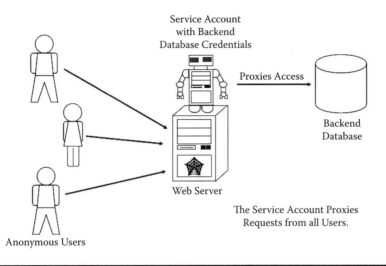

Figure 1.39   Proxy of anonymous users.

related content to user requests. Instead of users possessing a particular account, the Web server uses database credentials to access data on behalf of the anonymous users. Given the lack of accountability in this scenario and the potential for abuse, it is best that database implementations such as these not include sensitive data in the repository. Segregating data in this regard will ensure that vulnerabilities associated with the database or Web server will not potentially expose sensitive information.

In many cases, it is desirable to individually identify users. A front-end application is commonly used to retrieve and format data for user consumption. Users submit credentials, such as an identifier and authenticator, to access protected resources. Figure 1.40 illustrates this as proxied access. This three-tier application involves the client, a server layer, and the database tier. Perhaps the most common implementation of this architecture uses browsers at the client, Web servers in the middle, and a database at the back end. The browser provides end users with the capability to view and interact with the underlying data. The server commonly implements business logic or rules that provide an intermediate access control capability for the backend data. The database may further implement business rules to further restrict data access.

This multitier architecture design is a good way to enforce business rules and access control on elements within the database. Figure 1.41 shows one way this type of architecture could be implemented in an actual system. Note that all components are mutually joined through a central switch. Each network component is physically linked to the other. If the network switch does not have access control capabilities, each node is considered logically connected. Although this represents an efficient design for the architecture, it does afford some opportunities for abuse. For instance, if no network-based access controls are implemented, an insider or

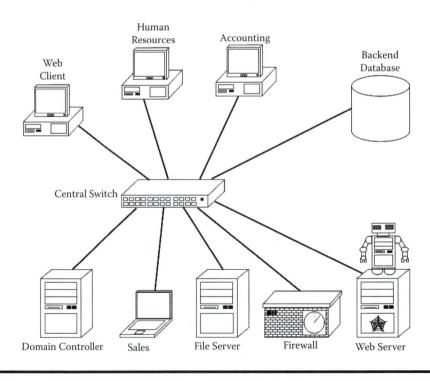

Figure 1.40 Proxy of authenticated users.

Figure 1.41 Typical network with a central switch.

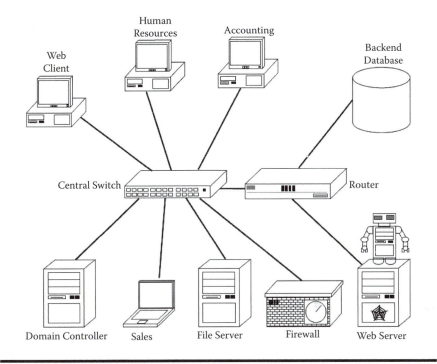

Figure 1.42   Improving security with router access control capabilities.

a compromised workstation would be able to launch attacks directly at the data-base server. Given this consideration, it becomes evident that the design lacks any defense in depth against these kinds of attacks. Furthermore, if the point of the design is to provide a layer of access control, then it seems reasonable that the logi-cal abstraction from Figure 1.41 should implement physical and other logical access controls as well.

This situation can be improved through the use of network segregation. Figure 1.42 demonstrates one way to accomplish this. In this diagram, a router is inserted to control the flow of network connections. Access controls within the router only allow traffic to flow from workstations to the server and from the server to the database. This effectively mitigates the potential for attacks focused directly on the database tier.

Accounts used to access data through a three-tier solution are not always those that are integrated with the system. This is a common situation when data access through this type of architecture is provided to external users. One way to authenti-cate users is to rely on business logic at the server layer. Identifiers and authenticators submitted from the client layer are evaluated at the server layer. Figure 1.43 pro-vides a graphic of this concept. The server looks up the user identification and pass-word either in a local file or from a database table. Users are granted access if their password matches an active account. Subsequent data requests from authenticated

Figure 1.43 Database access through proxy controlled authentication.

clients are frequently accessed through a common database account associated with the roles of the given user.

This approach provides a simple way of enabling a large number of users to access information within a database through a common account. There are some considerations when using this approach:

- *Password hashes*—Stored passwords will need to be hashed. It is best to imple-ment logic that causes the password to be hashed on the client side.
- *Identity management*—A capability should exist to match accounts with active system users. Detailed management aspects such as password history, complex-ity, and lifetime will also need to be handled along with account dormancy.
- *Back-end database access*—Access control on the network and within the back-end database should be implemented as added layers of protection.
- *Protection of access control business logic*—Any compromise of the software implementing the business rules may compromise all data within the data-base. The integrity of the business logic must be ensured.
- *Auditing may be challenging*—A separate audit mechanism may need to be developed to support accountability.

A more integrated approach is to rely on the authentication mechanism inherent within the DBMS. Figure 1.44 illustrates the use of a server that brokers access to the database by acting as an intermediary between user requests and database output. Here, the server proxies requests, but is not the primary access control mechanism. Database access control mechanisms, which include identification and

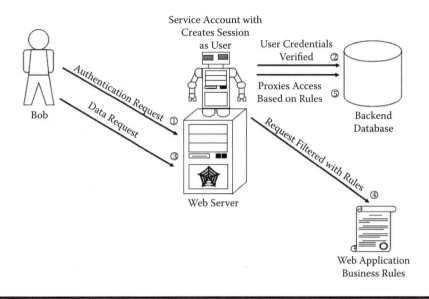

Figure 1.44   Proxy-facilitated database authentication and session.

authentication, are the mainline of defense for the data. Business logic built into the server has the potential to act as a secondary access control mechanism. This scenario has the following attributes:

Server:
  - *Session management*—The server matches a user session with a DBMS session. This allows clients to communicate with the database using foreign protocols.
  - *Information presentation*—The server provides query and other information in preformatted output for client consumption.
  - *Business rule enforcement*—Additional security measures or business logic can be applied by the server as an access control layer.

Database:
  - *Authenticates users*—Users connect to the database with accounts existing in the database.
  - *Primary access control*—Access control mechanisms within the database such as views, triggers, stored procedures, and other privileges are required to control data access.

As previously mentioned, the server in this situation is a secondary access control mechanism. This is because users may still be able to circumvent the server altogether and access the data. Using protocols known to the DBMS such as the Open Database Connectivity (ODBC), a user can access the data directly. In this case, access control is mostly dependent on the mechanism used within the DBMS.

From a security perspective, ODBC has a significant drawback. All communications are conducted in cleartext, which means passwords used to log into the database as well as other sensitive data associated with a session could be captured on the network. This weakness in ODBC is affected by the underlying drivers of the protocol. Some database vendors provide confidentiality for the authentication session in some instances. However, in most cases, SQL commands using ODBC are sent in cleartext. However, the weakness can be reduced if the connection is physically or logically segregated from the rest of the network. Physical segregation can be effected through the use of dedicated hardware devices and interfaces. Logical segregation can be accomplished using VPN, IPSec, or a VLAN, which either encrypt the traffic flowing over common links or pass traffic through links which are not in common. The goal is to prevent the cleartext messages from being captured by rogue or compromised devices configured to capture network traffic.

Three-tier Web-based applications are a frequently used architecture to provide controlled access to organizational data. Implementing this type of architecture has its benefits and drawbacks. A security architect will need to weigh these aspects when evaluating new designs and consider countermeasures and monitoring aspects for existing implementations.

Advantages:
- *Data presentation*—A common application, the Web browser, provides universal access and presentation of the data. Deployments of proprietary applications are not needed.
- *Centralized access*—This type of design makes it easier to connect users to multiple databases.
- *Communication protection*—Some DBMSs do not have link encryption. A Web-based three-tier architecture can make use of Secure Socket Layer (SSL) to protect sensitive communications.

Disadvantages:
- *Increased complexity*—Organizations must carefully manage code developed to support the architecture. Business rules coded in server-side logic should be controlled by change management activities.
- *Cross-site scripting attacks*—Poorly coded or poorly protected Web-based applications are subject to cross-site scripting attacks. This essentially allows an attacker to redirect user requests to other servers of ill repute.
- *Middle-tier security*—Any breach in the server may compromise all data accessible through the server. Aggressive access controls and monitoring of the server are imperative to prevent and detect attacks.
- *Accountability may be difficult*—Achieving the desired amount of accountability may require the development of an extensive access control mechanism. This may be fraught with challenges due to programming or implementation flaws. Although using accounts integrated within the

database may be desirable, this is also not always practical and may not provide sufficient auditing.

Inherent Rights

All accounts will have a default set of rights assigned to it. The inherent rights are the core set of account attributes. Account types are necessary to constrain human and automated aspects according to a security policy. Assigning a user or process more rights than necessary increases risk. This occurs when a user or process acts maliciously or operates as a conduit for another threat agent. Managing assigned rights is an important aspect of a system's overall risk management. The three most basic types of accounts are ordinary, administrator, and system:

- *Ordinary*—Normally, these accounts have very few rights in the system. Most users should be assigned this type of account. Where practical, automated processes and services supporting users should also be assigned an ordinary account. Although ordinary accounts are constrained, they could also violate security policies by exploiting a flaw in the system.
- *Administrator*—Only those individuals tasked with the maintenance of the system should be assigned this type of account. Administrators have substantial rights in the system; anyone with such rights could circumvent security policies.
- *System*—This account type supports system functionality. System accounts have enormous powers similar to those of an administrator. Threat agents exploiting weaknesses associated with an account with system privileges may be able to compromise all aspects of a system.

It is important to note that some system components, such as networking devices, commonly provide only one administrator account for management. In this situation, the account is typically shared among multiple individuals with system management responsibility. This can make accountability difficult. In cases like this, manual processes as well as physical and logical access control are needed to ensure appropriate device management. Secure such devices in a locked container or area. Implement processes that establish accountability for device access. This could be as simple as a key control log or as complex as an integrated facility access control system using two-factor authentication. In any case, where inherent rights cannot be separated and accountability is not automated, other processes will need to be implemented.

Granted Rights

Most accounts have the same rights granted to them even though they may have different resource permissions assigned. Accounts can ordinarily be grouped according to their type. Sometimes it is necessary to assign rights beyond those inherent for a given account by granting additional rights. This situation essentially creates an account with nonstandard rights. For instance, an ordinary user account may be granted additional rights so that it can be used as a system service. Altering the rights granted to a particular account can affect the overall security posture of the system. An attacker exploiting the properties of an account with nonstandard rights might be able to propagate an exploit more readily across a system. An account with nonstandard rights essentially establishes itself as a new type of account. The likelihood of a threat exploiting the new rights associated with the account should be properly assessed. Consider the following actions to manage the risk of creating accounts with nonstandard rights:

- *Document*—The rights of all accounts should be documented. When an account is given nonstandard rights, it is important that the reasons for the new rights be clearly enumerated. Risk associated with the changes should be documented as well. Documenting the reason and anticipated effects of the rights associated with the account will help future managers, administrators, and security personnel to understand the reasoning for the change and counter emerging threats when appropriate.
- *Authorize*—A change in account rights can pose new risks for the system. In this regard, management should authorize the change in writing. Ideally, alterations to account rights beyond what has been previously specified should be made using the system's change control process.
- *Monitor*—An account with nonstandard rights may end up an ideal target for an attacker. Actions of the account should be tracked to identify inappropriate activity or actions outside the scope of its intended use. Audit logs are an excellent resource that should be regularly reviewed for inappropriate account activity.

Just as rights can be granted for a particular account, they can be withdrawn as well. Reductions in rights support the concept of least privilege. There can be enormous security benefits to removing excessive or unused rights. This essentially helps eliminate or reduce possible attack vectors available to an authorized account. The trade-off comes with management overhead associated with reduced rights. If a selected right is removed for a security reason but is later restored to the account, then a previously mitigated weakness may reemerge on the system. Proper management steps should be followed whether rights are granted or curtailed. Following the previously mentioned steps of documenting, authorization, and monitoring will help manage any associated risk.

Change of Privilege Levels

Privileges are the combined rights and permissions allocated to interact with system resources. Altering object permissions and system rights for any given account has the potential to impact the overall security posture of the system. Changes in privileges should not be arbitrary and should only occur after consideration of the associated risk. Modification of permissions should include the involvement of resource managers or information owners. Similarly, altering account rights should only be done in coordination with the system owner or administrators. Inappropriate assignment of privileges can have undesirable consequences. When privileges are too lax, weaknesses may be introduced into the system that might expose sensitive information to abuse or compromise. Excessively rigid privileges can hamper operations, reduce system functionality, and frustrate users. A careful balance between usability and security is required to achieve the security goals of the system. Risk management is an important tool used by the security architect to strike the right balance.

Groups

Managing the security attributes for individual subjects and objects is an enormous undertaking. A system with hundreds of users and hundreds of thousands of objects is too difficult to manage individually. Thankfully, administrative tasks can be simplified when subjects and objects in common are manipulated simultaneously. Administrators make extensive use of groupings of subjects and objects to manage their vast numbers. Groups provide substantial advantages when managing large numbers of users and resources. This paradigm allows the convergence of management actions related to subjects and objects. The most common approach is to establish a group where membership is applied to particular objects or resources. Account membership in a group implies that different individuals have either a similar duty or need to access the same resource. Essentially, a group should be designed with the goal of accommodating accounts with

- Similar duties, but involving situations where they access different data. Here, a group is established to efficiently administer large numbers of accounts assigned permissions for a specific resource.
- Access to the same data, where each has different duties. This scenario is used to manage resource sharing among divergent types of users.
- Similar duties and data accesses. This type of group would essentially be the primary group used to manage a broad category of users such as Administrators or Ordinary users. However, more specific groups such as Accounting or Marketing could also be used.

Managing through the use of groups is indeed a double-edged sword. Although it provides substantial power to mitigate risk, when not properly managed it can cause other problems. Some issues facing a security architect when controls governing group management fail are the following:

- *Orphaned groups*—An excessive number of unused groups may appear on the system. Often, no one knows what the group was used for or if it should be retained. There is generally a reluctance to remove the group when no one is certain of the consequence.

- ◼ *Duplicated groups*—Often, multiple groups are created for the same purpose. They may have identical accounts and subgroups or nearly enough of the same members that the aggregate of different smaller groups equates to the sum of an existing group. Although particular members might be excluded from a given group, creating uniqueness, a lack of sufficient management reduces the advantages of the granularity provided.

- ◼ *Separation of duty violations*—It may occur that individuals included in the same group assigned to a given resource may ultimately violate separation of duties. Suppose a system administrator is included in a group of security officers managing audit logs. The administrator could potentially remove information in the logs associated with malicious activity. Adding members to groups without consideration of the use of the group can quickly result in unintended weaknesses.

- ◼ *Failures in least privilege*—Individuals might be given access to resources beyond the scope of their duties. Careless use of group assignments may result in the inclusion of individuals who should not have access to objects intended to be accessed by other members of the group. The haphazard or reckless addition of accounts may expose sensitive information to those who are not authorized or facilitate the introduction of malicious code such as a Trojan.

Administering group membership is an aspect of identity management. Processes should be implemented to control and monitor group assignments to prevent misuse or abuse. Some actions a security architect could take to establish management of group assignments include the following:

- ◼ *Identify purpose*—Record the reason for the group's existence. Indicate if the purpose is to group accounts according to function, data attribute, or both. Knowing the purpose for the existence of the group will help determine if future assignment to the group is appropriate.

- ◼ *Membership attributes*—Specify what types of members should be included in the group. Indicate if account types exist that would violate separation of duties or least privilege when included in the group.

- ◼ *Resource attributes*—List the various target resources that are to be associated with the group. Resource objects could be particular files, directories, or services. Indicate the permission levels to be assigned according to the type of object the group will be associated with.

- ◼ *Control changes*—Managing group memberships through a change control process is ideal, but may be difficult because changes may occur frequently. It is better to establish localized controls for changes. Assign one individual to approve changes and another to monitor compliance with the approvals.

Coordinate changes with other information and system owners when a change impacts their area of responsibility.

- *Periodic review*—Establish a time frame to reexamine all groups in the system. Determine if an application of a group fails to meet its purpose. Consider each member and assess if they still should be included as a member. Determine if the group has any inappropriate resource assignments.

One way to think about the application of groups is through the relation of accounts with the activity of their owners. In this way, a group can be established according to the types of duties assigned to a user or a particular job function. Groups can be viewed from two perspectives: role based or task based.

Role Based

A role represents an organizational duty. It may be the totality of a job position or it could be a particular function within an organization. Managing account access control through the use of roles is an ideal way to assign rights and permissions. People can more readily identify with the concept of a role as opposed to a security group. When a role is aptly named, people are likely to anticipate what access and capabilities are associated with it. For example, one may correctly assume that the *Advertising* role is associated with an organization's Marketing Department. We would further expect that this role would not have the same access as the *Chief Financial Officer* role. In this regard, access control based on roles may more likely appeal to those who are technical as well as those who are not.

Groups and roles are both a type of collection, but differ in their application. Groups are collections of users, while roles are collections of rights and permissions. In this regard, users are members of a group that can be assigned permissions for various resources. In contrast, a user assigned a role assumes a set of rights and permissions for designated resources. An RBAC implementation can be much more restrictive than those that rely on the use of groups.

An important aspect of an RBAC implementation is mutual exclusivity, which is the fundamental attribute used to establish separation of duties. Mutual exclusivity is a constraint in RBAC that specifies an incompatibility between roles; that is, two roles with mutual exclusivity have resource rights or permissions that must be kept apart to support separation of duties.

Assigning a single role to a user seems ideal, but it is difficult to do when using RBAC in a system or application with diverse types of resources. Limiting the number of roles in a system simply means more users must be assigned to the same role. This has the consequence of reducing the granularity of the access control implementation. Creating a role unique to each individual user seems like a good alternative. However, this has its problems as well. As the number of users and roles increases, it becomes more difficult to create new roles due to conflicts with existing roles. Furthermore, if mutual exclusivity is desired, then it can be difficult for users to even share data. Assigning a single role to a user in an RBAC implementation can work when the scope of the system or application is small. For instance, assigning a role to each user of a mobile or network device is reasonable. The limited functionality of the device and information that would be shared between users means there are fewer instances when sharing of rights or permissions is needed. Therefore, when mutual access to specific resources is uncommon, assignment of a single role to each user is less of a challenge. In cases where the number of rights and permissions is small, single roles may work well. However, assigning users a single role in a complex system with a diversity of data types will most likely result in a failed RBAC attempt.

Implementing an RBAC mechanism in a complex system will involve the creation and assignment of multiple roles. Rather than considering a role to match a particular individual or job function, we consider it to take on the attributes of the various activities associated with it. From this perspective, the organizational role of an individual is essentially the composition of many smaller roles. Suppose the organizational duty of a security officer is assigned the following roles:

- Conduct a security assessment
- Review audit logs
- Advise the CIO

In this example, rights and permissions on resources associated with these activities are assigned to each of the prescribed roles. An individual who is a security officer is allowed to use those roles within the system. This is not to say that a role contains other roles, but rather, that the activity of an individual comprises many smaller, more discrete roles. Reducing the activities of individuals to more discrete roles enables separation of duties while preserving the ability for mutual access. Considering the prior example, a system administrator and security officer would both be assigned the role to *Review Audit Logs*, but a system administrator would not be allowed to *Conduct a Security Assessment* or *Advise the CIO*. This exemplifies the need to define roles at a granular level.

An RBAC implementation with a rich diversity of roles should provide sufficient granularity of resource usage. However, an important consideration is the number of roles a subject possesses at any one time. This raises a couple of questions:

- Should a subject be allowed to hold multiple roles or only one role at a time?
- What is the impact of access control layering?

Some RBAC implementations only allow one role at a time, while others permit more. The security architect must decide if one role at a time is sufficient from a usability perspective. If it is too difficult to use, then multiple roles will be needed. However, the assignment of multiple roles must consider the possibility of violating separation of duties. A user concurrently possessing multiple roles might allow a separation of duty violation, whereas using one role at a time would not. If the underlying RBAC mechanism supports the ability to specify mutual exclusivity constraints for conflicting roles, then it may be possible to securely use multiple roles concurrently.

A well-designed RBAC implementation with highly granular role assignments and constraints may be made inconsequential when combined with other access control systems. When the access control systems of diverse system components are of different types or do not communicate, the incompatibility may reduce the overall effectiveness of the design. This is a concern when products with an access control capability do not integrate well with those of other applications. This situation is even more problematic when the access control mechanisms are of different types. For instance, an RBAC instance within a DBMS may have ideal role assignments and constraints. Users connecting to the DBMS do so from an operating system implementing DAC. Further, suppose that two particular users are assigned mutually exclusive roles to satisfy separation of duties. A problem may arise when one user copies information from the database into an operating system directory accessible by the other. Although this action may be prohibited by policy, it demonstrates that the system is incapable of enforcing the policy of separation of duties due to the incompatibility of the access control mechanisms. An architect must consider the effect of layering access controls and determine if a reduction in the desired control may occur. The ease with which a control may be bypassed is as important a consideration as the cost associated with its implementation and management.

Ultimately, these questions can be answered by examining organizational policy and goals for the system. The RBAC implementation should support system policy and goals. A valid access control approach should not violate the rules and desired implementation of the system.

RBAC, similar to DAC, is not exactly the same from one vendor to the next. Some vendor products claiming to support RBAC simply allow the designation of a group of rights and permissions as a role, while others make an effort to implement most of its desirable aspects. Ideally, an RBAC-enabled product will allow the allocation of multiple roles and the ability to specify mutual exclusivity. The decision to select an RBAC-enabled product should be driven by business requirements and its suitability for the intended purpose to enforce a security policy.

A true implementation of RBAC is predicated on a mechanism that enforces its attributes. However, this may not be practical or feasible for resource-constrained organizations using commodity systems that desire this type of access control. In these cases, groups could be used to mimic role-based access. Because the term *groups* generally implies the use of DAC, it is important to note that designing groups to be used as roles

- Requires management discipline. Those creating groups and assigning membership will need to strictly adhere to group usage specifications.

■ Will not enforce separation of duties. DAC does not have an inherent capability to enforce separation of duties. However, proper use of groups can come close to achieving the same effect without the assurance of enforcement.

User accounts can be administered on a role basis when sufficient planning, management, and monitoring are implemented. The following guidance provides some recommendations regarding the use of groups as roles:

■ *Create groups as if they were roles.* The mantra of fully documenting all aspects is essential here. A detailed listing of the attributes and uses of each group as a role is required. Inadequate or inconsistent specification for the design and use of groups as roles will yield less than desirable results.

■ *Map the new roles (groups) to specific permissions and objects.* Identify which objects in the systems should have permissions associated with the roles.

■ *Avoid assigning groups to groups.* This can quickly degrade the role-based effort. Assigning one role (group) to another will substantially add to the complexity needed and tracking required and should be avoided.

■ *Refrain from assigning account permissions on objects.* Maintaining role-based access means that individual accounts should be assigned permissions only through the use of roles. This may be problematic for service and system accounts, but in most cases should not be too difficult for accounts assigned to humans.

■ *Issue users multiple accounts.* This is necessary if varying levels of rights are needed. This does not mean a user must have an account for each role, but rather, the inclusion of a member in a "role" must not create a situation where an account can easily circumvent its intended use. In this regard, a solid identity management methodology increases in importance.

■ *Leverage system services.* Consider the implications of Web-based services, portals, databases, and other automation techniques that could act as intermediaries between subjects and objects. Designing services as a way to proxy access to objects without actually interacting with them can be used as a way to enforce role-based access for critical resources.

■ *Limit object permissions.* Avoid giving subjects too much control over existing objects. Providing excessive permissions will make it more difficult to prevent inappropriate assignment of rights with the matching of roles and permissions. Furthermore, curtail the use of multiple roles for any object. This will help simplify verification of access. However, this may require the creation of more roles or those with broader assignment.

■ *Monitor for inappropriate permissions.* Because object owners have full control over who can access their objects, it will be necessary to periodically check the permissions on all objects. Object permissions should match what has been documented for each role. An object should have a limited number of roles assigned to it. This will help ease role management and streamline its implementation.

■ *Audit for misuse.* Plan to use audit logs as a means to verify compliance. Look for events that indicate inappropriate assignment of rights or permissions. Use of rights capable of bypassing established permissions is another area worth monitoring.

Task Based

The output of an organization is a product, a service, or both. Either of these outputs is achieved by activity within the organization that transforms resources, such as raw materials or intellectual property, through effort exerted by its members. The activities associated with the resource conversions into outputs are called workflows. A task is a discrete activity in a workflow whereby people manipulate resources. A workflow may contain only one task or have multiple tasks. Some attributes of a task include time, sequence, and dependencies. A task may have to be conducted at specific times, but not necessarily in all cases. Most tasks will involve a series of steps and or events that may need to be accomplished in a particular order. An individual may not be able to conduct a task unless other tasks in the workflow are previously accomplished. For example, an editor cannot *edit* a document until the author has completed the *drafting* task. In this case, *edit* and *drafting* are tasks in the workflow of creating a document. Given the attributes of a task, an access control method supporting workflows is possible. These attributes can be specified as rules governing those aspects of the task. In this way, the rules can specify a subject, object, and permission in conjunction with a particular attribute. Task-based access control (TBAC) attributes consider

■ *Time*—This could be the amount of time allocated for a task as well as start and stop times. TBAC could specify a rule that requires a task to take no more than one hour, must be started between 6:00 AM and 8:00 AM, and is required to end by 9:00 AM. Days of a given week, month, or year could also be used as time parameters.

■ *Sequence*—A task may have elements that need to be performed in a certain order. If not, the task may produce erroneous output. The task sequence attribute of TBAC could specify the order of events or elements required to complete the task. A sequence can be enforced within a task by restricting access to elements until the ordering is correct.

■ *Dependencies*—Some tasks can only be performed after the work of a prior task in the workflow is completed. In this case, the task in question is dependent on the completion of the tasks before it. Similarly, subsequent tasks may also need to wait for the present task to complete. Like the previous example, a document editor cannot conduct the edit task until the author completes the drafting task. Edit has a dependency on drafting in this example. An obvious approach is to prevent the editor from accessing the draft before the author is finished. This may not work in all cases. Suppose the editor is required to periodically review the progress of the author. This may be a different task for the editor, but it is essentially part of the same overall workflow. By allocating permissions on objects according to their stage in a workflow, an editor could be given permission to read, but not write an object in the workflow given the requisite dependencies.

The concept of TBAC is still an emerging topic. Presently, there are no accepted standards or definitions of what TBAC entails. However, this does not detract from the usefulness of implementing access control according to the attributes of a task in a workflow. Indeed, many organizations already implement types of access control in workflows. A number of document collaboration suites implement workflows and make use of TBAC enforcement attributes. A security architect should consider methods of leveraging TBAC attributes to enforce access controls on organization-specific workflows.

At first glance, TBAC appears to be closely related to RBAC. This is somewhat true. The important difference arises in the fact that the attributes specified for TBAC are more granular than those for RBAC. For example, a time attribute for RBAC is nondeterministic. This is to say that there is no specification within RBAC that requires the assignment of a role to begin or end at a specific point in time. In contrast, TBAC can have an assigned start and stop time as well as duration. RBAC also does not specify a sequence of events within a workflow, but rather broadly defines an activity indicative of a role. Finally, RBAC does not consider dependencies in a task, whereas TBAC may prevent an individual from starting a task before all of the necessary elements are in place.

Implementing TBAC has many advantages for an organization. It can reduce confusion and errors by automating manual processes that may otherwise be chaotic. The attributes of TBAC can be expressed in any number of ways to support the goals of the organization. Business rules can be created for each attribute, which can yield efficiencies and reduce errors. Standardization of workflows is an important consideration when safety is a concern. For instance, establishing TBAC for vulnerability scanning tasks may be important to some organizations. Suppose a health care organization needs to scan its network for vulnerabilities, but must exclude medical monitoring devices attached to the network. Furthermore, the scanning must be done at nonpeak times. One part of the task may require a preliminary scan to detect nonmedical monitoring devices. The result is fed into the actual scan, which limits the bounds of the vulnerability scan. The actual vulnerability scan has a dependency on the preliminary scan. Implementing an automated process governed by TBAC to control the preliminary scan, subsequent vulnerability scan, and the timing of these events supports the organization's safety goal and provides a higher level of assurance against mistakes.

Dual Control

Some organizational activities are so sensitive that it is absolutely critical that no single person be able to control an event or access the information. Access control requiring the cooperation of two individuals participating jointly in a process to access an object is called dual control. Within dual control, access is granted after two subjects with the proper permissions jointly agree and perform a rigid procedure to access the protected object. The implementation of dual control involves not only individuals, but a detailed protocol as well.

Dual control is commonly used as an assurance mechanism to prevent a catastrophic event. It is frequently used as a control mechanism for nuclear weapons, large financial transactions, and certificate authority management activities. In each of these cases, a rogue individual with the ability to commit a transaction could precipitate an event with significant consequences. Launching of nuclear weapons by a single individual is certainly chilling. Granting an individual the power to make billions of investment dollars vanish into secret accounts is a misguided reliance on trust. Providing a person with unfettered access to cryptographic keys or certificates used to support e-commerce or the identity of individuals is potentially devastating and irresponsible.

The premise of dual control is that inappropriate access to a sensitive resource will only happen with collusion. Dual control is a hard-core implementation of separation of duties. All individuals participating in the dual-control protocol should have sufficient separation to prevent the possibility of one person unduly influencing another in the process. To further reduce the opportunity for collusion, it is necessary to periodically rotate one or both of the individuals participating in the dual-control protocol. Job rotations are a common procedural control used to identify abuse of access or ongoing collusion. When dual control is implemented as an access control measure to protect against a serious event or loss, it must be accompanied by rotation of the individuals as well.

Usage of the term *dual control* is somewhat misleading. The term implies that access control requires only two individuals. In fact, a dual control protocol may involve many more participants. Other individuals may be responsible for witnessing the event while others might be assigned to monitor the activities. In some cases, the individuals participating in the dual-control process release the asset so that yet another individual may temporarily access it. One might argue that the involvement of more than two individuals clouds the definition. In a pure sense, that is not the case. Essentially, the protocol is truly dual control when two individuals are needed to unlock the asset. However, there must be at least one more individual participating in the protocol as an auditor. This individual is responsible for auditing the actions of the participants to ensure some level of accountability. The auditor would not have the authority to interact with the asset and would most likely not be allowed in the area when it is unlocked. Nevertheless, accountability is still essential to the integrity of the dual-control protocol and must be followed by someone on the periphery of the actions of those accessing the sensitive item.

Security requirements that point to the need for dual control must be accompanied by management commitment to provide the necessary resources. In uncommon cases when extensive resources are available, it is not ideal to design dual control with enormously complex countermeasures. Complexity can introduce more opportunities for weaknesses. The design of the dual-control implementation should be sufficient to meet the goals and objectives of protecting the sensitive resource. The security architect must bear in mind that elaborate designs are more difficult to implement and enforce. Therefore, the use and design of dual control should be concise, yet sufficient for its purpose. The following are some points to keep in mind when developing dual access control:

- *A rigid protocol*—A successful implementation of dual control is highly dependent on the manual and automated processes supporting it. The interactions between people and machines should be designed to work in harmony. This can only be achieved when the processes used to protect the resource, control access, and monitoring work together without error. All processes supporting protection, access, and monitoring should be well defined in a thoroughly documented protocol. The steps in the protocol should be clear and concise. It should not be possible to execute steps out of sequence without detection of the violation. All errors or violations encountered during the protocol should be met with responses to ensure the appropriate protection measures of the resource have not been compromised. In other words, the protocol should be self-checking and have defense-in-depth countermeasures integrated within.
- *Layering of physical and logical controls*—A variety of controls should be used in layers. Defense in depth is an important strategy for controls implemented. The strategy should call for controls that continue to operate when another fails. There should be little or no dependency from one control layer to the next; that is, a failure in one layer will not make it easier to compromise the next. For example, IT systems are highly dependent on physical security controls. This situation is augmented with other controls, such as media encryption, to protect the system when physical security cannot be ensured. Consider these types of controls for use inside facilities when systems used to protect critical assets must have strong assurances even if a breach occurs at the physical layer.

Power Loss: The Universal Weakness

No matter how elaborate the complexity, redundancy, and failover measures planned by an organization are, they, like all modern systems, are vulnerable to a loss of electrical power. Organizations are heavily dependent on electrical grids for continuous power. Power disruptions occurring due to natural disaster are the most serious to deal with. Many sites plan for long-duration power outages by installing backup power generators. Most of these run off one fuel or another. However, during a natural disaster, fuel supplies may be disrupted. When the fuel dries up and the power goes off, the ability to monitor or control access to critical assets may be lost. Dual control may not even be possible to achieve in these instances. If access to a critical asset is necessary during such events, it is worth considering the use of manual methods to either supplement or replace electronic ones. Planning for the worst is imperative when the magnitude of harm from a loss of access control for a sensitive asset is significant.

- *Fail secure*—Ideally, the protocol and controls cannot be circumvented. Although it is not usually acceptable to rely on absolutes in the world of security, in the case of dual-control implementations, failing in a secure mode must be an important goal. Control failures are a reality. Nothing is perfect. Therefore, it is necessary to plan for imperfection. A failure in a control may indicate that an attack is under way and a breach is imminent. In this case, the protection of the asset is of paramount importance. The magnitude of harm that may occur due to its exposure should be met with a plan to prevent the catastrophic event. Fail-secure measures are alternative steps that further protect an asset from exposure. In the most critical cases, the asset is destroyed. A security architect implementing dual control should consider fail-secure measures that will deny unauthorized access to the resource when other controls fail.
- *Resource intensive*—It must be recognized and accepted that implementing dual control can be a costly endeavor. The involvement of multiple individuals, at a minimum, makes its usage inconvenient. Dual control is a form of access control that is best reserved for situations when the cost of a breach exceeds the cost of control by a large margin.
- *Frequency of use*—Use of the protocol should be kept to a minimum when possible. This will help keep adversaries who might be monitoring operations from analyzing the protocol and identifying weaknesses not previously considered. Ideally, the protocol will only be activated during special events that require access to the protected resource. Not only should use of the protocol be minimized, the timing of access should be varied as well. Vary the times and dates of initiating the protocol. This will help to further thwart adversarial activities. Unpredictability and randomness can increase the complexity of analysis by adversaries.
- *Keep protocol details confidential*—Centralize the entire documented protocol. Avoid distributing details of the entire protocol to its participants. Compartmentalize it to the greatest extent possible by only providing details to those who need to know what is necessary to execute their part.

■ *Auditing*—Those assigned to audit or monitor activities should not be provided with the capability to manage access control layers or interact with the protected resource. Those responsible for monitoring will need to have full knowledge of the details of the protocol for those areas monitored. This provides the auditor with the ability to assess situations and make a determination if the protocol was violated. A protocol violation is an indication of an actual attack, human error, or control flaw. The auditor must have sufficient understanding of the protocol and controls to be capable of making this determination.

■ *Key management*—To be certain, key management under dual control is not trivial. It is time consuming and should involve multiple participants to ensure integrity in the process. Nevertheless, keys should be periodically changed and must be controlled absolutely. Key management duties should be segregated outside of the scope of the individuals using the keys or managing any of the control layers.

Location

The physical attributes of system components provide yet another opportunity for the application of access controls. The locations of a subject versus the requested resource are often at different subnets, geographic locales, or devices. Access controls can be applied according to the location of the subject and the requested resource. Rule sets, policies, configurations, and network design can be implemented to dictate the extent of an access according to the origin and destination of the request. Locations have logical and physical attributes that can be used to enhance the granularity of other access control mechanisms.

Topology

Nodes in a distributed system are joined together through network topologies. The type of topology used in the network is influenced by the networking protocols and technology implemented. Regardless of the implementation, a common communication point will often be used that connects or routes network traffic between distant nodes. These junctures in the topology are the points in the network that are used to define locations. For instance, a router connecting the organizational network to the Internet defines internal and external locations. A wireless access point is another opportunity to define a location where trusted and untrusted traffic meet. The spans between the defining points are segments. The defining points that separate network subnets, geographical locales, or devices are where rules should be applied to establish location-based access controls.

Subnet

A subnet is used to logically segregate a network. In practice, a subnet is often associated with a particular grouping of users, devices, or areas within a network. The

Accounting
Workstations
192.168.10.0/24

Engineering
workstations
192.168.20.0/24

Marketing
workstations
192.168.30.0/24

Router

Permit	192.168.10.0/24	192.168.20.0/24
Permit	192.168.10.0/24	192.168.30.0/24
Permit	192.168.20.0/24	192.168.30.0/24
Permit	192.168.30.0/24	192.168.50.123

Sales Server
192.168.50.123

Router Access Control List

Figure 1.45   Using a router to establish access control.

implementation of a subnet is commonly applied to a particular network segment or an entire local area network. This often results in a given location having the same subnet mask. In this regard, the logical address is frequently associated with a particular physical location. This is not exclusively the case, though. Organizations using a virtual LAN (VLAN) may mingle logical addresses with different subnets in the same network segment. Associating subnet masks with their locations can be leveraged to control access. For instance, suppose a policy stipulates that a Sales server can only be accessed from the Marketing group within the LAN. If each major group within the network is allocated its own subnet, then an internal router can be configured to deny connections to all but the Marketing group based on their subnet. Figure 1.45 presents a diagram of this situation. A centralized router is configured to block subnet addresses that are not from Marketing. Because Accounting and Engineering are in different subnets, the router prevents them from accessing the server. This demonstrates a method of implementing access control based on the logical location of a subject and the resource.

Using subnets as a way to enforce access control is helpful, but not perfect. Abuse can still occur, and this type of control can be bypassed. Furthermore, usability can also be difficult in some situations given the structure of the organization. Some issues with this implementation include

- *Stealing IP addresses*—Insiders may be able to reassign the network address on their workstation. This would allow them to bypass the controls on the router unless subsequent routers are used to counteract this situation.
- *DHCP*—If all DHCP requests are handled by the same server, then this type of access control would be difficult to implement. Alternatively, a DHCP

server could be dedicated to the protected area to assign the protected range. This would also require the use of a router to block DHCP requests from traversing into or out of the protected subnet.

■ *Logon from nonstandard location*—Users allowed to login from different locations may not be able to access the resource. This would be particularly difficult to accommodate when users must frequently use different workstations at various locations.

■ *Network sniffing*—Sensitive-traffic-traversing network segments outside of the protected subnet range are vulnerable to capture. An insider might only need to record network traffic to obtain the information required rather than attacking the server itself.

Geographical Considerations

System nodes access resources from a given network segment. A node existing on a particular segment may access resources in the same segment or that of another. Each segment has a geographical location with respect to the organization's system. Consider a scenario where workstations, servers, and printers are physically joined to the network through switches. Nodes in a given area are clustered around a particular department within the organization. The switches joining the nodes in one department may connect to more switches or other networking devices, such as routers, enabling connectivity throughout the organization. The segments joining nodes and network devices are often contained in plenum areas such as ceilings, walls, and under floors, concealing their exact route. Although the exact path may not be known, the security architect and system engineers should know the area within a building serviced by a given segment. Knowing the approximate location serviced by a segment enables the application of access controls based on the physical location or a node. In this way, groupings of segments from a given networking device can be associated with a particular physical location. This could be used to control the types of traffic flows into and out of this area, based on the activities associated with the duties of those in the department.

Associating segments with node types is important, if only from an inventory perspective. However, this is less useful from a security standpoint if the types of activities in a segment are not known. For instance, security monitoring personnel may be tasked to conduct periodic port scans from their segment to the rest of the network. Given their duties, this is normal activity. However, port scanning would not be normal activity if it originated from the Accounting department segment. When the physical locations of nodes are associated with normal user activities, security policies can be applied accordingly. In this example, policy can be enforced for the Accounting department segment to prevent port scans from propagating across the network. Likewise, an intrusion detection sensor placed within the segment could be tuned to specifically look for activity that is known to be malicious, depending on the types of users within the segment.

Scheme = Device-IP/Floor/Department/Office

Figure 1.46 Network mapping using a tree diagram.

Applying restrictions based on physical location involves the use of logical access controls. The idea is to designate logical access controls based on physical locations rather than logical addressing. The approach simply requires the designation of access controls for a network segment and those behind it having the same nodes or subjects. Consider mapping a network using a tree diagram such as the one shown in Figure 1.46. Mapping a network in this manner can aid in the identification of areas to best apply physical restrictions.

Logical addressing and subnets enable one to support physical restrictions while still permitting organizational communications. The routing node is configured to only pass traffic for a given subnet that is exclusively dedicated to a particular group of subjects. The routing access control list specifies subnets or addresses that are accessible from a segment. The critical point here is that different segments should be physically separated until they are connected to the node applying the logical access controls. This prevents an insider from spoofing an address in an alternate subnet and bypassing access controls based on physical location. The interface on the network node used to apply the access controls must be exclusively connected to the intended segment.

Establishing access controls for physical segments is complicated when users are not stationary. Users with roaming profiles or mobile users who are allowed to login from any segment in the network make it more difficult to establish behavior patterns. When the scope of network activity is too broad, then the application of access controls based on node location can be too restrictive for organizational purposes.

The idea of using access controls for network segments assumes that requests for resource access originate from a node within the segment. Unfortunately, this is not always the case. A node that has been compromised by malicious code, such as a bot or a Trojan, will access resources according to the commands given by someone outside of the network. In this regard, a compromised node extends the activity of an attacker within the context of an authorized subject on the network segment, which essentially bypasses the restrictions of access control based on physical location. Access controls on the network segment may be of little help if the activity of the malicious code is similar to that of an authorized user. However, many types of malicious code do launch subsequent attacks to further compromise the network. In these cases, access control based on physical location has its benefits, by restricting the propagation. If auditing is enabled for the access control device, the violations will be reported, which provides an opportunity to identify the offending node and eliminate the malicious code.

Device Type

Applying access controls based on the type of device connected to the network is a desirable goal. A variety of device types are regularly attached to networks. Some common types include wired networking equipment, wireless devices, servers, workstations, laptops, and personal digital assistants (PDAs). The granularity of identification of the device type is based on the security policies or goals of the organization. For instance, it may be desirable to distinguish workstations according to who normally uses them. In this case, a workstation device type might be further decomposed into subsets such as administrator, security, and ordinary user workstations. Enabling access controls according to device type is dependent on two important factors:

■ *Device recognition*—Each device type must be recognizable in some way by the access control mechanism.
■ *Policy enforcement*—Access control decisions are made according to the device type recognized. Devices that are not recognized should not be allowed to connect and pass traffic in the network.

There are generally three approaches to solving any problem in IT. These involve solutions that are ad hoc, standards based, and proprietary. With respect to the application of access controls for device types, an ad hoc approach involves the use of physical and logical addresses. The use of network-based access control is a standards-based approach worth exploring. Third-party software frequently represents a plethora of proprietary techniques that can be used to solve perplexing problems.

Physical and Logical Addresses

Prior to connecting a device, its physical address is registered. In cases where the logical address is static, this address would be recorded as well. The rules regarding what the device is allowed to communicate with would be encoded into Layer 2 devices, Layer 3 devices, and monitoring devices. Layer 2 devices are configured to lock a port to a given physical address. This is applied for every network port in the organization. Ideally, static logical addresses are used to strongly associate a given port with a unique device. However, this would be difficult to administer in a large organization. When dynamic addresses are used, an assigned range for a given area of the network must be used. This means multiple DHCP servers will be necessary to control which addresses are available in a given segment. Layer 3 devices are used to enforce policies for an explicit device when the logical address is known, or for a range when applied to a particular device type. Network monitoring will be necessary to capture network communication activity. A log of network activity containing logical and physical addresses allows the security team to detect violations to policy and take actions when suspicious activity is detected.

Advantages:
- *Easy to implement*—This approach makes use of devices common to many organizational networks.
- *Cost-effective*—The costs associated with the design and implementation are minimal. Some additional cost may be necessary to place a sufficient number of devices to control and monitor access. However, these need not necessarily be top-of-the-line models.

Disadvantages:
- *Manual registration*—Each device must be manually registered. A centralized database of what is allowed must be maintained. Furthermore, activity on the network will need to be periodically compared to the database to detect violations. This could be automated, but that requires software development, which also may be costly.
- *Lack of scalability*—The manual aspects of this approach will not scale well. Implementing this approach in an organization with a large network may be impractical.
- *Limited enforcement*—A lack of integration with monitoring and enforcement mechanisms reduces the ability of this approach to fully enforce a policy. Unless the monitoring activity is automated and can create Layer 3 changes on the fly, the ability to fully support the policy is diminished.
- *Spoofing*—Insiders could spoof their media access control and logical addresses and thereby circumvent the control all together.

Network-Based Access Control

Another approach is to implement the 802.1X standard as a means of authenticating each device attaching to the network. As devices connect to the network, they are authenticated according to the certificate presented. A RADIUS server is used to support device authentication.

Advantages:

- *Standards based*—This approach relies on an existing protocol specifically designed to address the problem of device authentication.
- *Policy enforcement*—Only authenticated devices are allowed to connect to the network.
- *Auditing support*—Connection attempts can be recorded to identify misuse and abuse.

Disadvantages:

- *Not supported by all device types*—Some device classes such as PDAs may not support 802.1X. Existing network equipment internal to the organization also may not be capable of using the standard. Upgrading equipment to fully support this approach could be quite costly.
- *Manual registration*—Each device will still need to be individually issued a certificate. Prior to deployment, it must be ensured that the correct device is issued the appropriate certificate. For many devices, this may require an administrator to manually load the certificate or visually determine that the target device is that which is intended.
- *Certificate management*—The standard makes use of certificates that uniquely identify a given device. This implies the need to develop and maintain PKI to support 802.1X.
- *Authentication only*—The policy enforcement is limited to device authentication. Applying permissions for access to other resources necessitates logical access controls via other devices such as Layer 2 and Layer 3 network equipment.

Third-Party Software

As the problem of identifying device types and applying granular access control continues, it is certain that vendors will develop proprietary solutions to mitigate the problem. The solutions could be as varied as the number of available products. It is difficult to determine the exact advantages and disadvantages of using third-party products because one product may be quite different from another. However, it is surmised that some potential advantages and disadvantages will be common to products that are developed to specifically address the issue of allocating access controls based on the device type.

Potential Advantages:

- *Specialized*—A given technology may be uniquely designed to handle a given problem or task. In this regard, a vendor tool might prove quite useful and successful in enforcing organizational policy regarding device types in a network.
- *Technical support*—Most products have some sort of support built into their purchasing agreement. The support provided may be sufficient

to get the product deployed and staff adequately trained on its usage. Furthermore, vendor-supported products typically make updates available to address flaws or improve the native software.

- *Policy enforcement*—A tool that sufficiently supports the goals of the organization should support rule enforcement for a given device type.
- *Automated deployment*—Many products will have automated methods to deploy their tools to all intended targets. This can greatly simplify device management and expedite tool deployment.

Potential Disadvantages:

- *Cost*—Most tools may be too expensive for smaller organizations or departments with budgetary constraints. Reducing the scope of deployment to meet resource constraints may leave aspects of the policy unenforced.
- *Imaginary functionality*—The vendor marketing may be excellent, but the product could fail to live up to the hype. The vendor may overstate the actual capabilities of the product. The tool may not completely satisfy the intended security requirements specified by the acquiring organization.
- *May not support all device types*—A new product may not support all existing device types within an organization. Legacy operating systems and hardware may be outside the purview of the vendor's product. Furthermore, not all devices may be supported equally. The advertised functionality may not apply to all device types supported.

The aforementioned techniques to achieve location-based access control have various strengths and weaknesses. No individual technique is likely to be suitable for a moderate-sized organization or one that is geographically distributed. Location-based access control is best achieved through a combination of techniques. The design and implementation of location-based access control involves the following factors:

- *Join logical and physical*—Applying access controls based on location requires the use of logical and physical attributes of nodes and networking equipment. Identify all physical and logical characteristics that can be leveraged to achieve the desired level of access control.
- *Layer controls*—Use multiple techniques to achieve defense in depth.
- *Map and inventory the network*—Use scanning tools to identify all nodes in the network and the logical segments where they exist. Access controls in the network may prevent deep scanning. In these cases, it may be necessary to conduct scans from multiple locations. Conduct an inventory of all devices connected to the network. At a minimum, the media access control address, device type, and physical location will need to be collected.
- *Conduct traffic pattern analysis*—Observe traffic patterns to assess normal activity. This information can be used to apply access controls to prohibit

inappropriate connections from one area of the network to another. It can also constrain malicious code from propagating across the entire network.

■ *Know where segments exist physically*—Conduct physical surveys to verify where the Ethernet cable connects to the networking device and in what area of a building it terminates. Some organizations may already have this information, but it is still advisable to verify their locations.

■ *Implement rules on networking equipment*—Rely on networking equipment to enforce location-based rules. Ensure that the equipment is protected from logical tampering and located in physically controlled areas to prevent physical tampering. Trusting network nodes to enforce location-based access controls is less desirable unless it is integrated with network-based mechanisms such as 802.11X.

■ *Monitor compliance*—Assess the location-based access control mechanisms by reviewing network device configurations and logs, and watching traffic connections.

Authentication

The basis of access control relies on the proper identification of a subject. This occurs when several elements are joined together in a process that validates a claimed identity. The necessary components of identity verification include

■ *Entity*—A person or process claiming a particular identity.
■ *Identity*—A unique designator for a given subject.
■ *Authentication factor*—Proof of identity supplied by the entity. This element must be reproducible only by the entity.
■ *Authenticator*—The mechanism to compare the identity and authentication factor against a database of authorized subjects.
■ *Database*—A listing of identities and associated authentication factors. The database should be protected from tampering. Furthermore, the authenticator factors should also be protected from disclosure.

The Difference between an Entity and Subject

It is important to note that a distinction is made between an entity and a subject. An individual who is yet to be authenticated is referred to as an entity rather than a subject. This distinction is necessary because a subject represents someone or something with logical rights and permissions in a system. An entity has no logical rights before authentication. An entity graduates to a subject when successfully validated.

The act of an entity proving its identity is known as authentication. It is an exchange and validation of information that allows the entity further access into an environment. During authentication, an entity presents an identity and an authentication factor as proof that it is who it claims to be. The identity of the entity is verified by the authenticator comparing the authentication factor against a database of all identities. A successful match between the identity and authentication factor with an entry in the database supports the claim, and access is authorized. Once an entity is authenticated, it is recognized as a subject by the access control mechanism and is allowed access based on previously granted permissions and rights in the environment.

An authentication factor is essentially a key that opens a door into an environment. It is something tied to a specific identity and should only be reproducible by the entity. The three most common forms of authentication factors include something that is

- Known only by the entity. Passwords and passphrases are the most common.
- Held exclusively by the entity. An ATM card is an example of a token held by an owner.
- A physical attribute of the entity. Fingerprints are one type of physical attribute.

The most important point of an authentication factor is its reproducibility. Only the entity should be able to present the correct authentication factor. It should not be trivial for an attacker to reproduce the authentication factor and masquerade as the intended subject. Three qualities emerge that can be used to evaluate the suitability of an authentication factor in a given authentication mechanism. An authentication factor meeting at least one of these qualities will provide sufficient confidence that an attacker will not be able to easily masquerade as the intended subject. These three qualities are as follows:

- *It is known only to the entity*—No other individuals have cleartext access to the secret. This means that other means must be employed to capture or persuade the entity to disclose the secret as opposed to its being easily guessed or known by others.
- *Reproduction of it is infeasible*—It should be nearly impossible to create an illegitimate copy. Attributes of the authentication factor should be sufficiently complex or difficult to reproduce such that attempts to do so will have an extremely low likelihood of success.
- *It is computationally impractical to replicate*—Mathematical shortcuts to guess or reproduce the authentication factor should not exist. Brute force attacks should be met with a sufficiently large search space and an extremely small probability of finding the authentication factor over a long period of time.

Sometimes, authentication factors are not used appropriately. On occasion, some authentication mechanisms use the authentication factor as a form of identity as well. The problem with this approach is that a compromised authentication factor may make it difficult to uniquely identify the subject in subsequent environments. This is not an advisable practice and should be avoided when possible.

Strengths and Weaknesses of Authentication Tools

Passwords have long been an authentication factor of choice for many systems. They are cheap and easy to deploy. Generally, users find a password easy to remember and use with a system. However, passwords are not necessarily the best authentication factor. Users tend to choose weak passwords that can be guessed in relatively short periods of time. To counter this situation, organizations require passwords to be sufficiently complex that they are not easily guessed. At this point, users begin to rebel. Passwords are now more difficult. Indeed, they can become so complex that users write them down to remember them. Fortunately, advances in technology have made other authentication factors available for use. Two types of authentication factors that are finding their way into organizations are tokens and biometrics. Although some of these have strengths that may surpass fixed passwords, they each have their own unique issues that should be considered prior to rolling a new authentication system into an organization.

Token-Based Authentication Tools

A variety of devices are available that fall into the category of *something held exclusively by the entity*. These tokens rely on different types of technology to supply the authentication factor attribute.

Badges

These devices contain organization-specific designs, logos, and occasionally a picture of the authorized holder. Badges are most often used in conjunction with facility access control. Individuals posted at facility entry control points check the badge to ensure that it appears authentic, not expired, and is properly matched with the holder when an image is presented. Organizational staff should be trained to recognize badges to determine if an individual within the facility is either authorized facility access, a guest, or perhaps someone who inappropriately gained access. Plain badges are not used to interface with systems.

Strengths:
  - *Low cost*—Badge blanks and the equipment used to print them are affordable.
  - *Visually recognizable*—A unique design is recognizable by organizational members.

Weaknesses:
- *Easily spoofed*—The combined strengths are also a weakness. Attackers may be able to easily duplicate an organizational badge, which cannot be easily detected.
- *Relied upon as identification*—A badge lacking a feature or attribute permitting someone to verify its authenticity should not be used as an exclusive form of identification.

Considerations:
- *Mandate use of member pictures*—An individual's image ties the badge to the holder. Organizational members can at least determine that a badge is worn by the correct individual. Pictures also help validation at facility entry control points.
- *Manage badges like a credential*—Badges should be tracked and have a life cycle. Each badge should have a unique identifier tied to an individual. Those responsible for verifying identities at entry control points should be able to compare a badge number with an image of the holder. Periodically, change badge attributes to help visually detect frauds. Recover badges from those departing the organization.
- *Integrate machine-readable features*—Make the badge identifier machine readable using barcodes, magnetic strip, or proximity technologies.
- *Use different designs according to holder*—Use different colors and schemes to differentiate badge holders. Establish different badge holders by classes such as employees, contractors, visitors, maintenance crews, security personnel, escorts, and sensitive area access.

Magnetic Strip

This type of token normally has the same form factor as a credit card and has a magnetic tape stretching the length of the card. Magnetic strip cards are commonly used in facility access controls in a manner similar to that of door lock keys. In fact, the hotel industry makes extensive use of these tokens as room keys.

Strengths:
- *Cards are low cost*—Although the cards are relatively cheap, readers are moderately expensive.
- *Easy to use*—Most people have no problem using these cards.
- *Lock mechanism easily rekeyed*—Lock mechanisms are networked, so they can quickly be updated to reflect which magnetic strip cards can be used to gain entry.

Weaknesses:
- *Can be copied*—The magnetic strip is similar to the media used in audiocassette tapes. Readers can be easily procured to copy the magnetic information.

- *Vulnerable to magnetic fields*—Strong magnetic fields emanating from cell phones, cathode ray tube monitors and televisions, or permanent magnets can alter the information on the magnetic strip. Usually, the cards can be used after recoding.
- *Easily abused*—Magnetic strip cards are so easy to use that people often share them (whether voluntarily or involuntary). Many retail uses and facility access control implementations fail to employ techniques to detect masquerading or inappropriate use.

Considerations:

- *Use controls similar to those for badges*—Considerations listed earlier for badges apply to magnetic strip cards, given that the uses and form factors are similar.
- *Require two-factor authentication for sensitive areas*—A magnetic strip card alone represents a form of identification, but lacks an immediate way to authenticate without human intervention. Using another authentication factor, such as a PIN, strengthens the implementation, allows account-ability, and increases the overall level of assurance.
- *Institute a challenge response process for card recoding*—Uses of the card in situations where the user is not immediately known to the issuer should be coupled with controls and processes that track and validate magnetic strip recoding.

Proximity Cards

Many organizations employ proximity or "prox" cards for facility access control. Prox cards generally have the same form factor as a badge and use wireless techniques operating at either 125 kHz and 13.56 MHz. They provide a means to electronically identify a cardholder. Modern prox cards operate at the 13.56 MHz range and comply with ISO 14443. Prox card readers are capable of detecting a card up to several inches away. These cards contain no batteries, but are able to send their information in the presence of an electromagnetic field that powers the card, enabling transmission.

Strengths:

- *Double as ID badge*—The form factor of a prox card allows it to easily be used as an ID badge as well.
- *Simple management*—Access control systems implementing prox cards are relatively easy to use. Card activation and deactivation is a simple process.
- *Ease of use*—Prox card use is relatively intuitive. They can generally be used not only in office environments, but in areas that are exposed to the elements as well.

Weaknesses:

- *Readers are costly*—Although the cards themselves are relatively low cost, readers can be hundreds of dollars and more.

   – *Masquerading*—A card that is stolen or borrowed can be used to gain unauthorized access to areas granted to the intended cardholder.

   – *Can be spoofed*—Most cards are not capable of using encryption to prevent spoofing. Rogue readers with high output fields and strong sensitivity can be used to capture card identities as people pass by. This information can be passed to specially constructed devices that retransmit card information, allowing access to protected areas.

Considerations:

   – *Follow considerations given for magnetic strip cards*—Many of the issues applicable to magnetic strip cards apply to prox cards as well.

   – *Periodically reaffirm access*—Ensure that cardholders continue to require access and have not left the organization.

   – *Strategically deploy readers*—Prox cards and readers provide an efficient mechanism to implement access control and auditing. They are useful for controlling access and primary entry points and are a more preferred choice than physical keys for protecting sensitive areas.

   – *Protect controllers*—Central device controllers used with prox card readers and electronic locks/strikes should be protected from unauthorized access. Restrict access to the controller to only those individuals delegated the duty of managing the prox cards.

Common Issues with Token Management

Access control using physical tokens is a basic means of identifying a subject. However, they cannot always be relied upon to authenticate a subject according to something that is possessed. Security architects must consider several common factors when designing an access control system that uses tokens.

■ *Loss of token*—A lost token can deny an authorized subject access to a system or facility. A supply of spare tokens and the availability of support personnel should be planned for. Users are bound to discover their tokens are lost while on business trips after hours. Staffing decisions to deal with these eventualities will need to be addressed and planned for.

■ *Token damage*—An inoperative token may be apparent when it is presented to the security officer in multiple pieces. However, a malfunctioning token may not be physically evident and is bound to create some level of dissatisfaction and inconvenience for the subject attempting to use it; they will have difficulties accessing authorized resources or areas. Similar to the situation for lost tokens, the possibility that a token will become inoperative at the most inopportune time must be planned for. Further, the organization must have sufficient resources allocated to support end users.

- *Proprietary systems*—Tokens of the same type may not be able to interoperate with those of other vendors. This is especially true when tokens rely on proprietary protocols or form factors for proper operation. Locking into one vendor can prove expensive. Furthermore, vulnerabilities in one vendor product could affect an entire organization and be difficult and expensive to overcome.
- *Human resource management*—Tokens are issued to people who often move on to other opportunities. Those managing access control systems using tokens might not have been informed of the departure of the token owner. Timely revocation of the access provided by a token is a persistent problem in the real world. Security architects should seek ways to partner with human resource departments, payroll offices, and internal entities providing access to contractors and customers to identify when token holders depart the organization temporarily or permanently.
- *Binding tokens to owners*—Tokens without onboard microprocessors are not easily bound to the authorized individual. Most tokens are subject to theft and misuse. Unless the access control mechanism requires dual factor authentication, it is extremely difficult to ensure that a subject using a token is the authorized user. In this regard, tokens should be relied upon as a form of electronic identification, but not as a substitute for authentication.

Biometric Authentication Tools

The field of biometrics continues to grow and attract significant attention. Biometric authentication tools seek to uniquely identify an entity based on *something they are*. Regardless of the type of biometric targeted, a small amount of data is collected to form a template that describes the attributes of the individual measured with the biometric acquisition device.

Biometrics can be broadly categorized as either physical or behavioral. A physical biometric is a measurable attribute of an individual. It is something that is a tangible feature of a person. Fingerprints are an example of a physical biometric. In contrast, a behavioral biometric is something that is intangible about a person, but sufficiently unique that it can be used to identify an individual. For instance, the way each person uses a keyboard represents a biometric referred to as typing dynamics.

Users are included in a biometric system through an enrollment process. During this period, users present their biometric for measurement. This may involve several attempts. The acquisition device collects various data elements about the patterns that make up the individual's biometric. The collected data points are referred to as minutia, and are stored in a special template file. Multiple submissions during an enrollment are necessary to ensure that a sufficiently broad statistical representation of the biometric is collected. Minutia templates can be as small as 9 bytes or up to several kilobytes, depending on the type of biometric collected and the algorithms used by the acquisition device.

Performance Characteristics

When comparing various biometric options, it is important to consider the aspects and performance characteristics associated with the type of biometric:

■ *Accuracy*—This is the critical characteristic of a biometric. Accuracy is determined by the ability of a biometric acquisition device to correctly identify an enrolled individual and reject others who are not enrolled. This is arrived at through the use of statistical methods that look for error rates associated with incorrect associations made by the biometric system between the collected template and that held within its database. Type 2 errors, also known as false positives, occur when the biometric device incorrectly identifies an unenrolled individual as legitimate. Type 1 errors, called false negatives, occur when the biometric system incorrectly prevents an authorized individual from accessing the system. Plotting Type 1 and Type 2 errors on a graph reveals a cross-over error rate that represents the lowest possible trade-off between the two types of errors.

■ *Enrollment time*—This is an estimate of the amount of time needed to initially collect the necessary attributes that identify a person. The enrollment time is almost always longer than the verification time. Enrollment in some types of biometrics is challenging and requires multiple attempts. This adds to the base enrollment time for a given biometric.

■ *Response time*—This is the average amount of time needed for an acquisition device to collect the biometric and for the system to return a response to the user. In some cases acquisition can take a few seconds. Additionally, according to the type of biometric used, the search for a closely matching template could require more time as well.

■ *Security*—Spoofing is the primary attack technique used against a biometric. An acquisition device should include countermeasures that increase its resistance to spoofing or abuse. For example, fingerprint readers should measure heat and pulse to ensure a real person is interacting with the device.

Implementation Considerations

Other factors affecting the use of biometric tools should also be included in any review by the security architect:

■ *Cost*—To a large extent, biometric devices are expensive. Some types and technologies are substantially more expensive than others. For instance, fingerprint readers have good performance and are relatively low cost compared to retina scanners.

■ *Acceptance*—The user community should not be largely resistant to the use of the biometric. Individuals commonly have health and privacy concerns regarding biometric devices. Their concerns should be tempered with an appropriate amount of education on the benefits and any perceived risk of using a particular biometric acquisition device.

- *Storage*—Biometric data storage should be thought out well in advance. Will the biometrics be stored on a central server or distributed? Perhaps smartcards will be used instead. Wherever the biometric template is stored, there must be sufficient controls in place to protect the data from unauthorized changes or exposure. Access controls over these authentication factors becomes critical.
- *Changes*—People change due to behaviors, lifestyles, aging, injuries, and other medical conditions. These changes can affect the ability of the biometric system to accurately identify an individual.

Fingerprints

This type of biometric is the most well-known technical method of establishing an individual's identity. The uniqueness of a fingerprint is due to the differences in the ridges and furrows of a print. The characteristic differences commonly used as minutiae about a print include bifurcations, ridge endings, enclosures, and ridge dots. Other minutia include pores, crossovers, and deltas, which are also used to further emphasize the uniqueness of an individual print.

Fingerprint readers generally perform well, are low cost, and are generally accepted by the public. Enrollment time is generally quick, and the results are fairly accurate. Minutia files are relatively small. Collecting a sample minutia by a subject takes only a few seconds.

Although fingerprint recognition is one of the leading types of biometric authentication, it is not without its challenges. For instance, minutia templates are not entirely standardized and, therefore, vendor products do not always interoperate. Widely deploying biometrics may require reliance on a particular vendor. This can be problematic if the vendor goes out of business. This might require a massive reenrollment for all users. Fingerprints can be also faked. Given the fact that fingerprints can be captured in an environment and spoofed, their use as a trusted authenticator is risky. The fingerprints of some individuals are difficult to collect due to aging or from exposure to abrasive activity, which could make the print difficult to capture during an enrollment process.

Hand Geometry

The physical attributes of an individual's hand are sufficiently unique to be usable as a biometric. Considering the finger length, width, and thickness combined with surface area of a hand, it is possible to create rather small template files enabling unique identification. Hand geometry biometrics appears to be quite accurate, with little to no resistance from users to data acquisition. However, cost, size of the device, and its proprietary nature inhibit wide adoption and deployment.

Iris

The patterns within the iris of each eye are quite unique. An iris has many attributes characterized as freckles, furrows, and rings that can be used as data points for a minutia template. Eye color, the most obvious attribute, is not an element of iris detection technologies. The acquisition devices use black-and-white images to create the minutia templates of the iris.

Iris-based technologies have proved themselves to be one of the best forms of biometrics (Chirillo and Blaul, 2003). They have very low error rates and are very accurate. These types of biometric devices have a moderate-to-low cost. It is likely that cost will continue to decrease as usage increases globally. Although these devices have good performance, there are issues. Users are still somewhat reluctant to participate in iris-based biometrics. It seems that people fear that the acquisition device could damage their eyes due to the use of infrared technology. Eye movement, proximity, and angle of the acquisition device, as well as lighting, affect the quality of the minutia collected. These variations can hinder the enrollment process.

Retina

The vascular patterns at the back of an eye are used to form the retina template for this type of biometric. Retinal patterns are very consistent over time and not easily subject to surreptitious collection such as with fingerprint, facial recognition, and voiceprint. Retina templates have a higher minutia data point count that substantially adds to their uniqueness.

Retina recognition systems are very accurate and very expensive. Spoofing a retina pattern is considered difficult. Aside from cost, the biggest drawback to retina-based biometrics is user acceptance. Enrollment and authentication with a retina recognition device requires an individual to place the eye very close to the input device. Many users fear damage to their eye by the device or contracting an eye disease from a prior user. Eye glasses and contacts also interfere with the proper operation of a retina detection device. Due to cost and acceptance considerations, retina-based biometrics should only be used when a high level of security is essential.

Facial Recognition

The technology used for facial recognition is relatively new, but the application is not. Although fingerprint biometrics is sometimes touted as the oldest form of biometrics, the simple truth is that this is not the case. Early systems of identification using fingerprints, although technical, were not automated. Humans have, however, relied on facial recognition as an absolute form of identification for many aeons. In fact, facial recognition through photographs, such as those used on a driver's license, has enjoyed a much broader deployment than the use of fingerprints.

It is only recently that technology has advanced to the point that facial recognition can be sufficiently automated.

There are a number of techniques that can be used for facial recognition. Some of these techniques rely on grayscale image comparisons, thermal scanning to collect heat or blood vessel patterns, and local feature analysis based on differences in defined regions of a face.

Facial recognition technologies have acceptable performance, are low cost, and are not generally resisted by users. However, they do have some issues. Lighting, hairstyles, subject aging, cosmetics, accessories such as glasses or piercing, expressions, and facial hair can affect the accuracy of the detection process. Furthermore, some facial recognition techniques can be fooled with an image of the actual subject presented to the input device. Some facial recognition techniques also fail to distinguish between identical twins.

Authentication Tool Considerations

There is an important attribute of authentication factors that is sometimes overlooked. The strength attribute of an authentication factor lies in its ability to resist abuse; that is, a strong authentication factor is difficult to reproduce by anyone other than the owner. This is a major factor driving biometrics. Most people believe that something you *are* is superior to something you know or have. Indeed, this seems plausible. However, if something you are is reproducible or can be captured, then there is the risk of abuse. If authentication factors are considered in the context of cryptography, a different paradigm emerges. In cryptography, the algorithm is important, but the most critical aspect is key management. The key is what protects the confidentiality and integrity of the information. Protecting a cryptographic key is essential to the effective use of cryptography. With respect to cryptography, an authentication factor should be handled like a secret. No matter what authentication scheme or algorithm is used, the authentication factor must be protected from exposure. Given this line of thought, the use of authentication factors that can be publicly obtained undermines its strength. A difficult-to-capture or reproduced authentication factor is likely to be resistant to attack, which increases confidence in the authentication of a subject.

As time progresses, new attacks against biometrics will emerge. Spoofing of biometric features such as fake fingers or photographs of the victim will become more frequent. Countermeasures associated with biometric acquisition devices will be needed. Defense in depth involving people, processes, as well as technology will be necessary to help ensure biometrics uses are not abused. It is interesting to ponder the thought that biometrics has been hailed as an ideal replacement for weaker authentication factors such as fixed passwords. Time will tell if biometrics will prove more resistant to abuse than passwords.

However, there exists a more disturbing problem that will challenge biometric deployments. This problem is one that every security architect must carefully consider prior to recommending the acquisition or deployment of any biometric device. A threat that plagues passwords will likely have an equivalent counterpart affecting biometrics. Keystroke loggers are a particularly nasty threat to passwords. Those running within a system can capture all manner of authentication activity using a keyboard. Similarly, a Biometric Template Logger (BTL) could also be used to capture minutia attributes before they are sent over a network. A carefully placed BTL running as a device driver could intercept the biometric data before the resident application or service has an opportunity to encrypt the data. An attacker could effectively replay this data at a future data and masquerade as a user when the biometric is the sole authentication method. Attacks against stolen passwords are recoverable by removing the offending malware and creating a new password. However, it is not necessarily this simple with biometrics. How do we recover from an attack that exposes biometric minutia? A compromise to the database or interception of the minutia template at the collection point would result in a permanent exposure of the biometric. It's not yet evident that reenrollment would be sufficient to exclude malicious use of the captured biometric template. This disturbing problem should be taken into account in the design considerations and risk assessments associated with any biometric usage.

Fortunately, there exists an architectural design that can improve on the weaknesses of tokens and biometrics-based authentication tools. Using dual factor authentication is one technique that can frustrate the ability of an attacker to masquerade or steal the identity of an authorized user. Where possible and necessary due to the level of risk, a security architect should design dual factor methods into authentication schemes. This approach is an effective way to mitigate known weaknesses and impending attack vectors that are likely to emerge against tokens and biometrics in the future.

Design Validation

Evaluating the design of a system is an important step to ensure that it meets all expectations. Design validation provides the security architect with the opportunity to ask questions and make determinations regarding the sufficiency of the implementation. A validation seeks to determine if the system is adequate, sufficient, and complete. Questions and testing presented by the security architect seek to identify inadequacies regarding any requirements, operations, functionality, and weaknesses in the implementation. A broad perspective of this approach seeks to answer questions in areas such as

- *Requirements*—Have all requirements been addressed?
- *Operations*—Are organizational needs met?
- *Functionality*—Does it work as desired?
- *Weaknesses*—Can it be circumvented?

Requirements specify the minimum attributes that must be supported by a system. With respect to access controls, requirements tend to be very broad and can have multiple interpretations. Requirements are derived from a variety of sources. The most common sources of security requirements are laws, regulations, industry standards, and organizational policies. An efficient way to determine if a system meets access control requirements is to list all applicable security requirements in a matrix. Cull all access control policy statements from applicable sources. Attempt to make each requirement as granular as possible. This may result in a single sentence from a policy statement spanning multiple requirement records in the matrix. Within the matrix, rows are used to identify individual requirement records, and columns specify the record and requirement attributes. Column headings useful in this regard include

- *Unique identifier*—Create a unique numeric or alphanumeric designator to distinguish the requirement record one from another. When discussing security issues, a unique identifier helps organizational members to be clear on which requirement is affected.
- *Sources*—Requirements from different sources may be worded differently, but are essentially the same. Combine similar policy statements from multiple sources to eliminate duplication among matrix requirements.
- *Requirement*—Create a statement that best describes the target requirement. Be as granular as possible regarding what must be implemented from an access control perspective.
- *Interpretation*—Because policy statements tend to be broad enough to have multiple interpretations, it is helpful to provide additional information clarifying the requirement. Identify in the interpretation the breadth and depth necessary for the implementation. For instance, indicate which type of hardware, software, or operations must implement the requirement.

A review of access controls should determine if the implementation meets the mission and operations of the organization. Access controls that are not related to operations or are excessive may be wasteful. There may also be aspects of operations that are unique and not covered by existing requirements. In these cases, a gap in access control coverage may exist. The security architect must strive to have access controls that are sufficient, but not excessive.

The proper operation of implemented controls is a fundamental expectation. Individuals using the system will anticipate that the access control mechanism works without too much difficulty on their part. The two elements of functionality that a security architect should bear in mind when reviewing an access control mechanism are

- *Operational*—The access control must work as intended with the desired results.
- *Usable*—A difficult-to-use access control mechanism will ultimately prove ineffective.

A failure or misconfiguration may prevent an access control mechanism from functioning properly. Similarly, an access control mechanism that is too difficult to use is in some cases just as worrisome as one that is not functioning properly. System users may seek methods to circumvent difficult-to-use access control mechanisms, rendering them ineffective. Therefore, it is necessary to test access control mechanisms through a battery of tests to ensure they are operating as intended and are usable as well. Testing should attempt to exercise controls and evaluate settings to ensure they are properly configured and are not too difficult to use.

A properly configured access control mechanism may meet requirements, operational expectations, and pass testing, and yet still have weaknesses. Flaws in software or hardware supporting the access control mechanism may allow unauthorized subjects or entities the ability to bypass a mechanism. Changes in the environment may also introduce weaknesses into the access control mechanism. Authorized software may inadvertently violate least privilege or separation of duties, nullifying existing access control implementations. This indirect weakness in access control nonetheless affects the mechanism. This illustrates the need to consider testing that extends beyond the mechanism itself. Other dependencies in the system can impact access controls and should also be reviewed for induced weaknesses.

Architecture Effectiveness Assurance

The overall goal of access control design validation is to ensure that the questions regarding requirements, operations, functionality, and weaknesses are not left unanswered. A common thread among these questions is the problem of something missing. Certain requirements may have been missed and not integrated into the system. Some operational aspects may have recently emerged that are not covered by the access control mechanism. A functional aspect of the access control mechanism may not be available to all system users. Insufficient access control coverage introduces a weakness into the system. One way to determine architecture effectiveness is to look for aspects of these questions that are missing from the access control implementation:

- *Identify access control gaps*—The effectiveness of access controls are impacted by gaps in their coverage. Access control gaps can occur for a variety of reasons. Incorrect configurations or missing software components can create areas in a system where access controls are missing. Recent installations may have inadvertently changed access controls, exposing sensitive resources to those who are not authorized. In some cases, a necessary control might be missing altogether. Periodic reviews of access controls should be conducted to identify gaps that may exist.
- *Policy deficiencies*—Insufficient access control coverage can occur due to problems with policies. Policies governing an organization may not adequately

specify the requirements for access control. In this case, an organization may deploy ineffective access controls. This is a common problem for organizations that do not have access to seasoned information system security professionals. Another problem with policies involves their interpretation. A poorly worded policy that does not express the necessary access control depth and breadth may lead to weak implementations. In both of these cases, an incomplete policy can lead to poorly architected access controls.

■ *Look for obvious ways to circumvent controls*—Security is imperfect. With this understanding, it is evident that no control will be 100% effective. Furthermore, some controls may be easier to bypass than others. Attackers will certainly look for ways to get around access controls in a system. The security architect should also search for obvious ways to bypass existing access control mechanisms. One prime example is unencrypted passwords sent over the network. A number of commonly used protocols such as Telnet, Open Database Connectivity (ODBC), and Post Office Protocol (POP) transmit passwords in the clear. An attacker sniffing the network could easily capture these passwords and masquerade as the authorized user, effectively bypassing the intended purpose of the access control mechanism. Adding point-to-point encryption is one way to overcome this type of weakness. IPSec could be used between clients and servers to protect the passwords and still enable the use of these protocols.

Weaknesses are likely to occur through errors, omissions, or flaws in the design. These issues can be accommodated by forward thinking in the design process. Two ways to plan for emergent problems are to create contingency countermeasures and exploit defense in depth:

■ *Identify countermeasure strategies for emergent vulnerabilities*—Flaws in software continue to plague the IT world. Although the problem with buffer overflows has been known for quite some time, they still occur. It is best to anticipate that flaws in critical areas will be discovered. A security architect can help mitigate the eventual emergence of flaws by devising methods that limit exposures to a newly discovered vulnerability. Evaluate different techniques that could be used to block or slow the exploitation of a flaw. Identify ways to incorporate control layers in the various protocols and resources within the network to limit the scope of a exploited vulnerability.

■ *Use defense in depth to counteract weaknesses*—Fully leverage people, policies, and technology to detect and defend against weaknesses in access controls. Design layers into access controls such that a failure in one layer will not compromise another layer. Implement redundant and backup controls to counteract failures. For example, a VLAN can be used to segregate user network traffic, limiting access to particular resources. Suppose a network has resources that should not be accessed by those who are not authorized. In a network with no traffic restrictions, shared resources are frequently protected with file-system-based access control lists. However, if the access control list is accidentally altered, allowing inappropriate read access to the protected resource, then a compromise may occur. A VLAN that excludes the protected resource from those not authorized represents an additional measure protecting the resource from an inadvertent compromise. This supplemental control acts as a defensive layer protecting network-accessible sensitive resources from failures in file system access controls. Integrating a defense in depth strategy can reduce compromises due to inadvertent or malicious changes.

Testing Strategies

The effectiveness and assurance of an access control mechanism is determined through testing. The goal of testing to is to conclude if the access controls adequately support or enforce security policies. Testing is essentially a validation that the policies are integrated into the system through the application of countermeasures. Security requirements form the standards by which the access controls are compared. Compliance with a requirement supports assurances that the controls within the system are effective.

Supporting versus Enforcing Security Policies

In the world of information security, a "system" is the entire collection of equipment, software, facilities, people, and processes interacting with organizational information in the electronic environment. A system supports a security policy when aspects minimally provide an ability to direct policy compliance and can also be used to detect deviations. A security policy is supported if methods exist to guide user behaviors along activities meeting security requirements. For example, a "Rules of Behavior" guide directing users to create complex passwords supports policies underscoring the need for passwords that cannot be easily guessed. The guide is a tool, and training is the process by which users are informed of the policy and correct behavior. A system with automated mechanisms that disallow noncomplex passwords is said to enforce the security policy. From this perspective, policy enforcement occurs when the system prevents (or at least obstructs) users from not complying with established security requirements.

Testing Objectives

Testing seeks to identify the extent to which access controls support security requirements. Assurance of architectural effectiveness is predicated on the comprehensive testing of these objectives. Access control testing objectives in the following list help the security architect determine if the controls are

- *Implemented correctly*—System controls should support all security requirements. The implementation of the control should be in accordance with the appropriate depth and breadth to support the security policy of the system. Where applicable, access controls should enforce the security policy too. This objective is used to draw a direct link between policy and system. A correct implementation supports or enforces a security requirement as directed by policy.
- *Operating as intended*—The implementation of the control should meet the intent of the requirement and its design. Controls should be properly configured to support the intended operation as identified in the system design and relevant security requirements. Access controls should work as designed. This access control objective is used to assess the adequacy of the control's functionality.
- *Producing desired outcome*—Determining the degree to which access control supports operations and whether a weakness exists is the purpose of this objective. The implementation of a control alone, or in combination with others, satisfies the security requirements. Any gap within a control that is not supported by another control indicates that the control is not fully producing the desired outcome.

Testing Paradigms

Testing is conducted to evaluate to what extent an access control meets it objectives. Different testing paradigms are useful in determining the effectiveness of the control. Each type of testing approaches the control from a different angle. No single paradigm should be relied on exclusively. A security architect is encouraged to include aspects of each of the testing paradigms in the overall testing strategy to ensure that the objectives are met. The different testing paradigms include

- *Exercise controls*—It is important to know if the control is working properly. This type of testing primarily verifies if the control works as intended, but it can also determine if the implementation is correct, with the appropriate output. A determination is made by running test cases and reviewing the results to ensure that the result is what was expected. Consider a test that determines if the access control enforces an account lockout policy for failed logon attempts. The test involves a successful login followed by subsequent logins with an incorrect authentication factor. When the number of intentionally unsuccessful logins equals those specified in the policy, a review of the account properties is made. If the account is locked out, the test passes. If not, then the control fails. This type of testing is especially important for in-house software, such as Web-based applications that do not have the benefit of beta testers, such as other commercial off-the-shelf (COTS) products.

■ *Penetration testing*—The testing paradigm seeks to discover if an access control can be bypassed or overcome. A control is bypassed when the penetration tester is able to circumvent the control by creating an alternate path to access the target. This may involve exploiting other flaws in the system. Another tactic of this paradigm is to crash through an existing control using brute force techniques that overcome the control. A successful brute force attack often indicates a flaw in the access control mechanism. The main thrust of penetration testing is to confirm that the outcome of the control is correct. However, if the testing is properly designed, the results can be used to indirectly determine if the control is configured and operating correctly.

■ *Vulnerability assessment*—Identifying flaws in a system is a critical activity. This type of testing is essential to locate known software and configuration weaknesses that could be exploited. Vulnerabilities in software packages are discovered on a regular basis. The organization must regularly conduct vulnerability assessments to locate and correct flawed software. Some configurations in a system may also provide an attacker with avenues to compromise a system. Vulnerability assessments can be used to identify weak or inappropriate settings in the system, such as open file shares or weak ACL. This type of testing relies heavily on the use of automated tools. Manual methods can be used to identify vulnerabilities too, but are labor intensive.

Regardless of the testing paradigm followed, there must be sufficient testing conducted to determine if each of the testing objectives for each security requirement is met. A security architect is most likely to use all of the paradigms at one point or another to test an access control mechanism. Just as layering of security controls provides defense in depth, conducting an assessment from different perspectives can enhance test quality and results. Testing should be conducted using written test procedures that collectively evaluate the test objectives for each security requirement. Using a battery of paradigms will normally yield a comprehensive view of the control under test.

Repeatability

A hallmark of a quality-testing process is repeatability. This is a quality demonstrating that the testing process will provide the same or similar results when conducted by different individuals on a static system for a given standard. It is important to note that results may not always be identical. Minor changes on the system may yield slightly different results. So long as the results fall within the parameters of the standard specified by the security requirement, there is sufficient assurance that the testing methodology is sound. Test results that are substantially different on a static system indicate either a nonrepeatable testing process or a flaw in the system.

Methodology

A standardized methodology is needed to allow others to duplicate the access control testing. This can be accomplished by creating a process that allows the explicit specification of testing parameters while incorporating result tracking. Once again, a matrix approach is a useful way to organize this information. Suggested columns for a testing matrix include these items:

- *Test number*—A unique identifier to distinguish one test step from another.
- *Requirement number*—Matches the unique identifier in a Requirements Matrix.
- *Requirement*—This should replicate the associated statement in the Requirements Matrix. It is the standard driving the expected result.
- *Assessors*—The name or identification and contact information of those involved in conducting the test.
- *Test date*—The time frame of the test. A particular test might take a minute or a month to complete.
- *Test procedure*—The explicit sequence of actions to be performed. It should be put together in such a way that it evaluates each of the test objectives. A detailed test procedure supports repeatability.
- *Expected result*—This is the outcome of a test given the requirement is met.
- *Actual result*—The result of the test performed. For brevity, it is suggested that a short statement such as "Compliant" be used when no failures are noted. Report as much detail as appropriate for noted failures. Minimally report which aspect of the test failed, as well as the identification of the device, process, document, or interviewee associated with the failure.
- *Corrective action*—A detailed explanation of mitigating controls, corrections, or acceptance of risk for the failed test. An initial report of the failure should include a recommendation. The details of this item should reflect system management's decision to implement the recommendation or some other course of action.
- *Validating agents*—The name or identification of the individuals confirming that the corrective action was successfully performed.
- *Validation date*—The final date when the validating agents confirm that the corrective action was in fact fully implemented or approved.

Developing Test Procedures

Overall, testing determines if the system sufficiently supports the security policy. The vagueness of security policies can make this a difficult task. The intent of the policy can be lost when applied at a granular level. A truly focused test may lose sight of the purpose of the security requirement when the relationships between the elements of access control are not fully considered. The security architect should bear in mind the relationships between access control attributes when developing test procedures. Consider the following relationships when developing access control tests:

- *Entities and authentication factors*—Subjects are allowed access to the system or resources based on their ability to successfully authenticate. Accountability also relies on the correct association between an entity and subject via the authentication factor. Exposure of the authentication factor destroys accountability and threatens the other security goals as well. Access control testing should ensure that the link between an entity and authentication factor is resistant to compromise and tampering.
- *Subjects and rights*—All subjects in a system have been granted some rights. These rights should closely match the roles or duties assigned to the user or process. Access control testing should consider whether the rights associated with subjects of the test are appropriate or not. A weakness in an access control mechanism may allow subjects to directly or indirectly increase their rights in the system. Testing should determine if subject interactions with the system could result in the ability to increase rights or not.
- *Objects and permissions*—Determining if a given object has the correct permission is simple in execution, but challenging from an assessment perspective. This is particularly true for information repositories such as file systems. Top-level directories may have the correct ACL, but files deep within the structure may have the wrong permissions or be contained in an inappropriate location. Access control tests should consider objects and permissions, but in some cases, obtaining a valid assessment result with a high degree of confidence may be quite difficult. At a minimum, those objects that are particularly critical, such as password files, should have their permissions checked.

Risk-Based Considerations

An evaluation of the effectiveness of the access controls within a security architecture may reveal a variety of weaknesses. Some of the weaknesses may have been known prior to the testing, while others may not have been evident. In an ideal world, sufficient resources exist to implement effective countermeasures when weaknesses are discovered. Sadly, this is not usually the case, and often, an action must be taken that is less than ideal to address the problem. A security architect will frequently face this type of dilemma. Resource constraints, although problematic, need not be viewed as a crisis. Risk-based decisions are an effective way for managers to designate temporary or permanent alternatives to the problem. Achieving an optimal solution that keeps risk as low as is practical requires careful contemplation of the options. The following list provides some options that can be used to support risk-based decisions:

■ *Unconventional alternatives*—A security requirement may be met through a variety of methods. Identifying options to support risk-based decisions may call for some creative thinking. Solutions might involve the use of multiple tools or integration with manual methods to achieve the security requirement. Existing controls might be sufficient to mitigate the risk. Think about the different ways other controls could be used to achieve the same effect. This may simply necessitate enabling a software option or modifying an existing process or procedure.

■ *Enumerate risk*—Innovative options may incur new risk. Less than ideal solutions may be accompanied by new problems that were not previously considered. Any increase in risk associated with alternatives must be communicated to management for its consideration.

■ *Monitor weaker controls*—Insufficient controls can be bolstered with monitoring. An existing control that does not fully satisfy the testing objectives for a given requirement does not imply that it is flawed or useless. In some cases, monitoring combined with a weak control provides sufficient augmentation, allowing the requirement to be met. In instances when this is not the case, a carefully implemented monitoring scheme can still provide the ability to detect misuse and abuse. Monitoring can include automated or manual processes to support the weak control. The main point of the use of monitoring is to identify compromises that cannot be prevented through a weak control.

■ *Cost sensitivity*—Recommended control options for risk-based decisions should be practical from a resource perspective. The cost of a recommended tool or process should not exceed the value of the assets affected. When a tool is needed, compare costs and capabilities among various vendors. The most expensive tool might be ideal, but budget-conscious options may be suitable. It may be desirable to hire additional personnel to address the problem. This can also be an expensive alternative and is not always feasible. Automated mechanisms and alternatives must be leveraged to the greatest extent possible before requesting human resources.

■ *Manual processes*—Most automated processes can also be accomplished manually. Although automated processes are normally more efficient, their cost may be out of reach for an organization. Manual techniques may be sufficient when automation is not cost-effective. The implementation of manual access control methods must be supplemented with explicit documentation and sufficient end user training.

■ *Open source solutions*—The Internet is full of low-cost alternative tools. Open source tools, which are usually downloadable at no cost, are worth consideration. There are some excellent open source tools that can help augment or replace weak access controls. The downside to these solutions includes support and trust. An open source tool may not have any support and could conflict with other software in the organization's environment. Deployment and use of the tool may be complicated. Experimentation and learning may be a burden for the existing staff. Trust in the integrity of the tool is another consideration. Many open source organizations try to ensure their code does not contain backdoors or malicious aspects. When practical, an internal source code review of an open source tool should be conducted prior to compilation and deployment. Subsequent monitoring of the activity of the tool should be conducted when an internal source code review is not practical.

Concluding Thoughts on Access Control

The automation of access control techniques appears to have evolved beyond tight-fisted control of a floppy disk by incorporation of a rich variety of methods that support authentication, authorization, and accounting. The basic attributes of AAA can accompany a well-designed and well-implemented access control system. The essence of access control is to prevent information from falling into the wrong hands by controlling access to the data through techniques that allow accountability and verification of changes, or prevent tampering with our most precious information files. Possession of a floppy disk seems to be the ultimate form of access control. In this case, the security policy is known and invoked by the owner of the disk. The physical handoff of the disk in a face-to-face exchange is a strong form of authentication and authorization. Subsequent retrieval of the disk enables verification that the data is intact. Modern access controls provide techniques that allow information to be shared on an unprecedented scale. Implementations of strong cryptography associated with authentication mechanisms and protocols seem sufficient to provide a high level of confidence that access to the information is secured. Yet, given all of the potential techniques and implementations to achieve AAA, assurances are tenuous. Insider threats, malware, and other abuses can circumvent the best access control mechanisms and not prevent a loss of data confidentiality in most systems. In this light, it may seem that controlling information on a floppy is the best form of access control. However, it is not. The user borrowing the floppy disk could just as easily make inappropriate copies of sensitive files too. Trojan horse applications could have been used on the shared machine to further capture sensitive files. The problem has always been with us. Access control is helpful, but knowing where information flows is a highly relevant aspect of a system's use that is insufficiently monitored. Indeed, access control can be harnessed by the tenacity and creativity of a security architect dedicated to the cause of defending organizational information against exposure. Wherever information resides, access controls must be used to control information flows.

References

Aboba, B., Blunk, L., Vollbrecht, J., Carlson, J., and Levkowetz, H. (2004). RFC3748—Extensible authentication protocol (EAP). Retrieved from http://www.faqs.org/rfcs/rfc3748.html.

Bertino. E., and Sandhu, R. (2005). Database security—concepts, approaches, and challenges. *IEEE Transactions on Dependable and Secure Computing, 2*(1), 2–19.

Bishop, M. (2003). *Computer Security: Art and Science.* Boston, MA: Pearson Education.

Chirillo, J., and Blaul, S. (2003). *Implementing Biometric Security.* Indianapolis, IN: Wiley.

Finseth, C. (1993). RFC1492—An access control protocol, sometimes called TACACS. Retrieved from http://www.faqs.org/rfcs/rfc1492.html.

McCollum, C. J., Messing, J. R., and Notargiacomo, L. (1990). Beyond the Pale of MAC and DAC: Defining new forms of access control. *Proceedings of the1990 IEEE Symposium on Research in Security and Privacy*, 190–200.

Melnikov, A., and Zeilenga, K. (2006). RFC4422—Simple authentication and security layer (SASL). Retrieved from http://www.faqs.org/rfcs/rfc4422.html.

Park, J. and Sandhu, R. (2004). The UCONABC usage control model. *ACM Transactions on Information and System Security, 7*(1), 128–174.

Price, S. M. (2007). Supporting resource-constrained collaboration environments. *Computer*, 40(6), 108, 106–107.

Popescu, B. C., Crispo, B., and Tanenbaum, A. S. (2004). Support for multi-level security policies in DRM architectures. *Proceedings of the 2004 Workshop on New Security Paradigms*, 3–9.

Rigney, C., Willens, S., Livingston, Rubens, A., Merit, Simpson, W., and Daydreamer. (2000). RFC2865—Remote authentication dial in user servers (RADIUS). Retrieved from http://www.faqs.org/rfcs/rfc2865.html.

Sermersheim, J. (2006). RFC4511—Lightweight directory access protocol (LDAP): the pro. Retrieved from http://www.faqs.org/rfcs/rfc4511.html.

Stokes, E., Byrne, D., Blakley, B., and Behera, P. (2000). RFC2820—Access control requirements for LDAP. Retrieved from http://www.faqs.org/rfcs/rfc2820.html.

Zeilenga, K. (2006). RFC 4510—Lightweight directory access protocol (LDAP): Technic. Retrieved from http://www.faqs.org/rfcs/rfc4510.html.

Sample Questions

1. Which of the following represents the type of access given to a user?
    a. Permissions
    b. Subjects
    c. Objects
    d. Rights
2. Select the most widely adopted access control method:
    a. Discretionary access control
    b. Mandatory access control
    c. Rule-based access control
    d. Role-based access control
3. No read up and no write down are properties of
    a. Discretionary access control
    b. Mandatory access control
    c. Rule-based access control
    d. Role-based access control
4. Access control for proprietary distributable content is best protected using
    a. Discretionary access control
    b. Digital rights management
    c. Distributed access control
    d. Originator controlled
5. When designing least privilege in a system, a security architect should consider least
    a. Business requirements
    b. Organizational mission
    c. Affected usability
    d. Disaster recovery
6. Separation of duties are ideally implemented using
    a. Roles
    b. Permissions
    c. Rights
    d. Workflows
7. A good supplemental control for weak separation of duties is
    a. Intrusion detection
    b. Biometrics
    c. Auditing
    d. Training
8. Centralized access control
    a. Is only implemented in network equipment
    b. Implements authentication, authorization, and accounting
    c. Is implemented closest to the resources it is designed to protect
    d. Is designed to consider and accept business partner authentication tokens

9. Firewalls typically employ
   a. Centralized access control
   b. Decentralized access control
   c. Federated access control
   d. Role-based access control

10. A feature that distinguishes decentralized from centralized access control is its
    a. Audit logging
    b. Proxy capability
    c. Security kernel
    d. Shared database

11. Federated access control
    a. Is implemented with RADIUS
    b. Is designed to be mutually exclusive with single sign-on
    c. Is implemented closest to the resources it is designed to protect
    d. Is designed to consider and accept business partner authentication tokens

12. Lightweight Directory Access Control is specified in
    a. X.509
    b. X.500
    c. RFC 4510
    d. RFC 4422

13. Auditing seeks to record all of the following except:
    a. Who
    b. Why
    c. When
    d. What

14. This technique is commonly used to collect audit logs:
    a. Polling
    b. Triggers
    c. Workflows
    d. Aggregation

15. A word processing application, governed by DAC, executes in the security context of the
    a. End user
    b. Process itself
    c. Administrator
    d. System kernel

16. Peer-to-peer applications are problematic primarily because they
    a. Are prohibited by policy
    b. May be able to access all the user's files
    c. Are a new technology that is difficult to evaluate
    d. May be derived from untrustworthy open source projects

17. Business rules can be enforced within a database through the use of
    a. Proxy
    b. Redundancy
    c. Views
    d. Authentication
18. A well-designed demilitarized zone (DMZ) prevents
    a. Direct access to the DMZ from the protected network
    b. Access to assets within the DMZ to unauthenticated users
    c. Insiders on the protected network from conducting attacks
    d. Uncontrolled access to the protected network from the DMZ
19. Dual control is primarily implemented to
    a. Complement resource-constrained separation of duties
    b. Distribute trust using a rigid protocol
    c. Support internal workflows
    d. Supplement least privilege
20. A well-designed security test
    a. Requires penetration testing
    b. Is documented and repeatable
    c. Relies exclusively on automated tools
    d. Foregoes the need for analysis of the results

Chapter 2

Cryptography

Alex Golod and Mark J. Makowski

Contents

The cryptography domain requires security professionals to understand cryptographic methodologies and the use of cryptography to protect an organization's data storage and communications from compromise or misuse. This includes awareness of the threats to an organization's cryptographic infrastructure. The security professional must understand the importance of choosing, implementing, and monitoring cryptographic products and adoption of corporate cryptographic standards and policy. This may include oversight of digital signatures and PKI implementations and a secure manner of addressing the issues and risks associated with management of cryptographic keys. Key areas of knowledge include

- The application and use of cryptographic solutions
    - Interoperability of devices
    - Strength of cryptographic algorithms
- Cryptographic methodologies and methods
- Addressing key management issues
- Public Key Infrastructure
- Application-level encryption
- Design validation
- Defining cryptanalysis methods and threats
- Cryptanalytic attacks

Cryptographic Principles

Cryptography provides the bedrock for a multitude of security controls. The wide variety of applications where cryptography can be applied offers plenty of opportunity for security controls that provide an overall benefit. Its wide range of applications and uses also means there is more chance for a security control to be the weakest link in a chain. If cryptography is to be used effectively, the methodology and principles behind cryptography must be fully understood.

Applications of Cryptography

Benefits

While cryptography may not directly benefit the *availability* of information, the encryption of data is probably the most straightforward means of protecting its *confidentiality*. Hash functions such as MD5, SHA-256, and the new SHA-3 candidates [SHA-3] are used for *integrity* to protect against unauthorized modification of data and are cryptography's workhorses. The use of public key certificates and digital signatures are but two examples of cryptography providing a means of *Authentication*. This can include user authentication, data authentication, and data origin authentication—which is verification that a message received from a sender also originated from that sender. By binding a public key to its owner using a public key infrastructure (PKI), a *non-repudiation* service can also be provided. Non-repudiation offers protection from either the sender or the receiver of a message, denying that the message has been sent or received. Non-repudiation can be used to prove to a third party that a particular event took place and can prove to a third party that a particular event did or did not occur.

These benefits form four fundamental goals from which all the major benefits of cryptography are derived:

Confidentiality means the secrecy and privacy of information must be protected from unauthorized disclosure or access. Personal information, intellectual property, diplomatic and military communications, and credit card numbers are but a few examples of such data. Protection methods can utilize public-key/private-key pairs (asymmetric encryption) or secret-keys (symmetric encryption).

Integrity is concerned with guaranteeing data is not accidentally or maliciously changed. Integrity also relates to ensuring that the methods used for processing information perform with accuracy and completeness. One-way hash functions, while not necessarily the most effective, are the most common means used to ensure integrity.

Authentication is the broad goal of verifying that data is of undisputed origin and includes verifying the positive identity of users or other entities such as network devices. Passwords, PINs, and tokens also come into use here. Digital signatures are used to provide data origin authentication.

Non-repudiation involves preventing denial by one of the entities involved in a communication of having participated in all or part of the communication.

It is also used to prove to a third party that some kind of event or action did or did not occur. PKI certificates, where a digital signature binds together a public key with an individual's identity during a valid time period, can be used to provide a measure of cryptographic non-repudiation.

Uses

The need to use cryptography depends in part on the level of criticality of data being protected. While financial transaction data, such as credit card information or personal data and privacy information, could have a strong requirement for confidentiality provided by encryption, inventory data or public reference files in a central data store may have low confidentiality needs. The rationale for spending money on encryption controls depends on the data protection required. At the same time, technological improvements are lowering the costs of hardware and software encryption and making the controls provided by encryption ubiquitous. For example, at rest encryption for data stored within portable devices and in flight encryption for remote access VPNs have become common.

Cryptography remains at the heart of many logical information security controls. Cryptography is used in security controls that protect data during transmission over a network (data in flight), data residing in a storage medium (data at rest), data being processed within an application, user authentication, and device authentication.

Cryptography is not limited to uses in access control and telecommunications security. Business continuity planning lends itself to cryptographic uses for protecting data transferred to a hot site. A recovery site service provider may need to be one of the trusted parties having access to encryption keys for storage data, for instance.

Cryptography can depend on physical security as well. One example is the physical security of the master key in a media encryption system. Storage of the key may leverage physical security by splitting it into key shares (known as split knowledge; see section titled "Key Management"), with portions of the encryption key stored on separate smart cards in different safes, thereby limiting physical access to the master encryption key. To expound on this example further, the same key can reside within a hardware component of a cryptographic system, requiring specialized physical protection of the computing device itself. The National Institute of Standards and Technology (NIST) FIPS 140-2 defines standards for both hardware and software components of cryptographic modules. The specialized physical protection of cryptographic modules required by FIPS 140-2 may include tamper-proof enclosures and means of destroying or zeroizing keys upon physical opening.

The core areas that benefit from cryptography deal with keeping data confidential, maintaining its integrity, guaranteeing authenticity not only of data but of those accessing the data as well as those from whom the data originates, and of ensuring non-repudiation for data originators.

Message Encryption

Secure communication of messages is a traditional use of cryptography. Military communications have employed cryptography since at least the time of the Greco-Persian wars, with techniques such as hiding messages within wax tablets. Commercial messaging systems transmitting across untrusted networks also require encryption for privacy of messages. Corporate e-mail traffic may contain various types of sensitive information including financial data, personal information, intellectual property, or trade secrets. In addition to needing confidentiality for messages, e-mail can require authentication of the message recipient to the message, integrity of the message content, and non-repudiation of the message being sent or received.

Messaging security standards include

Secure Multi-Purpose Internet Mail Extensions (S/MIME): This extension of the MIME standards that specify e-mail formatting and encapsulation adds encryption of message content. S/MIME also uses a hashing algorithm for message integrity, public key certificates for message authentication, and digital signatures to provide non-repudiation of origin.

Privacy-Enhanced Mail (PEM): An early Internet Engineering Task Force (IETF)-proposed standard for securing e-mail using public-key cryptography with trusted distribution of public keys via PKI, PEM was never widely used for securing e-mail.

Only PEM's definition of header field format (PEM format) has found use as a common means of representing digital certificates in ASCII form.

Pretty Good Privacy (PGP): Originally developed by Phil Zimmermann in 1991, PGP is a cryptosystem utilizing symmetric key, asymmetric key, and message digest algorithms. When applied to securing e-mail, PGP provides message authentication by binding a public key to an e-mail address where the public key is distributed to a community of users who trust each other, commonly known as a web of trust. PGP with e-mail also provides message encryption, uses a hashing algorithm for message integrity, and digital signatures for non-repudiation.

Secure IP Communication

TCP/IP is a standard communication protocol for information systems today. Various cryptographic protections are provided for data traveling over IP networks by the IPSec suite of open standards developed by the Internet Engineering Task Force (IETF). The IPSec set of standard protocols provides cryptographic security services at Layer 3, the Network layer of the OSI model.

IPSec includes two protocols: Authentication Header (AH) and Encapsulating Security Protocol (ESP). The cryptographic benefits provided by them are

AH: Authentication Header provides data origin authentication and data integrity but does not provide confidentiality for the IP payload and header that it protects.

ESP: Encapsulating Security Protocol also provides data origin authentication and data integrity, and also offers confidentiality for the IP payload it protects.

IPSec operates in one of two modes:

Transport mode: In transport mode, only the IP payload is protected by the AH or ESP protections. Transport mode is used for end-to-end security between two systems, such as between a client and a server.

Tunnel mode: In tunnel mode, both the IP payload and the header are protected, and a combination of AH and ESP protections can be used. Tunnel mode sets up a virtual tunnel where multiple intermediaries may exist and is used for protecting traffic between hosts and network devices such as gateways or firewalls, routers, and VPN appliances.

Secure TCP/IP communication is not limited to IPSec. Transport Layer Security (TLS) and its predecessor, Secure Sockets Layer (SSL), are additional cryptographic protocols that provide communications security for TCP/IP. TLS/SSL provides confidentiality, integrity, and authentication for securing data traveling over IP networks. Authentication in TLS/SSL is commonly provided when an HTTP server proves to a client such as a browser that the server is authentic, and may also be used for mutual or server-to-server authentication. TLS/SSL is often used to provide secure HTTP (HTTPS), and is also used for securing data communicating over other application level protocols, such as File Transfer Protocol (FTP), Lightweight Directory Access Protocol (LDAP), and Simple Mail Transfer Protocol (SMTP).

Remote Access

Cryptographic controls are used when remote access is necessary. Examples include the need for integrity protection to prevent man-in-the-middle spoofing and hijacking attacks and vendor remote network access to a customer's data center, where the authentication and confidentiality of the network access are important. Likewise, remote access by telecommuting employees commonly uses virtual private networks (VPNs), which provide encryption and user authentication. Often, remote access means crossing boundaries where untrusted networks are present. In such cases, the need for confidentiality increases.

A VPN provides confidentiality by encrypting IP traffic and offering authentication between VPN endpoints. Because VPNs are often based on IPSec or SSL, the security benefits of the underlying protocols are provided. VPNs are implemented in the following architectures:

Remote access VPN: A remote access VPN provides security for remote users connecting to a central location via IP.

Site-to-site VPN: A site-to-site VPN provides communications security for separate locations in an organization that can connect over IP.

Extranet VPN: An extranet or trading partner VPN provides an organization with communications security when one or more separate organizations are connecting to that organization over IP.

Point-to-Point Protocol (PPP) is another means of establishing remote connectivity. PPP, operating at the data link layer of the OSI model, was designed to be used with network layer protocols such as IP or IPX. By default, PPP does not provide any security or rely on any cryptographic controls. However, PPP does include an optional authentication phase and an optional encryption feature, PPP Encryption Control Protocol (ECP).

A common protocol for remote access that involves cryptographic controls is Secure Shell (SSH), which operates at the application layer of the OSI model. SSH can be used in a client-server model for remote administration of servers, and in combination with other protocols such as Secure File Transfer Protocol (SFTP) or Secure Copy (SCP). SSH encrypts the data it transfers, and provides authentication using password- or public-key based methods. SSH also uses a keyed hash for integrity protection.

Secure Wireless Communication

Wireless networks are commonly used for enhancing user mobility and extending or even replacing wired IP networks. Their transmission is easily intercepted, so confidentiality is a must. Wireless transmissions can be more susceptible to man-in-the-middle attack than wired communication, so authentication is very important.

The most commonly used family of standards for wireless local area networks (WLANs) is Institute of Electrical and Electronics Engineers (IEEE) 802.11. 802.11 originally relied on the Wired Equivalent Privacy (WEP) security method to provide confidentiality and integrity. WEP has been proved insecure due to the way it implements its RC4 stream cipher algorithm; thus, WLANs using WEP are often vulnerable to eavesdropping and unauthorized access.

As a result, IEEE introduced a range of new security features designed to overcome the shortcomings of WEP in the IEEE 802.11i amendment [802.11i]. 802.11i introduces the concept of a Robust Security Network (RSN), an element of the protocol that allows a variety of encryption algorithms and techniques to be used for providing confidentiality and authentication. Prior to the introduction of 802.11i, the Wi-Fi Alliance, a global nonprofit industry association, created a protocol and certification program for wireless network components known as Wi-Fi Protected Access (WPA). WPA, based on a draft of IEEE 802.11i, securely implements the RC4 stream cipher for more effective confidentiality and authentication. The biggest difference between WPA and the draft is that WPA does not require support for the Advanced Encryption Standard (AES) strong encryption algorithm. WPA allows many existing IEEE 802.11 hardware components that cannot support the computationally intensive AES encryption.

At the same time the IEEE 802.11i amendment was ratified, the Wi-Fi Alliance introduced WPA2 [WPA2], its term for interoperable equipment that is capable of supporting IEEE 802.11i requirements. WPA2 certification is based on the mandatory elements of the IEEE 802.11i standard, but there are some differences. WPA2 extends its certification program to include interoperability with a set of common Extensible Authentication Protocol (EAP) methods. For example, WPA2 adds EAP-TLS, which is not a component of the 802.11i standard. WPA2 also excludes support for ad hoc networks, an 802.11i feature that allows peer-to-peer network device communication.

A short-range wireless protocol commonly used by many types of business and consumer devices such as mobile phones, personal digital assistants (PDAs), personal computer peripherals, cameras, and video game consoles is Bluetooth. The Bluetooth specification was developed, and is managed, by the Bluetooth Special Interest Group, a privately held trade association. By creating wireless personal area networks (PANs), Bluetooth enables ad hoc communication between multiple wireless devices. Bluetooth optionally encrypts, but does not provide integrity protection for the transmitted data. It is possible to easily modify a transmitted Bluetooth packet without being detected because only a simple cyclic redundancy check (CRC) is appended to each packet, and no message authentication code is used. Another security weakness with Bluetooth involves device pairing, the initial exchange of keying material that occurs when two Bluetooth-enabled devices agree to communicate with one another. In version 2.0 and earlier of the Bluetooth specification, pairing is performed over a nonencrypted channel, allowing a passive eavesdropper to compute the link key used for encryption. Version 2.1 introduced the use of Elliptic Curve Diffie–Hellman (ECDH) public key cryptography, which can be utilized by Bluetooth device developers for protection against a passive eavesdropping attack. The Bluetooth specification defines its own stream cipher called E0. Several weaknesses have been identified in Bluetooth's E0 stream cipher, which is not a Federal Information Processing Standards (FIPS)-approved algorithm and can be considered nonstandard [SP800-121].

Other Types of Secure Communication

Secure communication is not limited to IP networks. Plain Old Telephone Service (POTS), including voice as well as data, needs encryption for ensuring confidentiality. Encrypted telephones are no longer the domain of military communications. Portable/wireless telephone headsets that include encrypted transmission and reception are available in office supply stores for commercial use. Sensitive data, including personally identifiable information, trade secrets, and intellectual property, are routinely shared over telephone networks with limited protections.

While storage area networks (SANs) utilizing protocols such as FICON and Fibre Channel (FC) are thought to be less exposed and thus need less protection than the common TCP/IP networks, cryptographic controls are still necessary. A service provider hosting multiple clients in a data center may use encryption for privacy of data within a SAN. This can be done using Fibre Channel Security Protocol (FC-SP) [FC-SP], a security framework that includes protocols to enhance FC security in several areas, including authentication of Fibre Channel devices, cryptographically secure key exchange, and cryptographically secure communication between FC devices.

Depending on the criticality of the data, radio frequency communications of all types can require some measure of protection. Communication satellites, for instance, will require encryption, which may be in the form of hardware modules for securing telemetry, tracking, and control. Radio frequency identification (RFID) sensors and tags used for tracking and identification purposes can benefit from short transmission encryption to guarantee that the information they deliver is confidential, authentic, and unchanged.

Identification and Authentication

Cryptography is used for identification as well as user, device, and data origin authentication. An early use of cryptographic identification for distinguishing friendly aircraft was developed during WWII with the identification, friend or foe (IFF) system using coded radar signals to trigger a transponder on the aircraft. Modern military IFF transponders encrypt challenge and response messages, and include the use of key codes to prevent unauthorized use.

Similar to IFF, RFID relies on use of a transponder, or an RFID tag, to identify physical assets such as warehouse inventory when queried with a reader. RFID tags are finding their way into a wide range of applications such as libraries, transportation toll collection, and passports. Use of cryptography with RFID may become a necessity for privacy or to ensure authenticity.

Securely identifying physical items can prevent counterfeiting of bank notes, pharmaceuticals, computer parts, and a host of other products. While use of bar codes, holographic labels, and watermarks or signets is common, these methods often involve use of a simple code versus a cryptographic key and algorithm. Newer methods of applying cryptographic means include use of digital certificates, embedded encryption processing chips, and hardware security modules (HSMs) to securely identify components. One such application could involve use of a cryptographic component identification system to protect automotive components from theft, counterfeiting, or manipulation.

Securely identifying persons is necessary for user authentication and for access to information resources and processing systems. Authentication systems based on a user entering a password or a PIN are widely deployed and provide a low-cost but easily compromised means of authenticating users. A common method for user authentication involves comparing the results of a one-way hash operation performed on the password a user enters with the hash value stored in the authentication system.

User authentication can also be done with a software token. A software token can involve a user presenting a secret key during authentication, or may involve a system based on public key cryptography. Symmetric encryption is used in Kerberos, the MIT-developed authentication protocol commonly used for providing users single-sign on access to computing resources.

Using cryptographic hardware tokens for user authentication can provide increased security at a higher cost. Hardware tokens combined with passwords are commonly used for providing two-factor authentication. Hardware tokens may be able to generate and store private keys, support use of one-time passwords, and often contain cryptographic processing capabilities along with tamper resistance. Examples of hardware-token-based technologies include smart cards, Universal Serial Bus (USB) tokens, and special-purpose interfaces such as the NSA-developed Crypto Ignition Key (CIK) used in the STU-III family of secure telephones [CIK].

Authentication protocols used by Point-to-Point Protocol (PPP) include Password Authentication Protocol (PAP) and Challenge-Handshake Authentication Protocol (CHAP). PAP is a weak authentication method, transmitting a cleartext password and static identifier that does not protect against replay attack. CHAP transmits a hash that is computed based on a random challenge value and shared secret, providing replay protection and a stronger level of authentication. Another protocol originally developed to provide authentication services for PPP and commonly found in wireless network communication is Extensible Authentication Protocol (EAP). EAP is an authentication framework that supports a number of authentication mechanisms such as preshared keys, digital certificates, Kerberos, and others. These authentication mechanisms are implemented in a number of ways called EAP methods, for example, EAP-MD5 and EAP-TLS.

Storage Encryption

Storage encryption is typically known as encryption at rest. This includes file-level, file-system-level, and entire disk encryption. Storage encryption provides confidentiality of data, but it also requires authentication. For instance, a SAN may store its data in encrypted form, but the authorized hosts and devices that can access the data must be identified for the encryption to be effective. Cryptographic controls also provide integrity for storage media. For instance, Content Addressable Storage (CAS) provides file integrity via cryptographic methods.

Storage media encryption can be an excellent means of ensuring that removable media is protected during transit. Portable tape media, USB devices or "thumb drives," and notebook computers must be encrypted if they contain data that is not public. While secure data erasure should be depended upon to destroy data from disk drives that are decommissioned or that fail, disk encryption can also provide a degree of protection in those situations.

Storage encryption has a great reliance on proper encryption key management. Magnetic tape media must be encrypted when the criticality of the data warrants it, and especially when the tape is physically moved, such as via third-party carriers. Key management comes into play when the encrypted tapes must be read by a third party requiring access to a symmetric key that was used to encrypt the data. It should also be noted that using unique keys when encrypting multiple tape volumes provides greater protection than using a common key for a set of tapes, should the encryption key be compromised. Solutions being developed for managing keys for disk and tape encryption should take into account IEEE P1619.3. Being developed by the IEEE Security in Storage Working Group (SISWG), P1619.3 is an architecture specification for managing keys used for encrypting stored data across a distributed IT infrastructure.

Other standards produced by the IEEE Standards Association are applicable to disk and tape encryption products. The approved standard IEEE P1619 addresses data storage on disk drives, and the approved standard IEEE P1619.1 is for data encryption on tape drives. An additional standard in progress is P1619.2 for encrypting whole disk sectors [P1619].

While tape and disk encryption may be provided by software methods, appliances that perform encryption at hardware speed offer better performance, often with increased cost. Such specialized encryption appliances may continue to have a place; however, the trend is for tape, disk and network devices to provide the encryption functionality within the device itself.

Electronic Commerce (E-Commerce)

E-commerce consists of two or more parties using information technology infrastructures to execute financial transactions, and often involves the buying and selling of goods or services over networks such as the Internet. Examples include consumers accessing online services over the Internet or trading partners processing orders via an extranet. E-commerce includes the integration of Web-based IT applications in activities that do not directly involve buying and selling, such as in advertising, sharing production capacity information, or servicing warranties.

E-commerce business models are normally defined as

■ B2B (business to business)
■ B2C (business to consumer)
■ C2C (consumer to consumer)

A common infrastructure supporting e-commerce includes the following elements:

- Client: may be a web browser or customer's back-office network
- Front-end systems: may consist of one or more Web servers connected to the Internet and to back-end systems
- Back-end systems: may include application servers and databases necessary for supplying information to front-end systems (such as product information) and for receiving data from them (such as payment information)

For transactions to occur, there must be a level of trust between the trading parties and a level of assurance in the security of the transacting environment. The security requirements of the expansive and technologically entrenched use of e-commerce are supported by all the basic goals of cryptography: *confidentiality, integrity, authentication*, and *non-repudiation*. Cryptography also supports a number of detailed security requirements of e-commerce, including

Auditing: Accountability in financial transactions depends on secure audit logging records, and cryptographic methods such as hash functions and digital signing can ensure that records are not modified.

Authorization: E-commerce depends on being able to authorize transactions based on preassociated policies for a given user or other entity that is successfully authenticated. The access control mechanisms involved in authorization may involve cryptographic components such as digital certificates.

Privacy: Web-based transactions may include personal information. If this information is to be stored, cryptography can provide access control and secure storage.

B2B e-commerce still widely uses Electronic Data Interchange (EDI) [EDI], the decades-old set of standards for exchanging data between trading partners. EDI transmissions often occur using a value-added network (VAN), which acts as a gateway and clearinghouse for supporting the transmission. EDI can also be transmitted by a variety of methods including modems, FTP, e-mail, and HTTP. EDI transmission methods must include appropriate security methods, such as encryption for confidentiality or digital signing for authentication. One specification for protecting EDI transmitted over the Internet is Applicability Statement 2 (AS2), found in RFC 4130. AS2 specifies use of existing security methods including Secure/Multipurpose Internet Mail Extensions (S/MIME), Cryptographic Message Syntax (CMS) [CMS], and cryptographic hash algorithms in order to provide confidentiality, data authentication, and non-repudiation for EDI.

B2B, B2C, and C2C e-commerce often require Web Services Security (WS-Security) as part of the server-to-server protection mechanism involved in IP communications between front-end and back-end systems. WS-Security is an OASIS standard that builds a security layer to the Simple Object Access Protocol (SOAP). SOAP is used for exchanging XML-based messages over HTTP. WS-Security allows SOAP messages to be signed and encrypted, and adds Kerberos tickets or X.509 certificates as tokens for authentication [WS-Security].

Software Code Signing

While WS-Security uses digital signatures to ensure that an XML-based message is not altered during server-to-server transactions, client browser to Web server based transactions may require downloading a piece of code such as a Java applet, browser plug-in, or Microsoft ActiveX control. To ensure integrity of the code, digital certificates and cryptographic hash functions may be used, such as with the Microsoft Authenticode protocol.

One-way hash functions such as MD5 or SHA-1 are also commonly used for ensuring integrity when software such as source code or executables is distributed. While using a hash-function alone can provide integrity, unless the recipient knows the hash value is the same one supplied by the software provider, authentication of the software cannot be guaranteed. The software's authenticity is often protected by publishing the hash value separately.

Interoperability

Cryptographic interoperability means that the suite of cryptographic algorithms available is used in a manner that meets industry and governmental standards.

One example of a cryptographic interoperability objective is the United States National Security Agency (NSA) Suite B cryptography [NSA Suite B Cryptography]. NSA Suite B is a subset of cryptographic algorithms approved by NIST including those for hashing, digital signatures, and key exchange.

Suite B includes the following:

■ Encryption: Advanced Encryption Standard (AES)—FIPS 197
■ Digital Signature: Elliptic Curve Digital Signature Algorithm—FIPS 186-2
■ Key Exchange: Elliptic Curve Diffie–Hellman Draft NIST Special Publication 800-56
■ Hashing: Secure Hash Algorithm—FIPS 180-2

The goals of Suite B are to provide a common set of cryptographic algorithms that the commercial industry can use for creating products that are compatible in the United States as well as internationally.

Methods of Cryptography

So far we have described the practical advantages to using cryptography. Let us now review the basic principles behind common cryptographic systems, or cryptosystems. A cryptosystem contains the algorithm used as well as the key, and can include the plaintext and ciphertext. Because the algorithm or cipher is a mathematical function that produces a predictable result, using a key provides the ability

Figure 2.1   Elements of a cryptosystem.

to control the algorithm and limit predictability of the ciphertext. These elements are reflected in Figure 2.1.

A simple way to represent an encryption function is the following, where ciphertext "C" results from message "M" being encrypted by an algorithm together with a key denoted by "E_k":

$$E_k(M) = C$$

Symmetric Cryptosystems

Suppose the same key is used to decrypt the ciphertext. In the following decryption function, an algorithm together with the same key in our previous function, denoted by D_k, produces the original message M when the previous ciphertext is decrypted:

$$D_k(C) = M$$

We now have the elements of a symmetric cryptosystem, the primary element being use of the same secret key (see Figure 2.2).

In symmetric cryptosystems, the secret key used for decryption by the message recipient was also used for encryption by the sender. Confidentiality of the secret key becomes paramount, because knowledge of the key allows an unintended

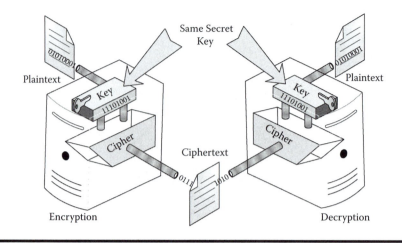

Figure 2.2   Elements of a symmetric cryptosystem.

individual the ability to see the message. With the secret key in hand, all the individual needs is the ciphertext and cipher to read the message. Thus, transport and protection of the secret key are important factors to consider in architectures using symmetric cryptosystems.

In a symmetric cryptosystem, management of keys can also become a problem. When a sender wishes to communicate with individual secrecy to multiple receivers, a symmetric cryptosystem requires the sender to distribute unique keys to each receiver. If the receiving parties share the same secret key, then the receiving parties would be able to access each other's messages from the sender, which the sender does not want. In such a case, where confidentiality is required between the sender and each receiver, the number of secret keys required becomes larger than the number of individuals. This is shown in Figure 2.3, where four individuals require six keys.

The number of keys is based on the number of communication channels, and increases dramatically. It is possible to determine the number of secret keys required for a given number of individual communication channels. In order to ensure secure communication between everyone in a group of n members, the number of keys is given by the following:

$$Keys = [n \times (n-1)]/2$$

Thus, while a group of 2 requires 1 secret key, a group of 100 requires 4950 keys.

While taking into account the problems inherent in management and distribution of secret keys, cryptographic solution development should be aware of the performance characteristics of symmetric algorithms. Symmetric key algorithms perform faster than asymmetric key algorithms. A few common examples of symmetric algorithms are the following:

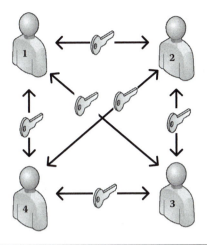

Figure 2.3   Management of secret keys problem.

- Advanced Encryption Standard (AES)
- Blowfish
- Data Encryption Standard (DES)
- IDEA
- RC2, RC4, RC5, and RC6
- Triple-DES (3DES)

Symmetric algorithms fall into two categories: block ciphers and stream ciphers. In block ciphers, plaintext is encrypted using the secret key in blocks of a certain size, for example, 128-bit block size. In stream ciphers, plaintext is encrypted one bit, byte, or word at a time using a rotating stream of bits from the key.

Block Cipher Modes

Symmetric key algorithms that operate as block ciphers are used in one or more modes of operation. Each block cipher mode provides a different level of security, efficiency, fault tolerance, or in some cases, provides a specific protection benefit such as confidentiality or authentication.

Block ciphers operate on blocks of plaintext of a certain size (often 64 or 128 bits) to produce ciphertext in blocks of the same size. The block size affects security (larger is better), at the cost of increased complexity. Secret key size also affects security, as larger keys increase the randomness of the keyspace. Block ciphers typically include an initialization vector (IV), a block of bits added to ensure that identical plaintext messages encrypt to different ciphertext messages.

There are several common block cipher modes of operation [Modes]. The following offer various degrees of security, a range of performance characteristics, and different levels of implementation complexity:

Electronic Code Book (ECB) Mode: The least complex mode; each block is operated on independently, and an IV is not used. Because identical plaintext
blocks result in identical ciphertext, this mode is not useful for providing
message confidentiality. ECB may be useful for short transmissions such as
key exchange. ECB is commonly, and erroneously, implemented by vendors
for bulk data encryption. This contradicts NIST guidance and puts customer
data at grave risk.

Cipher Block Chaining (CBC) Mode: Adds an IV and uses a chaining method such
that results of the encryption of previous blocks are fed back into the encryption
of the current block. This makes CBC useful for message confidentiality.

Cipher Feedback (CFB), Output Feedback (OFB), and Counter (CTR) Mode:
These modes are capable of producing unique ciphertext given identical
plaintext blocks, and are useful for message confidentiality. Because these
modes employ a block cipher as a keystream generator, they can operate
as a stream cipher. This may be desirable in applications that require low
latency between the arrival of plaintext and the output of the corresponding ciphertext.

The previous modes do not provide integrity protection; thus, an attacker may be
able to undetectably modify the data stream. Additional security benefits are provided by the following block cipher modes:

Cipher-Based Message Authentication Code (CMAC) Mode: This mode provides
data integrity and data origin authentication with respect to the original message source, allowing a block cipher to operate as a message authentication
code (MAC). The CMAC algorithm addresses security deficiencies found in
the Cipher Block Chaining MAC algorithm (CBC-MAC), which has been
shown to be insecure when using messages of varying lengths such as the
type found in typical IP datagrams. The CMAC algorithm thus offers an
improved means of using a block cipher as a MAC.

Counter with Cipher Block Chaining-Message Authentication Code (CCM) Mode:
This mode can provide assurance of both confidentiality and authenticity of
data by combining a counter mode with CBC-MAC.

Galois/Counter Mode (GCM): This mode also can provide assurance of both confidentiality and authenticity of data, and combines the counter mode with a
universal hash function. GCM is suitable for implementation in hardware for
high-throughput applications.

The following are some of the block ciphers currently in use, or that have been
popular at one time:

Advanced Encryption Standard (AES) [FIPS197]: Adopted as a standard by the
United States in NIST FIPS PUB 197, AES is one of the most popular block

ciphers. AES supports a fixed block size of 128 bits and a key size of 128, 192, or 256 bits.

CAST [RFC2144]: The popular CAST family of block ciphers uses a 64-bit block size and key sizes of between 40 and 128 bits. CAST-128 is a strong cryptosystem suitable for general-purpose use.

Cellular Message Encryption Algorithm (CMEA) [CMEA]: Designed for encrypting the control channel for mobile phones in the United States, CMEA is a deeply flawed encryption algorithm. The simple CMEA block cipher employs a block size of 16–64 bits and a 64-bit key.

Data Encryption Standard (DES) [SCHNEIER]: This once highly popular 64-bit block cipher, derived from Lucifer and modified to use a 56-bit key size, was called the Data Encryption Algorithm (DEA) in the FIPS 46-1 adopted in 1977. DEA is also defined as ANSI Standard X3.92. With the availability of increasing computing power, DES with its 56-bit key size was found to be insufficient at protecting against brute force attack. DES is more commonly implemented as Triple DES (3DES or TDES and also known as TDEA), offering a simple way to enlarge the key space without throwing away the algorithm. 3DES uses multiple keys in a block mode, allowing a key size of 168 bits. 3DES is specified in ANSI X9.52 and replaces DES as a FIPS-approved algorithm. 3DES is gradually being replaced by AES as an encryption standard.

GOST 28147-89 [GOST]: GOST is a strong 64-bit block size cipher using a 256-bit key in addition to 512 bits of additional secret keying material in the form of optional Substitution-boxes (S-box). GOST 28147-89 is the name of a government standard of the former Soviet Union, where the cipher was developed. GOST is now freely available, and used in software and hardware implementations in the former Soviet republics and elsewhere.

International Data Encryption Algorithm (IDEA) [SCHNEIER]: This 64-bit block cipher with 128-bit keys is used in the popular encryption software, Pretty Good Privacy (PGP). Commercial use of IDEA requires licensing from a Swiss company. Thus far IDEA has stood up to attack from the academic community.

LOKI [SCHNEIER]: The LOKI family of ciphers originated in Australia with LOKI89 and LOKI91, which use a 64-bit block and 64-bit key. LOKI91 is a redesign of LOKI89, which was shown to be especially vulnerable to brute force attack. The LOKI97 evolution has a 128-bit block size and offers a choice of 128, 192, or 256-bit key length. LOKI97 was rejected as a candidate for the AES standard, and was shown to be susceptible to cryptanalytic attack.

Lucifer [SCHNEIER]: Some of the earliest block ciphers originated at IBM by the early 1970s with the name Lucifer. Early variants operated on a 48-bit block using a 48-bit key, and a later version used 128-bit blocks with a 128-bit key. Even with a longer key length, Lucifer has been found vulnerable to cryptanalytic attack.

RC2, RC5, RC6: The RC algorithms, invented by Ron Rivest, are proprietary and largely unrelated to one another. RC2 is a variable key-size 64-bit block cipher intended as a replacement for DES. RC2 was found vulnerable to a related-key attack [RC2]. RC5 is a fast cipher with a variable block size (32, 64, 128-bit) and employs a variable key size (0 to 2040 bits). Brute force attack against RC5 is possible using distributed computing, and the level of security provided by RC5 is dependent upon how it is implemented [RC5]. RC6 was designed as a candidate for the AES standard, and is based on RC5 with improved performance, security, and a 128-bit block size and key sizes of 128, 192, or 256-bits. RC6 is a strong cipher with excellent performance characteristics [RC6].

Skipjack [SCHNEIER]: Invented by NSA, the now-declassified Skipjack algorithm uses a 64-bit block size with 80-bit key length. Skipjack was intended for implementation in tamperproof hardware using the Clipper chip as part of a now-defunct key escrow program that would allow U.S. government agency decryption of telecommunications. Skipjack is considered a strong cipher.

Tiny Encryption Algorithm (TEA) [TEA]: Designed at Cambridge University in England and first presented in 1994, TEA operates on 64-bit blocks and uses a 128-bit key. Corrected Block TEA (referred to as XXTEA) corrects weaknesses in the original version. Because TEA can be implemented in a few lines of code, it may be suitable for resource-constrained hardware implementations.

Twofish [Twofish]: A freely available 128-bit block cipher using key sizes up to 128 bits, Twofish was one of the finalists that was not selected for the AES standard. Cryptanalysis of Twofish continues to reveal that it is secure.

Stream Ciphers

In contrast to block ciphers, stream-based algorithms operate on a message flow (usually bits or characters) and use a keystream. Stream ciphers are applied where buffering may be limited or where data must be processed as it is received. While the case may exist for block ciphers to function as stream ciphers, and for block ciphers to be implemented in hardware, stream ciphers are generally less complex than block ciphers. Thus, stream ciphers may traditionally be found in hardware implementations of encryption.

Stream ciphers may be viewed as approximating the function of a one-time pad or Vernam cipher, which uses a random keystream of the same length as the plaintext. Due to the size of the keystream, a Vernam cipher is cumbersome and impractical for most applications. Traditional stream ciphers approximate the randomness of a keystream with a much smaller and more convenient key size (128 bits, for example). Encryption is accomplished by combining the plaintext with the keystream using the exclusive or (XOR) binary operation (see Figure 2.4).

Stream ciphers that operate in this fashion require sender and receiver to be in step during operations and are called synchronous stream ciphers for that reason. A benefit to using synchronous stream ciphers when the data transmission error rate is high is that if a digit of ciphertext is corrupted, only a single digit of plaintext is affected. However, this property is a disadvantage to security, because an

Figure 2.4 High-level view of stream cipher encryption.

attacker may be able to introduce a predictable error. Examples of synchronous stream ciphers are RC4 and HC-128.

Self-synchronizing or asynchronous stream ciphers overcome this security limitation by generating keystreams based on a set of former ciphertext bits. This allows resynchronization if ciphertext bits are corrupted, with loss of usually only a few characters. From a security standpoint, asynchronous stream ciphers are less susceptible to attack by attempting to introduce predictable error. Examples of asynchronous stream ciphers are ciphertext autokey (CTAK) and stream ciphers based on block ciphers in cipher feedback mode (CFB).

Asymmetric Cryptosystems

While the same key is used to decrypt the ciphertext in symmetric cryptosystems, asymmetric cryptosystems require use of a different key for decryption. In the following, the encryption key K1 is different from the corresponding decryption key, K2:

$$\textit{Encryption: } E_{K1}(M) = C$$

$$\textit{Decryption: } D_{K2}(C) = M$$

Use of a different key to encrypt the message than the key used to decrypt and the fact that it is infeasible to generate one key from the other are what distinguishes an asymmetric or public key cryptosystem (see Figure 2.5).

Asymmetric cryptosystems rely heavily on mathematical functions known as trapdoor functions. Such functions are easy to apply in one direction but extremely difficult to apply in the reverse.

Public key encryption can provide the benefits of confidentiality of message data, provide authenticity and data origin integrity of message data, and non-repudiation of data. Using public key encryption for the secure distribution of a secret key with a recipient is also possible, as long as a mechanism is used to authenticate the recipient and to ensure that the public key is authentic.

Figure 2.5 Asymmetric cryptosystem.

To review how confidentiality can easily be produced, let us ask Bob to send a secret message to Alice. We want Alice to be the only person who can read Bob's message. For this to occur, Alice must first generate a public/private key pair, and publish her public key for Bob to read in the local newspaper. Bob meticulously enters the public key into his asymmetric cryptosystem, and encrypts his plaintext message, "Hello this is Bob!"

When Alice uses the private key she generated earlier, she finds she can read the message. Because Alice has kept her private key secure, she is assured no one else was able to read Bob's message. However, Alice is not sure the message is really from Bob, because the public key is available to any newspaper subscriber.

So, to see how authenticity can be produced with an asymmetric cryptosystem, Bob's private key, not Alice's public key, must be used to encrypt the message. Bob generates a public/private key pair and publishes the public key. Bob uses his private key to encrypt the message "This message is from Bob!" Anyone, including Alice, can now obtain a copy of Bob's public key and decrypt the message. While there is no confidentiality of the message, using Bob's public key provides assurance the messages decrypted with it are from Bob. Thus, asymmetric cryptosystems can also be used for signing.

Because asymmetric cryptosystems tend to perform slower than symmetric cryptosystems, Alice and Bob can use their public/private key system to exchange the secret keys of a faster symmetric cryptosystem, using it for future communications.

The idea that separate keys for encryption and decryption could be used was presented in 1976 by Whitfield Diffie and Martin Hellman [DH]. This is the basis for the Diffie–Hellman (DH) key agreement protocol, also called exponential key agreement, which is a method of exchanging secret keys over a nonsecure medium without exposing the keys. The DH protocol is based on the difficulty of calculating discrete logarithms in a finite field.

While DH provides confidentiality for key distribution, the protocol does not provide authentication of the communicating parties. Thus, a means of authentication such as digital signatures must be used to protect against a man-in-the-middle attack.

The idea of a public-key cryptosystem and its use in digital signing was presented by Ron Rivest, Adi Shamir, and Leonard Adleman in 1977 [RSA]. RSA public and private keys are functions of a pair of large prime numbers. Recovering the plaintext from RSA encryption without the key would require factoring the product of two large primes, forming the basis for the security provided by the RSA algorithm. The keys must be generated in such a way that it is computationally infeasible to factor them; thus, proper creation of random prime numbers is a factor in how secure the cryptosystem is. An additional factor is the size of the key. Typically, key size of 1024 bits is required; however, 2048 or even 4096 bits may be used to provide additional security at the cost of performance.

Cryptosystems employ cryptographic primitives, which are the basic mathematical operations on which the encryption procedure is built. Primitives by themselves do not provide security. A particular security goal is achieved by employing the cryptographic primitives in what is known as a cryptographic scheme. Cryptosystems built using RSA schemes may be used for confidentiality, signing to provide authenticity, or key exchange.

Use of a different scheme can also provide a different level of security, including resistance to attack. The RSA Cryptography Specifications Version 2.1 combines the RSA encryption primitive (RSAEP) and RSA decryption primitive (RSADP) with particular encoding methods to define schemes for providing encryption for confidentiality and for digital signatures for providing authenticity of messages. While the current specification allows for use of earlier RSA schemes for compatibility reasons, it is highly recommended that the newer schemes be used for improved security. For instance, while the version 2.1 RSA Cryptography specification allows use of the version 1.5 scheme known as "RSAES-PKCS1-v1_5" for cryptographic applications requiring backward compatibility, if possible, the newer "RSAES-OAEP" scheme based on a more secure optimal asymmetric encryption padding encoding method should be used [PKCS #1]. Cryptosystems must consider not only the algorithm but the scheme to use for a given application.

While RSA and DH enjoy widespread use in applications such as for IPSec or for protecting AES private keys, their continued use will require improvements to the level of security they provide. Even if newer methods for attack against the fundamental problem of factoring large prime numbers or discrete logarithms are not created, computing power continues to increase significantly over time. As a result, implementing existing attack methods using special-purpose ultra-high-speed computers poses a theoretical threat to RSA and DH. To counter the threat, key size may be increased, which also requires additional computing power. Another option is to use a different asymmetric encryption algorithm altogether.

Another popular approach to public-key cryptography, which is more computationally efficient than either RSA or DH, is elliptic curve cryptography (ECC). For instance, recommendations by the National Institute of Standards and Technology (NIST) for protecting AES 128-bit private keys is to use RSA and DH key sizes of 3072 bits, or elliptic curve key size of 256 bits [NISTSP800-57-1]. Although ECC is slightly more complex than either RSA or DH, ECC has been shown to offer more security per bit increase in key size.

ECC schemes are based on the mathematical problem of computing discrete logarithms of elliptic curves. Because the algorithm is very efficient, ECC can be very useful in applications requiring limited processing power such as in small wireless devices and mobile phones.

Other asymmetric cryptosystems include El Gamal and Cramer–Shoup. El Gamal is based on the problem of computing discrete logarithms, and makes use of the Diffie–Hellman key exchange protocol. Cramer–Shoup is an extension of El Gamal.

Asymmetric cryptosystems that have been proved insecure and should not be used are those based on the knapsack algorithm. The first of these to be developed was the Merkle–Hellman Knapsack cryptosystem [Merkle–Hellman Knapsack]. The knapsack algorithm is based on having a set of items with fixed weights and needing to know which items can be combined to obtain a given weight.

Public key cryptosystems will continue to be necessary when secret key exchange is required. Common software protocols and applications where they are used include IPSec, SSL/TLS, SSH, and PGP.

Hash Functions and Message Authentication Codes

Hash functions are cryptographic algorithms that provide message integrity by producing a condensed representation of a message, called a message digest. Message authentication codes (MACs) are cryptographic schemes that also provide message authenticity along with message integrity by using a secret key as part of message input.

At a minimum, the following properties are present in a hash function:

Compression: The hash function H transforms a variable-length input M to a fixed-length hash value h. This is represented by

$$H(M) = h$$

Ease of computation: Given a hash function H and an input M, the hash value h is easy to compute.

In addition, the following properties of cryptographic hash functions exist:

Preimage resistance: Given a hash function *h*, it is computationally infeasible to compute what the input *M* was. This is known as the "one-way" property of hash functions.

Second preimage resistance: For a given input *M*, is computationally infeasible to find any second input which has the same hash value *h*.

Collision resistance: For hash function *h*, it is computationally infeasible to find any two distinct inputs that produce the same hash value.

Hash functions may be built from one-way compression functions, algorithms that exhibit the property of collision resistance. One-way functions are limited in their ability to provide collision resistance, however. A popular means of constructing the hash function and strengthen its collision resistance is the Merkle–Damgård technique, which involves breaking the message input up into a series of smaller blocks. A compression function is performed taking the first message block and an initial fixed value as inputs. The output is fed along with the next message block into the compression function being used. Successive outputs combine with respective message blocks as input to the collision-resistant compression function in an iterative fashion. This results in a fixed-length message digest. A simplified typical Merkle–Damgård construction is shown in Figure 2.6.

MD5 (Message Digest algorithm 5), designed by Ron Rivest in 1991, is one such hash function based on a one-way algorithm and utilizing Merkle–Damgård construction. While MD5 has been widely used, it has been found to be prone to collision weakness and is thus insecure [Tunnels].

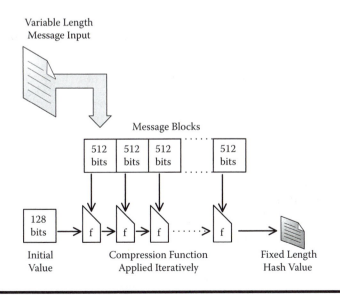

Figure 2.6   Merkle-Damgård strengthening.

A common replacement recommended for MD5, and which is also widely used, is SHA-1 (Secure Hash Algorithm), designed by the United States National Security Agency (NSA). SHA-1 is also based on a one-way function utilizing Merkle–Damgård, and produces a 160-bit message digest. It has been found possible to derive a collision (determine a pair of different inputs that produce the same hash value) with 2^{63} hash operations, which is less than the brute force strength of 2^{80} steps that would be necessary [SHA-1 Collisions]. To determine a collision in SHA-1 would still require significant computational resources, such as those provided by distributed computing.

An alternative to SHA-1 is RIPEMD-160, designed by Hans Dobbertin, Antoon Bosselaers, and Bart Preneel and which also produces a 160-bit message digest. RIPEMD-160 also replaces RIPEMD, which has been found to be prone to collision weakness [Collisions].

A summary of hashing functions based on one-way algorithms, along with their susceptibility to collision weakness, is summarized in Table 2.1.

Another means of creating a hash function is by using a block cipher algorithm. Thus, it is possible to use AES to create a cryptographic hash function. Block ciphers operate by encrypting plaintext using a private key to produce ciphertext. The ciphertext cannot be used by itself to recreate the plaintext, which resembles the one-way property of a hash function. However, because the block cipher's secret key and decryption algorithm would allow reconstruction of the plaintext, some additional operations must be added to a block cipher to turn it into a secure cryptographic hash function.

Table 2.1   Hashing Functions Based on One-Way Algorithms

Algorithm	Message Digest Output Size (bits)	Message Input Block Size (bits)	Collision Possible?
HAVAL	128/160/192/224/256	1024	Yes
MD4	128	512	Yes
MD5	128	512	Yes
RIPEMD	128	512	Yes
RIPEMD-128/256	128/256	512	Not yet
RIPEMD-160/320	160/320	512	Not yet
SHA-1	160	512	Yes
SHA-224/256	224/256	512	Not yet
SHA-384/512	384/512	1024	Not yet
Tiger	128/160/192	512	Not yet

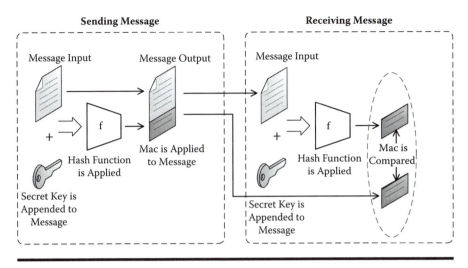

Figure 2.7   A hashed message authentication code (HMAC).

An example of a block cipher hash function is MDC-2 (Modification Detection Code 2, sometimes called Meyer-Schilling), developed by IBM, which produces a 128-bit hash. Another example is Whirlpool, which produces a 512-bit hash; it was adopted by the International Organization for Standardization (ISO) in the ISO/IEC 10118-3:2004 standard [Dedicated Hash].

Another use of a block cipher is in a MAC, which is a key-dependent hash function. A MAC adds to the input message the secret key used by the symmetric block cipher, and the resulting output is a fixed-length string called the MAC. Adding the secret key to the message produces *origin authentication*, showing that the message must have been constructed by someone with knowledge of the secret key. MACs also provide *integrity*, because any change to the message would result in a different MAC value. The most common form of MAC algorithm based on a block cipher employs cipher block chaining, and is known as a CBC-MAC.

A MAC may also be derived using a hash function, where the hash function is modified to incorporate use of a secret key to provide *origin authentication* and *integrity*. This is known as an MDx-MAC scheme, and can be based on a RIPEMD-128, RIPEMD-160, or SHA-1 hash function.

A hashed message authentication code (HMAC) is another case of a MAC derived using a hash function. In an HMAC, the underlying hash function is not modified, but is treated as a "black box." HMAC uses any iterative hash function and adds a secret key to the input message in order to obtain *origin authentication* and *integrity*. See Figure 2.7 for a simplified view of HMAC.

HMAC is used in a variety of applications from mobile phones to network-attached storage devices and in IPSec. The construction of HMAC was published in IETF RFC 2104. The use of HMACs is standardized in NIST FIPS PUB 180, the Secure Hash Standard, and in ISO/IEC 9797-2.

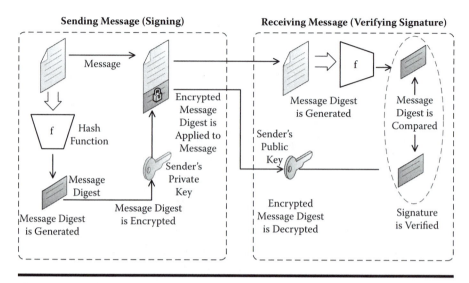

Figure 2.8   Digital signing and verifying.

Digital Signatures

MACs depend on use of a symmetric key that must be securely transmitted from the sender to the receiver. A digital signature may be thought of as a MAC that uses asymmetric cryptography, because a digital signature uses a private signing key and a public verification key.

A digital signature scheme operates in the following manner:

1. A message digest is generated using a hash function.
2. The message digest is encrypted with the sender's private key and attached to the cleartext message, signing it (note that a digital signature does not provide confidentiality).
3. The attached message digest is decrypted by the receiver, using the sender's public key. The receiver also compares this message digest with the message digest produced by hashing the cleartext message, to ensure that the message was not altered.

Figure 2.8 depicts digital signing and verifying.

A digital signature can provide *origin authentication*, *non-repudiation*, and *integrity*. By using a public/private key pair, the message is bound to the originator who used the private key. The originator can be bound to an individual using a mutual certification authority such as a PKI, thus assuring some measure of *non-repudiation* for the sender. *Integrity* is provided by using the cryptographic hashing function to make certain any alteration of the message can be detected.

A digital signature scheme contains the following elements:

- *Cryptographic hash function*: Hashing is done by the sending and receiving parties to determine integrity of the message.
- *Key generation algorithm*: Key generation produces a private key for signing and a public key for distribution to parties who will verify the digital signature.
- *Signing algorithm*: Signing produces a digital signature output using the private key and message.
- *Verification algorithm*: Verification uses the public key and digital signature to determine authenticity of the message.

Public key cryptosystems that are used to implement digital signature schemes include ECC, El Gamal, DSA, and RSA.

Standards that specify various schemes for digital signature algorithms exist. Digital Signature Algorithm (DSA) is a NIST standard specified for use in the Digital Signature Standard (DSS). DSS is defined in FIPS PUB 186. ISO/IEC 9696 and ISO/IEC 14888 specify a portfolio of digital signature schemes. Additional international standards specifying digital signature standards include ANSI X9.30.1, ANSI X9.62, and IEEE 1363.

Key Management

Historically, a lot of efforts in the field of cryptography have been devoted to the development and implementation of secure algorithms and protocols. They have been put through scrutiny at all levels. There are a lot of publications that give an estimation of an algorithm's strength. But it is very unlikely that a real attacker will prefer brute force to lower-hanging fruit in order to break a code. A real vulnerability can most likely be found in the key management methods. Key management in the real world is the most difficult part of cryptography [SCHNEIER]. It is much easier to find a flaw in one of the key management processes than to expend resources on sophisticated crypto attacks. It is not easy to design and implement a well-thought-out key management system. That is why the most successful crypto attacks have exploited poor key management. Moreover, the fact of using strong crypto algorithms and long keys very often creates a false sense of security that results in overlooking more mundane chores related to key management. Key management should provide the foundation for the secure generation, storage, distribution, and destruction of keys [NISTSP800-57-1]. Modern key management is usually an automated process, which helps to minimize human errors in the process of key generation, distribution and update, and also increases the key's secrecy. One of the principles of modern cryptography requires that keys not appear in cleartext outside the crypto module (except public keys, which are usually distributed within public key certificates).

The subject of key management is multidimensional because of different types of cryptography and the purposes they serve. Thus, asymmetric (public and private) keys are managed differently from symmetric keys. Likewise, data encryption keys are managed differently from signing keys. One of the goals of this section is to address these specifics.

Although the main purposes of cryptography have been reviewed from an application perspective earlier in this chapter, let us look at the main purpose from a key management perspective.

Purpose of the Keys and Key Types

Either as a stand-alone service or as a supporting part of another system, cryptography supports one or several security services or properties: *confidentiality, authentication, integrity, non-repudiation,* and *authorization*. Although they have been discussed in the first section of this chapter, here we will look at them from the key management perspective. The important characteristics of the cryptographic keys, such as key size and life span, are defined by the security services and type of cryptography these keys should support. One of the cryptographic principles is a preferred use of each key type for one designated purpose, although issuing and using a multipurpose key in real life is common.

Confidentiality is protection of information against unauthorized disclosure, and it is achieved by data encryption. Data to be protected may be either a human-readable text, or any type of binary, including other crypto keys. Both symmetric and asymmetric cryptography can be used. An unauthorized party should not be able to deduce or obtain the key for decryption. Keys for data at rest encryption may have a long crypto period; thus, they need to have a sufficient length and to be supported by a sophisticated and robust key management system (KMS). On the other hand, the keys for data in transit encryption may have a short life span, sometimes limited to one session. Their key length may be shorter and, thus, the KMS for this purpose may need to simply include a key generating and distributing mechanism.

The following key types support confidentiality:

- Symmetric data encryption key
- Symmetric key wrapping key; aka key encrypting key
- Public and private key transport keys
- Symmetric key agreement key
- Public and private static key agreement keys
- Public and private ephemeral key agreement keys

Broadly, *authentication* is a way to verify the origin of information. If the information is just data or an executable, authentication would verify its integrity as well as the identity of the person or system that created the information. If authentication is part of an access control system and the information consists of user or system identity, authentication will verify that identity in order to allow authorization services to make access control decisions. Both symmetric and asymmetric cryptography techniques may be used, such as digital signature and MAC. The main idea is that possession of the key proves the authenticity of an information originator. Both data at rest and in transit may employ key-based authentication.

The following key types support authentication:

- Private signature key
- Public signature verification key
- Symmetric authentication key
- Public and private authentication keys

Data integrity is a security feature that protects data against unauthorized alteration either in transmission or in storage. An unauthorized alteration may include substitution, insertion, or deletion and may be intentional or unintentional. None of these can happen unnoticed if data integrity control is in place. Both symmetric and asymmetric cryptography techniques, such as digital signature and MAC, may be used. The following key types support data integrity:

- Private signature key
- Public signature verification key
- Symmetric authentication key
- Public and private authentication keys

Non-repudiation is concerned with providing data integrity and authentication in a special way that allows a third party to verify and prove it. It is provided by asymmetric key cryptography and a digital signature relying on a signer's private key. This security feature requires an especially rigid control of the keys, because it should prevent a signing party from successfully denying its signature. The following keys may be found when non-repudiation is supported:

- Private signature key
- Public signature verification key

Authorization is the component of access control that is responsible for granting an object access to a particular resource after that object has already proved its identity (authenticated). A Kerberos ticket-granting service is a typical example of a key used for authorization. In more general terms, the following keys may be used for authorization:

- Symmetric authorization key
- Private authorization key
- Public authorization (verification) key

Cryptographic Strength and Key Size

The strength of cryptography depends on the strength of the algorithms, protocols, and keys and the strength of the security around the keys. In cryptographic applications that require key generation, key distribution, and encryption, whole suites of algorithms are used. For example, the first phases of IPSec and SSL include key negotiation and exchange, which may employ RSA cryptography. The following phases include generating a symmetric session key and using that key for encrypting data in transit with 3DES or AES. The strength of cryptography in this case is defined by the weakest link in this chain, so if in this example the key exchange employs very short public and private keys, the symmetric encryption key can be successfully intercepted and the transmitted data can be decrypted. Many factors should be considered, including the data and key's life span, volume of the data to be encrypted with the same key, the key size, and the way the keys are generated. For example, if a key is generated straight from a password, the entropy in the key is significantly reduced, because a smart brute force attack can generate just the keys deriving from ASCII characters that meet password policy requirements.

The difficulty of breaking a key using brute force grows exponentially with key length (i.e., number of bits), because each bit doubles a number of possible combinations for brute force. A long key gives better security but worse performance, so figuring an optimal key size is important. It should also depend on the projected key's lifetime. Temporary, or so-called ephemeral, keys generated for one session or one connection, may be shorter. The long-life keys protecting data at rest for years should be as long as possible.

One of the important characteristics of the keys is a crypto period. It is defined [NISTSP800-57-1] as the time span during which a specific key is authorized for use by legitimate entities, or during which the keys for a given system will remain in effect. Duration of a crypto period limits a "window of opportunity" for successful cryptanalytic or any other attacks and volume of information that can be exposed if the keys are compromised. Generally, the shorter the crypto period, the better security, although more frequent key generation, revocation, and replacement may be costly and may create additional risk. Many factors should be taken into consideration when the crypto period for each key type is defined. NIST recommendations [NISTSP800-57-1] regarding crypto period, which assume usage of the environment with the goal of achieving better operational efficiency, are in Table 2.2.

Originator usage period (OUP) is a period of time in the crypto period of a symmetric key during which cryptographic protection may be applied to data.

As was mentioned earlier in this chapter, both the continuous progress in cryptanalysis techniques and increasing computer power available for breaking the keys, should be considered. By Moore's law, computer speed doubles every 18 months, so the key size should be selected accordingly to protect the encrypted data against a brute force attack. If a computer is N time faster, the key size should increase by $\log_2 N$ bits.

Table 2.2 Recommended Crypto Periods for the Key Types

Key Type	Originator Usage Period (OUP)	Recipient Usage Period
Private Signature Key	1–3 years	1–3 years
Public Signature Key	Several years	Several years
Symmetric Authentication Key	< = 1–2 years	< = OUP + 3 years
Private Authentication Key	1–2 years	1–2 years
Public Authentication Key	1–2 years	1–2 years
Symmetric Data Encryption Key	< = 2 years	< = OUP + 3 years
Symmetric Key Wrapping Key	< = 2 years	< = OUP + 3 years
Symmetric Master Key	1 year	1 year
Private Key Transport Key	< = 2 years	< = 2 years
Public Key Transport Key	< = 2 years	< = 2 years
Symmetric Key Agreement Key	1–2 years	1–2 years
Private Static Key Agreement	1–2 years	1–2 years
Public Static Key Agreement	1–2 years	1–2 years
Private Ephemeral Key Agreement Key	One key agreement transaction	One key agreement transaction
Public Ephemeral Key Agreement Key	One key agreement transaction	One key agreement transaction
Symmetric Authorization Key	< = 2 years	< = 2 years
Public Authorization Key	< = 2 years	< = 2 years
Private Authorization Key	< = 2 years	< = 2 years

A successful brute force attack on a symmetric key algorithm, which in the case of perfect key entropy essentially consists of an exhaustive search of all the keys, would require on 2^N, divided by 2, where N is a size of the key in bits cycles. In addition to the key length, there is an effective key length factor. In the case of 3DES, which assumes total 3 * 56 = 168 bit key encryption, the effective key size is 80 bits if the first and third encryption rounds are performed using the same 56-bit key, and it is 112 bits if all three rounds employ unique 56-bit keys. As already discussed in the example of the keys derived from an ASCII or EBCDIC password, and as we will further see in the example of asymmetric key strength, there is another factor which impacts the strength in addition to the effective key length. This factor is a key space.

Table 2.3   Comparable Key Strength

Bits of Security	Symmetric Key Algorithms	FFC (e.g., DSA, D-H)	IFC (e.g., RSA)	ECC (e.g., ECDSA)
80	2TDEA	L = 1024; N = 160	k = 1024	f = 160–223
112	3TDEA	L = 2048; N = 224	k = 2048	f = 224–255
128	AES-128	L = 3072; N = 256	k = 3072	f = 256–383
192	AES-192	L = 7680; N = 384	k = 7680	f = 384–511
256	AES-256	L = 5360; N = 512	k = 5360	f = 512+

Breaking asymmetric key cryptography may need much less resources than breaking symmetric key cryptography. This stems from the nature of asymmetric key cryptography. For example, an RSA private key, which is a target of asymmetric cryptography attack, should be generated to meet certain RSA criteria. When this key is generated, as well as its counterpart public key, it is being derived from the space of large prime numbers. It means the key space for an exhaustive search is much smaller. Also, some advances in research of factoring large numbers indicates that increasing the size of public/private keys is required. RSA indicated that if an easy solution to the factoring problem is found and further increase of RSA key size beyond 2048 bits is required, then using the RSA algorithm may become impractical. Elliptic curve cryptography (ECC) is based on the elliptic curve discrete logarithm problem, which may take a full exponential time to solve. It is comparable with symmetric encryption strength. That is why ECC is considered the most likely successor of the RSA algorithm in the asymmetric cryptography area.

Comparison of symmetric, RSA, and ECC asymmetric cryptography and the corresponding key lengths are shown in Table 2.3 [NISTSP800-57-1].

Some observations regarding comments in this table [NISTSP800-57-1]

1. Column 1 indicates the number of bits of security provided by the algorithms and key sizes in a particular row. Note that the bits of security are not necessarily the same as the key sizes for the algorithms in the other columns, due to attacks on those algorithms that provide computational advantages. Because some combinations of 0 and 1 for 2TDES and 3TDES keys can be predicted, it takes less computational power to guess the key value, which is equivalent to a shorter key.
2. Column 2 identifies the symmetric key algorithms that provide the indicated level of security (at a minimum), where 2TDEA and 3TDEA are specified in [SP800-67], and AES is specified in [FIPS197]. 2TDEA is TDEA with two different keys; 3TDEA is TDEA with three different keys.
3. Column 3 indicates the minimum size of the parameters associated with the standards that use finite field cryptography (FFC). Examples of such

algorithms include DSA as defined in [FIPS186-3] for digital signatures, and Diffie–Hellman (DH) and MQV key agreement as defined in [ANSX9.42] and [SP800-56]), where L is the size of the public key, and N is the size of the private key.

4. Column 4 indicates the value for k (the size of the modulus n) for algorithms based on integer factorization cryptography (IFC). The predominant algorithm of this type is the RSA algorithm. RSA is specified in [ANSX9.31] and [RSA PKCS#1]. These specifications are referenced in [FIPS186-3] for digital signatures. The value of k is commonly considered to be the key size.
5. Column 5 indicates the size of the key for algorithms based on elliptic curve cryptography (ECC)

Key Life Cycle

Key life cycle should be analyzed for each key type in a crypto system in order to build a secure, cost-effective cryptographic architecture. Four major phases should be considered:

■ *Preoperational phase*: The key is not generated yet, but preactivation processes are taking place. It may include registering a user's attributes with the key management system, installing the key policies, and selecting algorithms and key parameters, and initial installation or update of the software or hardware cryptographic module with initial key material, which should be used just for testing and then replaced for production operation. Finally, the key material will be generated and optionally (depending on the application) distributed in a secure manner to other entities. For a more detailed description of these processes, see the sections "Key Creation" and "Key Distribution" of this chapter. The keys must be registered, which essentially includes binding them to the subject's identity. For PKI, it is implemented in the X509 certificate, which binds a public key with subject's name (usually DN), alternative name (usually e-mail) and some other attributes, and signs this binding by a digital signature of a trusted CA. For symmetric keys, it may be another mechanism, for example, implemented in a Kerberos Key Distribution Center (KDC).

■ *Operational phase:* Key material is ready for normal operational use (encryption, decryption, signing, etc.). In many cases, the key is stored in the crypto module hardware or disk storage that meets certain requirements; for example, FIPS 140-2 [FIPS 140-2]. Key material availability is important, and backup and recovery mechanisms should be used to support this requirement. However, if a key may be recovered by means other than backup/restore methods, such as regenerating or rederiving it, it reduces the probability of compromising the key's backups. Even if the key is not lost, it may need to be updated or changed during the operational phase. The main reasons are either the key policy regarding crypto period expiration or suspected or real key compromise. The key change may be accomplished either by simple rekeying, or replacing the old key with a completely independent new key, or updating the old key. The former method is used usually when a key is compromised, and it requires key redistribution. In the latter case, a new key is produced from the previous one, based on the protocol known to all parties, so no key redistribution is required. According to their policies, encryption/decryption and signing/verification key pairs have their own lifetime (crypto period). PKI applications automatically start trying to update the keys that enter into the transition period after a particular time interval, which is normally a percentage of the key lifetime.

■ *Postoperational phase:* Key material is not in operation, but access to the keys still may be needed. This need may be associated, for example, with the need to decrypt a document or verify a signature on the document after expiry of the crypto period. The keys for this purpose are stored in an archive in encrypted form, with access and integrity control. There is a special recovery process in place, usually available for designated administrators, to obtain the keys from archive. It is a good practice to have on-site and off-site (backup) archives. Not all the key types may, and should, be archived. Further destruction of the keys stored in the archive may be warranted by the applicable policies. More details about archiving, revocation, and destruction of the keys is in one of the following sections of this chapter.

■ *Key destruction* is performed either when the key is compromised or when its crypto period and retention in the archive have expired, according to the policy.

Key Creation

A key generation process is a part of the key establishment function of the key management preoperation phase [NISTSP800-57-1].

The security of cryptography is based on the secrecy of the keys and the virtual impossibility of deducing the keys from the cipher or other sources. Another principle of cryptography that relates specifically to key generation is to avoid weak keys and make a key space "flat," deriving from random numbers. Theoretically, any n-bit key's key space, based on the random number generator, is a 2^N. In reality, in many cases, it is significantly smaller, which translates into lower resources required to break the key by specialized brute force. The older basic encryption tools generated keys from ASCII characters [SCHNEIER], which reduced the key space at least by half and also invited dictionary attacks. In 1995, two PhD students found that a release of Netscape's SSL implementation chose the key from a recognizable subspace (bound to the clock) of the total key space. It significantly simplified attacks on SSL traffic. Another key generation weakness was discovered just recently [TECHREV-OPENSSL] in one open source system that used a "predictable random" number generator. Originating the keys only from true random numbers may help to avoid this flaw. Another potential weakness of keys stems from a specific algorithm and its implementation, when knowledge of just one portion of a key is enough to decrypt a cipher and deduce the whole key. As in the previous discussion about key size, we need to look at the process of key generation in context: type of the keys, purpose of the keys, crypto application, and operation environment. It may be difficult to evaluate these factors because some of them may be proprietary. For crypto systems that support applications for the federal government, the FIPS 140-2 [FIPS 140-2] and the coming draft FIPS 40-3 [FIPS 140-3] are clearly defining requirements for key generation. These standards give a good benchmark for commercial systems as well and help to avoid the crypto system design flaws as described earlier. As FIPS 140-2 defines [FIPS 140-2]:

> Random Number Generators (RNGs) used for cryptographic applications typically produce a sequence of zero and one bits that may be combined into sub-sequences or blocks of random numbers. There are two basic classes: deterministic and nondeterministic. A deterministic RNG consists of an algorithm that produces a sequence of bits from an initial value called a seed. A nondeterministic RNG produces output that is dependent on some unpredictable physical source that is outside human control.

A seed key, in its turn, is defined as "a secret value used to initialize a cryptographic function or operation." NIST has documented approved methods of producing random numbers [ANNEXC-FIPS 140-2]. It also has certain criteria of entering the seed during a key generation process, both for the case when the keys are generated inside a crypto module or outside. Entering the keys into the crypto module may be manual (e.g., keyboard) or electronic (e.g., smart cards, tokens, etc.). A seed key, if entered during key generation, may be entered in the same manner as cryptographic keys. Physical security requirements for the crypto modules that generate the keys are also described in FIPS 140-2 and 140-3 (draft) and include temper-resistant measures.

Although crypto key generation both for symmetric and asymmetric cryptography is based on RNG, the process is different for generating symmetric keys and asymmetric key pairs.

For asymmetric cryptography, the key pairs are generated according to the approved algorithms and standards. A static key pair can be generated by the end entity or by a facility that securely distributes the key pairs or by both the end entity and the facility in concert. A private signing key supporting the non-repudiation property should be generated on the end entity site and never leave that site. Ephemeral asymmetric keys are usually generated for the establishment of other keys, have a short life, and may be generated by the end entities and key distribution facilities. The following is a brief description of the RSA key pair, as one of the asymmetric key pair generation processes.

An RSA key pair consists of an RSA private key, which in digital signature applications is used to compute a digital signature, and an RSA public key, which in the digital signature applications is used to verify the digital signature. In encryption and decryption applications, the RSA private key is used to decrypt data and the RSA public key is used to encrypt the data. As described in [FIPS 160-3]:

> An RSA public key consists of a modulus n, which is the product of two positive prime integers p and q (i.e., $n = pq$), and a public key exponent e. Thus, the RSA public key is the pair of values (n, e) and is used to verify digital signatures. The size of an RSA key pair is commonly considered to be the length of the modulus n in bits (nlen). The corresponding RSA private key consists of the same modulus n and a private key exponent d that depends on n and the public key exponent e. Thus, the RSA private key is the pair of values (n, d) and is used to generate digital signatures. Note that an alternative method for representing (n, d) using the Chinese Remainder Theorem (CRT) is allowed as specified in PKCS #1. In order to provide security for the digital signature process, the two integers p and q, and the private key exponent d shall be kept secret. The modulus n and the public key exponent e may be made known to anyone. Guidance on the protection of these values is provided in SP 800-57. This Standard specifies three choices for the length of the modulus (i.e., nlen): 1024, 2048 and 3072 bits.
>
> A CA for signing certificates should use a modulus whose length nlen is equal to or greater than the moduli used by its subscribers. For example, if the subscribers are using an nlen = 2048, then the CA should use nlen ≥ 2048. RSA keys shall be generated with respect to a security strength S.

Parameters p and q are randomly generated and should be produced from seeds from a random or pseudorandom generator [NIST SP 800-90]. These prime numbers' seeds should be kept secret or destroyed after the modulus n is computed.

For symmetric cryptography, the keys may be generated from a random number generation method or regenerated from the previous key during a key update procedure. Another way is to derive the key from a master key using approved FIPS140-2 derivation functions, but eventually they are also coming from a random number. For secure key distribution purposes, split knowledge procedures can be used, and in that case, different components of the key may be generated in different locations, or may be created at one location and then split into components. Each key component will provide no knowledge of the entire key value (e.g., each key component must appear to be generated randomly). The principle of split knowledge is that if knowledge of k (where n is a total number of components and k is less than or equal to n) components is required to construct the original key, then knowledge of any $k - 1$ key components will not provide any information about the original key other than, possibly, its length. In addition, a simple concatenation of key components should not produce a key.

Key Distribution and Crypto Information in Transit

Key distribution mainly belongs to the key establishment function of the prepro-duction phase of key life cycle. By the NIST definition [NISTSP800-57-1], "it is the process of transporting a key and other keying material from an entity that either owns the key or generates the key to another entity that is intended to use the key." In many cases, it is a hard problem, which is solved differently for different types of keys. For example, data encryption keys are originated and distributed differently compared with signature verification keys, and public keys are distributed differ-ently from secret keys. This problem is more difficult for symmetric key applications, which need to protect the keys from disclosure. In any case, key distribution should use certain protection mechanisms to meet the following requirements, either the business dictates manual distribution or automated or a combination of both:

- Availability of the keys for a recipient after transmission by a sender (redundant channels, "store and forward" systems, and retransmission as a last resort).
- Integrity, which should detect modification of keys in transit. MAC, CRC, and digital signature can be used. Physical protection is required as well.
- Confidentiality. It may be achieved by key encryption or by splitting the key and distributing its components via separate channels ("split knowledge"). Physical protection should apply as well.
- Association of the keys with the intended application usage and related informa-tion may be achieved by appropriate configuration of the distribution process.

Symmetric Keys' Distribution

Symmetric keys may be distributed manually or electronically, by using a public key transport mechanism, or they may be previously distributed for transport using other encryption keys. Keys used only for encrypting data in storage should not be distributed at all, except for backup or other specially authorized entities. A descrip-tion of methods of symmetric keys distribution follows.

Splitting the keys. It is formally defined in FIPS 140-2 as a process by which a cryptographic key is split into multiple key components that individually share no knowledge of the original key. These components can be subsequently input into, or output from, a cryptographic module by separate entities and combined to recre-ate the original cryptographic key. Thus, FIPS 140-2 Level 3 requires

- A cryptographic module that separately authenticates the operator entering or outputting each key component.
- Cryptographic key components must be directly entered into or output from the cryptographic module without traveling through any enclosing or inter-vening systems where the key components may inadvertently be stored, com-bined, or otherwise processed.

■ At least two key components must be required to reconstruct the original cryptographic key.

In practical examples, several components of the key can be stored on devices with different ports and network connections, as well as on different crypto tokens that require individual authentication by designated security officers.

Manual key distribution. The process should ensure that the keys are coming from an authorized source and are received by the intended recipient. Also, the entity delivering the key should be trusted by both the sender and the receiver. A key in transit should be encrypted with a key intended for key wrapping.

Electronic distribution of wrapped keys (key transport). It requires a preliminary distribution of key-wrapping keys. In many implementations, a public key of an asymmetric key pair is used as a key-wrapping key; therefore, a recipient in possession of the private key will be able to "unwrap" the symmetric key. If symmetric cryptography is used for wrapping the keys, those key-wrapping keys should be distributed via a separate channel of communication.

Public and Private Keys Distribution

As was recalled earlier in our review of the methods of cryptography, one of the main advantages of using public and private key cryptography is easier key distribution of public keys. A party in possession of private keys can sign its message, and any receiving party who obtains the sender's public key can verify the signature. Likewise, any sender can obtain an encryption public key of a recipient, and only the recipient in possession of the counterpart private key can decrypt the encrypted data. While confidentiality of the public key is not needed, authenticity is. That is why public keys are usually distributed wrapped in public key certificates, issued and signed by a trusted certificate authority. The certificate, along with a public key, contains the subject's name and other attributes that indicate how the public key can be used. For easy access by relying parties, the certificates are either delivered with a signed message or made available in the directories and other publicly accessible distribution points.

Private keys are managed and distributed differently. If a signing private key must support non-repudiation, it should be generated and remain only in possession of the owner of this key, so no distribution applies. Although generating of public/private key pairs often takes place on a subject's node and the keys are placed in the crypto store on its hard drive or a hardware module, in some applications this is not the case. As described in the "Key Creation" section of this chapter, sometimes asymmetric key pairs, which do not have to support digital signatures with non-repudiation, may be generated on one of the servers of the public key infrastructure (either registration or distribution server), in cooperation between the servers and the subscriber, who is the owner of the keys. In such applications, private keys should be delivered to a subscriber via a secure encrypted channel with mutual authentication. Depending on policy, private decryption keys are also put in escrow, so that data may be decrypted if a subscriber leaves the organization or loses access to the keys.

When the public/private key pair is generated on the subscriber's site, there is no need to distribute the private key—it stays where it was generated and where it belongs.

A private key of a key pair generated on a central facility will be distributed only to the intended owner of that key, using either secure manual distribution or electronic distribution with security measures similar to those for symmetric key distribution, for example, authentication, encrypted channel, split knowledge, etc.

As was mentioned earlier, distributing static public keys does not require encrypted channels or split knowledge techniques, but it has its own specifics. A relying party, who obtains the keys either for verifying an owner's signature or for encrypting a message for the key owner, should have a high level of assurance that

- The key really belongs to the subject.
- The key is associated with certain attributes belonging to the subject.
- The key is valid.
- The key is allowed by its policy to be used for the intended purpose.

All of these issues are addressed by using Public Key Infrastructure (PKI) and issuing X.509 certificates containing the subject's public keys and attributes. The certificates are digitally signed by a PKI Certificate Authority and can be distributed via open channels, manually, or via e-mail or published by LDAP, HTTP, and FTP servers. Because each subject's certificate is signed by a CA, a relying party should treat that CA's certificate itself as an anchor of trust. Distribution of the trusted CA's certificate is usually done via other channels. It can be preinstalled by a software manufacturer or obtained from other distribution points. More details about asymmetric key management are provided in a separate PKI section later in this chapter.

Key Storage

The ultimate goal of key management is to prevent any unsanctioned access without impeding legitimate use of the keys by crypto applications and service and key life cycle management processes. Key storage should meet several requirements, which may be different for different type of keys [NISTSP800-57-1]. Generally, these requirements are broken into several categories.

Keys may be maintained within a crypto module when they are in active use, or they may be stored externally under proper protection and recalled when needed. The protection of the keys in storage should provide

- **Integrity** (by CRC, MAC, digital signature, checksums, parity check, etc.): In addition to logical integrity, the keys stored in HSM may be physically protected by the storage mechanism itself. For example, a crypto store may be designed so that once the key is installed, it cannot be observed from outside. Some key-storage devices (specifically those that meet FIPS 140-2 level 3) are designed to self-destruct when threatened with key disclosure or when there is evidence that the key device is being tampered with.

■ **Confidentiality** (by encryption, wrapping, and logical access control). Also, physical security is important (see earlier comments related to integrity).

■ **Association with application and objects** (making sure that the key belongs to a designated object; e. g., encapsulating public keys with the object DN in a signed certificate or storing private signing keys in the object's protected key store).

■ **Assurance of domain parameters** (making sure that domain parameters used in the PKI keys exchange are correct). Domain parameters are used in conjunction with some public key algorithms such as DSA and ECDSA (called p, g, and q parameter) to generate key pairs, to create digital signatures, or when generating shared secrets that are subsequently used to derive keying material.

Protection requirements by key types are in Table 2.4 [NIST SP 800-57].

In addition to key protection, the key store should also provide availability. Keys should be available for authorized users and applications for as long as data is protected by these keys. A secure key and escrow is usually used for this. After the crypto period expires, the keys should be placed in an archive, which can be combined with backup storage.

Overall security requirements and business reasons may define the type of crypto store. Keys stored in the computer files may be more easily accessible than those that are stored in the hardware such as smart cards, external token devices, or PCMCIA. Usually the vendors of crypto applications such as PKI CA or application gateways, which perform signing and decrypting of SOAP messages, provide the users with the choice, so the implementer may decide to either use a hardware security module as a key store or to store the keys in the files. An application's independence from hardware crypto device vendors is achieved by using standard RSA PKCS#11 compliant interfaces. A key file store is usually protected with an additional level of access control, so even a root user may not be able to access the key database if he or she does not have permissions and credentials for it.

Symmetric and private keys must be destroyed if they have been compromised or when their archive period (according to the policy) expires. Through the crypto period, when copies of the keys are made, these events should be documented; therefore, the keys' destruction should apply to all the copies. Specific methods used for key destruction are warranted by application and business requirements and acceptable risk. There are no specific requirements for destroying public keys. More specifically, processes for key destruction are described in NIST SP800-57 Part 2 [("Recommendation for Key Management—Part 2: Best Practices for Key Management Organization")]. *Zeroization* is a technical term for destroying

Table 2.4 Key Protection Requirements

Key Type	Security Service (Key Usage)	Required Security Protection	Required Association Protection	Period of Protection
Private signing key	Authentication; integrity; non-repudiation	Integrity; confidentiality	Usage or application; domain parameters; public signature verification key	From generation until the end of the crypto period
Public signature verification key	Authentication; integrity; non-repudiation	Archive; integrity	Usage or application; key pair owner; domain parameters; private signature key; signed data	From generation until no protected data needs to be verified
Symmetric authentication key	Authentication; integrity	Archive; integrity; confidentiality	Usage or application; other authorized entities; authenticated data	From generation until no protected data needs to be verified
Private authentication key	Authentication; integrity	Integrity; confidentiality	Usage or application; public authentication key; domain parameters	From generation until the end of the crypto period
Public authentication key	Authentication; integrity	Archive; integrity	Usage or application; key pair owner; domain parameters; private authentication key; authenticated data	From generation until no protected data needs to be authenticated

Continued

Table 2.4 (Continued)   Key Protection Requirements

Key Type	Security Service (Key Usage)	Required Security Protection	Required Association Protection	Period of Protection
Symmetric data encryption/ decryption key	Confidentiality	Archive; integrity; confidentiality	Usage or application; owner authorized entities; plaintext/ encrypted data	From generation until the end of the lifetime of the data or the end of the crypto period (whichever comes later)
Symmetric key wrapping key	Support	Archive; integrity; confidentiality	Usage or application; other authorized entities; encrypted keys	From generation until the end of the crypto period or no wrapped keys require protection (whichever comes later)
Symmetric and asymmetric RNG keys	Support	Integrity; confidentiality	Usage or application	From generation until replaced
Symmetric master key	Support	Archive; integrity; confidentiality	Usage or application; other authorized entities; derived keys	From generation until the end of the crypto period or the end of the lifetime of the derived keys (whichever comes later)
Private key transport key	Support	Archive; integrity; confidentiality	Usage or application; encrypted keys; public key transport key	From generation until the end of the period of protection for all transported keys

Public key transport key	Support	Integrity	Usage or application; key pair owner; private key transport key	From generation until the end of the crypto period
Symmetric key agreement key	Support	Archive; integrity; confidentiality	Usage or application; other authorized entities	From generation until the end of the crypto period or until it is no longer necessary to determine key (whichever is later)
Private static key agreement key	Support	Archive; integrity; confidentiality	Usage or application; domain parameters; public static key agreement key	From generation until the end of the crypto period or until it is no longer necessary to determine key (whichever is later)
Public static key agreement key	Support	Archive; integrity	Usage or application; domain parameters; key pair owner; private static key agreement key	From generation until the end of the crypto period or until it is no longer necessary to determine key (whichever is later)
Private ephemeral key agreement key	Support	Integrity; confidentiality	Usage or application; domain parameters; public ephemeral key agreement key	From generation until the end of the key agreement process. After the end of the process, the key should be destroyed

Continued

Table 2.4 (*Continued*) Key Protection Requirements

Key Type	Security Service (Key Usage)	Required Security Protection	Required Association Protection	Period of Protection
Public ephemeral key agreement key	Support	Integrity	Usage or application; domain parameters; private ephemeral key agreement key; key pair owner	From generation until the end of the key agreement process.
Symmetric authorization key	Authorization	Integrity; confidentiality	Usage or application; Other authorized entities	From generation until the end of the crypto period of the key
Private authorization key	Authorization	Integrity; confidentiality	Usage or application; domain parameters; public authorization key	From generation until the end of the crypto period of the key
Public authorization key	Authorization	Integrity	Usage or application; key pair owner; private authorization key; domain parameters	From generation until the end of the crypto period of the key

the keys by causing the storage medium to reset to all zeroes [NIST SP800-21]. Automatic zeroization is required when an attempt is made to access the maintenance interface or tamper with a device meeting FIPS 140-2 level 3 requirements [FIPS 140-2]. The key management policy should describe in detail the process of zeroization in a specific key management system.

If it is believed that an encryption key of data at rest was compromised, this data should be reencrypted with a new key. This whole process is called key rotation, and it includes decrypting data with the old encryption key (which is believed to be compromised) and rekeying this data with the new encryption key. With large volumes of data, data availability may be affected. That is why a lot of efforts are made to limit the need to rekey data. It is achieved by using a randomly generated value as an encryption key and making it unavailable directly for any user, including administrators. The application administrator may control encryption and decryption processes, but the key contents will never be disclosed.

Key Update

Modern key management is highly automated. For most phases of the key life cycle, manual steps are not required. Although creating a seed sometimes may require users to move a mouse or enter a long sequence of random key strokes, users do not manually select, communicate, or transcribe real crypto keys. Modern key management makes a periodic key update in accordance with key policies easier. One example is an automatic key and certificates rollover in the PKI. When a key or certificate is approaching the "valid to" date and time, an automated key update will kick off. Another example is session encryption keys. When an encrypted connection just starts, an initial key is negotiated and exchanged between parties using the key encryption key. When a session duration or volume of transferred data exceeds the limits, a new session is established between the same parties, and a new session key will be renegotiated and used for transactions. More frequent key updates will reduce the chance of a successful cryptanalytic attack and the volume of confidential data at risk. On the other hand, it may reduce system performance and increase the chance of key compromise in the case of misconfiguration. All the pros and cons should be evaluated, and keys' life span and frequency of key updates should be reflected in the policy.

Change of keys in the operational phase of the key life cycle may be caused by several reasons, as was alluded to earlier: key compromise, crypto period approaching the expiration date, or just a desire to reduce the volume of data encrypted with the same key.

- A new key may be produced by auto rekeying or by an automated function updating an existing key. Rekeying is producing a key that is completely independent on the key it replaces. Rekeying is applicable when an old key is compromised, the key approaches its expiration date, or a new session key must be established according to the requirements.

■ Another way of changing the keys is by applying a nonreversible function to an existing key. Updating an old key in this manner does not require new key distribution or exchange between parties, so it may be less expensive. Parties may agree to exchange the keys on a particular day and time or upon exchanging a certain volume of encrypted data or on other conditions. This method does not apply in the case of key compromise.

Key Revocation

Whenever a key is compromised, it cannot be trusted to provide required security, cannot serve its purpose, and should be revoked. Generally, the key is considered to be compromised if it is released to or discovered by an unauthorized entity or this event is suspected to have happened. A key may enter the compromised state from any state except the destroyed state. Although the compromised key cannot be used for protection, in some cases it still may be used to process cryptographically protected information, with reasonable caution and suspicion. For example, a digital signature may be validated if it can be proved that the data was signed before the signing key was compromised and that the signed data has been adequately protected.

Key revocation applies both to symmetric and asymmetric keys and the process should be formally described in the Key Management Policy. In the asymmetric key management systems and PKI, technically, a public key is revoked (or most often, a public key certificate, containing that key), but as a result, its counterpart private key is also getting automatically revoked.

Information about key revocation may be sent as a notification to the involved parties, which would indicate that the continued use of the key is not recommended. This notification should include complete information about the revoked key, the date and time of revocation, and the reason. Based on the revocation information provided, other entities could then make a determination of how they would treat information protected by the revoked keying material.

Another method is to provide the participating entities (i.e., relying parties) with the access point for obtaining the status of the key material. For example, if a signature verification public key is revoked because an entity left the company, the information may be published in the certificate revocation list (CRL). But an application may still honor the signature if it was created before the certificate was published in the CRL. (Note: Another problem is that many applications do not check CRLs by default [e.g., most Web browsers].) At the same time, if a signing private key was compromised in an unknown time frame, but eventually the public key certificate was revoked, the situation should be assessed more carefully. Certificate revocation in more detail will be reviewed in the section titled "Public Key Infrastructure."

A symmetric key that is used to generate a MAC may be revoked so that it is not used to generate a new MAC for new information. However, the key may be retained so that archived documents can be verified.

The recommended approach to the key revocation policy is to reflect it in the life cycle for each particular key. Thus, when a key is used in communication between just two parties, the entity revoking the key just informs another entity. On the other hand, if the key is used within an infrastructure with multiple relying parties, the revoking entity should inform the infrastructure, which should make the information about key revocation available to all relying parties.

Key Escrow

Generally, *escrow* is defined as something delivered to a third person (usually called an "escrow agent") to keep, and to be returned to the delivering entity under certain proof and conditions. This "something" may be a document, money, or a key.

In cryptography applications, a key escrow system operates with two components of one key, and these two components are entrusted to two independent escrow agents. For government applications [FIPS 185], these key components will be presented by the escrow agent to a requester, which may be an entity related to the owner of the key or a law enforcement organization, upon certain conditions, authorizations, and authentication.

This approach is implemented in electronic surveillance of encrypted telecommunications involving specific electronic devices. The key components obtained by the requester are entered into this device and enable decryption. Neither of the escrow agents can perform decryption, because it has just one component of the key. In applications for the private sector, the key components may be kept by two officers; therefore, if a key owner entity is not available, its encrypted information may be decrypted upon directions to the escrow officers from a higher official. Two types of risk exist in this schema: (1) collusion and (2) failure of reassembling and using the key for its intended purpose.

In order to support escrow capabilities in telecommunication, the U.S. government adopted the symmetric encryption algorithm SKIPJACK and a Law Enforcement Access Field (LEAF) method, which presents one part of a key escrow system enabling decryption of encrypted telecommunications. Both the SKIPJACK and the LEAF creation method are implemented in electronic devices. The devices may be incorporated in security equipment used to encrypt (and decrypt) telecommunications data.

Decryption of lawfully intercepted telecommunications may be achieved through the acquisition and use of the LEAF, the decryption algorithm, and the two escrowed key components.

Backup and Recovery

Backup

According to 800-57-2 [NISTSP800-57-2], key recovery is a stage in the life cycle of keying material; mechanisms and processes that allow authorized entities to retrieve keying material from key backup or archive. Key backup and recovery is a part of the KMS contingency plan, which according to 800-57-1 [NISTSP800-57-1],... "is a plan that is maintained for disaster response, backup operations, and post-disaster recovery to ensure the availability of critical resources and to facilitate the continuity of operations in an emergency situation."

As in the life cycle of any system, data can become unusable because of many reasons such as file corruption, hardware failure, configuration errors, etc. But in the case of cryptosystems management, backup should be considered only if there are no other ways (such as rekeying or key derivation) to provide continuity. These specific recommendations apply because of the risk associated with key backup, and the fact that key and other crypto information backup compromise is detrimental to the KMS operations. When planning key backup, the following questions should be answered: what key material needs to be backed up, where and how will the backup be stored, how will the backup and recovery procedures be performed, and who is responsible.

Not all the keys and cryptographic information should be backed up. For instance, private signing keys should not be backed up, to avoid any questionable situation with non-repudiation. However, in the specific case of the CA's signing key, this does not apply, because unrecoverable loss of this key would prevent new certificates from being issued until the CA was rekeyed. Special security measures apply for the backup of this key, such as storing it on a removable hardware crypto token protected by multiple keys and passwords that is stored in a safe under administrative control. Separation of duties in this schema prevents collusions and key compromise. Ephemeral keys and shared secrets, which are generated during key negotiations and used for one session for data in transit, do not need to be backed up. An RNG seed should not be backed up either, because it is not used immediately for data encryption and is needed only for key generation.

It is important to mention that the life span of the key backup should be equal to or longer than the life span of the encrypted or signed data. Another specific feature that makes key backup and recovery different compared with similar processes for other data is the criticality of a key's availability and, thus, backup redundancy. Both competing requirements for minimizing risk of the backed-up keys' disclosure and redundant storage for robust key recovery should be considered.

Key Recovery

Keys may not be available for cryptographic operations when the key material stored as a file in the system or on a hardware device/token is corrupted, the key owner either loses access to the key material (i.e., forgotten/lost password) or is not available when the organization needs access to the data, and some other situations. Keys may need to be recovered to enable decryption of data previously encrypted with a lost key or to verify the integrity and authenticity of previously signed data if a signature verification key is lost. The key recovery process acquires a key from backup storage and makes it available for the decryption or verification process.

Public Key Infrastructure

At this point, we assume that the reader preparing for ISSAP® certification has fundamental knowledge about asymmetric cryptography, public key certificates, and PKI. Therefore, we will analyze in more depth particular areas of this technology, which most likely lie outside the CISSP®-ISSAP® CBK, but may be useful for security architects. Before delving into the subjects in the following subsections, we should make several points that would influence the context of those subsections:

- The most important aspects of certificates, their life cycle, purpose, restrictions, and the way these certificates are supposed to be managed should be documented in the Certificate Policy (CP) and Certificate Practice Framework (CPF) [RFC 3647]. CPF includes one or more Certificate Practice Statements (CPSs) that address "... the practices that a certification authority employs in issuing, managing, revoking, and renewing or rekeying certificates."
- There are two categories of end entities that use PKI services: subscribers and relying parties. Subscribers are getting registered with PKI and subsequently generating or receiving private and public key pairs and receiving their certificates from a certificate authority (CA). Relying parties have access to the subscribers' public certificates, which they use for secure exchanges with subscribers. They trust the Certificate Authority, which is the heart of the PKI; hence, they rely on the PKI, which issues and supports certificates issued to subscribers.
- Depending on the policies that rule PKI and the need for relying applications, there may be one-key two-key, and sometimes multikey pair implementations. A single key pair PKI application uses one public/private key pair for all applications needs, chiefly for data decryption/encryption and signing/verification.
- Interoperability and integration of PKI with other IT infrastructure components and both client and server applications are very important issues for successful implementation and deployment. Although many relevant standards exist and are widely adopted, it should not be taken for granted that in the process of PKI enrollment, the keys will be placed in the right location on the client (subscriber) part and the certificate will be stored and published in a location that every relying party is aware of.

Key Distribution

The main reason why asymmetric cryptography and public certificates gained popularity is the manner in which they address the key distribution problem. Let us return to this discussion, begun earlier in this chapter. In order to support authentication and confidentiality, we would need each party to have its own symmetric keys dedicated for data exchange with one correspondent. If A is going to encrypt for B, C, and D, it would have to have individual keys for B, C, and D and send the keys to those parties in a secure manner. Each of B, C, and D would have to do the same. In sum, the two main problems of symmetric cryptography are the number of the required keys and the problem of their secure distribution. Public key cryptography solves both problems because of its nature. Keys come in pairs, and only the private key should be kept secret and should not be distributed. Its counterpart public key may be available to all parties, and hence may be published for public access on any server; that is, file server, LDAP, or Web server.

- For encryption, a recipient's public key may be used by any party wanting to encrypt data for that recipient, who is in possession of the counterpart private key. It guarantees that only this recipient in possession of that private key will be able to decrypt the data.
- For digital signature verification, each recipient may obtain a public verification key of the sender and be confident in the authenticity of the signature, because only the sender holds the private key that is used to produce the digital signature being verified.

The main problem that exists with public key distribution is to guarantee the key's integrity and binding to the identifier of the holder of the counterpart private key. This problem is solved by using X.509 public key certificates, which bind the subject name to a public key, and this binding is sealed by the signature of the PKI Certificate Authority. Because the CA signature is trusted by all parties, the integrity of the public key and its binding with the subject are trusted too.

Public key distribution, which is implemented via certificate distribution, boils down to publishing these certificates on a server accessible by relying parties or just attaching the certificate to an encrypted or signed message. Private keys should not be distributed at all.

Certificate and Key Storage

When talking about PKI certificates and the keys, we should always remember the guidance provided in CP and CPS documents. The purpose of the certificates and their keys will dictate how they should be handled and stored.

For two-key-pair applications, where the encryption key pair and the corresponding public-key certificate are created by the CA, the encryption public key certificates are most often placed in the subscriber's Directory entry and also in the PKI/CA database. Copies of the decryption private key and the encryption public key certificate will be securely sent to the subscriber and will be stored on the subscriber's machine on the disk or HSM. Decryption private keys should never be published, but they should be backed up. In a two-key-pair PKI, the subscriber generates the signing key on its machine and securely stores the signing private key on the disk or HSM. It sends only the verification public key to the CA in a secure manner. The signing private key is not sent to the CA, and it is never backed up in the CA's database. When the CA receives the verification public key, it generates a verification public key certificate. A copy of this certificate is stored in the CA database, and is also sent to the subscriber. Often, when the PKI subscriber sends a signed message to any recipient, it attaches the verification certificate to it. So, a relying party does not have to access the directory to retrieve this certificate, which is required for signature verification.

For one-key-pair applications, a dual-usage key pair is generated on the subscriber's machine and stored on the disk or HSM. A copy of the dual-usage private and public key will be sent to the CA. The private key will be stored in the CA database. The CA will use the public key to generate a dual-usage public key certificate and will put it in the user's Directory entry. A copy of this certificate will be stored in the CA database. It will be also sent to the subscriber and will be stored on its machine on the disk or HSM.

In sum, there are several places where certificates and public and private keys are stored: PKI/CA database, Directory server, and subscriber's machine. The specifics are highly dependent on PKI implementation and CPS directives.

PKI Registration

PKI consists of many components: Technical Infrastructure, Policies, Procedures, and People [PKIREGAG]. Initial registration of subscribers (either users, or organizations, or hardware, or software) for a PKI service has many facets, pertaining to almost every one of the PKI components. There are many steps between the moment when a subscriber applies for a PKI certificate and the final state, when keys have been generated and certificates have been signed and placed in the appropriate locations in the system. These steps are described either explicitly or implicitly in the PKI CPS.

Reference to the CP and CPS associated with a certificate may be presented in the X.509.V3 certificates extension called "Certificate Policies." This extension may give to a relying party a great deal of information, identified by attributes "Policy Identifier" and "Policy Qualifier" in the form of Abstract Syntax Notation One object IDs (ASN.1 OID).

One type of Policy Qualifier is a reference to CPF, which describes the practice employed by the issuer when registering the subscriber (the subject of the certificate). Here we focus on the following:

- How the subject proves its organizational entity
- How the person, acting on behalf of the subject, authenticates himself in the process of requesting a certificate
- How the certificate issuer can be sure that the subject, whose name is in the certificate request, is really in possession of the private key, to which the public key is presented in the certificate request along with the subject's name

How the Subject Proves Its Organizational Entity

Authentication requirements in the process of registration with PKI depend on relations between the CA and the organization, the nature of an applying end entity (EE) and CP, which is stating the purpose of the certificate. Thus, the organization may have its internal CA or may use a commercial CA to serve its all certificates needs. It may issue certificates of low assurance, which support just internal e-mail digital signature, or issue high assurance certificates, which encrypt and authenticate high value transactions between the organization and external financial institutions. Among end entities, there can be individuals, organizations, applications, elements of infrastructure, etc.

Organizational certificates are usually issued to the subscribing organization's devices, services, or individuals within the organization. These certificates support authentication, encryption, data integrity, and other PKI-enabled functionality when relying parties communicate. Among organizational devices and services may be

- Web servers with enabled TLS, which support the server's authentication and encryption
- Web services security gateways, which support SOAP messages' authentication and signatures' verification, encryption, and decryption
- Services and devices, signing content (software codes, documents, etc.) on behalf of the organization
- VPN gateways
- Devices, services, and applications supporting authentication, integrity, and encryption of Electronic Data Interchange (EDI), B2B, or B2C transactions
- Smart cards for end user authentication

Among procedures enforced within applying organizations (before a certificate request to an external CA is issued) are the following:

- An authority inside the organization should approve the certificate request.
- The authority should verify that the subject is who he or she claims to be.
- After that, an authorized person (authorized submitter) within the organization will submit a certificate application on behalf of the organization.
- The organizational certificate application will be submitted for authentication of the organizational identity.
- Depending on the purpose of the certificate, an external certificate issuer will try to authenticate the applying organization, which may include some but not all of the following steps, as in the following example [VeriSignCPS]:
  - Verify that the organization exists.
  - Verify that the certificate applicant is the owner of the domain name, which is the subject of the certificate.
- Verify employment of the certificate applicant and if the organization authorized the applicant to represent the organization.

A correlation between the level of assurance provided by the certificate and the strength of the process of validation and authentication of the EE registering with PKI and obtaining that certificate is always taking place.

How a Person, Acting on Behalf of the Subject, Authenticates to Request a Certificate (Case Studies)

Individual certificates may serve different purposes, for example: for e-mail signing and encryption, and for user authentication when they are connecting to servers (Web, directory, etc.) to obtain information or for establishing a VPN encryption channel. These kinds of certificates, according to their policy, may be issued to anybody who is listed as a member of a group (for example, an employee of an organization) in the group's directory and who can authenticate itself. An additional authorization for an organizational person may or may not be required for PKI registration.

An individual who does not belong to any organization can register with some commercial CAs with or without direct authentication and with or without presenting personal information. As a result, an individual receives his or her general use certificates. Different cases are now briefly described.

Online Certificate Request without Explicit Authentication

As in the example with VeriSign certificate of Class 1, a CA can issue an individual certificate (aka Digital ID) to any EE with an unambiguous name and e-mail address. In the process of submitting the certificate request to the CA, the keys are generated on the user's computer, and initial data for a certificate request, entered by the user (user name and e-mail address) is encrypted with a newly generated private key. It is all sent to the CA. Soon the user receives by e-mail his or her PIN number and the URL of a secure Web page to enter that PIN in order to complete the process of issuing the user's certificate. As a consequence, the person's e-mail address and ability to log into this e-mail account may serve as an indirect minimal proof of authenticity. However, nothing prevents person A from registering in the public Internet e-mail as person B and requesting, receiving, and using person B's certificate.

Authentication of an Organizational Person

The ability of the EE to authenticate in the organization's network (e.g., e-mail, domain) or with an organization's authentication databases may provide an acceptable level of authentication for PKI registration. Even just the person's organizational e-mail authentication is much stronger from a PKI registration perspective than authentication with public e-mail. In this case, user authentication for PKI

1. User enters to the corporate PKI/RA via intranet Web or GUI client.
2. User enters his name, e-mail address and other information pertaining to his authentication within corporate network.
3. PKI RA is using the data to authenticate the user against a corporate data IAW CPS policy
4. In the case of successful authentication an initialization request is forwarded to PKI CA
5. PKI/CA initiates the process of the user registration and issues authentication codes, bound to the user's distinguished name.
6. User receives the code, initiates key generation, sends to its certificate data to PKI/CA to complete the certificate issuing.

Figure 2.9   Authentication of an organizational person.

registration is basically delegated to e-mail or domain user authentication. In addition to corporate e-mail and domain controllers, an organization's HR database, directory servers, or databases can be used for the user's authentication and authorization for PKI registration. In each case, an integration of the PKI registration process and the process of user authentication with corporate resources needs to be done (see Figure 2.9).

A simplified case occurs when a certificate request is initiated by a Registration Authority upon management authorization. In this case, no initial user authentication is involved.

Individual Authentication

In the broader case, a PKI registration will require a person to authenticate potentially with any authentication databases defined in accordance with CPS. For example, to obtain a purchasing certificate from the CA, which is integrated into a B2C system, a person will have to authenticate with financial institutions, which participate in the Internet purchasing transactions. In many cases, an authentication gateway or server will do it, using a user's credentials (see Figure 2.10).

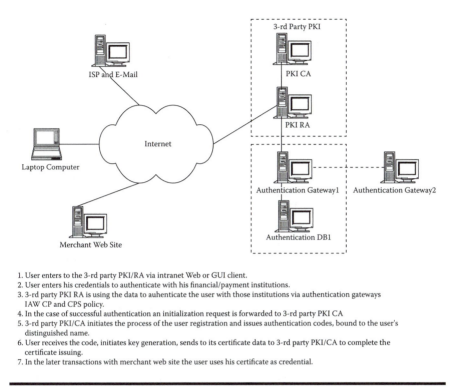

1. User enters to the 3-rd party PKI/RA via intranet Web or GUI client.
2. User enters his credentials to authenticate with his financial/payment institutions.
3. 3-rd party PKI RA is using the data to auhenticate the user with those institutions via authentication gateways IAW CP and CPS policy.
4. In the case of successful authentication an initialization request is forwarded to 3-rd party PKI CA
5. 3-rd party PKI/CA initiates the process of the user registration and issues authentication codes, bound to the user's distinguished name.
6. User receives the code, initiates key generation, sends to its certificate data to 3-rd party PKI/CA to complete the certificate issuing.
7. In the later transactions with merchant web site the user uses his certificate as credential.

Figure 2.10   Online certificate request with authentication gateways.

Dedicated Authentication Bases

In rare cases, when a PKI CPS requires user authentication that cannot be satisfied by the existing authentication bases, a dedicated authentication database may be created to meet all CPS requirements. For example, for this purpose a prepopulated PKI Directory may be created, where each person eligible for PKI registration will be challenged with his or her password or personal data attributes. Among possible authentication schemes with dedicated or existing authentication databases may be a password with additional personal challenge-response data, such as your mother's maiden name, make and year of your first car, biometrics, and others.

Face-to-Face

The most reliable, but most expensive method to authenticate an EE for PKI registration is face-to-face authentication. It is applied when the issued certificate will secure either high risk and responsibility transactions (certificates for VPN gateways, CA and RA administrators) or transactions of high value, especially when the subscriber will authenticate and sign transactions on behalf of an organization. To obtain this type of certificate, the individual must personally present and show his or her government-issued ID or badge and other valid identifications to the dedicated corporate registration security office and sign a document, obliging use of the certificate only for assigned purposes. All the procedures and sets of ID and documents that must be presented before an authentication authority are described in CPS.

Proof of Possession

A group of the key PKIX-CMP messages, sent by the EE in the process of initial registration, includes "Initialization Request," "Certification Request," and "PKCS10 Certification Request" messages. The full structure of these messages is described in [CRMF] and [PKCS10]. Certificate request messages, among other information, include "Public Key" and "Subject" name attributes.

The EE has authenticated itself out-of-band with the registration authority (RA) on the initialization phase of initial registration. Now an additional proof, that the EE, or the "subject," is in possession of a private key, which is a counterpart of the "public key" in the certificate request message, is required. It is a proof of binding, or so-called "Proof of Possession", or POP, which the EE submits to the RA.

Depending on the types of requested certificates and public/private key pairs, different POP mechanisms may be implemented:

- For encryption certificates, the EE can just provide a private key to RA/CA, or the EE can be required to decrypt with its private key a value of the following data, which is sent back by RA/CA:
  - In the direct method, it will be a challenge value, generated and encrypted and sent to the EE by the RA. The EE is expected to decrypt and send the value back.
  - In the indirect method, the CA will issue the certificate, encrypt it with the given public encryption key, and send it to the EE. The subsequent use of the certificate by the EE will demonstrate its ability to decrypt it, and hence the possession of the private key.
- For signing certificates, the EE just signs a value with its private key and sends it to RA/CA.

Certificate Issuance

A certificate can be looked at as an electronic equivalent of a subject's ID document, which is issued for particular purposes in accordance with the organization's policy. Technically, the sanctioned and expected usage of the certificate is represented in the X.509 certificate "Key Usage" attribute. A relying party application is capable of verifying this attribute; therefore, the certificate will be used only within the scope of its key usage. For example, encryption certificates are issued for encrypting data for a recipient whose name is in the certificate, and verification certificates are issued to verify a signature of the sender who signed the message. Very often, one certificate is issued to serve many purposes. In any case, a relying party has information to help decide how much security the certificate can support, provided that the issuance and management of this certificate is trustworthy. Two main issues relating to this question are: Is an issuing CA trustworthy and how is the information in the certificate secured?

- A certificate is digitally signed by an issuing CA, and it can be trusted only if the CA is trusted. A guard verifying a person's ID first looks to see what organization or country issued that ID and if the issuing authority is in the trusted list. In the same way, a relying party that verifies a certificate will verify if an issuing CA is in the trusted list. Technically, the application checks if that CA's certificate is installed in a designated storage and if it is not in the revocation list.

  Information in the certificate is secured by a digital signature of the issuing CA. Anybody can view and browse the certificate and each of its attributes, including the subscriber ("subject") name with its public key and the CA ("issuer") name with its key identifier and the thumbprint. The certificate binds together all the attributes, including the most important: the subject's name and its public key. The integrity of this binding is preserved by the signature of the trusted issuing CA. Some details of this process already have been mentioned in the previous section, "PKI Registration." Before signing that binding, the CA has to receive evidence that a subscriber public key is associated with the subscriber. One of the ways to obtain it is a proof of possession of the private key. The subscriber, who generated a key pair, signs a message containing its public key and its common name with its private key. The message is sent to the CA directly or via the registration authority (RA) and is used as material for the public certificate. Other certificate attributes and extensions are defined by certificates' templates. The format of the X509. V3 certificate is presented in Figure 2.11.

- Once all the attributes are filled in, the certificate is digitally signed by the CA and sent to the subscriber or published in the Directory.

Trust Models

One fundamental purpose of PKI is to represent the trust relationship between participating parties. When a verifying party verifies another participant's certificate, generally it verifies a chain of trust between that participant's certificate and the verifier's anchor of trust. If that party's certificate was issued by a CA that is directly trusted by the verifier, then that CA is an anchor of trust. Otherwise there are one or more intermediate CAs that constitute a chain between the anchor of trust and the party's certificate to be verified. In both cases, the anchor of trust is based on a preconfigured certificate, in most cases provided out of

Public Key Certificate

Version
Certificate Serial Number
Signature algorithm ID
Issuer DN
Validity Perion
Subject DN
Subject Public Key Info
Issuer Unique ID
Subject Unique ID
Extentions
Signature

Figure 2.11   Format of X509.V3 certificate.

band or as a configuration process. Several models described in the following text are available to provide chains of trust for PKI applications supporting multiple communities.

Subordinate Hierarchy

Very often, the current and long-term business reasons suggest putting two or more CAs into a hierarchical trust relationship. The CA hierarchy contains one root CA on top of the hierarchical tree and one or more levels of CA hierarchy of subordinate CAs (Figure 2.12). Each of the subordinate CAs has one immediate superior and may have one or more subordinates (the root CA is a top superior). A superior CA issues and signs CA certificates for its immediate subordinates. Only the root CA can issue and sign its own certificate. For crypto application operations, a subordinate issuing CA does not need to certify its superior. Each participant should know and trust a root CA, which establishes an anchor of trust. A relying party that trusts the root CA needs to validate a path from the root CA to the sender's certificate.

This model is good for internal enterprise applications, but the hierarchy may be hard to implement between enterprises because it must have in place the shared cross-enterprise certificate policies and one shared root of trust. For more details about certificate chains issued by hierarchical PKI, see the section titled "Certificate Chains" later in this chapter.

Cross-Certified Mesh

Cross-certified mesh is probably the most general model of trust between CAs and participating PKIs. The hierarchical model described earlier may be interpreted

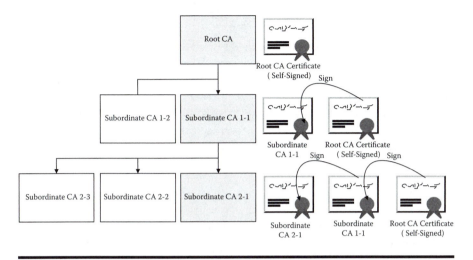

Figure 2.12   Hierarchical PKI CAs.

as a mesh with some constraints. The mesh model is good for intercommunity and dynamically changing enterprise PKI applications, especially for nonhierarchical organizations. When organizations need to establish trust relations, they cross-certify their CAs, which does not require a change of anchors of trust or other elements of existing PKIs. This model is also good for merging previously implemented PKIs into one PKI. Cross-certification includes an exchange of participating PKIs' public verification keys and having each participating PKI sign the received key by its internal root CA. When more than two PKIs participate in the mesh, they create a web of trust by mutually cross-certifying each to each. Although no changes to each participating PKI are required, certificate verification in this model of trust is more difficult to implement because there may be multiple certificate paths. More details are given in the section titled "Cross-Certification" later in the chapter.

Bridge CA

When a cross-certified mesh is too dynamic and grows too fast to include *n* CAs, it may not scale well because it is supposed to include and support $n(n-1)$ cross-certifications and also because of potentially ambiguous verification paths. A bridge CA model may be helpful in this case. A large and very comprehensive implementation of this model is Federal Bridge Certification Authority (FBCA), which is well described in [FBCACP] and [FPKIATO]. As in the FBCA example, any bridge CA issues and manages cross-certificates for participating PKIs. By creating a mesh of participating root CAs, the bridge CA model allows participating parties to mutually validate each other's certificate paths. More details are given in the section titled "Cross-Certification" later in this chapter.

Trusted List

The most well-known example of a Trusted List model is a set of publicly trusted root certificates embedded in the Internet browsers. When a client system verifies another party's certificate, it tries to chain that certificate to one of the certificates in the list of trusted roots. A fundamental difference between this model and the previously discussed hierarchical, mesh, and bridge models is in the fact that the parties to be verified have to accommodate the relying parties' trusted roots. It moves management overheads from PKI CAs to the clients and in an environment with many CAs, may require a large number of root certificates to be included in the list of trusted CAs.

Certificate Chains

Each CA's certificate is located in the certificate chain, which starts at the root CA certificate and includes the certificates of all superior subordinate CAs. Certificates of the issuing CAs that issue certificates for end entities are at the end of this chain (see Figure 2.13).

Several considerations should be taken into account:

- The validity of an issuing CA's certificate depends on the validity and life span of the whole certificate chain. If a root or an intermediate certificate at a higher level of hierarchy expires, validation of the end entity certificate issued by the issuing CA down the hierarchy should show negative. If any certificate in the chain is revoked, validation should show negative also. That is why the higher CA's certificates and certificate revocation lists (CRLs) usually have a life span that is significantly longer. The decreasing life span of the certificates in the chain is presented in Figure 2.13.
- The higher hierarchical CAs require higher security, because a compromise means revoking of all the subordinate and issuing CAs on lower levels as well as all the end entities' certificates. As a result, more certificates will be compromised and will require revocation. It is a common practice in PKI to take a root CA offline and lock its key storing medium in a secured safe store. It needs to be returned online only when its root certificate and immediate subordinate CA's certificates are approaching the end of life and need to be reissued to maintain validity of all subordinate chains or when a new immediate subordinate CA certificate should be issued or when one of the existing subordinate CAs is compromised and its certificate must be revoked. Another reason to put the root CA online is to let it update and publish the CRL when approaching the CRL expiration or when the CRL must be updated.
- The main purpose of the CA hierarchy and the use of certificate chains is to establish an anchor of trust (based on the root CA) and create a hierarchical model of trust. Distributing only a root CA certificate among all the relying parties is easier than distributing multiple CA's certificates. A relying party that needs to validate a certificate issued by an issuing CA in the hierarchical

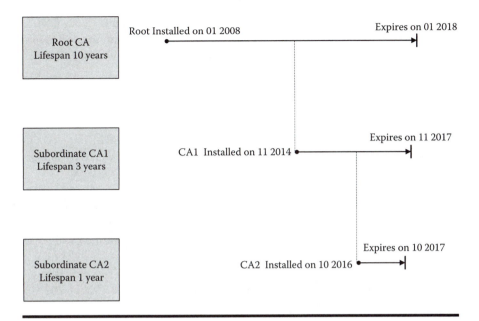

Figure 2.13 Hierarchical PKI certificate life span.

PKI starts walking up the chain until it reaches a root certificate, which is expected to be installed as a trusted CA certificate.

Certificate Revocation

When the private key of a subscriber is compromised or is suspected to be compromised, when an attribute of the certificate (e.g., rank) changes, or when trust between the CA and the subscriber is changed (for example, the employee holder of the certificate leaves the company), the issued certificate should be revoked immediately. The revocation process, from its origination to execution, should be described in the CPS. To inform relying parties, the revoked certificate is placed on a CRL, and the CA reissues, signs, and publishes the updated CRL. Regularly, or immediately after the revocation event, the latest CRL is published in a commonly available space (such as the directory server).

When a relying party (an application) receives a signed message, it should try to verify the signature. First, it checks to make sure the associated certificate has not expired, and second, it checks to make sure the certificate is still valid. Depending on business requirements, there can be two scenarios:

- A relying party is required to validate the certificate with the instantaneous revocation data. This is a real-time validation, and the relying party does not use any cache CRL.

■ A relying party is only required to use a valid nonexpired CRL. A CRL is considered valid if a trusted CA has signed it and the current time is between the "this Update" and "next Update" CRL attributes. So any caching mechanisms can be used to store the CRL on the validating site.

Traditional CRL Model

A relying party checks a certificate against the latest published CRL. If the certificate is not in the CRL, it is assumed valid. Two cases are possible when the application is making this check:

■ It does *not* have the current CRL in cache and has to retrieve it from a directory or other repository. This may also be the case if the real instantaneous certificate status is required. Requesting the CRL, the application will try to obtain the most current one.
■ It *does* have the current CRL in cache. In this case, no instantaneous status is required, and, therefore, certificate validation can be done without retrieving the CRL from a repository.

In applications with a large number of subscribers and relying parties and with a high revocation rate, the CRL request rate can be very high, and CRLs themselves can be very long. This may introduce network and CRL-repository performance problems.

Modified CRL-Based Models

Several methods described in [CRMOD] and in [DCRL] attempt to address the aforementioned problems.

Overissued CRLs Reduce Peak Request Rate

Importantly, when the cache CRL is acceptable, the CRL requests' distribution peaks exponentially at the moment when all relying parties try to request the CRL the first time or when they try to do it after their cached CRLs expire.

As described in [CRMOD], one remedy for reducing the peak of CRL requests may be to issue the CRLs before they expire or to overissue CRLs. Because the CRL validity time remains the same, new overissued CRLs will have a shifted "next update" expiration time. Hence, relying parties will request replacement of their expired CRLs at different times. In other words, this method will spread out CRL requests. As shown in [CRMOD], if a CRL is valid for 24 hours and is reissued every 6 hours instead of every 24 hours, the peak request rate is reduced almost four times. This method can be recommended for applications that allow CRL cache and for which the expected revocation rate is low.

Segmented CRLs Reduce CRL Size

The idea is to reduce the size of the CRL or the portion of the CRL that a relying party needs to download, although this measure cannot reduce the peak request rate. Certificates may be allocated to different CRLs, based on some criteria or at random. This method was implemented in CRL distribution points (CRLDP), as in [RFC2459]. X.509v3 certificates have a standard extension attribute called "CRLDistributionPoints" that provides the URI for the CRL, which is designated to the certificate if this certificate is revoked. When a relying party needs to validate the certificate, it requests this particular CRL. Designation of a particular CRL segment (CRLDP) to certificates is supported by CAs.

This method is recommended for applications that allow CRL caching and that have a high certificate-revocation rate. If instantaneous revocation data is required, it is also better than the method suggested earlier in traditional CRL or in the earlier section of this chapter titled "Over-Issued CRLs Reduce Peak Request Rate."

Delta CRLs

As was described earlier DCRL, the idea of using delta CRL was introduced to reduce the peak bandwidth in PKI applications, allowing caching but also requiring fresh certificate revocation information. A delta CRL provides only certificate revocation information changes since the full base CRL was issued. Base CRL is a traditional CRL containing all nonexpired revoked certificates. Its validity is much longer-lived than delta CRL, and a relying party does not request it frequently. Delta CRL validity is short. Hence, a relying party has to request it often. Because it contains only certificates revoked since the latest base CRL was issued, its size is supposed to be small. With delta CRL, an average request rate for the base CRL drops significantly, although the peak rate does not.

In DCRL, Cooper describes a further modification of delta CRL, which should allow a significant reduction of the base CRL request peak rate as well. It is a so-called sliding window delta CRL, which combines delta CRL with the CRL overissuing method. Every time a delta CRL is issued, a full CRL is reissued as well. As described in the section titled "Over-Issued CRLs Reduce Peak Request Rate," it spreads out CRL requests from relying parties and reduces peak base CRL requests.

This sliding window delta CRL method promises the ability to supply very fresh CRL data combined with relatively low values for CRL-based validation methods, peak request rate, and bandwidth. Choosing an optimal window size is crucial.

Online Certificate Status Protocol

The Online Certificate Status Protocol (OCSP) is presented in [OCSP]. A relying party sends to the validation server its request on the status of the certificate in question. The server returns its signed response. The request/respond formats are presented in the following text. Because the OCSP request and response data chunks are significantly smaller than with all CRL-based ones, the bandwidth required for OCSP is lower compared with the CRL models for the same validation rate. On the other hand, the need to sign all OCSP responses implies higher power requirements on the validation server.

The following three items are data structures. These represent OCSP transactions.

OCSP Request
  - Protocol version
  - Service request
  - Target certificate identifier
  - Optional extensions
OCSP Response
  - Version of the response syntax
    • Name of the responder
    • Responses for each certificate in a request
    • Optional extensions
    • Signature algorithm OID
    • Signature computed across hash of the response
  - Response for Each Certificate in a Request
    • Certificate identifier
    • Certificate status value (GOOD, REVOKED, UNKNOWN)
    • Response validity interval
    • Optional extensions

Unlike CRL-based models, an OCSP model is designed to provide instantaneous certificate status upon the certificate status request. Also, unlike CRL-based models, OCSP provides only the status of requested certificates, and it cannot be used by offline clients; for example, wireless devices wishing to authenticate the network to which they are attaching.

Cross-Certification

Cross-certification is a way of establishing trust between entities that are subscribers for different PKI certificates services and which have been issued certificates by different nonrelated CAs. In other words, it is a way of establishing a third-party trust. To make this happen, two CAs need to establish trust between each other, which is implemented via CA cross-certification. Cross-certification has a lot of implications. Complete understanding of Certificate Policy and Practice of each CA is required, because each party needs to know how much it can trust to the certificates issued by another CA, what are the enrollment, issuing, and revocation procedures of another CA, and what is the liability. Legal agreements and documents may be required as well.

How Applications Use Cross-Certification

If company A wants to trust company B, it should receive from company B its verification key, then issue a cross-certificate containing this verification key, and sign this certificate with company A's signing key. If an entity in company A receives a message signed by company B, it will trust the signature because A certified its verification key with its signature. Trust does not necessarily have to be mutual. If company B does not want to trust A, it does not have to cross-certify A, although A cross-certified B; that is why we should also be specific if cross-certification is one-way or two-way (or mutual) trust. In addition to cross-certification, the companies should provide each other access to the end users' certificates.

Now let us look at two cases when users of two companies that cross-certified their CAs will exchange secure messages (see Figure 2.14).

- An employee of A is going to send a signed and encrypted message to an employee of company B. He needs to find that employee and his certificate in the search base or through directory lookup.
- The employee of A verifies the cross-certificate issued by company A, to make sure that company B is still trusted. This is done by verification of its signature and validity dates and also checking if that certificate is not in the authority revocation list (ARL) of company A.
- Now the employee of A can verify if the encryption certificate of the recipient in company B is valid. It is done by checking integrity, validity dates, and presence in the CRL of company B. Also, the certificate should be signed by a key associated with the public key of the CA of company B, which is available in the cross-certificate.
- If all the foregoing verifications are successful, then a user in company A will send the message with its signature and will encrypt this message with the public key from the certificate of the user of company B.
- Recipient B, after decrypting the message, will try to verify the signature of sender A.
- It validates the issuer of the verification certificate attached to the message by comparing the signature with a public key of the CA of company A, which is available in the cross-certificate issued by company B. It also verifies if the cross-certificate is valid and is not in company B's ARL.
- The user of company B also validates the verification certificate's integrity, its validity dates, and presence in company A's CRL.

How Cross-Certification Is Set Up

With all the considerations mentioned at the beginning of this section, both mutual and unilateral cross-certification may be done online and offline.

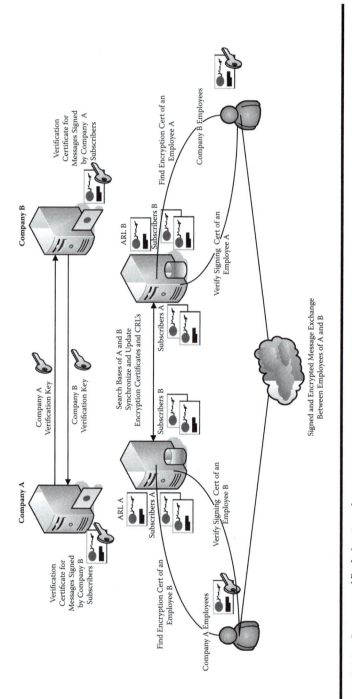

Figure 2.14 Cross-certified sites' exchange.

Online Cross-Certification

Online cross-certification requires TCP/IP connectivity between both CAs as well as their Directories. A company A, which wants to trust company B, has to give company B special access credentials (one time password, generated by CA A) to access A. A CA administrator of company B enters these credentials and connects to A to complete cross-certification. It securely sends online the CA B verification public key. CA A generates and signs a cross-certificate containing the public key of B. Depending on implementation and the PKI vendor, the process may be automated, and the new cross-certificate issued by A may be sent over to B and imported into its database and Directory.

Offline Cross-Certification

Offline cross-certification is the only method for CAs that does not have network connectivity. Nevertheless, the Directories should have connectivity for cross-certification as well as for online cross-certification. As in the case of online cross-certification, we assume that CA A wants to trust CA B, and CA B wants to be trusted by A. However, unlike in the online case, the offline cross-certification process is started by B generating its PKCS#10 certificate request with its verification public key and sending it to company A. After A verifies the request, it issues and signs the cross-certificate, stores it, and also sends it to B. The administrator of trusted CA B will import the cross-certificate issued by CA A into its database and Directory.

Once unilateral cross-certification is complete, the process may be repeated in the opposite direction if mutual cross-certification is required for business needs.

Cross-Certificates' Revocation

In order to break the trust between CAs, the cross-certified parties revoke the cross-certificates they issued. For example, if company A revokes the cross-certificate for company B, users of A will not be able to verify messages signed by users of B and will not be able to encrypt messages for users of B. Cross-certificates may need to be revoked for one of the following reasons:

- Partnership between companies A and B is terminated and their users do not need to use each other's certificates.
- The cross-certified CA is not trusted anymore.
- The cross-certified CA reissued its certificate and regenerated keys; thus, a new public key should be used for the cross-certificate.

Revoked cross-certificates are added to the ARL, which is used for any certificate verification as was mentioned earlier.

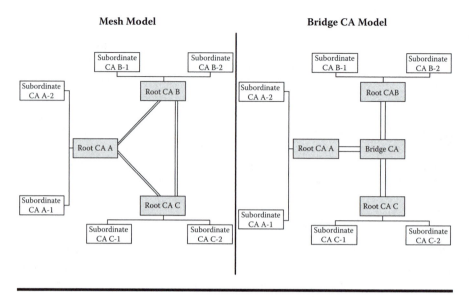

Figure 2.15   Cross-certified mesh and bridge CA models.

How Cross-Certification with a Bridge CA Is Implemented in Practice

The preceding example just described how cross-certification between two CAs works. With more than two CAs participating in this model and the CAs' mesh growing, certificate verification difficulties will start increasing. The bridge CA model helps to resolve these problems. Diagrams representing a cross-certified mesh and bridge CA are presented in Figure 2.15.

Let us use FBCA [FBCACP] as an example for the Bridge CA case study:

- FBCA can be looked at as a nonhierarchical hub that would allow trust paths between participating PKIs to be created.
- The FBCA would issue certificates to Principal CAs, which are CAs within participating PKIs, designated to cross-certify those PKIs directly with FBCA through the exchange of cross-certificates. The number of cross-certificates to support *n* PKIs is n * 2.
- Each PKI participating in FBCA, should be represented to FBCA by a single Principal CA. If a participating PKI is a hierarchical PKI, the Principal CA is typically its root CA. If a participating PKI is a mesh PKI, the Principal CA may be any designated CA within that PKI.
- The issued certificate will be posted in the FBCA directory. All cross-certified entities are notified by FBCA when the certificates are issued.
- Now, the subscribers of PKIs registered with FBCA may exchange signed and encrypted messages. The certificate's verification path will span FBCA and a sender's certificates.

■ The certificate trust path between one participating PKI and all others can be discontinued by revoking its FBCA cross-certificate. A new CRL will be published in the FBCA directory.

Design Validation

Review of Cryptanalytic Attacks

Attacking a cryptosystem reveals its weaknesses and flaws. Cryptanalysis can be used to improve the design of a cryptosystem and may result in the discarding of a cryptographic algorithm altogether. The ISSAP candidate should understand how cryptanalytic attacks can be used in validating cryptographic design as part of an architecture.

Attack Models

The following basic types of attacks are based on having some knowledge of the algorithm used. These attacks are characterized by the degree of plaintext and ciphertext the cryptanalyst has access to

Ciphertext-only attack: A sample of ciphertext, and preferably a large volume of ciphertext encrypted with the same algorithm, is required. While this is one of the most difficult attacks to execute, a successful attack reveals plaintext, and if completely successful, the key. This type of attack can reveal flaws in the algorithm. While cryptographic algorithms used in real-world applications must be vetted for weaknesses against ciphertext-only attacks, some protocols such as WEP have been found vulnerable to this type of attack.

Known-plaintext attack: Having some plaintext and the corresponding ciphertext is necessary. An objective of this type of attack is to determine the key and decipher all messages encrypted by it. This type of attack can be very practical when the corresponding plaintext is discoverable or can be deduced. Users of ZIP file archive encryption are very susceptible to this type of attack when a small portion of their archive is decrypted and becomes available for use in a known-plaintext attack.

Chosen-plaintext attack: This attack involves choosing the plaintext with the corresponding ciphertext.

Chosen-ciphertext attack: This attack involves choosing the ciphertext to be decrypted and gaining access to the resulting plaintext.

Symmetric Attacks

Variations on the attack models can be used in a controlled environment to reveal weaknesses in a cryptosystem and analyze an algorithm's strength. Two common attacks applied to the testing of symmetric ciphers are the techniques of differential cryptanalysis and linear cryptanalysis:

> *Differential cryptanalysis*: These techniques involve a chosen plaintext attack with the aim of recovering the secret key. The basic method of differential cryptanalysis involves investigating the differences in ciphertext produced from pairs of chosen plaintext having specific differences. While this type of attack was used for determining a theoretical weakness in DES, the amount of chosen plaintext necessary (in excess of 10^{15} bytes) makes it impractical. DES was designed to resist differential cryptanalysis [Coppersmith].
>
> *Linear cryptanalysis*: These techniques are based on a known-plaintext attack using pairs of known block-cipher plaintext and corresponding ciphertext in order to generate a linear approximation of a portion of the key. Instead of trying to keep track of differences propagated by chosen plaintext, linear cryptanalysis seeks to keep track of Boolean information in pairs of known plaintext and corresponding ciphertext to generate a probability in the confidence level of a specific key value. This method of attack is also commonly used to test block algorithms. While a theoretical attack against DES using linear cryptanalysis exists, it is considered impractical due to the amount of known plaintext–ciphertext required (2^{43} plaintexts) [Matsui].

Asymmetric Attacks

The algorithm in asymmetric cryptosystems is often based on solving some sort of mathematical problem such as the difficulty of integer factorization. As a result, applying the attack models to asymmetric cryptosystems can involve finding improved or faster methods of solving the various mathematical problems. Designing or integrating with a particular asymmetric scheme must take into account mathematical discoveries such as more efficient methods of finding discrete logarithms or integer factorization.

Hash Function Attacks

The principle applied in determining the collision resistance of hash functions is based on the birthday problem in probability theory. This type of attack is known as the *Birthday attack*. The term *birthday* pertains to the probability that in a set of randomly chosen people some pair of them will have the same birthday.

Many cryptographic hash algorithms such as MD5 and SHA-1 are built from one-way functions, which are limited in their ability to provide collision resistance. When validating security in cryptosystems, one must consider that hash functions are applied in digital signature schemes and used as building blocks in MAC construction.

Network-Based Cryptanalytic Attacks

Cryptanalytic attacks can be facilitated by network communications such as protocols involved in the transmission of data or in operations such as key exchange. The following network-based attacks target more than just the cryptographic algorithm and exploit weaknesses in areas such as communication protocols or transmission methods:

Man-in-the-middle attack: This technique involves intercepting and forwarding a modified version of a transmission between two parties. In this type of attack, the transmission is modified before it arrives at the receiving party. Safeguarding a protocol against this attack usually involves making sure authentication occurs at each endpoint in the communication. For example, in a Web service design, it may be necessary to require mutual SSL authentication involving use of a mutually trusted certification authority.

Replay attack: This attack involves capturing and retransmitting a legitimate transmission between two parties. Using this technique, impersonation or key compromise and unauthorized access to information assets may be possible. Protecting a protocol against this attack usually involves use of session tokens, time-stamping of data, or synchronization of transmission. For instance, IPSec provides an antireplay service using verification of sequence numbers, and the AH protocol in IPSec employs one-way hash functions to protect against impersonation.

Traffic analysis attacks: Observing traffic flow in encrypted communications can reveal information based on message volume or communication patterns, or show which parties are communicating. Protection against traffic analysis is a concern not only in the design of military signals intelligence systems, but in the design of commercial systems as well. For instance, SSH, when operating in interactive mode, transmits every key stroke as a packet. Packet analysis can therefore reveal information about the password lengths. A general countermeasure to protect against traffic analysis is to use traffic padding where feasible. Another approach to protecting messages traversing untrusted networks from traffic analysis involves anonymizing the message sender. This can be done by using a chain of proxy servers where the message is encrypted separately at each proxy in order to make the source and destination of the communicating parties more difficult to determine.

Attacks against Keys

An ideal goal for cryptanalysis is to extract the secret key. Observing how keys are used is important in validating a cryptographic design. Using the same key to encrypt larger volumes of data increases the success of a cryptanalytic attack. Also, the use of an appropriate key length is important, as noted earlier in the chapter.

Testing for weak keys during generation is another basic element of validating a cryptosystem. Understanding the ability of a random number generator to introduce entropy during key generation is an important factor in this, because greater randomness makes determining the key more difficult.

Secret keys must also be protected from unauthorized access and should remain encrypted when stored. In a cryptographic system where multiple secret keys are necessary, for example, with a tape encryption appliance device, it is common to encrypt individual working keys with a top-level master key. The storage of the top-level secret key used in such a cryptosystem can be done using key shares, a technique also known as split-knowledge. This involves splitting the key into multiple pieces and granting access to each share to separate individuals. This ensures that no one individual has access to the stored master key. To ensure security of this master secret key when it is in use within the cryptosystem, logical access controls and physical controls such as tamper-proof enclosures are used. In validating cryptosystems, it is essential to check that the subsystem components and processes that protect the secret key are functioning as intended.

The following attacks against keys are variations on the cryptanalytic attack models and are also important in validating cryptosystems:

Meet-in-the-middle attack: This attack applies to double encryption schemes such as 2DES and 3DES; it works by encrypting known plaintext using each possible key and comparing results obtained "in the middle" from decrypting the corresponding ciphertext using each possible key. This known plaintext attack was used against DES to show that encrypting plaintext with one DES key followed by encrypting it with a second DES key is no more secure than using a single DES key, and it reduces the strength of 3DES to only 112 bits.

Related-key attacks: These forms of attack involve relationships between keys that become known or are chosen while observing differences in plaintext and ciphertext when a different key is used. For instance, two keys that transform all plaintexts identically can be considered equivalent, a simple relation. It is beneficial to employ a related-key attack against stream ciphers because they typically employ a common key in combination with some varying nonsecret initialization vector (IV). An example of using a *related-key attack* to demonstrate that an encryption scheme is insecure is with WEP, in which the RC4 stream cipher uses a keystream comprising a WEP secret key and an exposed IV.

Brute Force Attacks

For a cryptosystem to be considered secure, a successful brute force attack must be computationally infeasible. For symmetric key ciphers, this involves an exhaustive search of the key space in order to determine plaintext. The result of the brute force is the secret key used for encrypting the ciphertext. Besides providing an indication of the security of the cryptosystem, a successful brute force attack involving a particular secret key would mean that any ciphertext encrypted with that particular key and potentially all future derived keys would become readable via the attack.

A brute force attack against asymmetric key ciphers involves applying computing resources to solving the underlying mathematical problem the algorithm is based on, such as in factoring large integers for RSA public-key encryption. The computational feasibility of solving a particular problem such as factoring an integer of a particular size gives an indication of the strength of the algorithm.

Side-Channel Cryptanalysis

Side-channel attacks are based on information gained from the physical implementation of the cryptosystem. These attacks mainly deal with obtaining and analyzing information that originates from the cryptosystem hardware rather than weaknesses in the cryptographic algorithm. Side-channel attacks can be based on the execution time of a cryptographic algorithm, power consumption within a cryptographic module, or electromagnetic emanations from a computer. Side-channel cryptanalysis requires substantial technical knowledge of the underlying hardware.

Susceptibility to side-channel cryptanalytic attack is an important consideration for any architecture where cryptography is applied. The following are some of these types of attacks:

Timing attacks: This attack requires the ability to accurately measure the time required to perform a particular operation within a cryptosystem. Timing attacks are based on detailed hardware performance characteristics such as memory cache hits and CPU instruction time for a given key and input data (plaintext or ciphertext). By using the baseline performance characteristics for a specific piece of hardware where the cryptosystem is implemented, successful attacks against protocols and algorithms such as Diffie–Hellman, RSA, DSS, and others can be executed [Kocher].

Differential fault analysis: This method involves introducing hardware faults into the cryptosystem in order to determine the state of internal data. This type of attack can be used to read the state of memory in order to determine a secret key. The technique can be applied to various types of semiconductor memory, including integrated circuits that are frozen and removed or to smart card memory that is read nondestructively [Samyde et al.].

Differential power analysis: In this method, power consumption measurements in a hardware device such as a smart card are made during encryption operations while ciphertext is recorded. The attack can be used to reveal a secret key [Kocher et al.].

Risk-Based Cryptographic Architecture

Computing power, which grows by the Moore's law; new developments in cryptanalysis; virtually borderless enterprise network topologies; wider than ever exposure to targeted attacks from different domestic and foreign entities—all these factors are constantly moving cryptographic standards higher. At the same time, the main purpose of cryptography—supporting confidentiality, integrity, and availability—should be served in the most productive and cost-effective manner. We move from DES to AES, from a key size of 56 bits to 256 bits, but as we stated in the section titled "Key Management," the strength of any crypto system or application is more than just strength of the algorithms and key size.

More often, crypto systems are compromised because of weaknesses in key management and processes around it. A risk-based approach to the crypto systems and applications design should help to architect a balanced and cost-effective solution that meets business requirements. Many areas of cryptographic architecture for government agencies are driven by regulatory compliance with appropriate prescriptive guidance documented in NIST FIPS publications referred to earlier. Designing cryptography for private sector industries, where regulatory compliance is less strict or not required at all, leaves more room for making architecture decisions. But it may be a good idea to follow a risk-based approach. We can use either qualitative or quantitative measures when assessing the risk. If quantitative risk assessment data is available, each design option may be assessed based on the cost, benefits, and the risk. Otherwise, qualitative methods should be used. Risk is assessed to determine the impact of given losses and the probability that these losses will occur.

The process of designing a cryptographic system is similar to the process used for any other IT system. The architecture should include appropriate crypto modules, components, and methods, and should be integrated with the surrounding infrastructure and supported applications in order to address the organization's needs and meet the requirements. Based on the requirements, several cryptographic methods may be needed. For example, both symmetric and asymmetric cryptography may be needed in a system, each performing different functions (e.g., symmetric encryption, asymmetric digital signature, and key establishment). It is important to be able to demonstrate traceability from the requirements back to the policies, goals, and risks to be mitigated.

The following areas may be considered for a cryptographic system high-level design:

- Hardware- and software-based components
- Security of cryptographic modules
- What cryptography should be used for a network environment
- What approved algorithms will be used, and key lengths
- Key management infrastructure
- Integration with hosting infrastructure and supported applications
- Interoperation with external organizations
- User interface
- User acceptance
- User training

It is important to develop confidentiality, integrity, and availability objectives. These objectives are at a high level and should address security, in general, and cryptography, specifically. The design should include software and hardware, procedures, physical security considerations, environmental requirements, etc.

After preliminary high-level and requirements-based architecture design is done, a preliminary risk assessment should be performed, and specific unique requirements associated with each component should be finalized. After the risk assessment has been performed, policies should be developed regarding the use of evaluated systems and cryptographic modules operating within the designed system.

Identifying Risk and Requirements by Cryptographic Areas

Risk management includes two components: assessing the risk and selecting and implementing appropriate countermeasures. The largest areas of risk addressed by cryptography are unauthorized disclosure and data modification, or confidentiality and integrity. Although the risks cannot be completely eliminated, they can be reduced to an acceptable level by using cryptographic controls. The risk management process ensures that the threats are known, as well as their impact, and that cost-effective countermeasures are applied. Risk assessment includes assessment of the assets and current protecting mechanisms, identification and assessment of the threats, assessment of potential losses and their likelihood, and their classification by criticality and sensitivity, and, finally, identification of potential mitigating controls and cost-benefit analysis.

Most often, the type of risk assessment that is performed is a qualitative analysis, rather than a formal quantitative analysis, and the results are used in developing the system requirements and specifications. The scope of risk analysis varies depending on the sensitivity of the information and the number and types of risks that need to be addressed. The next task is to identify categories of cryptographic methods and techniques that meet the requirements and mitigate the specific risks. There may be more than one method that can mitigate each risk.

Traceability from the requirements back to the policies and associated risk assessment is important. The following table is based on the data presented in the NIST SP800-21-1 [SP800-21-1] and demonstrates logical dependencies between risk and requirements for different cryptographic areas.

	Cryptographic Area	Risk	Technical and Assurance Requirements
1	Cryptographic Module Specification: Specify cryptographic boundary; specify cryptographic algorithms; diagram configuration; specify security policy; describe operational and error states	Incorrect implementation	Cryptographic requirements addressed in overall system/product requirements. Security policy (including security rules), configuration block diagram

	Cryptographic Area	Risk	Technical and Assurance Requirements
2	Cryptographic Algorithms (identify FIPS-approved algorithms and other cryptographic algorithms): Encryption	1. Unauthorized disclosure of data or undetected modification of data (intentional and accidental) during transmission or while in storage 2. Denial of service 3. Session capture 4. Man-in-the- middle attack	1. FIPS-approved AES algorithm or three key TDEA algorithm; conformance tests
3	Cryptographic Algorithms: Block Cipher Modes of Operation	Same as above	
4	Cryptographic Algorithms: Cryptographic Modules	Same as above	FIPS-approved cryptographic algorithms; conformance testing
5	Cryptographic Algorithms: Hash Functions	Same as above	Secure Hash Algorithm, message digest; conformance tests
6	Cryptographic Algorithms: Digital Signatures		Digital Signature Algorithm (DSA), RSA, ECDSA, digital signature generation/ verification; message digest; random/ pseudorandom number generation; hash function Algorithms for generating primes p and q; private key generation; conformance tests Cryptographic requirements addressed in overall system/product requirements
7	Cryptographic Algorithms: Random Number Generation		Algorithms for generating deterministic random bit generators; conformance tests
8	Cryptographic Module Ports and Interfaces: physical and logical input and output data paths	Unintentional output of plaintext data Design error	Physical/logical separation of data input /output ports, control input, status output, data input, data output; documentation of the interfaces and input and output data paths

	Cryptographic Area	*Risk*	*Technical and Assurance Requirements*
9	Roles, Services, and Authentication: Roles and associated services; authorization and access control mechanisms	1. Unauthorized access by authorized/ unauthorized individuals 2. Masquerade 3. Password compromise 4. Replay attacks	1. Role-based authentication mechanisms 2. Identity-based authentication mechanisms, maintenance-access interface; documentation of the authorized roles, services, operations, and functions 1. Token-based authentication 2. Biometrics-based authentication 3. Cryptographic authentication protocols (secret key and public key cryptosystems) 1. Digital signature algorithm 2. Digital signatures 3. Random/ pseudorandom number generator 4. Unilateral authentication protocol 5. Mutual authentication protocol Cryptographic requirements addressed in overall system/product requirements

	Cryptographic Area	Risk	Technical and Assurance Requirements
10	Physical Security: Specify physical security configuration and mechanisms; specify features or testing procedures (includes EFP/EFT)	1. Unauthorized physical access to the contents 2. Unauthorized use or modification, e.g., module substitution 3. Unusual environmental conditions or fluctuations that results in disclosures of critical security parameters 4. Unauthorized disclosure of plaintext critical security parameters	1. Production grade enclosures 2. Tamper evidence, or tamper resistance 3, 4. Tamper response of shutdown of the module; zeroization of plaintext security keys and other unprotected critical security parameters (CSPs) 1, 2, 3. Specification of the physical embodiment, description of the applicable physical security mechanisms 4. Specification of the environmental failure protection features, documentation of the environmental failure tests performed and the results
11	Operational Environment: Specify access, authorization, audit controls; identify critical security parameters (CSPs) and cryptographic data	1. Unauthorized access by authorized/ unauthorized individuals 2. Undetected modification of cryptographic component 3. Unauthorized modification, substitution, insertion, and deletion of cryptographic keys and other CSPs	Level 1: Single operator, executable code, approved integrity technique Level 2: Referenced PPs evaluated at EAL2 with specified discretionary access control mechanisms and auditing Level 3: Referenced PPs plus trusted path evaluated at EAL3 plus security policy modeling Level 4: Referenced PPs plus trusted path evaluated at EAL4

	Cryptographic Area	Risk	Technical and Assurance Requirements

12	Cryptographic Key Management: Specify random number generation, key generation, key establishment, key entry and output, key storage, and key destruction	1. Unauthorized disclosure, modification, and substitution of secret/ private keys
		
		2. Unauthorized substitution and modification of public keys
			Key entry/output: Levels 1, 2. plaintext. Levels 3, 4. encrypted keys or split knowledge for manual-distribution
			
			Key destruction: Zeroize all plaintext cryptographic keys and other unprotected CSPs
			
			Specification of the FIPS-approved key generation algorithm; documentation of the key distribution techniques
			
			  1. NIST-approved key generation algorithms
			
			  2. Use of error detection code (message authentication code)
			
			  1. Encrypted IVs
			
			  2. Key naming
			
			  3. Key encrypting key pairs
			
			  4. Random number generation
			
			Cryptographic requirements addressed in overall system/product requirements

13	EMI/EMC: identify FCC conformance requirements	Emanations	Conformance to FCC requirements Cryptographic requirements addressed in overall system/product requirements

	Cryptographic Area	Risk	Technical and Assurance Requirements
14	Self-Tests: Identify power-up and conditional tests	1. Module malfunction 2. Unauthorized disclosure of sensitive data	Cryptographic requirements addressed in overall system/product requirements Documentation on error conditions and actions to clear the errors; 1. Cryptographic algorithm test 2. Critical functions test. 3. Pair-wise consistency test (for public and private keys) 5. Software/firmware load test 6. Manual key entry test
15	Design Assurance: Describe the design of the software/hardware/firmware; explain the correspondence between the design and the security policy	Incorrect/invalid operation of the module	Cryptographic requirements addressed in overall system/product requirements Level 4. Formal model, informal proof

Note that the risk of each cryptographic area should be assessed for each individual system and application. If the risk is higher than an acceptable level, technical requirements should be strengthened.

Case Study

To clarify how all this information fits together, let us walk through a use case example and follow the process of defining requirements, identifying risks, and then proposing cryptographic methods that meet those requirements and mitigate the risks.

The use case involves secure communications for a device management function. Cryptography for communication between a management console and management server and between the management server and managed devices should support confidentiality, authentication, authorization, and integrity. For our scenario, we will consider the business function being performed to be firewall rule changes. So the management console will be a firewall administrator's workstation, the management server will be the system that affects firewall rulebase changes, and the managed devices will be firewalls. For simplicity's sake, our scope will

Firewall Rulebase Management

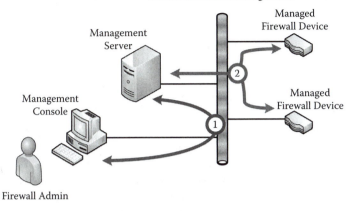

Figure 2.16   Firewall administration.

exclude firewall monitoring, audit logging, and device network configuration functions, and the design will be vendor neutral (refer to Figure 2.16).

Information flow in our use case is represented by flow "1" between the management console and management server, and by flow "2" between the management server and the managed devices. For our rulebase management scenario

- Managed devices may receive and store very sensitive configuration and corporate information, and its unauthorized disclosure may be detrimental.
- Integrity of the management data in transit and in store is crucial.
- Availability of these encrypted communication channels is important, but lost connectivity for a short time will not lead to major losses.

We have determined the functional requirements to be

- Provide secure communication between the manager's console and the management server.
- Provide secure communication between the management server and managed devices.

For this scenario we can define the following risks:

- Unauthorized disclosure of data in transit between the console and server and server and managed devices.
- Unauthorized and undetected modification of data in transit between the console and server and server and managed devices.
- An unauthenticated or unauthorized console gets access to the server.
- An unauthenticated or unauthorized server gets access to a managed device.

■ Data in transit is modified in a nonauthorized manner (man-in-the-middle attack).
■ Unauthorized disclosure, modification, and substitution of secret/private keys.
■ Unauthorized substitution and modification of public keys.

Our intent is to apply cryptography as the means to meet our requirements and address the risks. For our use case we might recommend

■ The management server includes an internal CA, which issues certificates for every console and managed device.
■ Key pairs are generated on each new console and device added to the system. After that, the keys are sent to the management server's CA for issuing certificates.
■ TLS tunnels with mutual authentication (MTLS) between the management server, and devices and console provide required access control, integrity, and confidentiality of the data in transit.
■ A FIPS 140-2-compliant hardware cryptographic module provides required physical and logical security, including protection of the private and secret keys, RNG, and AES 128 encryption for TLS sessions. Keys never appear in cleartext. These measures ensure mandatory key management.
■ Access to the consoles and management server with an internal CA requires 2 factor authentication. All data flows between the management server and console and devices goes encrypted via MTLS tunnels.

The recommendations we propose for our scenario fall into the following cryptographic areas. For a sound design, they should meet the following requirements:

Cryptographic Area:
  – Cryptographic algorithms (identify FIPS-approved algorithms and other cryptographic algorithms): Encryption.
  – Cryptographic algorithms: Digital signatures.
  – Cryptographic key management: Specify random number generation, key generation, key establishment, key entry and output, key storage, and key destruction.
Technical and Assurance Requirement:
  – FIPS-approved AES algorithm or three key TDEA algorithm; conformance tests.
  – Digital Signature Algorithm (DSA), RSA, ECDSA, digital signature generation/verification; message digest; random/pseudorandom number generation; hash function. Algorithms for generating primes p and q; private key generation; conformance tests. Cryptographic requirements addressed in overall system/product requirements.
  – Key entry/output: Levels 1, 2—plaintext. Levels 3, 4—encrypted keys or split knowledge for manual distribution.

- Key destruction: Zeroize all plaintext cryptographic keys and other unprotected CSPs.
- Specification of the FIPS-approved key generation algorithm; documentation of the key distribution techniques.
- NIST-approved key generation algorithms.
- Use of error detection code (message authentication code).
- Encrypted IVs.
- Key naming.
- Key encrypting key pairs.
- Random number generation.
- Cryptographic requirements addressed in overall system/product requirements.

It is important to look at the cryptographic areas and requirements both individually and as a whole. The following are some common design flaws that might be found in this or other scenarios:

- Using a strong cryptographic algorithm when the RNG supporting key generation is weak does not protect against key weaknesses and potential compromise.
- The RNG may be very strong, but key management has a flaw and does not provide sufficient protection for private and secret keys.
- Remote access control to the system incorporates strong two-factor authentication, but local access and physical access control are very weak.
- Bulk data encryption is performed on the management server data store using the wrong block cipher mode; for example, ECB for bulk data encryption.
- Encryption is implemented without any integrity checking; for example, HMAC.
- Key exchange is performed with weak or no authentication.
- Faulty key distribution methods; for example, sending the key in cleartext!
- Symmetric key is not changed when the IV or the counter space is exhausted.

An unbalanced architecture design produces a weak crypto system in which properly selected and designed components cannot compensate for the weak ones that introduce an additional risk.

Cryptographic Compliance Monitoring

A risk-based cryptographic architecture will employ components in a manner that meets business requirements while allowing for a business-defined acceptable level of risk. To manage this risk effectively, there must be control over the risk-impacting factors in designs of solutions employing cryptography. For instance, a digital signature scheme must employ an acceptable cryptographic hashing function, such as those specified in NIST FIPS 180-2, the Secure Hash Standard [FIPS 180-2]. So, cryptographic compliance monitoring in the context of design of a cryptosystem would mean assessing conformity to cryptographic standards.

Security requirements for an IT solution can include *confidentiality*, *integrity*, or one of the other benefits of cryptography. The source of these requirements can be regulations or standards specified by legal frameworks, corporate governance, or policies. For instance, corporate standards requiring confidentiality of personal information may require encrypting the information. So, cryptographic compliance monitoring in the design of an IT solution would mean measuring adherence to regulations in a larger context, where cryptographic controls are used to satisfy a regulatory requirement.

Cryptographic Standards Compliance

Cryptographic standards provide for assurance that a particular security level that is required can be maintained. An example is NSA Suite B, which includes FIPS-197 (AES) and complements encryption algorithms for hashing, digital signature, and key exchange that U.S. federal agencies must adhere to. Making certain that products follow the same standards such as NSA Suite B will also help ensure compatibility.

The Computer Security Division at NIST coordinates test suites for many of the NIST cryptographic standards. The Cryptographic Algorithm Validation Program (CAVP), established by NIST and the Communications Security Establishment Canada (CSEC), provide validation testing via accredited third-party laboratories for a number of cryptographic algorithms. CAVP validation of an algorithm used in a cryptosystem is a prerequisite for another validation program established by NIST, the Cryptographic Module Validation Program (CMVP). CMVP validates adherence of cryptographic modules to Federal Information Processing Standards (FIPS)140-1 Security Requirements for Cryptographic Modules, and other FIPS cryptography-based standards. CAVP and CMVP programs maintain and publish validation lists for algorithms and cryptographic modules. The CAVP list provides validated implementations of cryptographic algorithms showing vendor, validation date and certification number, operational environment, and other information such as key sizes and block cipher mode. The CMVP list shows FIPS-140 validated modules by vendor, validation date and certification number, and other details related to FIPS-140.

Cryptographic standards will also appear in corporate security policies and standards such as those indicating when to use encryption or specifying the level and strength of encryption to use, including key lengths and crypto periods.

Determining if cryptographic controls meet governmental or corporate standards is a function of compliance monitoring. Determining compliance with such cryptographic standards should be performed as part of an assessment of an IT system's design. It is important that this be completed during the requirements phase of an IT project, so that a given solution is developed to meet these standards.

Compliance with security standards for cryptography can also occur at the user level. For example, an organization may require that its personnel use encryption when sending certain types of data via e-mail. It should be noted that monitoring user-level actions such as these may be difficult, and require specialized services such as those provided by data leak protection solutions.

An additional area where compliance is associated with a cryptosystem is the notion of a compliance defect that may exist within a cryptosystem. A compliance defect may be thought of as the inability of a cryptosystem to securely perform one of its functions, and is a noncompliance in a more general sense. Don Davis defines a compliance defect in a cryptosystem as a rule of operation that is both difficult to follow and unenforceable [Davis]. According to Davis, public key cryptography has five unrealistic rules of use corresponding with the crucial moments in a key pair's life cycle. Davis calls these compliance defects and specifies them as follows:

1. Authenticating the user (issuance): How does a CA authenticate a distant user when issuing an initial certificate?
2. Authenticating the CA (validation): Public key cryptography cannot secure the distribution and validation of the root CA's public key.
3. Certificate revocation lists (revocation): Timely and secure revocation presents enormous scaling and performance problems. As a result, public key deployment is proceeding without a revocation infrastructure.
4. Private key management (single-sign on): The user must keep his long-lived private key in memory throughout his login session.
5. Passphrase quality (PW-Change): There is no way to force a public key user to choose a good passphrase.

Industry- and Application-Specific Cryptographic Standards Compliance

It is important that cryptographic controls themselves be compliant with standards. It is likewise important to satisfy the requirements of standards that specify how a cryptographic benefit must be employed. For instance, the California Information Practice Act (SB1386) specifies that if customer information is encrypted when it is stored and transmitted, it is exempt from costly notification procedures in the event of a breach. Regulations applying to information systems that include cryptographic requirements will often specify use of a cryptographic control in a general sense, such as needing "encryption" or requiring a "key management system."

Payment Card Industry Data Security Standard

One industry standard involving encryption is the Payment Card Industry Data Security Standard (PCI DSS), which requires protection and encryption of cardholder data. In the PCI standard, the essential requirement in protecting cardholder data is to not store it at all if possible. When it must be stored, the PCI standard specifies general attributes for cryptographic controls while enumerating the operational methods that must be employed. For instance, hash functions, cryptography, and key generation must be "strong." In relation to cryptographic requirements, PCI focuses on operational procedures and administrative controls such as key-custodian acceptance of responsibilities.

So, auditing a system for PCI compliance will include these types of cryptographic requirements. To see the PCI DSS 1.1 requirements relating specifically to encryption, refer to the portions of the standard that describe key management as well as protection and encryption of cardholder data at the PCI Security Standards Council Web site: https://www.pcisecuritystandards.org/security_standards/pci_dss.shtml [PCI DSS].

Health Insurance Portability and Accountability Act

A governmental regulation that includes requirements for the benefits that cryptography can provide are the provisions of the Health Insurance Portability and Accountability Act of 1996 (HIPAA) enacted by the U.S. Congress. These requirements are found in the Administrative Simplification provisions of the act (HIPAA, Title II), which among other things addresses the security and privacy of health data.

Requirements relating to cryptography are found in the Final Rule on Security Standards [Final Rule]. The Final Rule is where the U.S. Department of Health and Human Services stipulates three types of security safeguards required for compliance: administrative, physical, and technical. Within the technical safeguards, the Final Rule provides a set of security standards as follows:

- Access Control
- Audit Controls
- Integrity
- Person or Entity Authentication
- Transmission Security

These standards support the Final Rule by providing a minimum security baseline intended to help prevent unauthorized use and disclosure of Protected Health Information (PHI). Within each standard, policies, procedures, and technologies are either required and must be adopted, or are subject to individual evaluation (known as "addressable implementation specifications").

Encryption for data at rest falls under the Access Control standard, because encryption used with an appropriate key management scheme can be used to deny access to PHI, except for authorized individuals. The standards in the Final Rule state that encryption of data at rest is an addressable implementation specification, leaving it up to the system owner to determine whether it is required.

While the use of specific cryptographic technologies is not stipulated in the Audit Controls and the Integrity standards, meeting these standards is required by HIPAA. Thus, cryptographic hashing algorithms and digital signatures can be used as a basis for supporting the Integrity standard. The same cryptographic controls can support Audit Controls by ensuring that a change to a transaction log's integrity can be detected.

The Final Rule makes person or entity authentication a mandatory requirement without providing specifics. The Person or Entity Authentication standard does not specify use of any particular technology, allowing "covered entities to use whatever is reasonable and appropriate."

Transmission Security is required in the Final Rule, which stipulates

> The covered entity must implement technical security mechanisms to guard against unauthorized access to electronic protected health information that is transmitted over an electronic communication network.

The Transmission Security standard includes integrity controls to ensure that electronically transmitted PHI is not improperly modified. The standard also specifies encryption as a mechanism to protect electronic PHI being transmitted over open network such as the Internet. Both of these controls, integrity and encryption, are addressable implementation specifications and hence can be optional.

In addition to the Final Rule that is published, there is a proposed rule for Security and Electronic Signature Standards [Proposed Rule]. This HIPAA-proposed Security Rule, when published, will include recommendations for the use of electronic signatures in order to meet the requirement for non-repudiation. While the proposed rule will not mandate the use of electronic signatures, it will stipulate that if electronic signatures are used, they must be digital signatures employing the following implementation features:

- Message integrity
- Non-repudiation
- User authentication

So, when considering HIPAA compliance, one will certainly need to address whether or not cryptographic controls are required. Auditing a system for HIPAA compliance must take into account the basis for a decision when cryptographic controls are deemed unnecessary in meeting a HIPAA standard. In order to monitor cryptographic compliance for a system that processes, transmits, or stores data subject to HIPAA standards, these system-specific cryptography requirements must be defined.

International Privacy Laws

Not all industry or government regulations explicitly stipulate use of particular cryptographic controls such as encryption or digital signatures. Privacy laws, in particular, deal with confidentiality of data but generally do not stipulate that encryption be used as the means of control. Use of encryption to protect confidentiality is left to the detailed security requirements defined for a particular solution, based on the security risk present.

An example of a privacy law where confidentiality is required is Article 17 of the European Union Data Protection Directive [EU Data Protection] which states:

> Member States shall provide that the controller must implement appropriate technical and organizational measures to protect personal data against accidental or unlawful destruction or accidental loss, alteration, unauthorized disclosure or access, in particular where the processing involves the transmission of data over a network, and against all other unlawful forms of processing.

Audit Readiness and Compliance

Audit readiness and compliance oversight must take into account the requirements for cryptographic controls when addressing cryptographic compliance. In general, the need for cryptographic compliance with industry and government regulations is dependent upon criticality of data and security risk. For a given solution, the business requirements, type of data, and how the data will be accessed stored and transmitted all contribute to the need for compliance with such standards.

References

SHA-3 NIST. Announcing Request for Candidate Algorithm Nominations for a New Cryptographic Hash Algorithm (SHA–3) Family, Office of the Federal Register. National Archives and Records Administration. Available at http://csrc.nist.gov/groups/ST/hash/federal_register.html.

S/MIME IETF S/MIME Working Group. Internet Draft. Secure/Multipurpose Internet Mail Extensions (S/MIME) Version 3.2 Message Specification. Expires March 18, 2009.

PEM IETF Privacy-Enhanced Electronic Mail Working Group. RFC 1421, RFC1422, RFC 1423, RFC 1424. Proposed Standards. February 1993.

PGP Copyright © 1990-2001 Network Associates, Inc. and its Affiliated Companies. All Rights Reserved., *PGP Freeware for Windows 95, Windows 98, Windows NT, Windows 2000 & Windows Millennium User's Guide Version 7.0.* January 2001.

802.11 IEEE Std 802.11™-2007 (Revision of IEEE Std 802.11-1999). IEEE Computer Society. June 12, 2007.

WEP ibid.

802.11i IEEE Std 802.11i™-2004 (Amendment to IEEE Std 802.11™, 1999). IEEE Computer Society. July 23, 2004.

WPA B. Bing (Ed.). Understanding and achieving next-generation wireless security. *Emerging Technologies in Wireless LANs: Theory, Design, and Deployment.* Cambridge University Press, New York, 2008.

WPA2 ibid.

SP800-121 NIST Special Publication 800-121. Guide to Bluetooth Security. September 2008.

FC-SP H. Dwivedi. *SANs: Fibre Channel Security*. Securing Storage: A Practical Guide to SAN and NAS Security. 2005.

CIK Department of Defense Security Institute. *STU-III Handbook for Industry*. February 1997.

P1619 https://siswg.net/.

EDI NIST. Federal Information Processing Standards Publication 161-2. April 29, 1996.

CMS IETF Network Working Group. *Cryptographic Message Syntax (CMS)*. RFC 3852. Proposed Standard. July 2004.

WS-Security M. O'Neill et al. *Introduction to WS-Security*. Web Services Security. 2003.

NSA Suite B Cryptography http://www.nsa.gov/ia/industry/crypto_suite_b.cfm.

Modes A. Menezes, P. van Oorschot, and S. Vanstone. *Block Ciphers*. Handbook of Applied Cryptography. 1996.

RFC2144 C. Adams, Entrust Technologies. *The CAST-128 Encryption Algorithm*. RFC2144. Informational Memo. May 1997.

CMEA D. Wagner, B. Schneier, J. Kelsey. 17th Annual International Cryptology Conference. *Cryptanalysis of the Cellular Message Encryption Algorithm*. August 1997.

GOST State Standards Committee of the USSR. *Cryptographic Protection for Data Processing Systems, Cryptographic Transformation Algorithm, GOST 28147-89*. Government Standard of the U.S.S.R. July 1, 1990.

RC2 D. Wagner, B. Schneier, J. Kelsey. ICICS '97. *Related-Key Cryptanalysis of 3-WAY, Biham-DES, CAST, DES-X, NewDES, RC2, and TEA*. November 1997.

RC5 A. Biryukov, E. Kushilevitz. Advances in Cryptology—EUROCRYPT '98. *Improved Cryptanalysis of RC5*. June 1998.

RC6 R. Rivest, M.J.B. Robshaw, R. Sidney, Y.L. Yin. RSA Laboratories. *The RC6 Block Cipher*. August 20, 1998.

TEA http://143.53.36.235:8080/tea.htm.

Twofish http://www.schneier.com/twofish.html.

DH W. Diffie, M. Hellman. *New Directions in Cryptography. IEEE Trans. Information Theory*. Vol. 22, No. 6, pp. 644–654, November 1976.

RSA R.L. Rivest, A. Shamir, and L. Adleman. A method for obtaining digital signatures and public-key cryptosystems. *Commun. ACM*. Vol. 21, Issue 2, pp. 120–126, February 1978.

PKCS #1 B. Kaliski, J. Staddon, RSA Laboratories. *PKCS #1: RSA Cryptography Specifications Version 2.0*. RFC 2437. Informational Memo. October 1998.

Merkle-Hellman Knapsack A. Menezes, P. van Oorschot, and S. Vanstone. Public-key encryption. *Handbook of Applied Cryptography*. CRC Press, Boca Raton, FL. 1996.

Tunnels V. Klima. IACR ePrint archive Report 2006/105. *Tunnels in Hash Functions: MD5 Collisions within a Minute*. Version 2. April 2006.

SHA-1 Collisions X. Wang, Y.L. Yin, and H. Yu. *Finding Collisions in the Full SHA-1*. Advances in Cryptology, Crypto'05. 2005.

Collisions X. Wang, D. Feng, X. Lai, and H. Yu. IACR ePrint archive Report 2004/199. Collisions for Hash Functions MD4, MD5, HAVAL-128 and RIPEMD. August 17, 2004.

Dedicated Hash ISO/IEC 10118-3:2004. *Information technology—Security techniques—Hash-functions—Part 3: Dedicated hash-functions*. March 1, 2004.

SCHNEIER Bruce Schneier. *Applied Cryptography*. Second edition, John Wiley & Sons, New York, 1996.

NISTSP800-57-1 NIST Special Publication 800-57. Recommendation for Key Management—Part 1: General. NIST March 2007.

SP800-67 NIST Special Publication 800-67. Recommendation for the Triple Data Encryption Algorithm (TDEA) Block Cipher. Revised May 19, 2008.

FIPS197 Federal Information Processing Standards Publication 197. Announcing the ADVANCED ENCRYPTION STANDARD (AES). November 26, 2001.

SP800-56 NIST Special Publication 800-56A. Recommendation for Pair-Wise Key Establishment Schemes Using Discrete Logarithm Cryptography (Revised). March 2007.

RSA PKCS#1 PKCS #1 v2.1: RSA Cryptography Standard. *RSA Laboratories*. June 14, 2002.

FIPS 140-2 Federal Information Processing Standards Publication 140-2. Security Requirements for Cryptographic Modules. May 25, 2001.

TECHREV-OPENSSL Technology Review. Alarming Open-Source Security http://www. technologyreview.com/Infotech/20801/page1.

FIPS 140-3 Federal Information Processing Standards Publication 140-3 (DRAFT). (Will Supersede FIPS PUB 140-2, May 25, 2001).

ANNEX C-FIPS 140-2 Annex C Approved Random Number Generators For FIPS PUB 140-2. Draft. October 2007.

FIPS 160-3 Federal Information Processing Standards Publication. FIPS 160-3. Digital Signature Standard (DSS). March 2006.

SP800-90 NIST Special Publication 800-90. Recommendation for Random Number Generation Using Deterministic Random Bit Generators (Revised). March 2007.

NIST SP800-21 NIST Special Publication 800-21. Guideline for Implementing Cryptography in the Federal Government. November 1999.

FIPS 185 Federal Information Processing Standards Publication 185. Escrowed Encryption Standard. November 1994.

NIST SP800-56, 56A, 57 part 1 and 57 part 2.

FIPS186-3 FEDERAL INFORMATION PROCESSING STANDARDS PUBLICATION. Digital Signature Standard (DSS). March 2006.

ANS X9.42-2003 (Public Key Cryptography for the Financial Services Industry: Agreement of Symmetric Keys Using Discrete Logarithm Cryptography).

ANS X9.63-2001 (Public Key Cryptography for the Financial Services Industry: Key Agreement and Key Management Using Elliptic Curve Cryptography).

RFC 3647 IETF Network Working Group. RFC 3647. Internet X.509 Public Key Infrastructure Certificate Policy and Certification Practices Framework. November 2003.

PKIREGAG A. Golod, PKI registration. *Information Security Management Handbook*. 4th Ed., Auerbach Publications, Boca Raton, FL, 2003.

VeriSignCPS Verisign Certificate Practice Statement, version 2.0. 2001.

CRMF IETF Network Working Group. RFC 2511. Certificate Request Message Format. March 1999.

PKCS10

CRMOD Cooper, D. *A Model of Certificate Revocation*. Proceedings of the Fifteenth Annual Computer Security Applications Conference. December 1999.

DCRL Cooper, D. *A More Efficient Use of Delta-CRL*. Proceedings of the 2000 Symposium on security and privacy.

RFC2459 Housley, R., W. Ford, W. Polk, D. Solo, *Internet X.509 Public Key Infrastructure Certificate and CRL Profile*. RFC2459. January 1999.

OCSP M. Myers, R. Ankney, A. Malpani, S. Galperin, C. Adams, *X.509 Internet Public Key Infrastructure. Online Certificate Status Protocol—OCSP.* RFC2560. June 1999.

Coppersmith D. Coppersmith. The DES Encryption Standard (DES) and its strength against attacks. *IBM J. Res. Develop.*, Vol. 38 No. 3. May 1994.

Matsui M. Matsui, Advances in Cryptology—CRYPTO '94. The First Experimental Cryptanalysis of the Data Encryption Standard. 1994.

Kocher P. Kocher. *Timing Attacks on Implementations of Diffie–Hellman, RSA, DSS, and Other Systems.* Proceedings of the 16th Annual International Cryptology Conference on Advances in Cryptology , LNCS, Vol. 1109, pp 104–113, August 1996.

Samyde et al D. Samyde, S. Skorobogatov, R. Anderson, and J. Quisquater. *On a New Way to Read Data from Memory.* Proceedings of the First International IEEE Security in Storage Workshop, pp 65-69, December 2002.

Kocher, et al P. Kocher, J. Jaffe, and B. Jun. *Differential Power Analysis.* Proceedings of the 19th Annual International Cryptology Conference on Advances in Cryptology, LNCS, Vol. 1666, pp 388-397, August 1999.

FIPS 180-2 Federal Information Processing Standards Publication. FIPS 180-2. Announcing the Secure Hash Standard. August 1, 2002.

[Davis] D. Davis. *Compliance Defects in Public-Key Cryptography.* Proceedings of the 6th USENIX Security Symposium. July 1996.

[PCI DSS] PCI Security Standards Council, PCI Data Security Standard version 1.1, available at https://www.pcisecuritystandards.org/security_standards/download.html?id=pci_dss_v1-1.pdf.

[Final Rule] Department of Health and Human Services HIPAA Security Rule, Office of the Federal Register, National Archives and Records Administration, available at http://www.cms.hhs.gov/SecurityStandard/Downloads/securityfinalrule.pdf.

[Proposed Rule] Department of Health and Human Services HIPAA Proposed Security Rule, Office of the Federal Register, National Archives and Records Administration, available at http://frwebgate.access.gpo.gov/cgi-bin/getdoc.cgi?dbname=1998_register&docid=fr12au98-28.pdf.

[EU Data Protection] Directive 95/46/EC of the European Parliament and of the Council of 24 October 1995 available at http://eur-lex.europa.eu/LexUriServ/LexUriServ.do?uri=CELEX:31995L0046:EN:HTML.

[RIPEMD-160] http://homes.esat.kuleuven.be/~bosselae/ripemd160.html.

[RFC4301] S. Kent, K. Seo, BBN Technologies. Network Working Group. Proposed Standard. *Security Architecture for the Internet Protocol.* RFC 4301. December 2005.

[RFC2404] C. Madson, Cisco Systems Inc., R. Glenn, NIST. Network Working Group. *The Use of HMAC-SHA-1-96 within ESP and AH.* RFC2404. November 1998.

[RFC 2406] S. Kent, BBN Corp, R. Atkinson, @Home Network. Network Working Group. *IP Encapsulating Security Payload (ESP).* RFC2406. November 1998.

RFC4650 M. Euchner. Network Working Group. *HMAC-Authenticated Diffie–Hellman for Multimedia Internet KEYing (MIKEY).* RFC4650. September 2006.

FBCACP Certificate Policy for Federal Bridge Certification Authority http://www.cio.gov/fpkipa/documents/FBCA_CP_RFC3647.pdf.

FPKIATO Federal Public Key Infrastructure Architecture. Technical overview. 2005. http://www.cio.gov/fpkia/documents/FPKIAtechnicalOverview.pdf.

Sample Questions

1. What cryptographic hash function would be the acceptable replacement for MD4?
   a. MD5
   b. RIPEMD
   c. RIPEMD-160
   d. SHA-1

2. An IPSec Security Association (SA) is a relationship between two or more entities that describes how they will use security services to communicate. Which values can be used in an SA to provide greater security through confidentiality protection of the data payload?
   a. Use of AES within AH
   b. SHA-1 combined with HMAC
   c. Using ESP
   d. AH and ESP together

3. Suppose a secure extranet connection is required to allow an application in an external trusted entity's network to securely access server resources in a corporate DMZ. Assuming IPSec is being configured to use ESP in tunnel mode, which of the following is the most accurate?
   a. Encryption of data packets and data origin authentication for the packets sent over the tunnel can both be provided.
   b. ESP must be used in transport mode in order to encrypt both the packets sent as well as encrypt source and destination IP Addresses of the external entity's network and of the corporate DMZ network.
   c. Use of AH is necessary in order to provide data origin authentication for the packets sent over the tunnel.
   d. Source and destination IP Addresses of the external entity's network and of the corporate DMZ network are not encrypted.

4. What is the best reason a network device manufacturer might include the RC4 encryption algorithm within an IEEE 802.11 wireless component?
   a. They would like to use AES, but they require compatibility with IEEE 802.11i.
   b. Their product must support the encryption algorithm WPA2 uses.
   c. RC4 is a stream cipher with an improved key-scheduling algorithm that provides stronger protection than other ciphers.
   d. Their release strategy planning includes maintaining some degree of backward compatibility with earlier protocols.

5. What is true about the Diffie–Hellman (DH) key agreement protocol?
   a. The protocol requires initial exchange of a shared secret.
   b. The protocol depends on a secure communication channel for key exchange.
   c. The protocol needs other mechanisms such as digital signatures to provide authentication of the communicating parties.
   d. The protocol is based on a symmetric cryptosystem.
6. What is the main security service a cryptographic hash function provides, and what is the main security property a cryptographic hash function must exhibit?
   a. Integrity and ease of computation
   b. Integrity and collision resistance
   c. Message authenticity and collision resistance
   d. Integrity and computational infeasibility
7. What is necessary on the receiving side in order to verify a digital signature?
   a. The message, message digest, and the sender's private key
   b. The message, message digest, and the sender's public key
   c. The message, the MAC, and the sender's public key
   d. The message, the MAC, and the sender's private key
8. What is a known plaintext attack used against DES to show that encrypting plaintext with one DES key followed by encrypting it with a second DES key is no more secure than using a single DES key?
   a. Meet-in-the-middle attack
   b. Man-in-the-middle attack
   c. Replay attack
   d. Related-key attack
9. What is among the most important factors in validating the cryptographic key design in a public key cryptosystem?
   a. Ability of a random number generator to introduce entropy during key generation
   b. Preimage resistance
   c. Confidentiality of key exchange protocol
   d. Crypto period
10. What factor would be most important in the design of a solution that is required to provide at-rest encryption in order to protect financial data in a restricted-access file sharing server?
    a. Encryption algorithm used
    b. Cryptographic key length
    c. Ability to encrypt the entire storage array or file system versus ability to encrypt individual files
    d. Individual user access and file-level authorization controls

11. A large bank with a more than one million customer base implements PKI to support authentication and encryption for online Internet transactions. What is the best method to validate certificates in a timely manner?
    a. CRL over LDAP
    b. CRLDP over LDAP
    c. OCSP
    d. CRLDP over ODBC

12. A car rental company is planning to implement wireless communication between the cars and rental support centers. Customers will be able to use these centers as concierge services, and rental centers will be able to check the car's status if necessary. PKI certificates will be used to support authentication, non-repudiation, and confidentiality of transactions. Which asymmetric cryptography is a better fit?
    a. RSA 1024
    b. AES 256
    c. RSA 4096
    d. ECC 160

13. A key management system of a government agency's PKI includes a backup and recovery (BR) module. PKI issues and manages separate certificates for encryption and verification. What is the right BR strategy?
    a. Back up all certificates and private keys
    b. Back up all private keys and verification certificates
    c. Back up decryption keys and all certificates
    d. Back up signing keys and all certificates

14. A company needs to comply with FIPS 140-2 level 3, and decided to use split knowledge for managing storage encryption keys. What is the right method for storing and using the key?
    a. Store the key components on the encrypted media.
    b. Create a master key and store it on external media owned by the first security officer.
    c. Store key components on separate external media owned by a different security officer.
    d. Publish key components on an LDAP server and protect them by officers' asymmetric keys encryption.

15. An agency is using symmetric AES 128 cryptography for distributing confidential data. Because of its growth and key distribution problems, the agency decided to move to asymmetric cryptography and X.509 certificates. What is the optimal strength asymmetric cryptography to match the strength of the current symmetric cryptography?
    a. RSA 2048
    b. ECC 160
    c. ECC 256
    d. RSA 7680

16. One very large company created a business partnership with another, much smaller company. Both companies have their own PKI in-house. Employees need to use secure messaging and secure file transfer for their business trans-actions. What is the best strategy to implement this?
    a. The larger company creates a PKI hierarchical branch for the smaller company, so all parties have a common root of trust.
    b. The larger company enrolls all employees of the smaller company and issues their certificates, so all parties have a common root of trust.
    c. Companies should review each other's CP and CPS, cross-certify each other, and let each other access each other's search database.
    d. Employ an external third-party CA and have both company's employees register and use their new certificates for secure transactions.
17. When applications of cross-certified PKI subscribers validate each other's digitally signed messages, they have to perform the following steps:
    a. The signature is cryptographically correct, and sender's validation certifi-cate and sender's CA cross-certificate are valid.
    b. Validate CRL and ARL.
    c. Validate sender's encryption certificate, ARL, and CRL.
    d. The signature is cryptographically correct, and sender's CA certificate is valid.
18. A company implements three-tier PKI, which will include a root CA, several sub-CAs, and a number of regional issuing CAs under each sub-CA. How should the life span of the CA's certificates be related?
    a. Root CA = 10 years; sub-CA = 5 years; issuing CA = 1 year
    b. Root CA = sub-CA = issuing CAs = 5 years
    c. Root CA = 1 year; sub-CA = 5 years; issuing CA = 10 years
    d. Root CA = 5 years; sub-CA = 10 years; issuing CA = 1 year
19. Management and storage of symmetric data encryption keys most impor-tantly must provide
    a. Integrity, confidentiality, and archiving for the time period from key gen-eration through the life span of the data they protect or the duration of the crypto period, whichever is longer
    b. Confidentiality for the time period from key generation through the life span of the data they protect or duration of crypto period, whichever is longer
    c. Integrity, confidentiality, and archiving for the duration of the key's crypto period
    d. Integrity, confidentiality, non-repudiation and archiving for the time period from key generation through the life span of the data they protect or duration of crypto period, whichever is longer

20. Management and storage of public signature verification keys most importantly must provide
    a. Integrity, confidentiality, and archiving for the time period from key generation until no protected data needs to be verified
    b. Integrity and archiving for the time period from key generation until no protected data needs to be verified
    c. Integrity, confidentiality and archiving for the time period from key generation through the life span of the data they protect or the duration of crypto period, whichever is longer
    d. All of the above

Chapter 3

ISSAP® Physical Security Integration

Dr. Paul Baker, CPP

Contents

The key to a successful physical protection system is the integration of people, process, and technology. The Physical Security Integration domain recognizes the importance of physical security and personnel controls in a complete information system security model. The security professional is required to demonstrate understanding of the risk and tools used in providing physical security. This includes secure management, administration and deployment of physical access controls, and whether to prevent, detect, or react to suspicious activity. Key areas of knowledge include

- Identification and protection of restricted work areas, including traffic control, access control, and monitoring
- Selecting the locations of and designing secure facilities
- Addressing facility infrastructure risk and requirements, including identity management and facility protections
- Remediation of risks associated with portable data processing and storage devices

Physical Security Risks

The *Merriam-Webster* online dictionary defines *risk* as "a chance of encountering harm or loss; hazard; danger." Risk is the potential for a loss of or damage to an asset. It is measured based on the value of the asset in relation to the threats and vulnerabilities associated with it. Risk is based on the likelihood or probability of the hazard occurring and the consequences of the occurrence. Nevertheless, risks can be reduced or managed.

Physical security is often described as the "forgotten side of security," and yet it is a key element of an overall protection strategy. Protection of restricted work areas is important to the overall functionality of the company's operation. Proprietary, sensitive, and classified material must be protected from the general population or from other employees who do not need to know. In the case of a company, such areas may be protected by restricting unauthorized personnel from entering the area. General traffic flow to the area must be diverted away to minimize the entry of unauthorized personnel. Personnel who are authorized to enter these restricted areas must have a company badge that quickly identifies them as authorized. Moreover, these authorized personnel must be on an access roster that the guards can use to verify their credentials. If the area is a large area where vehicles are used, guards at the sentry post have to verify the vehicles being used to enter the premise along with personal identification. Verification may be accomplished by using access rosters for both vehicles and personnel. By applying these preventive measures, the risk of loss or damage is reduced.

Many organizations spend thousands of dollars on IT hardware and software, only to forget about securing the actual building that houses them. Remember:

Even if no one can steal or corrupt your data over the network, they may still be able to walk out your front door with it. Do not neglect physical security in your attempts to lock down data.

Unauthorized Access

Access control is the regulation of movement into, from, and within a designated building or area. The primary objective of controlling entry into a facility or area is to ensure that only authorized persons are allowed to enter. Unauthorized access in simple terms is trespassing, which is defined as making an unwarranted or uninvited incursion; to enter unlawfully the land of another. A security professional's mantra is protecting property, information, and personnel. Keeping unwanted intrusion away from the facility is paramount, and the function of the security professional is to incorporate knowledge, technology, vigilance, and professionalism into a sound security program.

Traffic Monitoring

Geographically speaking, what are the physical bounds of security concerns? Does one stop at the end of the parking lot or the fence line? Does one have to venture beyond the property line and the community in order to maintain a visual watch for potential threats? The farther one can observe, the more time one has to react. The design of roads and parking lots influences the security at the building site.

Traffic monitoring can be accomplished in several ways, from the design of the roadway to monitoring with CCTV. The most controlled way is to have an entry control point or guard building serving as the designated point of entry for site access (Figure 3.1). It provides a point for implementation of desired or required levels of screening and access control. The objective of the entry control point is to prevent unauthorized access to the facility while maximizing the rate of authorized access by foot or vehicle. Designs should be flexible to allow implementation of increased security controls when organizations are placed on high alert as well as easing of controls at lower threat levels.

Roadway Design

There is not a facility anywhere that does not have roadways and vehicular traffic. Employees, visitors, and deliveries have requirements to bring their vehicles close to the facility. The concept of designing streets and roadways as a way to curtail unauthorized access or prevent sabotage and structural damage to the facility is never thought of as the first line of defense. Streets are generally designed to minimize travel time and maximize safety, the end result typically being a straight path between two or more endpoints. Although a straight line may be the most efficient course, designers should consider a roadway system to minimize vehicle velocity,

Figure 3.1   Traffic monitoring can be accomplished in several ways, from the design of the roadway to monitoring with CCTV. The most controlled way is to have an entry control point or guard building serving as the designated point of entry for site access.

thus using the roadway itself as a protective measure. This is accomplished through the use of several strategies.

First, straight-line or perpendicular approaches to the facility should not be used, because this gives a vehicle the opportunity to gather the speed necessary to ram and penetrate buildings. This can also occur by accident when a gas pedal sticks and the driver panics. Instead, approaches should be parallel to the perimeter of the building, with natural earthen berms, high curbs, trees, or other measures used to prevent vehicles from leaving the roadway. Existing streets can be retrofitted with speed bumps, barriers, swing gates, or other measures to force vehicles to travel at a slow pace as they approach the facility. The front of the building can be equipped with decorative bollards (Figure 3.2 through Figure 3.4) to keep vehicles from running into the facility. In high-security areas, "delta barriers" are used to control vehicle traffic into secured areas.

Parking

Parking restrictions can help to keep potential threats away from a facility. In downtown settings, underground parking is often necessary and sometimes difficult to control. Mitigating the risks associated with parking requires creative design measures, including parking restrictions, perimeter buffer zones, barriers, structural hardening, and other architectural and engineering solutions.

Visitor parking should be located in front of the facility in full view of the reception or guard desk. There should be limited space availability for guests and

Figure 3.2   The front of the building can be equipped with decorative bollards to keep vehicles from running into the facility.

Figure 3.3   In high security areas, "delta barriers" are used to control vehicle traffic into secured areas.

visitors. Some facilities host large meetings, and in this situation designated areas should be cordoned off specifically for those events.

Facilities should also encompass a clear zone area. This can be achieved with perimeter barriers that cannot be compromised by vehicular ramming. A continuous line of security should be installed along the perimeter of the site to protect it from unscreened vehicles and to keep all vehicles as far away from the facility as possible.

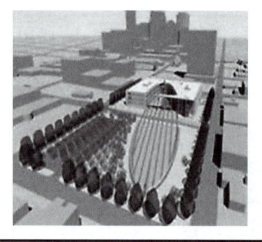

Figure 3.4   Security measures, such as setbacks, bollards, protective glazing, and structural hardening, are incorporated into the design of the new Oklahoma City Federal Building, located north of where the former Alfred P. Murrah Federal Building once stood.

According to FEMA (Federal Emergency Management Agency), the following critical building components should be located away from main entrances, vehicle circulation, parking, and maintenance areas. If this is not possible, harden as appropriate:

- Emergency generator, including fuel systems, day tank, fire sprinkler, and water supply
- Normal fuel storage
- Telephone distribution and main switchgear
- Fire pumps
- Building control centers
- Uninterrupted power supply (UPS) systems controlling critical functions
- Main refrigeration systems if critical to building operation
- Elevator machinery and controls
- Shafts for stairs, elevators, and utilities
- Critical distribution feeders for emergency power

Parking Garages — If the facility has an underground parking facility (Figure 3.5), the security professional will have to understand that there will be two primary safety threats: crime and vehicles hitting pedestrians. Notwithstanding the current threat—terrorist bombing—this can also be addressed with proper security measures.

Start by controlling access to the garage area. This can be accomplished with automatic controlled gate arms (Figure 3.6) that are activated by using a transponder

Figure 3.5 **If the facility has an underground parking facility, the security professional will have to understand that there will be two primary safety threats: crime and vehicles hitting pedestrians.**

or a badge reader. The badge reader can be incorporated into the overall access control system and use the same badge that will be used within the facility. It is imperative that with an underground parking facility, only authorized employees be allowed access. Visitors and all deliveries should be rerouted to outside areas. A car bomb can hold up to 500 pounds of explosive. "Therefore, the most effective tool a designer has against a high-explosive terrorist attack is to force the terrorist to detonate the explosive as far from the building as possible."[1]

Figure 3.6 **Controlling access into the garage area can be accomplished with automatic controlled gate arms that will be activated by using a transponder or a badge reader.**

Figure 3.7   For additional security, quick-access roll-ups doors have dramatically reduced the time it takes for the doors to open and close.

For additional security, there have been industry advancements that have led to the development of quick-access roll-ups doors, which have dramatically reduced the time it takes for the doors to open and close. With this system, an access card is inserted and the door opens within 7 seconds, and then immediately closes. This system is a vast improvement over traditional roll-up doors, which take anywhere from 20 to 25 seconds to come back down again, allowing time for unauthorized individuals to follow cars into the building on foot.

Signage can direct vehicles and pedestrians to the exit points or the entrance of the facility. The only entry points into the garage should be for vehicles. Inside the garage, there should be easily identifiable signs to direct pedestrians toward elevators and stairs. CCTV cameras should be used for monitoring events, and emergency call boxes should be placed throughout the garage. Generally, when the parking floor is only 200 to 250 feet long, only one camera needs to be used at the end of each aisle. For floors over 250 to 400 feet long, a second camera can be placed midway down the aisle so that the cameras do not have to be manipulated for telephoto or tilt zoom. Cameras should also be positioned to capture activity in and around elevator lobbies and in stairwells.

Installing bright lights is one of the most effective deterrents to both accidents and attacks. It is recommended that lighting levels be at least 10 to 12 foot-candles over parked cars and 15 to 20 foot-candles in walking and driving aisles.

It is also advisable to install high lighting levels to illuminate the exterior of the parking facility, particularly in areas that experience high pedestrian traffic. As a rule, exterior lights should be placed approximately 12 feet above ground, and they should point downward to illuminate wide areas along the ground. Another

Figure 3.8   Open surface parking areas are common in rural or industrial areas. The way to provide measured security is with initial parking access control.

method for increasing visibility is to paint the walls of the structure white to reflect light. Lighting fixtures should also be strategically placed to bounce light off the walls and reduce dark corners where criminals could hide.

With garages under the facility, elevators or walk-ups should all empty into the lobby, outside of the controlled space. Having all employees and visitors pass through the controlled receptionist area will maintain the integrity of the facility. In this way, the elevators going into the core of the building will only be accessible from the lobby and not from the garage levels.

It is always best to install emergency communications systems, such as intercoms, telephones, etc., at readily identified, well-lighted, CCTV-monitored locations to permit direct contact with security personnel.

Open Area Parking

Open surface parking areas (Figure 3.8) are common in rural or industrial areas. The way to provide measured security is with initial parking access control. Only allow employees access to specific segregated parking areas. Again, this can be accomplished with the use of automatic gate arms that will be activated by using a transponder or a badge reader. Both devices would allow access to the parking area. It is best to have an entry-only or exit-only design that will maintain a one-way circulation within a parking lot to facilitate monitoring for potential aggressors. To maintain a secured parking area, it is best to locate parking within view of occupied buildings while maintaining stand-off zones and prohibit parking within the stand-off zone. The parking lot could also utilize control arms for controlling access by employee vehicles only.

Loading Docks

All facilities will require deliveries, and loading docks and service access areas are typically desired to be kept as invisible as possible. For this reason, special attention should be devoted to these service areas in order to avoid intruders. Who controls the deliveries to the facility? Is it a security guard making sure that all deliveries are recorded? Does security work in conjunction with a warehouse, mail room, or shipping and receiving group to coordinate deliveries on the loading dock platform? The operation should control the overhead doors to the loading dock just as it would protect perimeter doors. When these doors go up, a physical security presence needs to be in place. From the standpoint of a perpetrator, this would be the ideal location to gain entry. Daily deliveries and pickups are made all day, and workmen and contractors move supplies in and out of the facility.

Some organizations design their loading docks using interior door control. In this scenario, the loading dock doors are controlled by a card reader that would only allow authorized persons to operate the roll-up doors. When the overhead doors go up, the interior door that leads into the facility is controlled to lock and cannot be opened until the loading dock doors are shut. This maintains a secure perimeter even when deliveries are being made.

Proper loading dock security starts with comprehensive policies and procedures for shipping and receiving operations. Here are some examples of simple steps to improve operations that many organizations fail to implement:

- Secure loading dock overhead doors and entry doors.
- Implement personnel screening processes to ensure that only authorized personnel access the loading dock areas.
- Institute detailed logging of all items entering or leaving the facility.
- Implement security awareness training programs for nonsecurity personnel in order to communicate the message that security is everyone's responsibility.[2]

Signage

Signs are an important element of any facility layout. Signage is necessary to direct visitors, deliveries, and employees to their respective parking areas. They are also meant to keep intruders out of restricted areas and notify "No Trespassing" instructions. Signs should be located at the street entry of the facility, explaining current entry procedures for drivers and pedestrians. They should give traffic regulatory and directional details that control traffic flow and direct vehicles to specific appropriate points. Post easily understandable signs to minimize accidental entry by unauthorized visitors into critical areas. In areas where English is one of two or more languages commonly spoken, warning signs must contain the other languages in addition to English. The signs should be posted at intervals of no more than 100 feet and should not be mounted on fences, posts, or light poles.[3]

Surveillance Devices

Depending on the extent of security required to protect the facility, exterior or perimeter sensors will alert you to any intruders attempting to gain access across your open space or attempting to breach the controlled area zone. These may provide security personnel ample opportunity to evaluate and intercept any threat. Intrusion sensor performance is described by three fundamental characteristics: probability of detection, nuisance alarm rate (NAR), and vulnerability to defeat.

In general, open terrain sensors work best on flat, cleared areas. Heavily or irregular contoured areas are not conducive to open terrain sensing systems. Open terrain sensors include infrared, microwave systems, combinations (dual technology), vibration sensors, and new emerging video content analysis and motion path analysis systems.

Infrared Sensors

Passive infrared sensors are designed for human body detection, so they are great for detecting when someone approaches. Passive infrared sensors detect the heat emitted by animate forms. Because all living things emit heat, a system of recording measurable changes in a specific area provides a means of detecting unauthorized intrusions. When the unit registers changes in temperature in its area of detection, it relays the information to a processor that measures the change according to detection parameters. If the change falls outside the parameters, the processor sends a signal to the unit's alarm.

Active infrared sensors transmit an infrared signal via a transmitter. The location for reception is at a receiver. Interruption of the normal IR signal indicates that an intruder or object has blocked the path. The beam can be narrow in focus, but should be projected over a cleared path.

Microwave

Microwave sensors come in two configurations: bistatic and monostatic. Both bistatic and monostatic sensors operate by radiating a controlled pattern of microwave energy into the protected area. The transmitted microwave signal is received, and a base-level "no intrusion" signal is established. Motion by an intruder causes the received signal to be altered, setting off an alarm. Microwave signals pass through concrete and steel and must be applied with care if roadways or adjacent buildings are near the area of coverage. Otherwise, nuisance alarms may occur due to reflected microwave patterns. A bistatic sensor sends an invisible volumetric detection field, which fills the space between a transmitter and receiver. A monostatic microwave sensor (Figure 3.9) uses a single sensing unit that incorporates both transmitting and receiving functions. It generates a beam radiated from the transceiver that creates a well-controlled, three-dimensional volumetric detection

Figure 3.9   A monostatic microwave sensor uses a single sensing unit that incor-porates both transmitting and receiving functions. It generates a beam radiated from the transceiver that creates a well-controlled, three-dimensional volumetric detection pattern with adjustable range.

pattern with adjustable range. Many monostatic microwave sensors feature a cut-off circuit, which allows the sensor to be tuned to only cover the area within a selected region. This helps to reduce nuisance alarms.

Coaxial Strain-Sensitive Cable

These systems use a coaxial cable woven through the fabric of the fence. The coaxial cable transmits an electric field. As the cable moves due to strain on the fence fabric caused by climbing or cutting, changes in the electric field are detected within the cable, and an alarm condition occurs.

Coaxial strain-sensing systems (Figure 3.10) are readily available and are highly tunable to adjust for field conditions due to weather and climate character-istics. Some coaxial cable systems are susceptible to electromagnetic interference and radio frequency interference, which can generate nuisance alarms. Possible defeat measures include tunneling, jumping, or bridging across the fence system. Careful climbing at corner posts may not generate sufficient vibration to generate an alarm condition.

Taut-Wire System

This system consists of micro switches or turnbuckles connected to tension wire installed on fence posts. This aligns an internal magnetic contact in the closed loop state. Cutting the fence wires, spreading them, climbing over them on a ladder or through them, cutting the communication cable, or trying to tamper with the sen-sor itself will all cause an immediate alarm.

Figure 3.10 Coaxial strain-sensing systems are readily available and are highly tunable to adjust for field conditions due to weather and climate characteristics. Some coaxial cable systems are susceptible to electromagnetic interference and radio frequency interference, which can generate nuisance alarms.

Due to the fact that a force of less than about 33 lb will not activate the sensor, small animals such as rabbits, dogs, snakes, birds, etc., will not trigger the alarm. A taut-wire system is the most costly fence mounting system available. It has a very high probability of detection and nearly a zero false alarm rate.

Time Domain Reflectometry Systems

Time domain reflectometry (TDR) systems send induced radio frequency (RF) signals down a cable that is attached to the fence fabric. Intruders climbing or flexing a fence create a signal path flaw that can be converted to an alarm signal. When the conductor cable is bent or flexed, a part of the signal returns to the origination point. This reflected signal can be converted to an intrusion point by computing the time it takes for the signal to travel to the intrusion point and return. The cable can be provided in armored cable, which requires more than a bolt cutter to sever the sensing cable. These systems require their own processor unit and can be configured in a closed loop, such that if the cable is cut, it can be detected by the other return path.

Prudent application of TDR-based alarm systems should begin from the perspective of project objectives, liability, and risk aversion. The technology is capable of monitoring movement over large lateral extents and to great depths with a high density of monitoring points. Similar to other systems, it should be expected that 70% to 90% of calls will be "false" in that an alarm condition exists that is spurious and not associated with actual deformation. Responsible personnel must gain experience with the system and develop the ability to make decisions using minimal information followed by more detailed analysis of the TDR waveform.[4]

Closed Circuit TV (CCTV)

Now that you have been notified that there is a potential intrusion, the next step is to get visual confirmation. The idea of dispatching a reaction force for every alarm is not reasonable or cost-effective. The use of CCTV is an effective means of evaluating and observing activities inside your protective area. A comprehensive CCTV system will consist of cameras, DVR recorders, switches, keyboards, and monitors that allow viewing and recording of security events. The CCTV system is normally integrated into the overall security program and centrally monitored at the security central station.

Within the past several years, there have been enhanced developments in the CCTV industry, particularly: better picture resolution, microprocessor-based video switchers, and the ability to transmit video over networks with a compressed bandwidth ratio.

CCTV provides a highly flexible method of monitoring, surveillance, and deterrence. One advantage is its immediate output. There is never a question of whether the equipment works properly or not. In addition, it can be adapted through the use of remote control devices, recorders, and computer imaging to guard against virtually any crime including burglary, unauthorized entrance, and employee theft.

Uses of CCTV systems for security services include several different functions:

Surveillance. CCTV cameras can be used to enable a viewer to watch events at multiple locations from a centralized remote viewing area. CCTV camera technology makes visual information available that would normally only be available through multiple (possibly roving) human resources.

Assessment. When alerted by an alarm notification, CCTV cameras allow the security control center operators or other viewers to assess the situation and make a determination as to what type of response may or may not be required. An example would be an intrusion alarm at a remote facility. Visual assessment may indicate an unannounced maintenance crew at work. This situation will be handled differently than if the operator viewed an unknown individual removing a laptop from the facility.

Deterrence. Although more effective against unsophisticated burglars, as opposed to trained covert insurgents, CCTV cameras may deter burglary, vandalism, or intrusion due to fear of discovery and prosecution.

Evidentiary archives. Retrieval of archived images may be helpful in the identification and prosecution of trespassers, vandals, or other intruders. DVRs are now capable of holding months of video data; a standard 16-port DVR is typically sold with a 500 GB hard drive as the standard. Most DVRs are provided with self-contained CD burners for archival or removal of stored data. Most security specifications require a CCTV system to be able to retain a minimum of 45 days of camera images.

Digital Video Recorder (DVR)

In current CCTV systems, the digital video recorder (DVR) has become the bread and butter of the system. The DVR is used principally for the download of camera images onto a hard drive for recording and storage of historical information. Older systems used VHS tapes, but these have largely been phased out. This system required tapes to be changed every day for storage, and when an incident occurred, someone had to sit in front of the monitor and review the entire tape. DVRs currently have memory storage capability starting at 80 GB to 1 TB with expansion options to increase storage by using additional hardware. DVRs typically come in 8-port or 16-port versions, meaning that 8 or 16 cameras can be recorded at one time. Most DVRs are provided with self-contained CD burners for archival or removal of stored data. Most security specifications require a CCTV system to be able to retain a minimum of 45 days of camera images. The amount of storage required for 45 days is dependent on a number of factors, including the number of cameras, the compression ratio, the resolution, and the frame rate. Typically, these systems can be configured to detect motion and hence will not fill up the database with useless images. For example, is it necessary for the DVR to record the loading dock area from midnight until 4 AM if there is no activity? Once there is motion in front of the camera, the system will begin recording. This does not mean that the monitoring officer cannot see the real-time images; it just will not store irrelevant images. This is an optional feature that can be used by security professionals.

Video Content Analysis and Motion Path Analysis

The newest technology for intrusion detection is sophisticated software analysis of camera images such as video content analysis and motion path analysis. CCTV camera systems are increasingly being used as intrusion detection systems. The application of complex algorithms to digital CCTV camera images allows CCTV systems to detect intruders. The software programming is smart enough to detect pixel changes and differentiate and filter out normal video events (leaves blowing, snow falling) from true alarm events. The application of software rules can further evolve to differentiate between a rabbit hopping across a parking lot and a person trespassing in the parking lot, which needs to be addressed. The application of complex software algorithms to CCTV digital images takes on the aspect of an artificial camera, whereby the camera and processors become "smart video" and start to emulate a human operator. The differences between a smart camera and a human operator are principally twofold. It takes a lot of complex software programming and associated rules to enable camera systems to differentiate and assess video events compared to the processing ability of the human mind.

With more and more project applications, the gap is closing as the camera systems come closer to emulating the capabilities of a fully alert, very motivated, intelligent security guard fresh into the shift. The advantage of video content analysis and motion path analysis is that camera systems do not get tired. Studies have demonstrated that after 20 minutes, the ability of a guard to discern an abnormal event is severely degraded. Video content analysis systems do not suffer fatigue and remain "alert" after monitoring hundreds of video events during a shift. Video content analysis systems can monitor more cameras, more effectively, with fewer operators at a reduced cost. Fewer dispatch center and command center staff will be required if technology and the human factor are combined.

Guard Force

With surveillance devices, the human element is necessary for determination of whether the event is critical and requires intervention or response. Security officers are the physical presence and the deterrence to unauthorized entry into the facility along with being the response force to an alarm activation. With all the alarm technology, it still requires human intervention to respond to an alarm, make contact with an intruder, interact with employees, and provide first-aid when necessary.

According to the U.S. Department of Labor, "Security guards, also called security officers, patrol and inspect property to protect against fire, theft, vandalism, terrorism, and illegal activity. These workers protect their employer's investment, enforce laws on the property, and deter criminal activity and other problems."[5]

Security officers are required to conduct foot patrols of building interiors, exteriors, and parking areas. Some officers are assigned a fixed or stationary position at entrances and other designated areas in order to prevent unauthorized entrance or the introduction of prohibited items. Another security officer responsibility is to control access to the facility by checking employee identification badges, issuing temporary badges, and registering visitors. Officers are required to respond to fire, security, and medical emergencies, and render assistance when needed as well as submit written or oral reports regarding significant events to security management. They also escort designated visitors, usually construction and maintenance contractors, who require nonbusiness-hour access to facilities or access to areas where classified or proprietary information is accessible. They must immediately report potentially hazardous conditions and items in need of repair, including inoperative lights, leaky sprinkler heads, leaky faucets, toilet stoppages, broken or slippery floor surfaces, trip hazards, etc.

Access Control System

The primary function of an access control system (ACS) is to ensure that only authorized personnel are permitted inside the controlled area. This can also include the regulation and flow of materials into and out of specific areas. Persons subject to control can include employees, visitors, customers, vendors, and the public. Access control measures should be different for each application to fulfill specific security, cost, and operational objectives.

Control can begin at the facility property line to include such areas as parking lots. Exterior building entrances can then be controlled. Within the facility, any area can be controlled at the discretion of management. However, the applied control is normally consistent with identified risk, and the protective value that is desired. Protected areas can include street level entrances, lobbies, loading docks, elevators, and sensitive internal areas containing assets such as customer data, proprietary information, and classified information.

The goal of an access control program is to limit the opportunity for a crime to be committed. If the potential perpetrator of a crime cannot gain access to financial assets, data files, computer equipment, programs, documentation, forms, operating procedures, and other sensitive material, the ability to commit a crime against the institution is minimized. Thus, only identified, authorized personnel should be permitted access to restricted areas.

The basic components of an ACS are shown in Figure 3.11. They include card readers, electric locks, alarms, and computer systems to monitor and control the ACS.

In order for the system to identify an authorized employee, an ACS needs to have some form of enrollment station to assign and activate an access control device. Usually, a badge is produced and issued with the employee's identifiers, with the enrollment station giving the employee specific areas that will be accessible.

In general, an ACS compares an individual's badge against a verified database. If authenticated, the ACS sends output signals that allow authorized personnel to pass through controlled areas such as a gate or door. The system has the capability of logging and archiving entry attempts (authorized and unauthorized).

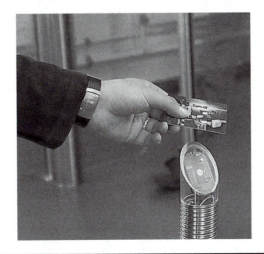

Figure 3.11 The basic components of an access control system include card readers, electric locks, alarms, and computer systems to monitor and control the ACS.

A second scenario is to have an ACS reader next to a guard's desk, so that when the individual places his badge on the reader, a picture is generated from the ACS system and verifies to the guard that the person holding the badge is in fact the correct card holder and his or her card is valid. This eliminates the chance of a perpetrator stealing or finding a badge and falsely using it to gain entry.

Another safeguard is to use a card reader with a personal identification number (PIN) pad. This requires the user to utilize a unique PIN number that will be needed in connection with the badge in order for the access point to open. Coded devices use a series of assigned numbers commonly referred to as a PIN. This series of numbers is entered into a keypad and is matched to the numbers stored in the ACS. This style of reader is mostly used at employee entrances that are not manned by guards and higher-security areas within the facility. This provides additional security because if a badge is lost or stolen, it will not grant entry into a controlled area without the proper PIN number, similar to an ATM bank card.

Another feature the access control system can provide is an event tracking/event log. These are lists or logs of security events recorded by the access control system that indicate the actions performed by an individual with an access badge and monitored by the system. Each event log entry contains the time, date, and any other information specific to the event.

Card Types

Magnetic stripe (mag stripe) cards consist of a magnetically sensitive strip fused onto the surface of a PVC material, specific to a credit card. A magnetic stripe card is read by swiping it through a reader or by inserting it into a position in a slot. This style of card is old technology; it could be physically damaged by misuse and its data can be affected by magnetic fields. In terms of overall security measures, magnetic stripe cards are easy to duplicate.

Proximity cards (prox cards) use embedded antenna wires connected to a chip within the card. The chip is encoded with the unique card identification. Distances at which proximity cards can be read vary by manufacturer and installation. Readers can require the card to be placed within a fraction of an inch from the reader to six inches away. This will then authenticate the card and will release the magnetic lock on the door. Proximity cards are moderately difficult to duplicate.

Smart cards are credential cards with a microchip embedded inside. Smart cards can store enormous amounts of data, such as access transactions, licenses held by individuals, qualifications, safety training, security access levels, and biometric templates. This card can double as an access card for doors and can be used as an authenticator for a computer. The federal government has mandated smart cards to provide Personal Identity Verification (PIV) to verify the identity of every employee and contractor in order to improve data security. The card will be used for identification, as well as for facility and data access. Smart cards are hard to duplicate.

Badge Equipment

Employee badges are an excellent method of control for both identification and access. The badges need to be created and encoded by security personnel. The badges need to be maintained and accounted for, similar to key controls. These badges will allow entry into the facility, and they must be protected and controlled. The equipment necessary for a badging access control system will include

1. Camera for capturing photographs.
2. Software for creating badge images.
3. Badge printer capable of printing a color ID template on the front and back of the badge, and capable of encoding a magnetic stripe or smart card (where applicable). There are new-technology printers that are capable of printing pseudo holograms on the clear protective laminate, which may be considered for higher-security applications.
4. Computer for retention and programming of the security credential database. This computer may be a stand-alone or client workstation that is connected to the ACS server database in a client–server architecture.

The badges that fit the needs of the operation, either magnetic, proximity, or smart, can be purchased in bulk and can be encoded and printed when needed.

Biometrics

Biometric devices rely on measurements of biological characteristics of an individual, such as a fingerprint (Figure 3.12), hand geometry, voice, or iris patterns. Biometric technology involves data that is unique to the individual and difficult to counterfeit. Selected individual characteristics are stored in a device's memory or on a card, from which stored reference data can be analyzed and compared with the presented template. A one-to-many or a one-to-one comparison of the presented template with the stored template can be made, and access granted if a match is found.

Biometric readers verify personal biological metrics of an individual. Biometric readers may be used in addition to credential devices or with a PIN code. This type of security technology is more likely found in high-security areas such as data centers and Sensitive Compartmented Information Facilities (SCIFs).

Biometric readers are the future trend of security systems. Current gains in large-scale production of some types of biometric readers have brought biometrics close in cost to conventional card readers.

According to David Fisch, a security consultant with International Biometric Group LLC, another advantage of this layered approach is that if someone loses his or her ID card, or if the card is stolen, the need for a fingerprint will ensure that the data center remains secure. Also, the ID card and fingerprint combination means that someone enrolled at one site can access another site without having to reenroll, because the metrics are on the card.

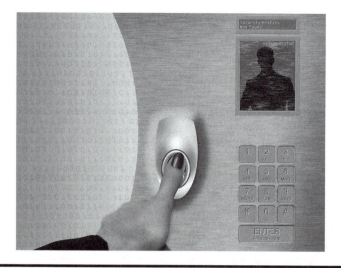

Figure 3.12 Biometric technology involves data that is unique to the individual and is difficult to counterfeit. Biometric devices rely on measurements of biological characteristics of an individual, such as a fingerprint, hand geometry, voice, or iris patterns.

However, there is a downside to biometrics. Tsutomu Matsumoto, a Japanese cryptographer, has demonstrated the problem. He took a latent fingerprint left on a piece of glass, enhanced it with a cyanoacrylate adhesive, and then photographed it with a digital camera. Using PhotoShop, he improved the contrast and printed the fingerprint onto a transparency sheet. Then, he took a photo-sensitive printed-circuit board (PCB) and used the fingerprint transparency to etch the fingerprint into the copper, making it three-dimensional. (You can find photo-sensitive PCBs, along with instructions for use, in most electronics hobby shops.) Finally, he made a gelatin finger (the stuff they use to make Gummi Bears) using the print on the PCB. By simply forming the clear gelatin finger over his own finger, an intruder can hide the gelatin finger as he presses his own finger onto the sensor. After the intruder is allowed in, he would eat the evidence. This also fools fingerprint detectors about 80% of the time.

Using only one type of security access device involves potential for compromise; with any security system, the more layers there are, the better the protection.

Access Control Head End

The application software housed in the CPU is the physical intelligent controller where all access control systems are activity monitored, recorded into history, commanded, and controlled by the operator. Current state-of-the-art access systems, such as Lenel OnGuard or Software House CCURE System, allow each local security panel to hold the system logic for its associated devices. The CPU retains the system-specific programming to allow entry (access) for authorized personnel and deny access to unauthorized personnel.

Communications failure between the CPU and the local access control panel could result in new users not being permitted entry; however, the system is set so that the panel will recognize personnel already installed and will grant access to an authorized badge holder.

These systems have advances that can integrate with CCTV and provide instant visual recognition along with visual alarm activation in order to provide the security console operator visual information before dispatching a security response team.

Another feature of an access control system is it can provide event tracking/event logs, which are lists or logs of security events recorded by the access control system that indicate the actions performed by employees as they enter or attempt to enter a controlled area. Each event log entry contains the time, date, and any other information specific to the event. This is useful when identifying who has access to a specific area and verifying with management if that employee still needs access.

Facility Risk

It is the responsibility of every security profession to identify the facility risks and do everything possible to mitigate them. A vulnerability assessment tour of a facility is designed to gather information regarding the general layout of the facility, the location of key assets, information about facility operations and production capabilities, and locations and types of physical protection systems.

Facility risk assessments have an enormous potential to improve the safety of a facility by recognizing and eliminating potential problems. Restricted area physical security is not just about keeping bad people out with biometrics and retinal scans. It is also about keeping out the fires, floods, and hurricanes that can ravage your facility—and your data. An acceptable risk profile can only be achieved by identifying hazards and assessing the associated risks and control measures.

According to Eric Maiwald, security analyst for Burton Group's new Security and Risk Management Strategies, "If physical access to a computer system can be achieved, gaining logical access to the information on that computer system is guaranteed and an attacker can use either electronic or physical means to gain access to information, so the two disciplines must work together to help the organization manage risk."

There are many potential risks that can take out a facility, from human error, natural disasters, to corporate espionage. A security professional needs to be aware of all types of risk and take the necessary steps to mitigate and prepare for potential hazards.

The purpose of a data security program is to ensure adherence to four basic tenets:

- **Confidentiality:** Only authorized people should be able to see the data.
- **Integrity:** Only authorized people should be able to change the data and then, only in authorized ways.

- **Availability:** Authorized persons should be able to access the data whenever they are allowed to do so.
- **Accountability:** Managers should be able to discover who has done what to the data.

Compromises may be necessary to provide a level of security that does a fair job of keeping out intruders but does not make the information inaccessible to authorized users. A comprehensive security program must include written policies and procedures, access control systems, user authentication technologies, auditing systems, encryption, and content security.

In order to understand how physical security dovetails with IT security, it is necessary to fully understand the basic concepts of the following:

1. Threat—Anything that can harm your assets
2. Vulnerability—Anything that allows the harm to occur or a weakness that allow security breaches to occur
3. Counter measure—Steps taken to reduce the risk of the occurrence or magnitude of asset loss

The following measures outline the requirements that physical security must satisfy to provide the necessary facility protections and the means to protect the personnel, information, and other assets of an organization.

Low Profile

One way to reduce the risk of casual or opportunistic intrusion is not to broadcast out to the world where you are and what business you are engaged in. If you are in a business that requires direct sales, such as Sears or Best Buy, this would not be the approach you would want to take. However, if you are in a business that permits anonymity and obscurity from the general public, then having a low profile is the way to go. A plain building with only street numbers on the façade of the building serves well for a facility that does not want to attract unwelcome interest. There should be no art sculpture, water feature, or architectural design in front of the building. There should not be any benches or waiting areas that would give the impression of an invitation to the facility. A low-profile building is plain and unimaginative, it blends into the landscape, and is not noticed. This does not mean that the inside will not be warm and welcoming for staff and visitors, but rather, the goal is to deflect unwanted attention.

Personnel will need to be educated on operational security measures; this will include concealing their identification badges when they leave the facility. Do not discuss the type of work that goes on inside the facility; being discreet will keep potential thieves away. These are standard security measures that all employees should be briefed on annually. If a parking sticker is required for employees, a nondescript sticker should be utilized, with nothing on it that would identify the company by name. However, this will not help stop targeted attacks, and this control is brittle. The difficulty is in recovering security once your presence is revealed, as it eventually will be.

Location Hazards

What is the threat? A threat (hazard) is any indication, circumstance, or event with the potential to cause loss of, or damage to, an asset. It is important to understand who are the people who intend to cause us harm; or who, by process, materials, or proximity, can cause indirect harm to the facility.

In order to identify and locate hazards, a security assessment needs to be completed. A security assessment is a comprehensive overview of the facility, including physical security controls, policy, procedures, and employee safety. At the beginning, a good assessment requires the security professional to determine specific protection objectives. These objectives include threat definition, target identification, and facility characteristics.

So when the question is asked, "What is the threat or hazard?," the security professional will go down the list of probable threats to the organization or facility. Is it vandals, hackers, terrorists, internal employees, corporate spies, or a combination of these? Explicitly stating the threat will identify how adversaries can impact assets and will provide guidance on developing a sound physical protection system.

Target identification involves identifying the most valuable asset that needs to be protected. Assets can be personnel, property, equipment, or information. To identify assets to be protected, it would be prudent to prioritize the assets or establish a matrix and identify the asset in conjunction with the probability of attack, along with the question: what would be the impact and consequence of the loss of the asset?

Sample of Defined Threat Matrix

Asset	Probability of Attack	Consequence of Loss
Data center server	Medium	Very high
Portable laptops (critical staff)	High	High
Copy machine	Low	Low
Portable laptops (nonessential personnel)	High	Low
Power control unit (PCU)	Medium	High
Classified containers	Low	High

Walking a team of security professionals though a facility will provide a static picture of how to protect it. However, one of the best ways to build a comprehensive approach toward protecting the facility is by doing on-site interviews. Everyone has an opinion on security, and it is amazing that often the best insight and information on what needs to be protected and how it should be protected comes from interviewing the staff. One of the most astute and insightful persons I have interviewed was the midnight security officer. He has all the time in the world and walks the facility without interruption, seeing things that are clearly visible only at night.

The American Institute of Architects has established some key security questions that need to be addressed while performing a security assessment.[6]

1. What do we want to protect?
2. What are we protecting against?
3. What are the current or expected asset vulnerabilities?
4. What are the consequences of loss?
5. What specific level of protection do we wish to achieve?
6. What types of protection measures are appropriate?
7. What are our protection constraints?
8. What are the specific security design requirements?
9. How do the integrated systems of personnel, technologies, and procedures respond to security incidents?

Once these questions have been answered and a thorough facilities evaluation and staff interview completed, it is time to develop and outline a physical protection system for the facility.

Threat Assessment

A threat assessment is a continual process of compiling and examining all available information concerning potential threats and manmade hazards. The product of a threat assessment is a list of threats and hazards with a threat rating assigned. The threat rating is a subjective judgment based on existence, capability, history, intention, and targeting. Often, information is sketchy and analysts must rely more on the judgment of experts, statistical probability, and occasionally, assumptions to help quantify and qualify the threat. The assessment of any vulnerability of a facility or building should be done within the context of the defined threats and the value of the organization's assets. That is, each element of the facility should be analyzed for vulnerabilities to each threat, and a vulnerability rating should be assigned. You would not install $10,000 worth of security equipment in order to protect $100 worth of assets. It should be noted that a vulnerability assessment may change the value rating of assets due to the identification of critical nodes or some other factor that makes the organization's assets more valuable. The following ratings could be assigned:

Very High—One or more major weaknesses have been identified that make the organization's assets extremely susceptible to an aggressor or hazard.

High—One or more significant weaknesses have been identified that make the organization's assets highly susceptible to an aggressor or hazard.

Medium High—An important weakness has been identified that makes the organization's assets very susceptible to an aggressor or hazard.

Medium—A weakness has been identified that makes the organization's assets fairly susceptible to an aggressor or hazard.

Medium Low—A weakness has been identified that makes the organization's assets somewhat susceptible to an aggressor or hazard.

Low—A minor weakness has been identified that slightly increases the susceptibility of the organization's assets to an aggressor or hazard.

Very Low—No weaknesses exist.

Sample of Vulnerability Matrix

Main Facility	Vulnerability
Front Entrance	Medium
Receptionist	High
Access Control	Low
Response to Alarms	High
CCTV	Medium
Classified Containers	Low

Site Planning

The primary goal of a physical protection program is to control access to the facility. In the concept of defense in depth, barriers are arranged in layers with the level of security growing progressively higher as one comes closer to the center or the highest protective area. Defending an asset with a multiple posture can reduce the likelihood of a successful attack; if one layer of defense fails, another layer of defense will hopefully prevent the attack, and so on. This design requires the attacker to circumvent multiple defensive mechanisms to gain access to the targeted asset.

The single most important goal in planning a site is the protection of life, property, and operations. A security professional needs to make decisions in support of this goal, and these decisions should be based on a comprehensive security assessment of the threats and hazards so that planning and design countermeasures are appropriate and effective in the reduction of vulnerability and risk.

Technology is not the only answer to heightened security needs. It is essential to start by first looking at the way the facility is laid out and then assessing what electronic devices are needed to achieve enhanced overall security. The positioning

Figure 3.13 If it were only up to security in designing a facility, it would look like a fortified stronghold.

of security personnel for presence and response capability is a key to the overall success of a comprehensive security protection program.

There is a natural conflict between making a facility as convenient and open as possible for staff and visitors and maintaining a secure facility. If it were left to security to design a facility, it would look like a fortified stronghold (Figure 3.13).

However, with most applications and design requirements, there needs to be cooperation between several departments. Expediency should be considered during the different phases of the design review; however, the requirement for security should not be sacrificed for convenience. Proper security controls will reduce the flow rate and ease of entry and egress into and out of a facility, but will also allow for rapid evacuation in case of emergency. These issues must be addressed in the initial planning to facilitate additional entry points or administrative requirements. Once a process has been established and there is buy-in from the employees, the acceptance of operational policy is generally embraced.

Designing a new building to mitigate threats is simpler and more cost-effective than retrofitting an existing building. Important security benefits are achieved not by hardware and electronic devices but by shrewd site selections, proper placement of the building on the site, and careful location of building occupants and functions to minimize exposure to threat. These factors also have the benefit of reducing operating expenses over the lifetime of the building, such as limiting the number of entrances to the site that must be monitored, staffed, and protected.

When there are changes to the design after the fact and personnel are used to doing something a certain way, there will be reluctance, questions, and push back. Humans like stability and have a need for things to be a certain way. For example, for years an employee entrance was in the rear of the building, and security recommended closing it down because of guard cost and lack of use. This entrance was converted to an emergency exit only, and even employees who did not use it when it was an entry point wanted to know why. This is because it takes away from their norm or comfort zone and becomes a change factor in their routine. However, if a sound security explanation is presented, it will not take long for the grumbling to end, and a new routine will take its place.

To maximize safety and security, a design team should implement a holistic approach to site design that integrates security and function to achieve a balance among the various design elements and objectives. Even if resources are limited, significant value can be added to a project by integrating security considerations into the more traditional design tasks in such a way that they complement the design.

The movement of people and materials throughout a facility is determined by the design of its access, delivery, and parking systems. Such systems should be designed to maximize efficiency while minimizing conflicts between the entry and departure of vehicles and pedestrians. Designers should begin with an understanding of the organization's requirements based on an analysis of how the facility will be used. The design process of a security plan for a new facility should begin with the interior, then the exterior, and finally the outer perimeter.

When designing the data center, make sure that only durable materials are used that can exceed normal design loads. At a minimum, the facility must be capable of withstanding 200 mile per hour winds and driven rain or snow. Material such as masonry and concrete will afford the most protection to your facility, along with fire resistance. Include only necessary windows in the structure. Make sure that you have 20-foot high ceilings for tolerance of over-temperature conditions.

Restricted Work Areas

Sensitive Compartmental Information Facilities (SCIF)

In highly restricted work areas or government SCIF, there is a requirement to increase the security blanket to ensure stricter access control to these areas. The physical security protection for a SCIF is intended to prevent as well as detect visual, acoustical, technical, and physical access by unauthorized persons. Your organization may not be required to maintain government classified information; however, the company's profitability and your employment may be tied to proprietary information that requires the same level of security.

SCIF walls will consist of three layers of 5/8 inch drywall and will be from true floor to true ceiling. There will typically be only one SCIF entrance door, which will have an X-09 combination lock along with access control systems. All SCIF perimeter doors must be plumbed in their frames and the frame firmly affixed to the surrounding wall. Door frames must be of sufficient strength to preclude distortion that could cause improper alignment of door alarm sensors, improper door closure, or degradation of audio security. All SCIF primary entrance doors must be equipped with an automatic door closer.

Basic HVAC requirements are that any duct penetration into the secured area that is over 96 square inches will require man bars so as to prevent an intruder from climbing through the ducts.

White noise or sound-masking devices need to be placed over doors, in front of plenum or pointed toward windows to prevent an eavesdropper from listening to classified conversations. Some SCIFs use music or noise that sounds like a constant flow of air to mask conversation.

All access control must be controlled from within the SCIF. Intrusion detection is sent out to a central station with the requirement that a response force will respond to the perimeter of the SCIF within 15 minutes.

Data Centers

When discussing the need to secure the data center, security professionals immediately think of sabotage, espionage, or data theft. While the need is obvious for protection against intruders and the intentional harm caused by intentional infiltration, the hazards from the ordinary activity of personnel working in the data center present a greater day-to-day risk for most facilities.

Personnel within the organization need to be segregated from access areas where they do not have a "need to know" for that area. The security director will have physical access to most of the facility but has no reason to access financial or HR data. The head of computer operations might have access to computer rooms and operating systems, but not the mechanical rooms that house power and HVAC facilities. It comes down to not allowing wandering within your organization. If you were working in the data center and you saw the line cook from the cafeteria walking through, how good would you feel about security and the protection of information?

As data centers grow, the need for physical security at the facility is every bit as great as the need for cyber security of networks. The data center is the brains of the operation and, as such, only specific people should be granted access.

The data center should have signs at the doors marking the room as "restricted access" and prohibiting consumption of food and drink, and smoking in the computer room. There should be a mandatory authentication method at the entrance to the room such as a badge reader.

The Network Operations Center (NOC) is the central security control point for the data center (Figure 3.14). This is the internal gatekeeper for the data center. It must have fire, power, weather, temperature, and humidity monitoring systems in place. The NOC must have redundant methods of communication with the outside world, including telephone, cell phone, or two-way radio system. The NOC must be manned 24 hours a day.

Figure 3.14   The Network Operations Center (NOC) is the central security control point for the data center.

Access to the data center should be restricted to those who need to maintain the servers or infrastructure of the room. Service engineers must go to the NOC to obtain access to the computer room.

Cleaning crews should work in groups of at least two. Cleaning crew should be restricted to offices and the NOC. If cleaning staff must access a data center for any reason, they will be escorted by NOC personnel.

The standard scenario for increased security at a data center would consist of the basic security-in-depth: progressing from the outermost (least sensitive) areas to the innermost (most sensitive) areas. Security will start with entry into the building, which will require passing a receptionist guard, and then using a proximity card to gain building entry. Access to the computer room or data center will now require the same proximity card along with a PIN and a biometric device (Figure 3.15).

Combining access control methods at an entry control point will increase the reliability of access for authorized personnel only. Using different methods for each access level significantly increases security at inner levels, because each is secured by its own methods as well as those of outer levels that must be entered first. This would also include internal door controls. For a data center, the use of an internal mantrap or portal would provide increased entry and exit control. A portal (Figure 3.16) allows only one person in at a time and will only open the inner door once the outer door is closed. The portal can have additional biometrics within the device that must be activated before the secured side door opens.

According to Kevin Beaver, principal security consultant of Principle Logic LLC, there are ten common mistakes companies make when it comes to the physical layout of their data center[7]:

Figure 3.15   Card reader requiring a PIN.

Figure 3.16   A portal allows only one person in at a time and will only open the inner door once the outer door is closed.

1. **Weak or missing security policies:** Do not take the time to develop security policies only to put them on a shelf and forget about them. It's important to make sure security policies are effectively communicated to employees. A good security policy includes a simple introduction that conveys the purpose of the policy, the policy statement itself, and information about how compliance will be measured. It should also include information about what sanctions will be taken against those who fail to comply.

2. **Poor physical access controls:** To ensure that everyone entering the data center has a reason to do so, implement strong visitor sign-in procedures and then enforce those rules. If keycards are required to enter the data center, check regularly to make sure they work. Companies that have no receptionist should consider hiring guards around the clock.

3. **Specific security concerns:** Constantly check the data center for vulnerabilities. Look to see how many access points there are and if people tend to leave doors open. Do not leave media such as CD-ROM or documentation lying around. Try to make sure that wires are not exposed. For companies that outsource their data center, make sure the third party secures documentation about your infrastructure.

4. **Location and layout:** There is much debate over which floor of an office building is best for housing a data center. First-floor data centers are vulnerable to car crashes, while second-floor data centers may be vulnerable to fires that start below. Either way, try to be aware of where your data center resides in the building, and develop disaster recovery plans accordingly.

5. **Unsecured computers:** Always lock screens when employees get up and walk away from their computer. Locking screensavers are recommended.

6. **Utility weakness:** Confirm that the proper fire protection policies are in place. Also, make sure there are working back-up generators or battery power in the event of an electrical outage.

7. **Rogue employees:** Everyone inside the data center should have a reason to be there. Do not assume people are trustworthy just because they have gained access to the data center. To solve the problem of rogue employees, vendors, and others passing through the data center, refer to internal policies or create them if necessary. Next, have some awareness training for employees. Finally, make it a human resources (HR) issue.

8. **Separation of physical and logical security:** Physical and logical security should be merged into one because they are both equally important. After all, there is a lot of overlap between the two. Both require risk assessment and countermeasures to mitigate risks. The goal of both is to keep the bad guys out and the good guys honest.

9. **Outsourcing all data center security responsibilities:** Companies should never outsource 100% of their data center's security responsibilities to a third-party company. Rather, put someone in charge of making sure the third party is properly handling your physical security, compliance and other needs.

10. **No third-party security assessments or audits:** The security of data centers is a continually evolving process. Every time a new technology is introduced, a new vulnerability appears that needs to be addressed. That is why it is important to occasionally bring in a third-party auditor or consultant. Companies that outsource data center operations should consider sending auditors to the third-party company in question.

Entrances and Exits

All operations require personnel, visitors, vendors, contractors, and guests to have the ability to enter and leave as required by the facility. Typically, employees will have accessible areas that are not intended for visitors. Vendors and contractors will have requirements to make deliveries and need access to loading docks or basement entrances. An organization will not want the soft drink vender walking through their lobby with a handcart full of products, right alongside guests or business associates. It is best to designate specific entry and exit points with the use of signage to direct pedestrian traffic to the correct locations.

Lobby Entrances

Companies having a main entrance and lobby area typically use it as the main thoroughfare for employees, but it is also designated for guests and visitors. The receptionist at this post is a vital component of the access control system and gives visitors their "first impression" of the company (Figure 3.17). It is always necessary to have this post staffed with a professional who is friendly, positive, and polite. This person will also be the gatekeeper for the main entrance and needs to be vigilant against unauthorized entries.

Overall, the requirements of a sound visitor management system are about controlling access to the facility, knowing who is in the building, and making employees accountable for their visitors. It requires all visitors entering the facility to be greeted by the receptionist. The receptionist will then determine who the visitor is to meet. They will contact the intended employee and verify that they are indeed expecting a visitor. Have the employee they are visiting personally come to the lobby and meet the guest and escort them to the business meeting or function.

I find this to have two benefits. One, it is common courtesy to your guest to not have him or her traverse the hallways searching for the right conference room or office. The other is a common security measure: do not let visitors have unconditional access to your facility. There should be some type of controlled waiting area within the lobby, so the receptionist can keep track of the visitors and can direct the employee to them, in the event they have never met previously.

There are many businesses where lobby and entry security is nonexistent, and guest or visitors would be allowed unescorted entry into the facility. This approach is not an acceptable security practice, for so many reasons. One, you have no idea who is inside

Figure 3.17   The receptionist at the main entrance and lobby area is a vital component of the access control system and gives visitors their "first impression" of the company.

your facility. From the standpoint of employees, it can be unnerving to turn around and have an uninvited salesman standing at their door or even in their cubicle. It is in everyone's best interest to have a sound visitor management system in place.

Visitors are given temporary badges, but this badge does not double as an access card. The temporary badge will be issued at an entry control point only after the visitor discloses the purpose of the visit and is approved by the employee being visited. In some organizations, only certain employees may approve visitor access, along with the day and time of the visit. In many operations, the visitor is escorted at all times while inside the facility. When the visitor arrives, he or she will present a form of photo identification, such as a driver's license to the receptionist for verification. Some visitor badges are constructed of paper and may have a feature that causes a void line to appear after a preset time period. Typically, the pass is dated and issued for a set period, usually one day. In most cases, visitors will wear conspicuous badges that identify them as visitors and clearly indicate whether an escort is required (often done with color-coded badges). If an escort is required, the assigned person should be identified by name and held responsible for the visitor at all times while he or she is on the premises.[8]

A visitor management system can be a pen-and-paper system that records basic information about visitors to the facility. Typical information found in an entry includes the visitor's name, reason for the visit, date of visit, and the check-in and check-out times.

"The lobby is the single-most important security point in any building or facility where protection of personnel and property is paramount," says Richard Grassie, a Certified Protection Professional (CPP) and president of TECHMARK Security Integration, Inc. "Security around visitor management has to be nearly flawless." Grassie says a complete lobby system must be in place that supports security physically, electronically, and procedurally. Visitor management systems are an integral element of the total system and must be capable of

- Accurately and quickly capturing visitors' pictures, signatures, business cards, and drivers' license information
- Authenticating their ID or credentials
- Performing discreet security checks using watch lists
- Creating one-time-use visitor badges that feature the visitor's photo, name, affiliation, host name, and authorized areas of access, as well as the badge's expiration time
- Allowing employees to register visitors online ahead of time—and be notified electronically or by phone when a visitor arrives

There are many software products available for visitor management and visitor control. It is the responsibility of the receptionist to initiate contact and proceed with identifying visitors and processing them into the visitor management system that has been established for the company. There are companies that utilize a standard log book for maintaining records of visitors and depending on the amount of visitors and the requirements of the organization, this may be functional.

An automated visitor control system offers benefits beyond security. In addition to strengthening facility security, visitor management systems also

- **Improve productivity**—Visitors are preregistered electronically, and multiple visitors can be processed simultaneously. The system can be integrated with the facility's existing e-mail system, as well as other business and security systems. It also can be used to set up meetings and attendee lists.
- **Enhance your image**—Badges should be professionally made. Visitors are processed efficiently and professionally, eliminating large waiting lines in the lobby.
- **Improve visitor service**—Because they are preregistered or can be registered quickly, visitors are made to feel expected and welcome.
- **Control resources**—The system can track assets and deliveries, and provide traffic reports for resource planning.
- **Enhance emergency response**—If the building must be evacuated, the system can be used to determine the presence and location of visitors within the facility.

"A digital system is a more secure way for a lobby guard to authorize a visit—rather than through word of mouth or the visitors' claim," Grassie says. "An automated system, used properly and effectively by lobby personnel, can significantly heighten facility security—and process visitors quickly."

Other types of visitor management systems use a computer-based system or specific visitor software product. They can either be manually inserted into the system by the receptionist or on a higher-end visitor management system, the visitor provides the receptionist with identification, such as a driver's license, or a government or military ID. The receptionist then swipes the person's identification through a reader. The system automatically populates the database with ID information and recognizes whether the ID is properly formatted or false. The receptionist registering the guest identifies the group to which the person belongs: guest, client, vendor, or contractor. Then the badge is printed.

There are other functions that can be enabled with a reusable visitor badge that has been programmed into the access control system from the receptionist desk. In this scenario, even after an employee who is escorting the visitor proceeds into the facility, the visitor will still be required to use the visitor badge to gain entry. There will then be an electronic time stamp of when this visitor went into the facility, and if the badge is not returned, it can be deactivated so that it will not be able to be used for access. It is then just a worthless piece of plastic.

For facilities that have large meetings with outside guests, it is recommended that the initiating internal group that is putting on the meeting prepare a visitor log with the individual's name and organization. This will assist the receptionist in preparing badges in advance and having them ready for the meeting day. The same principle of escorting individuals applies, and from a security standpoint, one escort employee can properly control five visitors.

Lobbies are the central meeting point and entry area for a facility. This area can be quite busy, and an opportunistic attacker could take advantage of a lone receptionist who is busy with a legitimate guest, and walk into the facility unnoticed. In this case, it is better to have a receptionist desk manned by two persons during busy hours. The receptionist desk should be positioned so that the entire lobby and the entry and exit doors are visible. The receptionist during peak hours can concentrate on guests and visitors, and a guard can concentrate on entry control measures. Ensure that all personnel entering the facility have a valid access badge and that the picture matches the holder. An access visitor management system can be incorporated so that the guard can identify if the badge is valid by scanning the badge prior to entry. When an employee/contractor swipes his or her badge, a picture, name, employee number, and badge status will appear on the monitor for the guard to verify.

Turnstiles and Mantraps

A common and frustrating loophole in an otherwise secure access control system can be the ability of an unauthorized person to follow through a checkpoint behind an authorized person, called "piggybacking" or "tailgating."

Figure 3.18 One solution to the "piggybacking" or "tailgating" problem is an airlock-style arrangement called a "mantrap," in which a person opens one door and waits for it to close before the next door will open.

The traditional solution is an airlock-style arrangement called a "mantrap" (Figure 3.18) in which a person opens one door and waits for it to close before the next door will open. A footstep-detecting floor can be added to confirm there is only one person passing through. A correctly constructed mantrap or portal will provide for tailgate detection while allowing for roller luggage, briefcases, and other large packages to pass without causing nuisance alarms. People attempting to enter side by side are detected by an optional overhead sensing array. The mantrap controller prevents entry into secured areas if unauthorized access is attempted.

Another system that is available is a turnstile (Figure 3.19), which can be used as a supplemental control to assist a guard or receptionist to control access to a protected area. Anyone who has gone to a sporting event has gone through a turnstile. In this approach, the individual's badge is used to control the turnstile arm and allow entry into the facility.

A higher-end turnstile is an optical turnstile (Figure 3.20) that is designed to provide secure access control in the lobby of a busy building. This system is designed as a set of parallel pedestals that form lanes, which allow entry or exit. Each barrier is equipped with photoelectric beams, guard arms, and a logic board.

To gain access to the interior of the building, an authorized person uses his or her access card at the optical turnstile. When the access card is verified, the guard arm is dropped, the photoelectric beam is temporarily shut off, and the cardholder passed without generating an alarm.

The concept behind these options is to create a secure perimeter just inside the building to ensure that only authorized people proceed further into the building, thereby creating a secure working environment.

Figure 3.19   A turnstile can be used as a supplemental control to assist a guard or receptionist while controlling access into a protected area.

Figure 3.20   A higher end turnstile is an optical turnstile, which is designed to provide a secure access control in the lobby of a busy building.

Anti-Passback

In high-security areas, a card reader is utilized on both entry and exit sides of the door. This keeps a record of who went in and out. Anti-passback is a strategy in which a person must present a credential to enter an area or facility, and then again use the credential to "badge out." This makes it possible to know how long a person is in an area, and to know who is in the area at any given time. This requirement also has the advantage of instant personnel accountability during an emergency or hazardous event. Anti-passback programming prevents users from giving their cards or PIN number to someone else to gain access to the restricted area. In a rigid anti-passback configuration, a credential or badge is used to enter an area, and that same credential must be used to exit it. If a credential holder fails to properly "badge-out," entrance into the secured area can be denied.

Two-Man Rule

This is a security strategy in which two people must be in an area together, making it impossible for a person to be in the area alone. Two-man rule programming is optional with many access control systems. It prevents an individual cardholder from entering a selected empty security area unless accompanied by at least one other person. Use of the two-man rule can help eliminate insider threats to critical areas by requiring at least two individuals to be present at any time. It is also used for life safety within a security area; if one person has a medical emergency, there will be assistance present.

Doors

Perimeter doors should consist of hollow steel doors or steel-clad doors with steel frames. Ensure that the strength of the latch and frame anchor equals that of the door and frame. Permit normal entry and egress through a limited number of doors, if possible, while accommodating emergency egress. Ensure that exterior doors into inhabited areas open outward. Locate hinges on the interior of restricted areas. Use exterior security hinges on doors opening outward to reduce their vulnerability.

If perimeter doors are made of glass, make sure that the material is constructed of a laminate material, or even stronger material. Ensure that glass doors only allow entry into a public or lobby area of the facility. High-security doors will then need to be established within the lobby area, where access will be controlled.

All doors that are installed for sensitive areas such as telephone closets, network rooms, or any area that has access control will require the door to have an automatic door closing device.

Door Locks

Electric Locks

The electric lock is a very secure method of controlling a door. An electric lock actuates the door bolt. For very secure applications, dual locks can be used. In some cases, power is applied to engage the handle, so that the user can retract the bolt instead of the electric lock door operator actually retracting the bolt. Most electric locks can have built-in position switches and request-to-exit hardware. Although offering a high security level, electric locks are expensive. A special door hinge that can accommodate a wiring harness and internal hardware to the door is required. For retrofit applications, electric locks usually require the purchase of a new door.

Electric Strikes

The difference between an electric strike and an electric lock lies in the mechanism that is activated at the door. In an electric-lock door, the bolt is moved. In an electric-strike door, the bolt remains stationary, and the strike is retracted. As in electric locks, electric strikes can be configured for fail-safe or fail-secure operation. The logic is the same. In fail-safe configuration, the strike retracts when de-energized on loss of power. This allows the door to be opened from the public side. In fail-secure configuration, the strike remains in place, causing the door to be locked from the public side, and thus requiring manual key entry to unlock the door from the public side. Again, as with electric locks, unimpeded access is allowed for in the direction of egress by manual activation of the door handle/lever when exiting from the secure side. For retrofit situations, electric strikes rarely require door replacement, which can often be done without replacing the door frame.

Magnetic Locks

The magnetic lock (Figure 3.21) is popular because it can be easily retrofitted to existing doors. The magnetic lock is surface-mounted to the door and door frame. Power is applied to magnets continuously to keep the door closed. Magnetic locks are normally fail-safe.

Figure 3.21   The magnetic lock is popular because it can be easily retrofitted to existing doors. The magnetic lock is surface-mounted to the door and doorframe. Power is applied to magnets continuously to hold the door closed. Magnetic locks are normally fail-safe.

Magnetic locks do have a security disadvantage. In requirements for life safety codes, doors equipped with magnetic locks are required to have one manual device (emergency manual override button) and an automatic sensor (typically, a passive infrared sensor (PIR) or request-to-exit) to override the door lock signal when someone approaches the door in the exit direction. All locks are controlled by a card reader that when activated will release the secured side portion of the door and allow entry into the facility. While enhancing overall building safety, the addition of these extra devices allows possible compromise of the door lock. In the scenario, where a REX (request to exit device) is used with magnetic locks, it not only turns off the alarm when the individual exits but also deactivates the locking device. This can be a problem if an adversary can get something through or under the door to cause the REX to release the magnetic lock.

Exit Technologies

While access control is principally concerned with entry requirements, it is a fundamental responsibility to provide for safe egress from the facility. Life safety codes in most jurisdictions dictate that personnel cannot be locked in such that they cannot freely exit. When an opening is locked from the outside and free exit is required from the inside or secure side, there are several methods that can be employed.

The simplest door hardware is a "crash bar." This strictly mechanical device merely requires exiting personnel to hit the "push-to-unlock" bar. If an electric strike is used as a door lock, generally the door has a twist door-knob handle that allows free exit.

If magnetic locks are used to secure the door, then both an automatic and manual method of existing the door must be provided. Generally, the manual method is a Request to Exit button, sometimes abbreviated as a REX. When this device is pressed, power to the door locks is shunted, allowing exit. The most common form of an automatic sensing device that will release the door lock when a person approaches a door in the exiting direction is a passive infrared sensor (PIR). This device senses the infrared heat signature of a person and automatically shunts door lock power, allowing free exit. PIRs have a significant security loophole in that any person passing by or loitering in the sensing area of the opening can activate the PIR and shunt door lock power. For this reason, magnetic locks should be the designer's last choice for door-locking mechanisms.

The access control system can also be tied into the fire control system. In the event of a fire alarm, the doors with electric strikes can be set for "fail secure," which allows the door to maintain security integrity by keeping the doors locked to prevent entry but allowing free egress from the facility. The system can also designate the doors to be "fail safe," which releases all locking devices and allows for a free flow in or out until the alarm is cancelled. The downside is that it can allow unauthorized entry into the building if the fire alarm is pulled.

Mobile Devices

Laptops

When using a piece of portable equipment, such as a laptop, regardless of whether it is being used inside the facility or is being removed for legitimate business outside of the facility, simple protection methods need to be employed in order to maintain the security of the equipment. "No laptop should contain sensitive information on the hard drive or the hard drive should be removed and carried separately from the machine. It is estimated that one in four laptops will be stolen, so this is a very real threat. Let the machine go but make sure there is no company information going with it." [9] However, this may not be a practical approach, depending on your business. There are many options available for the protection of laptops. Other methods of maintaining the security of your laptop are as follows:

Use a cable lock: Cable locks are a simple means of protecting a laptop regardless of whether it is used in the office or at a hotel during travel. They deter casual theft, and as long as you pick something secure to lock your laptop to, you will not have to fret about it at work when you leave for lunch or back at the hotel when you head out to dinner. Be sure to lock up your laptop whenever you have to leave it unattended.

Do not leave your laptop unattended: For example, when you are going through security at the airport, and they make you put your laptop through the x-ray machine, send it through last, and then stand there and wait for it so no one can grab it while you are taking off your shoes, and so forth.

Use strong passwords: Do not use an easily guessable password. The stronger your password is, the less likely it is that an attacker can gain access to your machine. Make up a combination of numbers, letters, and symbols for your password, which will make life much more difficult for malicious users and password-guessing programs.

Encrypt your data: If your computer gets stolen or hacked, it will be next to impossible for thieves and hackers to access the sensitive data. Besides, apart from the potentially painful expense of having to replace your laptop, you might have just handed over some very expensive corporate data or personal information that far outweighs the cost of the hardware.

According to Crisp Report,[10] "Lost Laptops = Lost Data," there are seven steps to prevent laptop loss:

Step 1: Conduct an audit to determine where laptops are used within the organization. This audit determines specific information about a company's laptops, such as where they are being used in the organization, how many are in the inventory, who is using them, for what purpose, and what type of data is residing on each one.

Step 2: Determine whether specific employees need a laptop to do their jobs. If a laptop is not required, it should be replaced with a desktop unit. If the laptop is an essential part of the employee's work, the next steps should be pursued.

Step 3: Classify data on the laptop according to organizational guidelines. The classification scheme should be specific to the organization and its culture. A number of classification models are available. The one selected should be clearly understood, implemented, and followed by all employees.

Step 4: Determine if data residing on each laptop is necessary for employees to complete their jobs. If not, the data should be removed. If the data is necessary, the next step should be pursued.

Step 5: Conduct a risk assessment to determine possible theft scenarios for the data stored, processed, or transmitted by laptop. Devise appropriate security measures to protect both the data and the laptop. The assessment puts the required physical, procedural, and electronic security measures into perspective, as well as the necessary security awareness training. Obviously, the higher the classification of the data, the more the security measures that should be in place.

Step 6: Implement the required protection strategies. These detailed lists provide templates for implementing a comprehensive security program. Protective strategies start with security awareness programs; employees must understand their obligation to use the security measures required to protect laptops and data. Employees should be required to indicate, in writing, that they understand the established laptop and data protection guidelines. Department managers and senior managers should show their support for the policy by signing similar forms. Both facility and IT security personnel have special responsibilities for implementing the policy, and should indicate their willingness to assist on the appropriate forms.

Step 7: Create a loss response team to monitor laptops and data. Should a loss occur, the affected employees should be required to report the loss in writing. The team then responds to the report by investigating the loss and determining the scope of the data breach. In addition, the team should be regularly educating users, conducting audits to ensure compliance, annually assessing data needs, and destroying or removing data when it is no longer required. This process is cyclical, because new laptops and data enter and leave the organization on a regular basis.

Lo-Jack for Laptops: While there are plenty of products that help prevent theft, there are very few tools that will help to recover your laptop in the event of a theft. Several companies offer software that can be installed into the BIOS of your laptop. If your laptop is stolen, you would initiate a police report and contact the software company's monitoring station, which will activate the tracking software inside the laptop. If the laptop is connected to the Internet, the tracking software will locate the laptop and notify law enforcement.

Cell Phones

The cell phone has become an indispensable piece of equipment. It provides for instant communication with staff, clients, and family and stores a wealth of information that would be beneficial to subversive entities. The cell phones of today not only have information on phone activity but text messaging along with e-mail capacity. To prevent your phone from being stolen, always keep it in sight. It is amazing how fast a cell phone can disappear in a public area even if you take your eyes off it for a few seconds. If you carry your phone in a cell phone case or pouch attached to your belt, consider a belt loop type case or pouch. A belt either wraps around your belt or you thread your belt through the loop.

Many people believe that using cell phones protects their conversations from unwanted listeners. This depends on the phone you are using, who you are calling, and the cell phone he or she is using. All digital phones, such as GSM/PCS types, the ones that use a smart chip, are essentially impossible to monitor over the air. No over-the-air intercepts have been publicly recorded. These mobile phones use a strong encryption scheme that encodes voice traffic flowing between the mobile and the cell site. However, always remember that if you need privacy, watch what you say over the phone.

However, as with the incident involving Paris Hilton's cell phone, cell phones can be hacked and information retrieved. According to Hackingalert.com, cell phone hackers have apparently found a glitch in the way the chips are manufactured. The good news, though, is that it only applies to the first-generation models of cell phones that use the Global System for Mobile communications (GSM). Another requirement is that the hacker have physical access to the cell phone for at least 3 minutes, which is a real good reason to not let it out of your sight. Currently, although the problem has been remedied (at least for now) in the second- and third-generation phones, it seems that about 70% of existing cell phones are unprotected.[10]

Bluetooth: The common uses of Bluetooth technology include

- Using a wireless mobile phone headset during a call while keeping a phone in the bag
- Synchronizing a calendar, phone book, and other information between a PDA and a PC
- Connecting a printer, keyboard, or mouse to a PC without cables
- Transferring photos or ring tones between mobile phones

A hacker using off-the-shelf components such as a LinkSys BT100 USB Bluetooth Adaptor and 19Dbi Panel Antenna can walk around with his computer and can literally pick up your cell phone data if it is turned on. This is more applicable to cell phones that use Bluetooth technology.

There are some common tasks connected with Bluetooth security that for most users require the "pairing" of devices. This is how two devices on a crowded street associate with each other and do not link up with all the other Bluetooth devices carried by everyone else.

Another simple setting is to have your Bluetooth set to a "nondiscoverable" mode, which prevents the device from appearing on the list during a Bluetooth device search process.

According to *Computerworld*, when using Bluetooth devices, the following security precautions are critical for protecting the system:

1. The device and its software must be configured according to tested and established policies. Never leave the device in its default configuration.
2. Choose a PIN that is strong, long, and unsystematic. If the PIN is out of band, it is impossible for the attacker to intercept.
3. To protect the BD_ADDR and its keys, set up the device in nondiscoverable mode until pairing and then set it back to the same mode after pairing. Use a PIN to access the device before communication begins—this protects the user if the device is lost or stolen.

Personal Digital Assistants (PDAs)

PDAs are now becoming as prevalent as laptops and are in many cases preferred for short trips. These devices are being used to store and manage more and more sensitive and critical data. Physical loss or theft is without doubt among the primary concerns; do not keep things on a PDA that you cannot afford to lose. And be vigilant—do not let it get lost or stolen.

According to Mark Desman, more and more corporate information is being loaded and stored on privately owned computer systems. PDAs are being beefed up to the level where desktop computers were a few years ago, and they are starting to look like mini mainframes. Due to their portability and, therefore, attractiveness to thieves, they present many significant problems.[11]

One of the best policies dealing with the protection of PDAs is to set a reasonable policy for inactivity on the PDA device that balances locking the device for protection and frustrating the user with frequent password requests. This will prevent someone who acquires one of your corporate PDAs from obtaining anything more than just the hardware.

Just as you protect your laptop data by using antivirus and firewall software, you have to take the same precautions with your PDA. The data it contains is equally valuable to both you and your company, so take the time to make sure you are doing and using all that is available to protect your PDA and the data stored on it. Although most PDAs offer password protection, passwords alone are not always enough. Encrypting your data is essential, and there are several vendors that have encryption products which will protect all data—including e-mails, attachments, contacts, calendars, and appointments—by fully encrypting it on the device using the AES-256 encryption algorithm.

Security Awareness Programs

All companies large or small can benefit from a security awareness program. A security awareness program aims to make all the employees understand and appreciate not only the value of the company's information assets but also the consequences if these assets are compromised. Knowledge is power, and educating your employees about the risks and benefits of using secure practices can only save your company time and money. The overall goal is for each employee to understand the required security measures and the importance of security to the company as a whole.

> Awareness is not training. The purpose of awareness presentations is simply to focus attention on security. Awareness presentations are intended to allow individuals to recognize IT security concerns and respond accordingly.[12]

About.com[13] states that a security awareness program can help with viruses, spyware, hacking attempts, physical premise access, and even emergency procedures for fire, etc. Some companies believe that this will never happen to them, but the statistics for monetary loss due to security breaches show that it happens all the time. Hackers who write malware or break into computer systems are no longer doing it for fame and prestige; it is now about making money. With that in mind, here are some basic precautions that a company can include in its security awareness program to keep it and its employees safe.

Just as you protect your laptop data by using antivirus and firewall software, you have to take the same precautions with your PDA. The data it contains is as valuable to you as it is to your company, so take the time to make sure you are using all that is available to protect you and your data. When looking at antivirus and firewall protection, you may find programs that work on both your laptop and PDA. Using antivirus and firewall protection should be made company policy and enforced.

Fire

Threats from fire can be potentially devastating and can affect an organization beyond the physical damage. Not only fire, but the heat, smoke, and water can cause irreversible damage. This type of damage can keep a company from ever regaining its market share and is the leading cause of environmental failures for a company.

From the National Achieves and Records Administration[14] report:

- Forty-three percent of businesses suffering a fire disaster never recover sufficiently to resume business. Of those that do reopen, only 29% are still operating two years later.
- Ninety-three percent of businesses that lost their IT (information technology) capacity to do business for more than 9 days had filed for bankruptcy within 1 year of the disaster.

- Fifty percent of those that found themselves without their data for more than 9 days filed for bankruptcy immediately thereafter.

The fire protection system should maintain life safety protection and allow for safe evacuation from the building. A facilities fire protection water system should be protected from a single-point of failure. The incoming line should be encased, buried, or located 50 feet away from high-risk areas. The interior mains should be looped and sectionalized. Water can be your main fire suppression tool; however, for electronic equipment it will cause extreme damage.

Fire Control

To protect your server room from fire, you need to have smoke detectors installed and linked to a panel with enunciators that will warn people that there is smoke in the room. Also, it should be linked to a fire suppression system that can help put out the fire with no damage to equipment from the chemical itself. The room itself should be built with fire retardant material to decrease the chance of fire. The installation of limited combustible cabling (LCC) should be used. This product is jacketed and insulated with a fluoropolymer resin, and can hang on for as long as 20 minutes before it begins to catch fire, up to 10 times longer than a typical communication metallic plenum-rated cable.

Fire Detection/Alerting

Fire detection and alarm systems are designed to provide warning of a fire outbreak and allow for appropriate fire-fighting action to be taken before the situation gets out of control, resulting in serious damage to property and possible loss of lives.

The fire alarm panel (Figure 3.22) is the hub of the fire alarm system in a building. It is usually located on the ground floor near an entrance close to the nearest road. The fire alarm panel senses the presence of a fire by way of smoke and heat detectors. Each detector is linked back to the panel, advising of the relevant zone of the building where the fire has been detected. The panel automatically notifies the fire department of an alarm when one of its sensors locates a fire.

A smoke detector is one of the most important devices to have to warn of a pending fire, coupled with a good signaling device. A detector in proper working condition will sound an alarm and give all occupants a chance to make it out alive. There are two main categories of smoke detectors, optical detection (photoelectric) and physical process (ionization). Photoelectric detectors are classified as either beam or refraction. Beam detectors operate on the principle of light and a receiver. Once enough smoke enters the room and breaks the beam of light, the alarm is sounded. The refraction type has a blocker between the light and the receiver. Once enough smoke enters the room, the light is deflected around the beam to the signal.

Figure 3.22   The fire alarm panel is the hub of the fire alarm system in a building.

The ionization-type detector monitors the air around the sensors constantly. Once there is enough smoke in the room, the alarm will sound.

The use of smoke detectors is very crucial; most deaths that occur in a fire are not from the fire or the flames. Most deaths are from smoke inhalation, heat, the toxic gasses produced by fires, and explosion or panic. According to the National Fire Prevention Association,[15] in 2006 alone there were 3,245 deaths caused by fire, over 16,000 injuries due to fire, and over 11 billion dollars in property damage. Nationwide, there is a civilian death due to fires every 162 minutes. With these statistics, we cannot afford to ignore the need for a proper fire execution plan.

Remember the old saying "where there is smoke, there must be fire"? There are three main types of fire detectors: they are flame detectors, smoke detectors, and heat detectors. There are two main types of flame detectors, and they are classified as infrared (IR) and ultraviolet (UV) detectors. IR detectors primarily detect a large mass of hot gases that emit a specific spectral pattern in the location of the detector; these patterns are sensed with a thermographic camera, and an alarm is sounded. Additional hot surfaces in the room may trigger a false response with this alarm. UV flame detectors detect flames at speeds of 3–4 milliseconds due to the high-energy radiation emitted by fires and explosions at the instant of their ignition. Some of the false alarms of this system include random UV sources such as lightning, radiation, and solar radiation that may be present in the room.

There are heat detectors that include fixed temperature or rate of rise detectors. This is a real simple concept for all users. The user will set a predetermined temperature level for the alarm to sound. If the room temperature rises to that setting, the alarm will sound. Rate of rise temperature will detect a sudden change of temperature around the sensor. Usually this setting is at around 10–15 degrees per minute. Nothing more is really required of the consumer except routine checks for battery life and operational status. Heat detectors should not be used to replace smoke detectors; each component in fire safety serves its purpose and should be taken seriously. The combination of devices and knowledge of procedures is the only way to deal successfully with a possible fire.

Fire Suppression

Fire requires three elements to burn: heat, oxygen, and a fuel source. Fire extinguishers and fire suppression systems fight fires by removing one of the three elements. Fire extinguishers are divided into five categories, based on different types of fires[16]:

- **Class A** extinguishers are for ordinary combustible materials such as paper, wood, cardboard, and most plastics. The numerical rating on this type of extinguisher indicates the amount of water it holds and the amount of fire it can extinguish.
- **Class B** fires involve flammable or combustible liquids such as gasoline, kerosene, grease, and oil. The numerical rating for a class B extinguisher indicates the approximate number of square feet of fire it can extinguish.
- **Class C** fires involve electrical equipment, such as appliances, wiring, circuit breakers, and outlets. Never use water to extinguish class C fires: the risk of electrical shock is far too great! Class C extinguishers do not have a numerical rating. The C classification means the extinguishing agent is nonconductive.
- **Class D** fire extinguishers are commonly found in a chemical laboratory. They are for fires that involve combustible metals, such as magnesium, titanium, potassium, and sodium. These types of extinguishers also have no numerical rating, nor are they given a multipurpose rating—they are designed for class D fires only.
- **Class K** fire extinguishers are wet chemical discharge type and are found in a restaurant kitchen environment. The Class K extinguisher is hand portable and is the ideal choice for use on all cooking appliances, including solid fuel char broilers.

All buildings should be equipped with an effective fire suppression system, providing the building with around-the-clock protection. All facilities should have portable fire extinguishing equipment (Figure 3.23) conveniently located on each floor and especially within sensitive areas such as the data center. There is an acronym for using a fire extinguisher PASS. This stands for

Pull—the pin on the fire extinguisher
Aim—at the base of the fire

Figure 3.23   All facilities should have portable fire extinguishing equipment conveniently located on each floor and especially within sensitive areas such as the data center.

Squeeze—the handle on the extinguisher
Sweep—from side to side of the fire

Traditionally, fire suppression systems employed arrays of water sprinklers that would douse a fire and surrounding areas. Sprinkler systems are classified into four different groups: wet, dry, preaction, and deluge.

■ **Wet** systems have a constant supply of water in them at all times; these sprinklers once activated will not shut off until the water source is shut off.
■ **Dry** systems do not have water in them. The valve will not release water until the electric valve is stimulated by excess heat.
■ **Preaction** systems incorporate a detection system, which can eliminate concerns of water damage due to false activations. Water is held back until detectors in the area are activated.
■ **Deluge** systems operate in the same function as the preaction system except that all sprinkler heads are in the open position.

Water may be a sound solution for large physical areas such as warehouses, but it is entirely inappropriate for computer equipment. A water spray can irreparably damage hardware more quickly than encroaching smoke or heat. Gas suppression systems operate to starve the fire of oxygen. In the past, halon was the choice for gas suppression systems; however, halon leaves residue, depletes the ozone layer, and can injure nearby personnel.

There are two gas suppression systems that are recommended for fire suppression in a server room or anywhere electronic equipment is employed:

1. Aero-K uses an aerosol of microscopic potassium compounds in a carrier gas released from small canisters mounted on walls near the ceiling. The Aero-K generators are not pressurized until fire is detected. The Aero-K system uses multiple fire detectors and will not release until a fire is "confirmed" by two or more detectors (limiting accidental discharge). The gas is noncorrosive, so it does not damage metals or other materials. It does not harm electronic devices or media such as tape or discs. More important, Aero-K is nontoxic and does not injure personnel.
2. FM-200 is a colorless, liquefied compressed gas. It is stored as a liquid and dispensed into the hazard as a colorless, electrically nonconductive vapor that is clear and does not obscure vision. It leaves no residue and has acceptable toxicity for use in occupied spaces at design concentration. FM-200 does not displace oxygen and, therefore, can be safely used in occupied spaces without fear of oxygen deprivation. The advantage of FM-200 is that it is safe. People can be in the room when it goes off and it is totally harmless to electronic equipment, but the downside is the cost.

Defense In Depth

The primary goal of a physical protection program is to control entry into the facility. With defense in depth, barriers are arranged in layers with the level of security growing progressively higher as one comes closer to the center or the highest protective area (Figure 3.24). Defending an asset with a multiple posture can reduce the likelihood of a successful attack; if one layer of protection fails, another layer of protection will hopefully prevent the attack, and so on.

A defense-in-depth system, by design, has more features and layers, which the adversary would need to defeat in order to gain access to the objective of the system design. An adversary would spend more time trying to defeat the multiple levels of protection, thereby increasing his chances of being caught by security personnel. Because a defense-in-depth system is designed with greater emphasis on deter, delay, and response, the chances of being caught increase with every level of the system.

This design requires the attacker to circumvent multiple defensive mechanisms to gain access to the targeted asset. "Implementing protection-in-depth requires that the security practitioner understand the goals of security. Essentially, security can be distilled down to three basic elements: availability, integrity, and confidentiality.

Figure 3.24 The primary goal of a physical protection program is to control access into the facility. In defense in depth, barriers are arranged in layers with the level of security growing progressively higher as one comes closer to the center or the highest protective area.

Availability addresses the fact that legitimate users require resources, which should be available to the users as needed. Integrity relates to the concept that information is whole, complete, and remains unchanged from its true state. Confidentiality can be defined as ensuring that data is available to only those individuals that have legitimate access to it." [17]

For example, consider the layers of security at a local bank; there are many redundant measures to protect personnel and assets. The fortress-like appearance and protective reputation that is synonymous with banking is likely to deter some would-be bank robbers but, of course, not all. The next line of defense that serves as both a deterrent and as a means for suspect apprehension and asset recovery is security cameras. This layer of security obviously has a level of failure; how many times have we seen video of bank robberies showing a suspect who was never caught. If the cameras are considered ineffective, the next layer is an armed security guard present both as a deterrent factor, and to physically defend the bank. This too is not 100% effective as the security guard can be neutralized by the intruder.

If the security guard is overpowered, the next layer involves hardware, such as bulletproof glass and electronically locked doors. Of course, not all branch offices are fortified in this manner, leaving the bank tellers vulnerable. In this case, the teller must rely on the silent alarm button, dye packs, and robbery training. Some branches also have double time-release doors where people are slightly delayed during ingress and egress.

The vault itself has defense in depth through multiple layers of defense, such as opening only at certain controlled times, its heavy metal construction, and multiple compartments that require further access.

The defense-in-depth principle may seem somewhat contradictory to the "secure the weakest link" principle, because we are essentially saying that defenses taken as a whole can be stronger than the weakest link. However, there is no contradiction; the principle "secure the weakest link" applies when components have security functionality that does not overlap. But when it comes to redundant security measures, it is indeed possible that the sum protection offered is far greater than the protection offered by any single component.[18]

Of course, all of these defenses collectively do not ensure that the bank will never be successfully robbed, even banks with this much security. If the bad guy wants to rob the bank, he is going to give it his best effort. Nonetheless, it is quite obvious that the sum total of all these defenses results in a far more effective security system than any one of these defenses alone. This does not mean that every known defensive measure should be indiscriminately applied in every situation. Using risk, vulnerability, and threat assessment, a balance has to be found between security provided by the defense-in-depth approach, and the financial, human, and organizational resources management is willing to expend.

The key to a successful system is the integration of people, procedures, and equipment into a system that protects the targets from the threat. A well-designed system provides defense in depth, minimizes the consequences of component failures, and exhibits balanced protection.[19]

Physical protection is no different from computer security and, in fact, dovetails into the processes: you perform a threat analysis, design a system that involves equipment and procedures, and then test it. The system itself typically has a number of elements that fall into the essence of *deter–detect–delay–respond.*

Deter is meant to make a facility an unattractive target so that an adversary abandons attempts to infiltrate or attack. Examples of deterrence are the presence of security guards, adequate lighting at night, signage, and the use of barriers, such as fencing or bars on windows. While deterrence can be very helpful in discouraging attacks by adversaries, it cannot stop an adversary who chooses to attack regardless of your defenses. Nothing is going to stop the bank robber who is bent on robbing the bank. The deterrent value of a true physical protection system can be very high while at the same time providing protection of assets in the event of an attack.

Detect involves the use of appropriate devices, systems, and procedures to signal that an attempted or actual unauthorized access has occurred. It will have one or more layers of barriers and sensors that will be utilized to keep out casual intruders, detect deliberate intruders, and make it difficult for them to defeat your defensive security easily.

Delay involves delaying a perpetrator by the use of layered defenses. This will delay the attack for a sufficient period of time to allow a response force time to confront and intercept the intruder.

Response requires communication to a response force that an unauthorized person is attempting to or has entered the facility. The response force is required to intercept the adversary before an attack has occurred or has been completed.

Security systems are often designed utilizing multiple barriers—"rings of protection"—encircling the protected asset. Layered barrier designs are advantageous when increased knowledge, skill, and talent are required to circumvent them. A group of attackers with the necessary skills must be assembled, and because group secrecy is hard to maintain, the likelihood of being discovered is increased. Layered barriers also afford a greater time delay because each safety layer requires time to circumvent. This helps to provide the necessary delay in the event that the response time is relatively slow.

A system with defense in depth is one that has a number of protective devices in sequence. This is a great advantage because an adversary not only has to avoid or defeat one system, he has to avoid or defeat several. The actions and times required to penetrate each of these layers may not necessarily be equal, and the effectiveness of each may be quite different, but each will require a separate and distinct action by the adversary moving along the path. Each of these systems will require the adversary to use a separate and distinct action as he moves through. The effect produced on the adversary by a system that provides defense in depth over one that is very secure at one level is: it will increase uncertainty about the system; it will require more extensive preparations prior to attacking the system; and it will create additional opportunities for the adversary to fail or abort the mission.

Protection Plans

The primary foundation of effective building security requires careful planning, design, and management of the physical protection system, in order to integrate people, procedures, and equipment into the process. Protecting a building, its occupants, and related assets can pose a complex problem, and there is no perfect defense to all of the potential threats a target may face. Optimizing building security with respect to performance, cost, and efficiency ultimately requires compromise and balance in the application and consideration of people, procedures, and equipment. The fundamental aspects of building operations, however, are built upon three basic components: people, procedure, and technology. The combination of these elements contributes to overall organizational security as well as providing the basis for effective emergency preparation and response.

People are the most important consideration for any security plan. People are not considered expendable assets. Yes, people can be replaced with new personnel, but they are still an asset that must be protected to the greatest extent possible. Personnel within an organization have specific functions depending on the department in which they work and the expertise they possess. A successful plan takes into consideration which departments need to be functional in the shortest amount of time possible. It is important to understand the pattern of movement of a building's occupants. This will help to ensure the procedures outlined in the plan take into account where the highest concentration of personnel may be located. With the examination of people within an organization, it is important to determine the type of security personnel an organization will use. Contract or proprietary personnel can be utilized. The most effective and efficient methods and locations to deploy those security personnel assets must also be determined.

The other category of people is those who provide protection. In the people element of security operations, the integration of people as a layer of security in the form of security guards and other security personnel is another consideration. The architectural layout of the building can be designed to influence the movement of people for rapid evacuation, limited congregation, increased visibility, and to limit the need for a large amount of security personnel.

Security is a dynamic process, and for it to be effective, it must be procedural in nature. For example, emergency response and business continuity plans must be developed well in advance of a critical incident and must define the plan of action or steps to be taken in a logical, orderly, and procedural manner. The development of procedures involves planning for such events as evacuation, emergency response, and disaster recovery in response to fires, natural disasters, and criminal intrusions. Policies and procedures are then developed to assist with the proper response and recovery actions in the event a crisis strikes. It should be noted that policies and procedures are guides to actions that should be taken in the event of an emergency, and should not be inflexibly construed. No critical incident is the same, and it would be impossible to develop a procedure for every possible event that could occur. Procedures should be written in such a way that they can be adapted to any application.

The third element of the security operation, technology, involves hardware, electronics, and other equipment used in the security mission. In building security design, technologies can be built in or retrofitted into the existing structure to perform a variety of functions such as access control, surveillance, personnel screening, intrusion detection, and fortification. Technology has also advanced competitive intelligence and espionage. Global positioning systems and high-resolution surveillance are pushing security to new levels. There is technology now that can track an item taken from a facility via GPS with a tiny sensor attached or scanned onto it.

These elements of security, people, procedures, and technology are interdependent because they rely on each other to be effective. For example, the behaviors and needs of people dictate what procedures and equipment may be deployed; procedures depend on people to be effective; and equipment requirements depend on the particular procedures to be followed in a critical incident. A cost-effective and comprehensive plan necessitates a balance of these three elements, taking into account their particular contribution to the mission; one application may be security personnel intensive, where as another may be equipment intensive.

Evacuation Drills

From the days when we were all in grade school, we have all been aware of the need to have fire drills. Every organization should have an emergency management plan developed in partnership with public safety agencies, including law enforcement, fire, and local emergency preparedness agencies. The plan should address fire, natural, and manmade disasters. An organization's plan should be tailored to address the unique circumstances and needs of the operation. For example, organizations on the east coast of the United States do not need to prepare for earthquakes, but all operations in California will put this as one of their top-priority drills.

Staff training, particularly for those with specific responsibilities during an event, will include a combination of security personnel, facilities, and selected employees designated as floor fire wardens. Holding regularly scheduled practice drills, similar to the common fire drill, allows for plan testing, as well as employee and key staff rehearsal of the plan, and increases the likelihood of success in an actual event.

If the organization has a visitor management software program incorporated with access control, this will provide a system for knowing who is in your building, including customers and visitors.

In the United States, the FEMA Emergency Management Guide for Business and Industry outlines specific areas that need to be addressed and implemented during an evacuation of a facility:

1. Decide in advance who has the authority to order an evacuation. Create a chain of command so that others are authorized to act in case your designated person is not available. If local officials tell you to evacuate, do so immediately.
2. Identify who will shut down critical operations and lock the doors, if possible, during an evacuation.
   - Choose employees most able to make decisions that emphasize personal safety first.
   - Train others who can serve as a backup if the designated person is unavailable.
   - Write down, distribute, and practice evacuation procedures.
3. Locate and make copies of building and site maps with critical utility and emergency routes clearly marked.
   - Identify and clearly mark entry–exit points both on the maps and throughout the building.
   - Post maps for quick reference by employees.
   - Keep copies of building and site maps with your crisis management plan and other important documents in your emergency supply kit and also at an off-site location.
   - Make copies available to first responders or other emergency personnel.

4. Plan two ways out of the building from different locations throughout your facility.

5. Consider the feasibility of installing emergency lighting or plan to use flashlights in case the power goes out.

6. Establish a warning system.
   - Test systems frequently.
   - Plan to communicate with people who are hearing impaired or have other disabilities and those who do not speak the local language.

7. Designate an assembly site.
   - Pick one location near your facility and another in the general area in case you have to move farther away.
   - Talk to your people in advance about the importance of letting someone know if you cannot get to the assembly site or if you must leave it.
   - Ensure the assembly site is away from traffic lanes and is safe for pedestrians.

8. Try to account for all workers, visitors, and customers as people arrive at the assembly site.
   - Take a head count.
   - Use a prepared roster or checklist.
   - Ask everyone to let others know if they are leaving the assembly site.

9. Determine who is responsible for providing an all-clear or return-to-work notification. Plan to cooperate with local authorities responding in an emergency.

10. Plan for **people with disabilities** who may need help getting out in an emergency.

11. If your business operates out of more than one location or has more than one place where people work, establish evacuation procedures for each individual building.

12. If your company is in a high-rise building, an industrial park, or even a small strip mall, it is important to coordinate and practice with other tenants or businesses to avoid confusion and potential gridlock.

13. If you rent, lease, or share space with other businesses, make sure the building owner and other companies are committed to coordinating and practicing evacuation procedures together.

There are also special requirements if you are in a high-rise building, which is a building with more than seven floors:

1. Note where the closest emergency exit is.
2. Be sure you know another way out in case your first choice is blocked.
3. Take cover against a desk or table if objects are falling.
4. Move away from file cabinets, bookshelves, or other objects that might fall.
5. Face away from windows and glass.
6. Move away from exterior walls.
7. Listen for and follow instructions.

8. Take your emergency supply kit, unless there is reason to believe it has been contaminated.
9. Do not use elevators.
10. Stay to the side while going down stairwells to allow emergency workers to come up.

There may also be requirements to shelter-in-place. There may be situations when it is best to stay where you are to avoid any uncertainty outside. There are other circumstances, such as during a tornado or a chemical incident, when specifically how and where you take shelter is a matter of survival. You should understand the different threats and plan for all possibilities. FEMA has developed a system to put into place if you are instructed by local authorities to take shelter.

Determine where you will take shelter in case of a **tornado warning:**

1. Storm cellars or basements provide the best protection.
2. If underground shelter is not available, go into an interior room or hallway on the lowest floor possible.
3. In a high-rise building, go to a small interior room or hallway on the lowest floor possible.
4. Stay away from windows, doors, and outside walls. Go to the center of the room. Stay away from corners because they attract debris.
5. Stay in the shelter location until the danger has passed.

If local authorities believe the air is badly contaminated with a chemical, you may be instructed to "shelter-in-place" and seal the room (Figure 3.25). The process used to seal the room is considered a temporary protective measure to create a barrier between your people and potentially contaminated air outside. It is a type of sheltering that requires preplanning.

1. Identify a location to "seal the room" in advance.
   - If feasible, choose an interior room, such as a break room or conference room, with as few windows and doors as possible.
   - If your business is located on more than one floor or in more than one building, identify multiple shelter locations.
2. To seal the room effectively:
   - Close the business, and bring everyone inside.
   - Lock doors, and close windows, air vents, and fireplace dampers.
   - Turn off fans, air conditioning, and forced air heating systems.
   - Take your emergency supply kit unless you have reason to believe it has been contaminated.
   - Go into an interior room, such as a break room or conference room, with few windows, if possible.
   - Seal all windows, doors, and air vents with plastic sheeting and duct tape. Measure and cut the sheeting in advance to save time.

Figure 3.25   Shelter-in-place is a process used to seal a room as a temporary protective measure to create a barrier between your people and potentially contaminated air outside. (Source: www.ready.gov/america/makeaplan/stayingput.html.)

- Be prepared to improvise, and use what you have on hand to seal gaps so that you create a barrier between yourself and any contamination.
- Local authorities may not immediately be able to provide information on what is happening and what you should do. However, you should watch TV, listen to the radio, or check the Internet often for official news and instructions as they become available.

Incident Response

An incident response plan takes its place beside business continuity and disaster-recovery plans as a key corporate document that helps guarantee that companies will survive whatever glitch, emergency, or calamity comes their way.

According to George McBride, director of IT Risk Consulting, "The typical response to trouble—the deer-caught-in-the-headlights look—is exactly why companies need such a plan. And while a business continuity plan aims to preserve operations in the face of adversity and a disaster recovery plan details what to do in case of a disaster, an incident response plan is broader, laying out how to respond to scenarios as diverse as data security breaches and network crashes."

Plans and procedures, including recovery plans, emergency response, and evacuation, are deployed in response to different kinds of security and safety threats such as earthquakes, explosions, lightning damage, and fires. Once the plans and procedures have been established, policies can be deployed to show how security personnel respond to the foregoing threats and to assist in recovery from other incidents that may occur.

Technology involves where and how screening of personnel and materials will be accomplished, and what kinds of systems and equipment will be used. The technology must be suitable for the operations or mission of the facility.

Some communities rely on businesses to generate jobs and tax revenue and to nurture an environment that is healthy and suitable. When a business protects itself from natural disasters, it also protects one of the community's most valuable assets. There is no way to prevent a natural disaster from occurring; however, you can take action to avoid the most devastating damage your business may face. The lack of knowledge and fear of the unknown about what to do in the case of emergency has caused businesses to fail or increased their cost due to an extended recovery time. Companies have to learn to identify the risk and hazards facing their business, and determine what types of training are useful, and deal with and categorize the risk rationally. The goal of emergency preparedness is to be reasonably prepared and not to be swept up in the sea of confusion.

The best time to respond to a disaster is before it happens. A relatively small investment of time and money now may prevent severe damage and disruption of life and business in the future. Every area of the world is subject to some kind of disaster; you do not have to live on the coast to experience a severe event. Floods, hurricanes, earthquakes, ice storms, and landslides could happen anytime. With global warming and other unnatural events happening all over the world, we businesses must prepare for all possible occurrences. Every one responds to disasters differently; however, business owners can take advantage of typical human behavior in the aftermath of an event. Seek out those individuals who rise above the chaos, and get them trained and involved in recovery activities. This will improve the organization's chances for a shorter recovery time, and a successful recovery effort.

The security professional needs to put together a plan of action, and in doing so will identify areas that need to be addressed when an incident response is required. There are five topics that can be initiated and prepared for before an actual Incident Response becomes necessary.

1. **Identify what can happen**—If you have completed a security survey or risk assessment, then you have made determinations on what hazards are possible. However, you cannot possibly anticipate what will happen in a crisis or during the aftermath, but that does not mean you cannot plan for one.

2. **Put together the team**—You need to put into place the team that will be utilized during an incident response and what roles each person will play when something happens.

3. **A communication plan**—When the decision is made to initiate the incident response, how will you get in touch with the team? The plan should include the individual contact information for team members that goes well beyond office e-mail addresses and phone extensions. There should also be home phone numbers and e-mails along with mobile phone numbers.

4. **Identify who does what and when**—Good incident response plans do not just name the members of the response team; rather, they lay out who will have which responsibilities and authority so they can get right to work.

5. **Test your plan**—You do not want to find holes and glitches in your incident response plan when dealing with a fire, burst water pipe, or a bomb threat. That's why it is so important to test it ahead of time.

Design Validation

Penetration Tests

A penetration test is the best way to test your security operation. From an IT standpoint, the idea of a penetration test is immediately connected to testing the network defenses by attempting to access a system from the outside using hacker techniques. However, from the physical security aspect, there is a much more "in your face" and personal approach that needs to be addressed. There are several variations of physical penetration methods used by perpetrators, including dumpster diving, lock picking, social engineering, physical access compromise, and simulated sabotage. While these techniques may seem extreme, it is important to remember that bad guys do not follow the rules, and they do not play nice.

> Tests should be designed with the purpose of the system and the specific type of prevention desired in mind. In addition, threats evolve so quickly that penetration testing should be a regular occurrence, not just a one-time event.[20]

There are many benefits to conducting a penetration test on your facility. It will identify vulnerable areas that need to be immediately addressed. In order to determine the effectiveness of the security apparatuses in place, a penetration test is essential. It easy to say we have outstanding security personnel and a security program in place, but it is another matter to verify and confirm.

- Will the guard at the front desk actually look for a perpetrator or an individual without a badge?
- Can the guard spot a forged badge or if the picture on the badge is the same as the individual?
- Will employees stop and question someone who looks out of place inside the building? Will they contact security and notify that there is someone on their floor who does not belong?
- Will employees hold open a door for someone trying to enter through an employee-only entrance or will they make them use their access card; and does the employee-only entrance require a dual-technology badge and pin number?

Having an outside entity attempt the penetration is the best method. They look for easy accesses into the facility or they try and mingle with the crowd during morning hours when everyone is coming into work. If your facility utilizes a contract guard force, this can be done with the coordination of their upper management. There are also several companies that specialize in penetration testing. In a penetration test that I was associated with, the penetration tester was given several fake badges that had a picture on the badge that was similar to their looks but was obviously not them. If the guard was to scrutinize the badge and compare it with the holder, it would be obvious. The penetration tester was instructed to show the badge to the receptionist and attempt to enter as though they belonged. The first attempts were successful, and the penetration tester gained entry. After the receptionists were made aware and counseled by management on their assigned duties and responsibilities, a second test was conducted two months later, and this time a 70% reduction in successful penetrations resulted. Once the receptionists and guards are made aware of tests and that their response will affect their performance rating, they became true guardians of the gate.

This test was done to see if the facility can stop a person from gaining entry from a physically manned entry–exit point. But from the perspective of an all-inclusive test, there needs to be more emphasis on an all-out penetration attack.

Another perimeter area to look at: is there construction going on? Can a perpetrator put on a hard hat and walk in with the construction crew, then discard the construction gear and walk into the facility as though he belongs? How are construction, contractors, and vendors controlled?

Are secured areas truly secured? Are there layers of security within the structure or is it considered an M&M candy—hard on the outside but soft on the inside? These facilities place all the emphasis on the outer security perimeter, but once you have navigated through into the building, there are virtually no security measures.

A penetration test can determine if security measures are enforced within the building. Are all employees required to wear identification badges in plain sight while they are inside the building? Are security awareness posters displayed?

After an intruder has entered through the perimeter, can he walk into areas within the facility and go through an employee area without being disturbed? Will anyone confront him and question his presence in the area?

The penetration test will identify vulnerabilities at the perimeter, but what about exiting the facility—are there any safeguards set up to deter the removal of classified information or property from the facility?

> Does the company check for theft of sensitive material when employees exit the facility? Are laptop computers or other portable devices registered and checked when entering and exiting the building? Are security guards trained not only on what types of equipment and information to look for, but also on how equipment can be hidden or masked and why this procedure is important?[21]

Other methods used in penetration testing include a social engineering scheme, in which the attacker relies on human nature to gain access to unauthorized network resources. This could be in the form of eavesdropping or "shoulder surfing" (looking over your shoulder) to obtain access information. The basic goals of social engineering are the same as hacking in general: to gain unauthorized access to systems or information in order to commit fraud, network intrusion, industrial espionage, identity theft, or simply to disrupt the system or network. Computer Security Institute [22] gives an example of how to use social engineering to gain critical information:

The facilitator of a live Computer Security Institute demonstration neatly illustrated the vulnerability of help desks:

> He dialed up a phone company, got transferred around, and reached the help desk.
>
> *"Who's the supervisor on duty tonight?"*
> *"Oh, it's Betty."*
> *"Let me talk to Betty." [He's transferred.]*
> *"Hi Betty, having a bad day?"*
> *"No, why?"*
> *"Your systems are down."*
> She said, *"My systems aren't down, we're running fine."*
> He said, *"You better sign off."*
> She signed off.
> He said, *"Now sign on again."*
> She signed on again.
> He said, *"We didn't even show a blip, we show no change. Sign off again."*
> She did.
> *"Betty, I'm going to have to sign on as you here to figure out what's happening with your ID. Let me have your user ID and password."*
> *So this senior supervisor at the help desk tells him her user ID and password.*

Figure 3.26 "Dumpster diving" is the practice of searching through the trash of an individual or business in attempts to obtain something useful.

The natural human willingness to accept someone at his or her word leaves many of us vulnerable to attack. There is an old saying, "In God we trust, all others we verify." This needs to be instilled in staff. All employees should be trained on how to keep confidential data safe. The simple statement "I'm sorry but I do not know who you are and I will not be providing that information over the phone" will provide for a level of security.

Another of the penetration tests is the simple task of checking your trash. "Dumpster diving" is the practice of searching through the trash of an individual or business in an attempt to obtain something useful (Figure 3.26). It can also include data aggregation by looking for passwords written on sticky notes, unwanted files, letters, memos, photographs, IDs, and other paperwork that has been found in dumpsters. This oversight is a result of many people not realizing that sensitive items such as passwords, credit card numbers, and personal information they throw in the trash could be recovered anywhere from the dumpster to the landfill.

Every business has information that is confidential and must be disposed of properly. Carelessly discarded correspondence, financial statements, medical records, credit card statements, photocopies and computer printouts are all easily removed from the trash. Should this data get into the wrong hands, it can cause acute embarrassment, financial loss, or legal action. Loss of government data can result in a serious breach of national security.

Your personal information in the wrong hands can be just as damaging. Protecting your privacy is a vital necessity, and shredding has become standard practice in offices as well as homes. There are several methods for proper destruction of information. Your company can contract with a licensed and bonded shredding company that will come to your site with a mobile shredding truck and dispose of your classified material and sensitive information while you watch and verify the destruction (with a photo), or you can shred on site depending on the volume of information that needs to be destroyed. Shredding services can also have the capacity to irretrievably destroy hard drives and physical components.

The following table lists some common intrusion tactics and strategies for prevention:[23]

Area of Risk	Hacker Tactic	Combat Strategy
Phone (help desk)	Impersonation and persuasion	Train employees/help desk to never give out passwords or other confidential information by phone
Building entrance	Unauthorized physical access	Tight badge security, employee training, and security officers present
Office	Shoulder surfing	Do not type in passwords with anyone else present (or if you must, do it quickly!)
Phone (help desk)	Impersonation on help desk calls	All employees should be assigned a PIN specific to help desk support
Office	Wandering through halls looking for open offices	Require all guests to be escorted
Mail room	Insertion of forged memos	Lock and monitor mail room
Machine room/phone closet	Attempting to gain access, remove equipment, or attach a protocol analyzer to grab confidential data	Keep phone closets, server rooms, etc., locked at all times and keep updated inventory on equipment
Phone and PBX	Stealing phone toll access	Control overseas and long-distance calls, trace calls, refuse transfers
Dumpsters	Dumpster diving	Keep all trash in secured, monitored areas, shred important data, erase magnetic media

Area of Risk	Hacker Tactic	Combat Strategy
Intranet–Internet	Creation and insertion of mock software on intranet or Internet to snarf passwords	Continual awareness of system and network changes, training on password use
Office	Stealing sensitive documents	Mark documents as confidential and require those documents to be locked up
General–psychological	Impersonation and persuasion	Keep employees on their toes through continued awareness and training programs

Access Control Violation Monitoring

When doors are not physically controlled by a guard, there is a tendency for personnel to violate entry procedures. Violation of access control systems, when controlled by card reader, may occur by "tailgating" or "piggybacking," where an authorized employee with a valid entry card is accompanied by a closely spaced nonauthorized perpetrator or an authorized employee who inadvertently failed to follow proper entry procedures without considering the security consequences.

If your operation has an employee entrance that does not have a mantrap or turnstile entry system and has only a single door, there are products available to announce when a tailgate has occurred. This could be a buzzer local to the door that sounds to alert a valid cardholder to challenge someone tailgating behind them.

In higher-end security systems, the alarm may be used to alert a control room operator and trigger live closed circuit television (CCTV) images allowing immediate action to be taken. When coupled with a modern integrated security management system, a full alarm event history can be produced indicating the date, time, and location of the alarm, the cardholder who allowed someone to tailgate, and the digital CCTV images of the person tailgating.

This is why a defense-in-depth approach is necessary. If a perimeter door is compromised and an individual has gained entry into the facility, the area that has been entered will not be a high-value area, and a response team can cordon off the area that has been breached and make contact with the violator.

Maintaining an audit trail of improper entry attempts or entry violations (allowing tailgating) is a way to identify employees who need additional training on proper security entry requirements; more drastically, for continual violations, notify their supervisor, and if all else fails, revoke their badge and require them to be escorted all day. This is a drastic move, but they will only need to be escorted once by a fellow worker before they get the message and will adhere to proper security procedures.

References

1. *Security Planning and Design* (The American Institute of Architects. 2004). 92.
2. J. Gompers (7/1/2004). *Security Hot Spot: Loading Docks.* SecuritySolutions.Com.
3. FEMA. Mitigate Potential Terrorist Attacks Against Buildings. 2003/426-2.6.
4. K. O'Conner. *TDR 2006.* https://engineering.purdue.edu/TDR/Papers/10_Paper.pdf.
5. http://stats.bls.gov/OCO/OCOS159.HTM.
6. *Security Planning and Design* (The American Institute of Architects. 2004).
7. M. Brunelli (6/3/2004). *Data Center Security: 10 things not to do.* SearchCIO.com. Web site: http://searchdatacenter.techtarget.com/news/article/0,289142,sid80_gci1071551_tax305172,00.html.
8. L. Fennelly. *Effective Physical Security*, 3rd edition (Butterworth-Heinemann, 2004). 195.
9. M. Desman. *Building an Information Security Awareness Program* (Auerbach Publications, 2001). 73.
10. http://www.hackingalert.com/hacking-articles/cellphone-hacking.php. Phones fall within the first-generation category.
11. M. Desman. *Building an Information Security Awareness Program* (New York: Auerbach Publications, 2001). 72.
12. NIST Special Publication 800-16. http://csrc.nist.gov/publications/nistpubs/800-50/NIST-SP800-50.pdf.
13. http://bizsecurity.about.com/od/staffingandsecurity/a/SAwarenessP.htm.
14. http://sema.dps.mo.gov/04%20Business%20plan.pdf.
15. http://www.nfpa.org.
16. http://www.fire-extinguisher101.com/.
17. Cramsession.com (2007). *Building a Defense in Depth Toolkit.* Retrieved March 1, 2007. Website: http://www.cramsession.com/articles/get-article.asp?aid=1105.
18. J. Viega and G. McGraw. *Building Secure Software: How to Avoid Security Problems the Right Way.* (Boston, MA: Addison-Wesley. 2002).
19. M. Garcia. *Vulnerability Assessment of Physical Protection Systems* (Boston, MA: Butterworth-Heinemann, 2006). 35.
20. J. Tiller. *The Ethical Hack: A Framework for Business Value Penetration Testing* (New York: Auerbach Publications, 2004).
21. H. Tipton and M. Krause. *Information Security Management Handbook* (New York: Auerbach Publications, 2006). 181.
22. S. Granger. (12/1/2001). *Social Engineering Fundamentals, Part I: Hacker Tactics. http://www.securityfocus.com/infocus/1527.*
23. S. Granger (1/9/2002) *Social Engineering Fundamentals, Part II: Combat Strategies.* http://www.securityfocus.com/infocus/1533.

Sample Questions

1. The primary function of a physical protection system is
   a. Determine, direct, and dispatch
   b. Deter, detection, delay, and response
   c. Display, develop, initiate, and apprehend
   d. Evaluate, dispatch, and detain
2. The single most important goal in planning a site is
   a. Protection of life, property, and operations
   b. Threat definition, conflict control, and facility characterization
   c. Risk assessment, threat identification, and incident review
   d. Threat identification, vulnerability appraisal, and access review
3. Intrusion sensor performance is described by three fundamental characteristics:
   a. Balanced magnetic switches (BMSs), passive infrared sensors (PIRs), and video motion detectors (VMDs)
   b. Interior boundary penetration, critical infrastructure facility, and proximity sensors
   c. Probability of detection, nuisance alarm rate (NAR), and vulnerability to defeat
   d. Capacitance proximity, intrusion detection rate (IDR), and boundary penetration frequency
4. The strategy of forming layers of protection around an asset or facility is known as
   a. Secured perimeter
   b. Defense in depth
   c. Reinforced barrier deterrent
   d. Reasonable asset protection
5. The regulation of movement into, from, and within a designated building or area is called
   a. Restricted access
   b. Access control
   c. Security access
   d. Security control
6. The key to a successful physical protection system is the integration of
   a. People, process, and technology
   b. Technology, risk assessment, and human interaction
   c. Protecting, offsetting, and transferring risk
   d. Detection, deterrence, and response

7. What is the primary objective of controlling entry into a facility or area?
   a. Provide time management controls for all employees.
   b. Ensure that only authorized persons are allowed to enter.
   c. Keep out potential hazards and dangerous material that could be used to commit sabotage.
   d. Identification purposes.

8. The best way to test your security operation is by
   a. Observation
   b. Penetration test
   c. Security survey
   d. Risk assessment

9. CCTV technologies make possible three distinct yet complementary functions. The first is visual assessment of an alarm or other event. This permits the operator to assess the nature of the alarm before initiating a response. What are the other two functions of CCTV?
   a. Surveillance and deterrence
   b. Intrusion detection and response
   c. Optical and lighting
   d. Monitoring and inspection

10. High-tech integrated technologies not only offer greater protection opportunities but also help minimize cost by
   a. Reducing electrical costs
   b. Reducing reliance on multiple operators and guard force
   c. Providing government tax incentives for increased physical protection systems
   d. Increasing capital value of property

11. A vulnerability assessment tour of a facility is designed to gather information regarding the general layout of the facility, the location of key assets, and information about facility operations, production capabilities, and locations and types of physical protection systems. During this tour—and subsequent tours—the vulnerability assessment member or team should be looking to
   a. Determine where all the fire exits are located.
   b. Examine the locations of physical protection system components.
   c. Count the number of employees within the facility.
   d. Determine the structural strength of the perimeter walls.

12. Designing a new building to mitigate threats is simpler and more cost-effective than retrofitting an existing building. Important security benefits are achieved not by hardware and electronic devices but by shrewd site selections, proper placement of the building on the site, and careful location of building occupants and functions to minimize exposure to threat. These factors also have the benefit of reducing operating expenses over the lifetime of the building. An obvious example of this is planning for
    a. Limiting the number of entrances to the site that must be monitored, staffed, and protected
    b. Reducing the cost associated with energy needs in providing the physical protection system
    c. Giving employees easy access to the facility without their knowledge of the security components used in monitoring their activities
    d. Blast reinforcement film on all perimeter windows

13. How must classified material and sensitive information be disposed of?
    a. Torn in half and thrown in the trash can
    b. Shredded
    c. Removed to a decontamination room
    d. Marked declassified and thrown in a trash can

14. Building security involves more than bars on windows, a guard in a booth, a camera on the ceiling, or locked doors and gates. Effective security solutions call for systematic integration of
    a. Design, technology, and facility operations and management
    b. Reducing vulnerability by protecting, offsetting, or transferring the risk
    c. Operational readiness, physical protection systems, standard operating processes
    d. Increase awareness, environmental design, and physical security

15. In which order should the designing of a security plan for a new complex progress?
    a. Outer perimeter, interior, exterior
    b. Interior, outer perimeter, exterior
    c. Interior, exterior, outer perimeter
    d. Exterior, interior, outer perimeter

16. Physical security is applied by using _____ of physical protective measures to prevent or minimize theft, unauthorized access, or destruction of property.
    a. Layers
    b. Methods
    c. Varieties
    d. Types

17. Employee badges are an excellent method of control. Two functions they serve are
    a. Identify and credit
    b. Payroll and identification
    c. Identification and access
    d. Access and personal information

18. Which security control is most effective in curtailing and preventing "piggybacking" or "tailgating" as a means of unauthorized access?
    a. Cameras
    b. Turnstiles
    c. Security guards
    d. Mantraps

Chapter 4

Requirements Analysis and Security Standards/ Guidelines Criteria

Robert B. Batie, Jr.

Contents

Domain Description

A secure information systems architecture depends on diligence and attention to standards, awareness of threats, and identification of the risk and value of data. The CISSP®-ISSAP® should know and follow the best practices and standards for network and information systems design and implement an architecture that will provide adequate security and reliability for the enterprise. This requires the evaluation and selection of different architectures and understanding the risk associated with each type of design. Key areas of knowledge include

- Analysis of design requirements
  - Value of data
  - Design architecture
- Understanding information systems security standards and guidelines
- Assessment of the information systems security design effectiveness
  - Attack vectors

Requirements analysis begins with gathering requirements that are designated by the customers who submit statements of work (SOW), contract documents, system specifications, service level agreements (SLA), requests for proposals (RFP), legal and regulatory documents, or other types of systems development requirements. The ISSAP may also need to help his or her customers and stakeholders identify, define, and document these system requirements. These documents spell out the customers' expectations regarding the delivery of security services provided by the information system. The security features and functionalities the customers expect to see are based on their business needs and view of the world. The customers may or may not be well versed in understanding security countermeasures and data protection needs in such matters. In either case, they are relying on you, the ISSAP, to deliver a system that is safe and secure to operate, and one that protects their data.

Requirements come in the form of business or mission needs of the customer, who is looking to automate a particular set of capabilities and functions. These requirements reflect those needs and desires. They are also driven by the need to satisfy business policy and regulatory compliance.

Security requirements complement system functional requirements by addressing the needs to provide protection of the information systems, its data, and its users. Security requirements flow down from the functional requirements. They are typically addressed separately from functional requirements but complement the functional requirements at the same time. They complement the functional requirement by addressing concerns regarding the confidentiality, integrity, availability, and accountability of the information system, and the system protection needs.

Requirements analysis is critical to the success of a project. In systems design, requirements analysis encompasses those tasks that go into determining the conditions that must be met by new or altered products, taking into account any conflicting requirements from various stakeholders. It is sometimes referred to as *requirements gathering, requirements capture,* or *requirements specification.* The term *requirements analysis* can also be applied specifically to the analysis proper (as opposed to elicitation or documentation of the requirements, for instance). Requirements must be actionable, measurable, testable, related to identified business needs or opportunities, and defined to a level of detail sufficient for system design.

Requirements are captured in a variety of ways. Usually, they are captured in a table, spreadsheet, or database. Spreadsheets and databases offer the more convenient way to manage requirements. Products such as Rhapsody, Systems Architect, and DOORS are common products used to capture requirements. They also contain features that allow the requirements to be traced to the solution, develop test cases, and contain pointers back to the requirement to ensure validation.

Security requirements typically come from two sources: security best practices that are industry standards for safety and security and regulatory requirements that are mandated by federal, state, local, or international policy. Rarely do customers want a set of requirements that are not motivated by one of these two sources; however, additional requirements are sometimes included that may be considered unnecessary but may be forward looking for future growth. Security requirements, similar to all requirements, cost money to implement, so customers rarely want to add cost by adding unnecessary features or functionality. In the absence of functional, legal, or regulatory requirements levied on the system, at a minimum, the ISSAP should recommend and insist on implementing industry best practices as a measure of due diligence and ethics.

Risk Analysis

A risk analysis should be conducted to determine the requirements and any risk to the system or data processed, stored, or transmitted. Risks should be mitigated to an acceptable level. There are numerous risk analysis methods including Operationally Critical Threat, Asset, and Vulnerability Evaluation (OCTAVE), National Institute of Standards and Technology (NIST) Special Publication 800-30, and ISO/IEC 27005.

Risk Theory

It is unrealistic to think that 100% protection against all possible threats, at all times, is attainable or even desirable. Organizations require a risk-based management process that weighs potential impacts or losses, which may be expected to occur in the presence of a given vulnerability (with a particular threat likely), against the business resource cost of mitigating or eliminating the risk. The qualitative expression of this approach is as follows:

$$R_{(risk)} = \frac{V_{(vulnerability)} \times T_{(threat)} \times I_{(impact)}}{C_{(countermeasures)}}$$

Risk assessments evaluate the sensitivity and criticality of the system or application data to the vulnerabilities, threats, impacts, and potential countermeasures that may exist in its environment. A risk analysis includes the following activities:

- Develop a business case.
- Perform system characterization.
- Conduct threat analysis.
- Perform impact analysis.
- Perform vulnerability and control analysis.
- Develop a risk mitigation strategy.
- Determine the risk level.
- Report the residual risk.

By conducting these risk assessment activities, the CISSP-ISSAP can focus security countermeasures where they provide the most protection for the system and data.

No matter what the size of the enterprise may be, the following steps should be completed when defining the security requirements:

Step 1. Identify requirements—Requirements come from formal proposals, statements of work, specifications, industry best practices, and other sources to form a baseline set of requirements. Also included are user needs discussions with managers, and review of existing documentation for the operational system. The results should be presented and discussed with the business owners and stakeholders.

Step 2. Verify and validate requirements—Before finalizing the baseline requirements, they should be verified and validated with the stakeholders to gain consensus. This is crucial because stakeholders' understanding of the requirements and the vetting process will help avoid scope creep, schedule delays, and general confusion.

Step 3. Document the requirements—The requirements documentation provides a basis for architecting and designing the solution. Key personnel who are present at the beginning of the project may not be there throughout the development life cycle. Therefore, it is an excellent idea to get the requirements signed off by the stakeholders.

In defining requirements, careful consideration should be given to how a requirement is crafted. It is worth the extra time to develop and vet good requirements. So, you might say why is this important? Well, experience has shown that incomplete or missing requirements are the major reasons for unsuccessful projects, resulting in a greater number of system defects. These defects eventually surface late in the development phase or after delivery to the users and end up as punch list items that must be addressed before final sign-off. System defects are very time consuming and expensive to correct. Poorly written requirements can also lead to a continuous stream of new requirements designed to fill the gaps and inadequacies found throughout the project. New requirements cause a great deal of rework and extend development time and costs. This is a form of scope or requirements creep that should be avoided.

Requirements that are ambiguous, untestable, and not capable of fully satisfying needs of the users cause higher development costs, schedule slippage, and unhappy customers. Therefore, organizations must emphasize the importance of requirements definition to ensure that they are clear, meaningful, effective, and efficient.

Table 4.1 provides an example of two requirements that are analyzed to interpret the meaning of the requirement: what it takes to satisfy the requirement and the validation of the requirement. In this case, we looked at identification and authentication and access control. Extensive details are given to explain and understand the requirement and a number of ways it can be satisfied and validated.

Attack Vectors

The ISSAP should be intimately familiar with the most common types of attacks in order to select countermeasures that will combat them. An attack vector is a path or means by which a hacker or cracker can gain access to a computer or network server in order to deliver a payload or malicious outcome. They enable hackers to exploit system vulnerabilities, including the human element. Attack vectors include viruses, e-mail attachments, Web pages, pop-up windows, instant messages, chat rooms, and deception. All of these methods involve programming or, in a few cases, hardware, except deception, in which a human operator is fooled into removing or weakening system defenses.

To some extent, firewalls and antivirus software can block attack vectors. But no protection method is totally attack proof. An effective defense method today may not remain so for long, because hackers are constantly updating attack vectors and seeking new ones, in their quest to gain unauthorized access to networks and computer systems. Some of the most common malicious payloads are viruses, Trojan

Table 4.1 Requirements Analysis and Validation Insert in Chapter 1 Requirements Analysis Section

Requirement	Requirement Meaning and Comments	Review and Validation: Details

An Identification and Authentication (I&A) management mechanism that ensures a unique identifier for each user and that associates that identifier with all auditable actions taken by the user. The following must be specified:*
 	
[*Alternative controls, such as biometrics or smart cards, may be used. These alternative methods may have similar requirements. For example, the electronically stored version of biometric authentication patterns needs to be protected, as do password authenticators.]
 	
• Initial authenticator content and administrative procedures for initial authenticator distribution
	To meet this requirement you must:
	
	• Provide an I&A management mechanism that:
	
	  • Provides a unique identifier for each user
	
	  • Provides an association of all auditable actions taken by a given user
	
	• System documentation must describe the mechanism used to ensure that every user can be uniquely identified and authenticated and that the identity is associated with all auditable actions.
	
	• System documentation must describe how the initial authenticator is delivered to the user.
		Documentation Inspection Required:
		
		• System documentation must describe the identification and authentication management mechanism used to ensure that every user can be uniquely identified and authenticated and that the identity is associated with all auditable actions in an immutable way.
		
		• System documentation must describe the type of authenticator(s) that are being utilized.
		
		• System documentation must describe the management mechanism used to distribute the initial authenticator (must be delivered to a unique user).
		
		• System documentation must describe how the initial authenticators are delivered to the user.

Continued

Table 4.1 Requirements Analysis and Validation Insert in Chapter 1 Requirements Analysis Section (Continued)

Requirement	Requirement Meaning and Comments	Review and Validation: Details
• Individual and Group authenticators. (Group authenticators may only be used in conjunction with an individual/unique authenticator, that is, individuals must be authenticated with an individual authenticator prior to use of a group authenticator).	• System documentation must describe appropriate authenticator change process.	• System documentation must describe the use of any group authenticators utilized by the system, and how the system is configured to prevent direct login with a group authenticator.
• Length, composition, and generation of authenticators.	• System documentation must describe appropriate mechanism or process designed to disable the authenticator after a certain period of time.	• System documentation must fully describe the type of authenticator(s) used within a system (their length, composition, and generation).
• Change Processes (periodic and in case of compromise).	• System documentation must describe how changes to the authenticator content is tracked and configured to prevent the reuse of authenticators.	• System documentation must describe the authenticator change process, both periodic and in case of compromise.
• Aging of static authenticators (i.e., not one-time passwords or biometric patterns).	• System documentation must describe how authenticators are protected to preserve confidentiality and integrity.	• System documentation must describe authenticator aging, reuse preclusion (generation checking/history).
• History of authenticator changes, with assurance of non-replication of individual authenticators, per direction in approved System documentation.		• System documentation must provide detailed description regarding how authenticator history is tracked by the system and configured to prevent its reuse from compromising the nonreplication of individual authenticators.
• Protection of authenticators to preserve confidentiality and integrity.		

- System documentation must describe how authenticators and their corresponding content are protected at rest and in transit over the network.
- Demonstration or Test Required:
- Demonstrate/Verify IA management mechanism works as described.
- Demonstrate/Verify that each user has a unique identification and that identification must be directly attributable to all auditable actions taken by that user.
- Demonstrate how dissemination of authenticators (i.e. passwords, SecureID, etc.) is handled
- Demonstrate that if Group authenticators are being utilized, that one cannot log in directly with a group authenticator.
- Demonstrate how password strength is enforced (review password management within the system):
- Review system configuration files, mechanisms, etc. that control the generation of authenticators.

Continued

Table 4.1 Requirements Analysis and Validation Insert in Chapter 1 Requirements Analysis Section (*Continued*)

Requirement	Requirement Meaning and Comments	Review and Validation: Details
		• Demonstrate/Verify that a "weak" authenticator cannot be generated by the system • Demonstrate how password aging is implemented (review password management within the system). • Demonstrate how Authenticator Histories are tracked. • Capture and Review network data and storage locations for passwords that are stored or transmitted in an unsecured open manner that would offer simple compromise.
Access control, including: • Denial of physical access by unauthorized individuals unless under constant supervision of technically qualified, authorized personnel. Procedures controlling access by users and maintainers to IS resources, including those that are at remote locations.	To meet this requirement you must: • Deny physical access to unauthorized individuals. • Supervise any unauthorized individuals with authorized personnel if the unauthorized individual ever needs physical access. • Have procedures that control authorized access to IS resources.	Documentation Inspection Required: • How-To: • System documentation must address and include a physical construct of the space where all components of the IS are located.

• Apply same protections/procedures to any users, maintainers, and IS resources at remote locations.	• System documentation must provide description of physical protection measures employed to prohibit unauthorized access (unless escorted properly).
	• System documentation must describe procedures that are utilized to control access to IS resources.
	• Demonstration or Test Required: (Site Inspection)
	How-to:
	• Demonstrate/Verify how IS resources are physically protected by unauthorized personnel (including any IS resources at remote locations), examples:
	• Badge/Card Reader access to room(s) containing IS resources
	• Approved combination locks on door(s) to rooms containing IS resources
	• Locked cabinets, equipment racks, etc.
	• Demonstrate/Verify that procedures for access control (as defined in the System documentation) are in use at the facilities.

horses, worms, and spyware. These attack vectors are not a completely exhaustive list but a general list of the most common ones.

Methods of "Vector" Attack

Attack "vector" refers to the method of attack: the attacker's choice of weapon. E-mail attachments are a prime example. It is often easy to get them past the firewall. In most cases, the human element is the end target. Users are the weakest link in the network. They just love clicking on the button to open attachments, making this form of attack popular.

Do not confuse attack vectors with payload. Worms, for example, always count on some vector to let them in. They usually carry spyware, a virus, or a Trojan as their payload. "Worm" alludes to how they replicate. Worms wiggle into a computer, replicate, and crawl out over a network (local net or Internet) to infect other computers. Trojan horses, spyware, dialers, hijackers, etc., are the kind of payloads worms can deliver. All attacks combine a payload with a vector.

While ordinary virus attacks have been declining, Trojan horses and spyware attacks have been on the rise, as hostile software developers move to more damaging types of attacks. The number of attacks has increased dramatically. The attack vectors described in the following text are how most of them are being launched today.

Attack by E-Mail

E-mail messages themselves have become vectors, even though attacks using attachments are still more common. The hostile content is either embedded in the message, or linked to the message. Sometimes, attacks combine the two vectors, so that if the message does not get you, the attachment will. E-mail provides a convenient delivery vehicle for deception. The weak spot is the ignorance or credulity of the computer user, not the computer itself. E-mail attacks continue to advance in sophistication. Criminals are combining their tricks with the techniques of spammers to make these attacks more effective. Millions of messages can be sent out in the hope that a large number of people will be duped.

Spam is almost always a carrier for scams, fraud, dirty tricks, or malicious actions of some kind. Any link that offers something "free" or tempting is suspect. Acting on a spam message usually leads to an outcome that is negative if not downright unpleasant. Attachments (and other malicious files) are the most powerful ways to attack a PC. They are a simple way to deliver a highly effective payload. They are being overtaken by Web page trickery, but attachments are still a major threat.

Attack by Deception

Social engineering in the form of deception is aimed at the user/operator as the vulnerable entry point. It is not just malicious computer code that you need to watch out for. Fraud, scams, hoaxes, and to some extent spam, not to mention viruses, worms, and such, require the unwitting cooperation of the computer user to succeed. Social engineering is the art of convincing people to do something they would not ordinarily do, such as giving up a valuable secret. Malware developers use social engineering techniques in spam to con people into doing careless things, such as opening attachments that carry viruses and worms or using the telephone to get passwords or other sensitive information.

Hoaxes

Hoaxes are another form of deception that is often an attack vector too. Ignorance and credulity are the target. They can result in an exponentially growing number of messages that can easily swamp an e-mail system. Other hoaxes trick people into damaging their own PC by deleting files.

Hackers

Originally, *hacker* was a term of respect for experts who could do "cool" things with computers. Some hackers crossed over to the dark side. These villains are more properly known as *crackers*. The distinction is not often made in the popular press. That annoys hackers, who like to think of themselves as white-hats, aka, good guys. Hackers are a formidable attack vector because, unlike ordinary malicious code, people are flexible, and they can improvise. They use a variety of hacking tools, heuristics, and "social engineering" to gain access to computers and online accounts. They often install a Trojan horse so that they can commandeer the computer for their own use.

Web Page Attack

Counterfeit Web sites are often used to extract personal information from people. They look very much like the genuine Web sites they imitate. You think you are doing business with someone you trust, but you are really giving your personal information, such as your name, address, and credit card number to a scam artist. They are often used in conjunction with spam, which gets you there in the first place.

Pop-up Web pages can install spyware, adware, hijackers, dialers, Trojans, or other scamware. They may even close your Internet connection, and then make a *very* expensive phone call using your modem. All of these activities are malicious.

Attack of the Worms

Many worms are delivered as attachments, but network worms use holes in network protocols directly. Window's DCOM vulnerability is a prime example. Any remote access service, such as file sharing, is likely to be vulnerable to this sort of worm.

These worms propagate without relying on victims to open attachments. In most cases, a firewall will block system worms, or you can disable the vulnerable service.

Many worms install Trojan horses. Some can disable ordinary antimalware software, and then install the worm's payload. Next, they begin scanning the Internet from the computer they have just infected, looking for other computers to infect. If the worm is successful, it propagates rapidly. The worm owner soon has thousands of "zombie" computers to use for more mischief.

Malicious Macros

Many documents such as those generated by Word and Excel, for example, allow the use of macros. A macro can automate spreadsheets, forms, or document templates, for example. The problem is that macros can also be used for malicious purposes. They can attack your computer directly. Keeping your software patched and antivirus programs active are the best ways to mitigate malicious macros. You can get a malicious macro from anybody. If they have picked one up, their documents will contain a copy of the malicious macro.

Instant Messaging, IRC, and P2P File-Sharing Networks

These three Internet services rely on cozy connections between your computer and other computers on the Internet. If you use them, the special peer-to-peer (P2P) software that you install makes your machine more vulnerable to hostile exploits. Just as with e-mail, the most important things to be wary of are attachments and Web site links.

Spyware is a software that adds hidden components to your system on the sly. It is often bundled with some attractive software or other bait. The stealth process is installed without your knowledge. Sneak software often hijacks your browser and diverts you to some "revenue generating opportunity."

Viruses

Viruses are malicious computer code that hitches a ride. That makes them the payload. The original virus vector, floppy disks, would carry the infected files. Now, virus vectors include e-mail attachments, downloaded files, worms, and more [Happy Trails 2009].

Asset and Data Valuation

In the world of data protection, prevailing practices imply that every piece of an organization's data is equal to every other piece. This also holds true for all other company assets. Companies do not always see the same value in intangible assets that they do in tangible ones. They tend to use a "one-size-fits-all" approach in both cases, for instance, ensuring that hardware, software, and data are included in the recovery plan for backup, redundancy, business continuance, and other data protection. As a result, priceless data may be poorly protected, whereas relatively unimportant files consume disproportionate amounts of time and resources. What is missing is the concept of asset and data valuation as part of the initial business assessment.

This assessment should take into account the physical infrastructure, information systems (hardware), people, facilities, and the like. Architecting the system depends on more than just protecting the data. Let us consider the defense-in-depth approach. It calls for policies, procedures, technology, and personnel to be considered in the system security development process. The customer requirements as well as the regulatory and statutory requirements must also be satisfied within the design functions. As you better understand the needs of customers and what they are contracting you to do, requirements analysis is a significant factor that if not done right can make or break your projects.

Different types of data have different values when placed in the context of their business use. One way of determining the value of specific information is in conducting a Business Impact Assessment (BIA) based on how individual departments or business units would be affected if their systems were compromised under a denial-of-service attack, or the data was lost or deleted. How quickly could the system be brought back into service? How long would it take to restore the data in the event of such a loss? Only then can the individual or the enterprise determine the appropriate data protection, storage services, and redundancy required for each type of data.

Context and Data Value

Let us take a look at the concept of data valuation in more detail, beginning with an examination of the importance of organizational data. What data merits the greatest data protection investment? According to common practices, core company databases and mission-critical data files are the most obvious choices. As these are typically housed on central servers, information technology (IT) departments tend to devote their energies to backing up these files at specific periods (often on a daily or weekly basis), while also providing redundancy through Redundant Array of Inexpensive/Independent Disks (RAID) or server replication and other advanced means of data protection. While this approach is certainly better than leaving everything to fate, it neglects the concept of value. For instance, just how impacted would the organization be if it suffered a catastrophic failure of corporate systems? Perhaps you have all the database records immediately recoverable, but what about the operating system and applications harnessing that database? Without those, the database is useless. For example, what is the maximum allowable downtime? If the organization can survive a few days "under the weather" while operating systems and applications are reinstalled and database files restored, then it may not need to invest in high-availability redundant data storage or protection methods to continue doing business. However, if the company would effectively "die" due to such an event, or would suffer massive losses, then investment in a high-availability redundant system should be a high priority to mitigate such threats.

Corporate versus Departmental: Valuation

Another aspect of context is relative position on the organizational chart. From the standpoint of the enterprise, perhaps only key database files deserve the highest priority in data protection. While that may be correct for the company as a whole, departments or remote offices may require different priorities. Thus, each echelon of management should consider its own data protection needs and take actions accordingly.

In Company X, for example, the sales and marketing database may be assigned the greatest importance. However, at a local level, a software engineering department would probably have a completely different set of priorities and, therefore, different data protection needs. While the corporate IT department may be taking care of database backup and protection, local IT personnel management needs to ensure that their critical information is safeguarded, either by handling storage management locally or by justifying the need to protect that data to the corporate IT department.

Business, Legal, and Regulatory Requirements

Business requirements vary depending on the type of business or enterprise. Parts of the U.S. healthcare industry must comply with Health Insurance Portability and Accountability Act (HIPAA). Other U.S. organizations that handle personal/privacy data may have Sarbanes–Oxley Act of 2002 compliance requirements. Organizations that process credit card information must comply with Payment Card Industry Data Security Standard (PCI DSS). Other U.S. businesses or government agencies requirements include compliance with Gramm–Leach–Bliley Act (GLBA) and FISMA.

Most European countries' data protection laws follow principles detailed in two EU directives, whether or not these countries are part of the European Union. These directives are (1) Directive 95/46/EC of the European Parliament on the Protection of Individuals with Regard to the Processing of Personal Data and on the Free Movement of Such Data (commonly called the Data Protection Directive) and (2) Directive 2002/58/EC Concerning the Processing of Personal Data and the Protection of Privacy in the Electronic Communications Sector. The first directive applies to the collection, storage, disclosure, and other uses of personal data. The second directive addresses the use of "cookies" and places, restrictions on spam, telemarketing, and interception of communications and traffic data [IT Law Group].

As stated earlier, the ISSAP need to understand what is specifically called out in national and international policies that affect the systems. For instance, privacy laws in one country differ from those of another. Interconnection agreements between other countries must be considered as well as some ground rules that express an understanding of how these countries can operate effectively across international borders. Typically, the most stringent policy prevails because it covers the more loosely coupled policy. But what if there is a disagreement among international parties? How does it get resolved? Memorandums of agreement or memorandums of understanding can help identify a mutually acceptable solution.

Product Assurance Evaluation Criteria

The Common Criteria (CC) was born out of the necessity to expand product security assurance programs in the United States, Canada, United Kingdom, France, and Germany. The goal of the program was to establish a high degree of assurance that products would consistently perform the security function safely and securely when handling data and that failures would not result in the compromise of sensitive information. The expansion of the program also provided a broader market for those products completing the evaluation process by allowing international sales to the nations participating in the program. Some participating nations mandate the use of these products in their information systems. This mandate has translated into requirements for the system under development.

Product evaluations began in the United States with the Orange Book (TCSEC), which was the criteria for evaluating secure systems and vendor products. The Orange Book had an assurance range from D2 up to A-3. The D class had the least amount of rigorous testing, and A class consisted of more formal evaluation methods.

The Orange Book only addressed confidentiality. It was part of the Rainbow series, a set of security guidance named after its colorful covers. Each colored cover addressed a different security topic. The Orange Book and the Rainbow series were developed by the National Security Agency (NSA), and all products were tested by them. Over time, a backlog of evaluations made the delay in product evaluation less cost-effective. By the time the product reached evaluation, it may already be at the end of the life cycle. Businesses began to lose interest in this process because there was little return on investment in time and money. They were interested in selling their secure products in the international market as well.

The next evaluation criteria, the ITSEC, was created by Canada, United Kingdom, France, Spain, and Germany, which the United States adopted and participated in. This evaluation criteria addressed integrity as well as confidentiality and was a step in the right direction. ITSEC had classes of assurance products, but the process did not go far enough. So, discussions began to develop a common set of standards that could be agreed to by a consortium of countries and the CC was established.

Using these evaluated products is mandated by law for all countries that have signed the arrangement discussed in the following text. For instance, a device such as a firewall seeking an Evaluation Assurance Level (EAL) 4 certification must meet all the requirements set in the criteria for that level of assurance. While conducting a requirements analysis, the ISSAP must include the functional requirements for that device as identified in the CC [Common Criteria, 2006].

Common Criteria (CC) Part 1

The CC philosophy is to provide assurance based on an evaluation (active investigation) of the IT product that is to be trusted. Evaluation is the traditional means of providing assurance and is the basis for prior evaluation criteria documents. The CC proposes to use expert evaluators to measure the validity of the documentation and the resulting IT product with increasing emphasis on scope, depth, and rigor. It does not comment on the relative merits of other means of gaining assurance. Researchers continue looking for alternative ways of gaining assurance. As mature alternative approaches emerge from these research activities, they will be considered for inclusion in the CC.

The CC provides a common set of requirements for the security functionality of IT products and for assurance measures applied to the IT products during a security evaluation. These IT products may be implemented in hardware, firmware, or software. The evaluation process establishes a level of confidence that the security function of IT products as well as the assurance measures applied to these IT products meet these requirements. The evaluation results may help the ISSAP, and the consumers determine whether these IT products fulfill the security needs.

The CC is useful as a guide for the development, evaluation, or procurement of IT products with security functionality. It addresses protection of assets from unauthorized disclosure, modification, or loss of use. The categories of protection relating to these three types of failure of security are commonly called confidentiality, integrity, and availability, respectively. The CC may apply to risks arising from human activities (malicious or otherwise) and to risks arising from nonhuman activities. It may also be applied in other areas of IT depending on the nation's security policies, but makes no claim of applicability in these areas [Common Criteria 2006].

The latest version of the CC is version 2.3. It is based on version 2.2, with updates that include a number of interpretations and editorial changes with no impact on the technical content. These standards have also been published as International Organization for Standardization (ISO) and the International Electrotechnical Commission (IEC) 15408:2005 and ISO/IEC 18045:2005. This version is the last of the version 2 series, to be used until March 2008, and maintenance based on this version during a further 18 months, that is, until September 2009. CC consists of three parts:

Part 1. Introduction and general model is the introduction to the CC. It defines general concepts and principles of IT security evaluation and presents a general model of evaluation. Part 1 also presents constructs for expressing IT security objectives, for selecting and defining IT security requirements, and for writing high-level specifications for products and systems. In addition, the usefulness of each part of the CC is described in terms of each of the target audiences.

Part 2. Security functional requirements establish a set of functional components as a standard way of expressing the functional requirements for the Target of Evaluation (TOE). Part 2 catalogs the set of functional components, families, and classes.

Part 3. Security assurance requirements establish a set of assurance components as a standard way of expressing the assurance requirements for the TOE. Part 3 catalogs the set of assurance components, families, and classes. Part 3 also defines the evaluation criteria for Protection Profile (PP) and Security Target (ST) and presents evaluation assurance levels that define the predefined CC scale for rating assurance for the TOE, which is called the EAL.

The purpose of this arrangement is to advance those objectives by bringing about a situation in which IT products and protection profiles that earn a CC certificate can be procured or used without the need for further evaluation. It seeks to provide grounds for confidence in the reliability of the judgments on which the original certificate was based, by requiring a Certification/Validation Body (CB) issuing Common Criteria certificates meet high and consistent standards [Common Criteria Part 1, 2006].

A management committee, composed of senior representatives from each signatory's country, was established to implement the arrangement and provide guidance to the respective national schemes conducting evaluation and validation activities. The list of current arrangement members is discussed in the following text.

In October 1998, after 2 years of intense negotiations, government organizations from the United States, Canada, France, Germany, and the United Kingdom signed the historic recognition arrangement for Common Criteria-based IT security evaluations. The arrangement officially known as the *Arrangement on the Mutual Recognition of Common Criteria Certificates in the Field of IT Security* was a significant step forward for government and industry in IT product and protection profile security evaluations. The U.S. Government and its foreign partners in the arrangement share the following objectives with regard to evaluations of IT products and protection profiles:

■ Ensure that evaluations of IT products and protection profiles are performed to high and consistent standards and are seen to contribute significantly to confidence in the security of those products and profiles.

■ Increase the availability of evaluated, security-enhanced IT products and protection profiles for national use.

■ Eliminate duplicate evaluations of IT products and protection profiles.

▪ Continuously improve the efficiency and cost-effectiveness of security evaluations and the certification/validation process for IT products and protection profiles.

In October 1999, Australia and New Zealand joined the Mutual Recognition Arrangement, increasing the total number of participating nations to 7. Following a brief revision of the original arrangement to allow for the participation of both certificate-consuming and certificate-producing nations, an expanded Recognition Arrangement was signed in May 2000 at the 1st International Common Criteria Conference by Government organizations from 13 nations. These include the United States, Canada, France, Germany, the United Kingdom, Australia, New Zealand, Italy, Spain, the Netherlands, Norway, Finland, and Greece.

The State of Israel became the 14th nation to sign the Recognition Arrangement in November 2000. As of March 2008, 25 countries are currently part of the Common Criteria Recognition Agreement (CCRA). Thirteen countries (United States, Australia, Canada, France, Germany, Japan, Netherlands, New Zealand, Norway, Spain, South Korea, Sweden, and the United Kingdom) are Certificate Producers, and twelve countries (Austria, Czech Republic, Denmark, Finland, Greece, Hungary, India, Israel, Italy, Malaysia, Singapore, and Turkey) are Certificate Consumers.

The CC-evaluated products begin the process by being evaluated in a certified laboratory. These commercial laboratories agree to use stringent principles and test methods that are approved by the National Information Assurance Partnership (NIAP) members. The National Voluntary Laboratory Accreditation Program (NVLAP) provides third-party accreditation to testing and calibration laboratories. The NVLAP is established in response to Congressional mandates or administrative actions by the federal government or from requests by private-sector organizations.

The NVLAP provides third-party accreditation to testing and calibration laboratories. NVLAP accreditation programs are established in response to Congressional mandates or administrative actions by the federal government or from requests by private-sector organizations. The NVLAP must be in full conformance with the standards of the ISO/IEC, including ISO/IEC 17025 and Guide 58. NVLAP is required before becoming a Common Criteria Testing Laboratory. The accreditation ensures that the Common Criteria laboratories meet the requirements of ISO/IEC Guide 25, General Requirement for Competence of Calibration and Testing Laboratories, and specific Common Criteria Evaluation and Validation Scheme requirements for IT security evaluations [Common Criteria, 2006].

CC Part 2

Part 2 of the CC defines the Security functional components. It is really the heart of the CC process. The security functional requirements are expressed in a PP or ST. These requirements describe the security behavior the TOE is expected to meet. The requirements describe security properties that users can detect by direct interaction (i.e., inputs, outputs) with the TOE or by the IT response to stimulus. Security functional components express security requirements intended to counter threats in the assumed operating environment of the TOE and cover any identified organizational security policies and assumptions.

This part of the CC and the associated security functional requirements are not meant to be a definitive answer to all the problems of IT security. Instead, it offers a set of well-understood security functional requirements used to create trusted products reflecting the needs of the market. These security functional requirements are presented as the current state of the art in requirements specification and evaluation [Common Criteria, 2006].

This part of the CC contains a catalog of security functional requirements that may be specified for a TOE. A TOE is a set of software, firmware, or hardware possibly accompanied by user and administrator guidance documentation. A TOE may contain resources such as electronic storage media (e.g., main memory, disk space), peripheral devices (e.g., printers), and computing capacity (e.g., CPU time) that can be used for processing and storing information and is the subject of an evaluation. The TOE evaluation is concerned primarily with ensuring that a defined set of Security Functional Requirements (SFR) are enforced over the TOE resources. The SFR defines the rules by which the TOE governs access to and use of its resources, and thus information and services controlled by the TOE.

The SFR may also include multiple Security Functions Policy (SFP). Each SFP has a scope of control that defines the subjects, objects, resources, or information, and operations controlled under it. All SFP are implemented by the TOE Security Functionality (TSF), whose mechanisms enforce the rules defined in the SFR and provide necessary capabilities.

Those portions of a TOE that must be relied on for the correct enforcement of the SFR are collectively referred to as the TSF. The TSF consists of all hardware, software, and firmware of a TOE that is either directly or indirectly relied upon for security enforcement.

The Target of Evaluation (TOE)

The CC is flexible in what to evaluate and is, therefore, not tied to the boundaries of IT products. Instead of the term *IT product*, the CC uses the term *TOE (Target of Evaluation)*. While there are cases where a TOE consists of an IT product, this need not be the case. The TOE may be an IT product, a part of an IT product, a set of IT products, a unique technology that may never be made into a product, or a combination of these. The precise relation between the TOE and any IT product is only important in one respect: the evaluation of a TOE containing only a part of an IT product should not be misrepresented as the evaluation of the entire IT product. Examples of a TOE include

- A software application
- An operating system
- A software application in combination with an operating system
- A software application in combination with an operating system and a workstation
- An operating system in combination with a workstation
- A smart card integrated circuit
- The cryptographic coprocessor of a smart card integrated circuit
- A local area network including all terminals, servers, network equipment, and software
- A database application excluding the remote client software normally associated with that database application [Common Criteria Part 2, 2006]

Table 4.2 lists the primary classes of the security functional requirements. Note that the abbreviations for the classes for the security functions begin with an "F"—this denotes its reference to the functional requirements. (Assurance class acronyms begin with an A.) This can be helpful if you just see the acronym, such as FPR. Drop the F, and PR makes sense as an acronym for privacy. FAU would indicate Functional (F) and Audit (AU). The functional class description is spelled out in the Security Functional Class column.

Evaluation Assurance Level (EAL) Overview

Table 4.3 represents a summary of the EALs. The columns represent a hierarchically ordered set of EALs, while the rows represent assurance families. Each number in the resulting matrix identifies a specific assurance component where applicable. As outlined in the next section, seven hierarchically ordered evaluation assurance levels are defined in the CC for the rating of a TOE's assurance. They are hierarchically ordered inasmuch as each EAL represents more assurance than all lower EALs. The increase in assurance from EAL to EAL is accomplished by the substitution of a hierarchically higher assurance component from the same assurance family (i.e., increasing rigor, scope, or depth) and from the addition of assurance components from other assurance families (i.e., adding new requirements).

These EALs consist of an appropriate combination of assurance components as described in Chapter 7 of this CC Part 3. More precisely, each EAL includes no more than one component of each assurance family, and all assurance dependencies of every component are addressed. While the EALs are defined in the CC, it is possible to represent other combinations of assurance. Specifically, the notion of "augmentation" allows the addition of assurance components (from assurance families not already included in the EAL) or the substitution of assurance components (with another hierarchically higher assurance component in the same assurance family) to an EAL. Of the assurance constructs defined in the CC, only EALs may be augmented. The notion of an "EAL minus a constituent assurance component"

Table 4.2   Security Function Requirement Classes

Security Function Class (Fxx)	Description
Audit (FAU)	Security auditing involves recognizing, recording, storing, and analyzing information related to security activities. The class includes families that define requirements for the selection of auditable events, the analysis of audit records, their protection, and their storage.
Communications (FCO)	Provides two families concerned with verifying the identity of a party participating in data exchange. The families are concerned with non-repudiation by the originator and by the recipient of data.
Cryptographic support (FCS)	Used when the TOE implements cryptographic functions. The two families cover the operational use and management of cryptographic keys.
User data protection (FDP)	This class contains families specifying requirements related to the protection of user data. These families address user data within the TOE during import, export, and storage. It also covers security attributes related to user data.
Identification and authentication (FIA)	The requirements for I&A ensure the unambiguous identification of authorized users and the correct association of security attributes with users and subjects. Families in this class deal with determining and verifying user identity, determining their authority to interact with the TOE, and with the correct association of security attributes with the authorized user.
Security management (FMT)	This class is used to specify management of the product's security function's attributes, data, and functions. For example, different management roles and their interaction, such as separation of capability, can be defined. The class is also used to cover the management aspects of other functional classes.
Privacy (FPR)	Privacy requirements provide a user with protection against discovery and misuses of his identity by other users. The families in this class are concerned with anonymity, pseudonymity, unlinkability, and unobservability.

Continued

Table 4.2 (*Continued*) Security Function Requirement Classes

Security Function Class (Fxx)	Description
Protection of the TOE security functions (FPT)	This class is focused on protection of TOE security functions data, rather than protection of user data. The class relates to the integrity and management of the TOE security function mechanisms and data.
Resource utilization (TRU)	Resource utilization provides three families that support the availability of required resources, such as processing capability and storage capacity. The families detail requirements for fault tolerance, priority of service, and resource allocation.
TOE access (FTA)	This class specifies functional requirements, in addition to those specified for I&A, for controlling the establishment of a user's session. The requirements for TOE access govern such controls as limiting the number and scope of user sessions, displaying the access history, and the modification of access parameters.
Trusted path/channels (FTP)	This class is concerned with trusted communications paths between the users and the TOE security functions, and between TOE security functions. Trusted paths are constructed from trusted channels, which exist for intertrusted security function communications, which provide a means for users to perform functions through a direct interaction with the trusted security function. The user of trusted security function can initiate the exchange, which is guaranteed to be protected from modification by untrusted applications.

Source: Hansche, S. *The Official Guide to the CISSP-ISSEP CBK,* New York: Auerbach Publications, 2005.

is not recognized by the standard as a valid claim. Augmentation carries with it the obligation on the part of the claimant to justify the utility and added value of the added assurance component to the EAL. An EAL may also be augmented with extended assurance requirements.

EALs are augmented to show increased assurance capabilities or functionality. The additional functions are added from the next higher EAL and show compliance with parts of that level placing emphasis on certain functions. The augmented function should be listed as part of evaluation so that stakeholders will understand what additional capabilities were tested.

Table 4.3   Evaluation Assurance Level Summary

Assurance Class	Assurance Family	Assurance Components by Evaluation Assurance Level						
		EAL1	EAL2	EAL3	EAL4	EAL5	EAL6	EAL7
Development	ADV_ARC		1	1	1	1	1	1
	ADV_FSP	1	2	3	4	5	5	6
	ADV_IMP				1	1	2	2
	ADV_INT					2	3	3
	ADV_SPM						1	1
	ADV_TDS		1	2	3	4	5	6
Guidance Documents	AGD_OPE	1	1	1	1	1	1	1
	AGD_PRE	1	1	1	1	1	1	1
Life-Cycle Support	ALC_CMC	1	2	3	4	4	5	5
	ALC_CMS	1	2	3	4	5	5	5
	ALC_DEL		1	1	1	1	1	1
	ALC_DVS			1	1	1	2	2
	ALC_FLR							
	ALC_LCD			1	1	1	1	2
	ALC_TAT				1	2	3	3
Security Target Evaluation	ASE_CCL	1	1	1	1	1	1	1
	ASE_ECD	1	1	1	1	1	1	1
	ASE_INT	1	1	1	1	1	1	1
	ASE_OBJ	1	2	2	2	2	2	2
	ASE_REQ	1	2	2	2	2	2	2
	ASE_SPD		1	1	1	1	1	1
	ASE_TSS	1	1	1	1	1	1	1
Tests	ATE_COV		1	2	2	2	3	3
	ATE_DPT			1	2	3	3	4
	ATE_FUN		1	1	1	1	2	2
	ATE_IND	1	2	2	2	2	2	3
Vulnerability Assessment	AVA_VAN	1	2	2	3	4	5	5

The next section contains a list of the EALs followed by a more detailed description of each EAL. The list of EALs and its short title is as follows:

- Evaluation assurance level 1 (EAL1)—functionally tested
- Evaluation assurance level 2 (EAL2)—structurally tested
- Evaluation assurance level 3 (EAL3)—methodically tested and checked
- Evaluation assurance level 4 (EAL4)—methodically designed, tested, and reviewed
- Evaluation assurance level 5 (EAL5)—semiformally designed and tested
- Evaluation assurance level 6 (EAL6)—semiformally verified design and tested
- Evaluation assurance level 7 (EAL7)—formally verified design and tested

Evaluation Assurance Level 1 (EAL1)—Functionally Tested

EAL1 is applicable where some confidence in correct operation is required, but the threats to security are not viewed as serious. It will be of value where independent assurance is required to support the contention that due care has been exercised with respect to the protection of personal or similar information. EAL1 requires only a limited security target. It is sufficient to simply state the SFRs that the TOE must meet, rather than deriving them from threats, OSPs, and assumptions through security objectives. EAL1 provides an evaluation of the TOE as made available to the customer, including independent testing against a specification and an examination of the guidance documentation provided. The goal is for an EAL1 evaluation to be successfully conducted without assistance from the developer of the TOE, and for minimal investment. An evaluation at this level should provide evidence that the TOE functions in a manner consistent with its documentation.

Evaluation Assurance Level 2 (EAL2)—Structurally Tested

EAL2 requires the cooperation of the developer in terms of the delivery of design information and test results, but should not demand more effort on the part of the developer than is consistent with good commercial practice. As such, it should not require a substantially increased investment of cost or time. EAL2 is, therefore, applicable in those circumstances where developers or users require a low to moderate level of independently assured security in the absence of ready availability of the complete development record. Such a situation may arise when securing legacy systems, or where access to the developer may be limited.

Evaluation Assurance Level 3 (EAL3)— Methodically Tested and Checked

EAL3 permits a conscientious developer to gain maximum assurance from positive security engineering at the design stage without substantial alteration of existing sound development practices. It is applicable in those circumstances where developers or users require a moderate level of independently assured security, and require a thorough investigation of the TOE and its development without substantial reengineering. EAL3 provides assurance by a full security target and an analysis of the SFRs in that ST, using a functional and interface specification, guidance documentation, and an architectural description of the design of the TOE, to understand the security behavior.

The analysis is supported by independent testing of the TSF, evidence of developer testing based on the functional specification and TOE design, selective independent confirmation of the developer test results, and a vulnerability analysis (based on the functional specification, TOE design, architectural design, and guidance evidence provided) demonstrating resistance to penetration attackers with a basic attack potential.

Evaluation Assurance Level 4 (EAL4)—Methodically Designed, Tested, and Reviewed

EAL4 permits a developer to gain maximum assurance from positive security engineering based on good commercial development practices that, though rigorous, do not require substantial specialist knowledge, skills, and other resources. It is the highest level at which it is likely to be economically feasible to retrofit to an existing product line. It is, therefore, applicable in those circumstances where developers or users require a moderate to high level of independently assured security in conventional commodity TOEs and are prepared to incur additional security-specific engineering costs.

EAL4 provides assurance by a full security target and an analysis of the SFRs in that ST, using a functional and complete interface specification, guidance documentation, a description of the basic modular design of the TOE, and a subset of the implementation, to understand the security behavior.

Evaluation Assurance Level 5 (EAL5)— Semiformally Designed and Tested

EAL5 permits a developer to gain maximum assurance from security engineering based on rigorous commercial development practices supported by moderate application of specialist security engineering techniques. Such a TOE will most likely be designed and developed with the intent of achieving EAL5 assurance. It requires additional costs attributable to the EAL5 requirements, relative to rigorous development without the application of specialized techniques.

EAL5 is applicable in circumstances where developers or users require a high level of independently assured security in a planned development and require a rigorous development approach without incurring unreasonable costs attributable to specialist security engineering techniques. It provides assurance by a full security target and an analysis of the SFRs in that ST, using a functional and complete interface specification, guidance documentation, a description of the design of the TOE, and the implementation, to understand the security behavior. A modular TSF design is also required [Common Criteria Part 2, 2006].

Evaluation Assurance Level 6 (EAL6)—
Semiformally Verified Design and Tested

EAL6 permits developers to gain high assurance from application of security engineering techniques to a rigorous development environment in order to produce a premium TOE for protecting high-value assets against significant risks. It is, therefore, applicable to the development of security TOEs for application in high-risk situations where the value of the protected assets justifies the additional costs [CC Part 2].

EAL6 provides assurance by a full security target and an analysis of the SFRs in that ST, using a functional and complete interface specification, guidance documentation, the design of the TOE, and the implementation, to understand the security behavior. Assurance is additionally gained through a formal model of select TOE security policies and a semiformal presentation of the functional specification and TOE design. A modular and layered TSF design is also required.

The analysis is supported by independent testing of the TSF, evidence of developer testing based on the functional specification, TOE design, selective independent confirmation of the developer test results, and an independent vulnerability analysis demonstrating resistance to penetration attackers with a high attack potential.

EAL6 also provides assurance through the use of a structured development process, development environment controls, and comprehensive TOE configuration management, including complete automation and evidence of secure delivery procedures. This represents a meaningful increase in assurance from EAL5 by requiring more comprehensive analysis, a structured representation of the implementation, more architectural structure (e.g., layering), more comprehensive independent vulnerability analysis, and improved configuration management and development environment controls.

Evaluation Assurance Level 7 (EAL7)—
Formally Verified Design and Tested

EAL7 is applicable to the development of security TOEs for application in extremely high-risk situations or where the high value of the assets justifies the higher costs. Practical application of EAL7 is currently limited to TOEs with tightly focused security functionality that is amenable to extensive formal analysis. EAL7 provides assurance by a full security target and an analysis of the SFRs in that ST, using a functional and complete interface specification, guidance documentation, the design of the TOE, and a structured presentation of the implementation, to understand the security behavior. Assurance is additionally gained through a formal model of select TOE security policies and a semiformal presentation of the functional specification and TOE design. A modular, layered, and simple TSF design is also required.

The analysis is supported by independent testing of the TSF, evidence of developer testing based on the functional specification, TOE design and implementation representation, complete independent confirmation of the developer test results, and an independent vulnerability analysis demonstrating resistance to penetration attackers with a high attack potential. EAL7 also provides assurance through the use of a structured development process, development environment controls, and comprehensive TOE configuration management, including complete automation and evidence of secure delivery procedures. This EAL represents a meaningful increase in assurance from EAL6 by requiring more comprehensive analysis using formal representations and formal correspondence, and comprehensive testing.

CC Part 3: Assurance Paradigm

CC Part 3 begins with a philosophy of the approach to assurance that will permit the reader to understand the rationale behind the assurance requirements. This philosophy is that the threats to security and organizational security policy commitments should be clearly articulated and the proposed security measures be deemed sufficient for their intended purpose.

Measures should be adopted that reduce the likelihood of vulnerabilities, the ability to exercise (i.e., intentionally exploit or unintentionally trigger) a vulnerability, and the extent of the damage that could occur from a vulnerability being exploited. Additionally, measures should be taken to facilitate the subsequent identification of vulnerabilities and to eliminate, mitigate, or provide notification that a vulnerability has been exploited or triggered.

Significance of Vulnerabilities

There are threat agents that will continue to actively seek to exploit opportunities to violate security policies for illicit gains. These threat agents may also accidentally trigger security vulnerabilities, causing harm to the organization. Because of the need to process sensitive information and the lack of trusted products, there is significant security risk to IT systems that is likely to cause security breaches resulting in significant loss.

IT security breaches come from the intentional exploitation or unintentional triggering of vulnerabilities in the application of IT within business concerns. Steps should be taken to prevent vulnerabilities in IT products. To the extent feasible, vulnerabilities should be

- Eliminated, by taking steps to expose, remove, or neutralize all exercisable vulnerabilities
- Minimized, by taking steps to reduce to an acceptable level residual potential impact of any risks or vulnerability
- Monitored, by taking steps to ensure that any attempt to exercise a residual vulnerability will be detected so that steps can be taken to limit the damage

Cause of Vulnerabilities

Vulnerabilities are due to any number of reasons, including inadequate requirements definition, defects in hardware or software, or misconfigured equipment security settings. The system developer or customer may not adequately define the security requirements, which can lead to inadequate security countermeasures. Vulnerabilities may be introduced into the system as a result of poor development standards or incorrect design choices. An IT product may possess all the functions and features required of it and still contain vulnerabilities that render it unsuitable or ineffective with respect to security. IT products placed in operation may have been configured according to the correct specification, but vulnerabilities may have been introduced as a result of inadequate controls upon the operation. These are not a list of all inclusive reasons for vulnerabilities but a general idea of the types of causes that may affect the security of the system.

CC Assurance

Assurance is the foundation for confidence that an IT product meets its security objectives. It can be derived from a reference to sources, such as unsubstantiated assertions, prior relevant experience, or specific experience. However, the CC provides assurance through active investigation. Active investigation is an evaluation of the IT product in order to determine its security properties [Common Criteria Part 3, 2006].

Assurance through Evaluation

Evaluation is the traditional way of gaining assurance. It serves as the basis of the CC approach. Evaluation techniques can include, but are not limited to

- Analysis and checking of processes and procedures
- Checking that processes and procedures are being applied
- Analysis of the correspondence between TOE design representations
- Analysis of the TOE design representation against the requirements
- Verification of proofs
- Analysis of guidance documents
- Analysis of functional tests developed and the results provided
- Independent functional testing

- Analysis for vulnerabilities, including flaw hypothesis
- Penetration testing

The CC Evaluation Assurance Scale

The CC philosophy asserts that greater assurance results from the application of greater evaluation effort, and that the goal is to apply the minimum effort required to provide the necessary level of assurance. The increasing level of effort is based on

- **Scope**—That is, the effort is greater because a larger portion of the IT product is included.
- **Depth**—That is, the effort is greater because it is deployed to a finer level of design and implementation detail.
- **Rigor**—That is, the effort is greater because it is applied in a more structured, formal manner.

The ISSAP should understand the basic EAL structure and levels as well as where to find evaluated products. Currently, a list of these evaluated products can be found on the National Information Assurance Partnership (NIAP) Web site. This site contains the following types of information:

- List of evaluated products currently on the market, evaluating country, and the EAL level
- List of products in the test cycle
- List of products no longer on the active products list
- List of available protection profiles
- The CC Parts 1–3
- Other useful information about CC EAL and assurance

ISO/IEC 27000 Series

ISO/IEC 27000 is part of a growing family of ISO/IEC ISMS standards. This series is the number reserved for a new international standard, which currently has the provisional title: *"Information technology—Security techniques—Information security management systems—Overview and vocabulary."* The standard is known informally as "ISO 27000." The standard is being developed by a subcommittee of the Joint Technical Committee (JTC1) of the International Organization for Standardization and the International Electrotechnical Commission. ISO 27000 provides an overview of standards related to the ISO/IEC 27000 Information Security Management Systems (ISMS) family of standards that provide uniformity and consistency of fundamental terms and definitions (vocabulary) used throughout the ISMS family. Information security, similar to so many technical subjects, continues to develop a complex web of terminology. Relatively few authors take the trouble to define precisely what they mean, an approach that is unacceptable in the standards arena as it potentially leads to confusion and devalues formal assessment and certification. As with ISO 9000 and ISO 14000, the base "000" standard is intended to address this.

Although ISO/IEC 27001:2005 does not specifically address requirements analysis, organizations may require compliance with this document from the standpoint of implementing best security practices, which in turn may be interpreted as a requirement. Meeting ISO standards is generally good for business as they lend credibility to the company's commitment to quality and excellence. Customers may seek out organizations that meet the ISO standards and may require compliance for their information systems.

ISO/IEC 27001:2005 covers a variety of organizations including commercial enterprises, government agencies, and nonprofit organizations. If compliance with this standard is made mandatory by the contract or statement of work, the ISSAP will need to evaluate the contents of this code of practice to ensure that they are adequately addressed. ISO/IEC 27001:2005 specifies the requirements for establishing, implementing, operating, monitoring, reviewing, maintaining, and improving a documented Information Security Management System within the context of the organization's overall business risks. It specifies requirements for the implementation of security controls customized to the needs of individual organizations or parts thereof.

ISO/IEC 27001:2005 is designed to ensure the selection of adequate and proportionate security controls that protect information assets and give confidence to stakeholders. ISO/IEC 27001:2005 is intended to be suitable for

- Use within organizations to formulate security requirements and objectives
- Use within organizations as a way to ensure that security risks are cost-effectively managed
- Use within organizations to ensure compliance with laws and regulations
- Use within an organization as a process framework for the implementation and management of controls to ensure that the specific security objectives of an organization are met
- The definition of new information security management and governance processes
- The identification and clarification of existing information security management processes
- Use by the management of organizations to determine the status of information security management activities
- Use by the internal and external auditors of organizations to determine the degree of compliance with the policies, directives, and standards adopted by an organization

- Use by organizations to provide relevant information about information security policies, directives, standards, and procedures to trading partners and other organizations with whom they interact for operational or commercial reasons
- The implementation of business-enabling information security
- Use by organizations to provide relevant information about information security to customers

Software Engineering Institute—Capability Maturity Model (SEI-CMM) Key Practices Version 1.1

Introducing the Capability Maturity Model

The Capability Maturity Model (CMM) for Software is a framework that describes the key elements of an effective software process. The CMM describes an evolutionary improvement path from an ad hoc, immature process to a mature, disciplined process. The model covers practices for planning, engineering, and managing software development and maintenance. When followed, these key practices improve the ability of organizations to meet goals for cost, schedule, functionality, and product quality. It establishes a yardstick against which it is possible to judge, in a repeatable way, the maturity of an organization's software process and compare it to the state of the practice of the industry [Paulk et al., 1993a]. The CMM may also be used by organizations and the ISSAP to plan improvements to its software process.

Sources of the CMM

The Software Engineering Institute (SEI) developed an initial version of a maturity model and maturity questionnaire at the request of the government and with the assistance of the MITRE Corporation. Throughout the development of the model and the questionnaire, the SEI has paid attention to advice from practitioners who are involved in developing and improving software processes. The objectives are to provide a model that

- Is based on actual practices
- Reflects the best of the state of the practice
- Reflects the needs of individuals performing software process improvement, software process assessments, or software capability evaluations
- Is documented
- Is publicly available

Additional knowledge and insight into software process maturity has been gained since the earlier versions of the maturity model. This insight has been gained by

- Performing and observing software process assessments and software capability evaluations
- Studying nonsoftware organizations
- Participating in meetings and workshops with industry and government representatives
- Soliciting and analyzing change requests to the model
- Soliciting feedback from industry and government reviewers

Using this additional knowledge, the CMM and its practices have been revised, creating CMM v1.1.

Structure of the CMM

The CMM is composed of five maturity levels. With the exception of Level 1, each maturity level is composed of several key process areas. Each key process area is organized into five sections called *common features*. We will not look at each key feature of the model but review a summary of the practices. The common features specify the key practices that, when collectively addressed, accomplish the goals of the key process area. This structure of the CMM is illustrated in Figure 4.1.

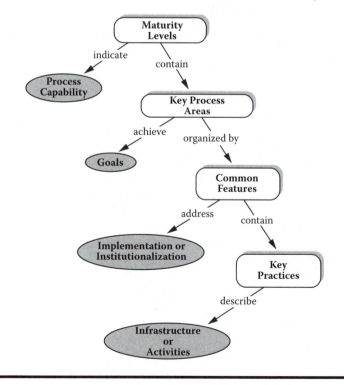

Figure 4.1   The structure of the Capability Maturity Model.

Developing reliable and usable software that is delivered on time and within budget is a difficult endeavor for many organizations. Products that are late, over budget, or that do not work as expected also cause problems for the organization's customers. As software projects continue to increase in size and importance, these problems are amplified. They can be overcome through a focused and sustained effort at building a process infrastructure of effective software engineering and management practices.

To build this process infrastructure, organizations producing software need ways to appraise their ability to perform their software process successfully. They also need guidance to improve their process capability. Customers, such as the Department of Defense (DoD), need ways to effectively evaluate an organization's capability to perform successfully on software engineering contracts. Prime contractors need ways to evaluate the capability of potential subcontractors.

To help organizations and customers such as the DoD and prime contractors, the Software Engineering Institute (SEI) has developed the CMM for Software, which delineates the characteristics of a mature, capable software process. The progression from an immature, unrepeatable software process to a mature, well-managed software process also is described in terms of maturity levels in the model. The CMM may be put to the following uses:

- Software process improvement, in which an organization plans, develops, and implements changes to its software process
- Software process assessments, in which a trained team of software professionals determines the state of an organization's current software process, determines the high-priority software process-related issues facing the organization, and obtains organizational support for software process improvement
- Software capability evaluations, in which a trained team of professionals identifies contractors who are qualified to perform the software work or monitor the state of the software process used in an existing software effort

This SEI CMM document describes the key practices that correspond to each maturity level in the CMM. It is an elaboration of what is meant by maturity at each level of the CMM and a guide that can be used for software process improvement, software process assessments, and software capability evaluations.

The key practices of the CMM are expressed in terms of what is expected to be the normal practices of organizations that work on large government contracts. In any context in which the CMM is applied, a reasonable interpretation of how the practices would be applied should be used. Guidelines on interpreting the CMM are contained in Chapter 4 of the CMM document. The CMM must be appropriately interpreted when the business environment of the organization differs significantly from that of a large contracting organization. The role of professional judgment in making informed use of the CMM must be recognized. The SEI CMM should be used by

- Organizations wanting to understand and improve their capability to develop software effectively
- Professionals wanting to understand the key practices that are part of effective processes for developing or maintaining software
- Anyone wanting to identify the key practices that are needed to achieve the next maturity level in the CMM
- Acquisition organizations or prime contractors wanting to identify the risks of having a particular organization perform the work of a contract
- Instructors preparing teams to perform software process assessments or software capability evaluations
- The SEI as the basis for developing process products, such as the maturity questionnaire

Version 1.0 of the CMM was released in August of 1991 in two technical reports. This initial release of the CMM was revised during 1992. To understand and use the current version of the CMM, two documents are needed:

- "Capability Maturity Model for Software, Version 1.1" [Paulk93a]
- "Key Practices of the Capability Maturity Model, Version 1.1" [Paulk93b]

Capability Maturity Model for Software, Version 1.1, contains an introduction to the model, descriptions of the five maturity levels, an operational definition of the CMM and its structure, a discussion of how organizations can use the maturity model, and some remarks on the future directions of the CMM. "Key Practices of the Capability Maturity Model, Version 1.1" contains the key practices that correspond to the key process areas at each maturity level of the CMM and information to help interpret the practices.

The maturity questionnaire and other process products are derived from the key practices of the CMM. Other SEI process products that support software process improvement, software process assessment, and software capability evaluation include training courses, handbooks, and site visit guides.

CMM Level 2

Beginning at CMM Level 2, processes must be repeatable in the areas of project planning, tracking, oversight, contracts management, QA, configuration management, process definition, and training. Requirements Management is established to foster a common understanding between the software project requirements and the customer. This involves establishing and maintaining an agreement with the customer on the requirements for the software project. This agreement is referred to as the "system requirements allocated to the software." The "customer" may be interpreted as the system engineering group, the marketing group, another internal organization, or an external customer. The agreement covers both the technical and nontechnical requirements. It forms the basis for estimating, planning, performing, and tracking the software project's activities throughout the software life cycle [Paulk93a].

The allocation of the system requirements to software, hardware, and other system components, including humans, may be performed by a group external to the software or systems engineering group. The software engineering group should have no direct control of this allocation except within the constraints of the project; the software engineering group takes appropriate steps to ensure that the system requirements allocated to software are documented and controlled.

The purpose of Software Project Planning is to establish reasonable plans for performing the software engineering and for managing the software project. Software Project Planning involves developing estimates for the work to be performed, establishing the necessary commitments, and defining the plan to perform the work.

The software planning begins with a statement of the work to be performed and other constraints and goals that define the software project. The software planning process includes steps to estimate the size of the software work products and the resources needed, produce a schedule, identify and assess software risks, and negotiate commitments. This plan provides the basis for performing and managing the software project's activities and addresses the commitments to the software project's customer according to the resources, constraints, and capabilities of the software project [Paulk93a].

Software Project Tracking and Oversight provides visibility into actual progress so that management can take effective actions when the software project's performance deviates significantly from the plans. Project Tracking and Oversight involves tracking and reviewing the software accomplishments and results against documented estimates, commitments, and plans, and adjusting these plans based on the actual accomplishments and results.

A documented plan for the software project is used as the basis for tracking the software activities, communicating status, and revising plans. These activities are monitored by the management. Progress is determined by comparing the actual software size, effort, cost, and schedule to the plan when selected work products are completed and at selected milestones. Other CMM Level 2 activities include

- Software Subcontract Management which selects qualified software subcontractors and manage them effectively in cases where these activities are monitored and managed as if the work was done in-house
- Software Quality Assurance, which involves reviewing and auditing the software products and activities to verify that they comply with the applicable procedures and standards as well as providing the project managers with the results of these reviews and audits
- Software Configuration Management which involves identifying the configuration of the software at given points in time, systematically controlling

changes to the configuration, and maintaining the integrity and traceability of the configuration throughout the software life cycle

By establishing the plans, standards, procedures, and configuration management, the organization helps ensure that the project's needs are met, the development is controlled and consistent, and verifies that they will be useful for performing reviews and audits throughout the development life cycle [Paulk93a].

A software baseline library is established containing the software baselines as they are developed. Changes to baselines and the release of software products built from the software baseline library are systematically controlled via the change control and configuration auditing functions of software configuration management. The practice of performing the software configuration management function identifies specific configuration items/units that are contained in the key process areas.

CMM Level 3

At CMM Level 3, the process must be repeatable in all the Level 2 task areas and have defined processes for organizational process focus, process definition, training, integrated software management, intergroup coordination, and peer reviews. (Most medium to large organizations reach Level 3 with relative ease once they decide that CMM is a value worth the investment.)

Process Definition involves developing and maintaining the organization's standard software process, along with related process assets, such as descriptions of software life cycles, process tailoring guidelines and criteria, the organization's software process database, and a library of software process-related documentation [Paulk93a].

These assets may be collected in many ways. For example, the descriptions of the software life cycles may be an integral part of the organization's standard software process or parts of the library of software-process-related documentation that may be stored in the organization's software process database. The organization's software process assets are available for use in developing, implementing, and maintaining the projects' defined software processes.

The training program is a key process area for developing the skills and knowledge of individuals so that they can perform their roles more effectively. Building training programs involves first identifying the training needed by the organization, projects, and individuals, and then developing or procuring training to address the identified needs. The project evaluates its current and future skill needs and determines how these skills will be obtained. Some skills are effectively obtained or upgraded using on-the-job training and informal mentoring, whereas other skills need more formal training such as computer-based or classroom training. Other times, a combination of approaches is used, including self-study.

The purpose of integrated software management is to integrate the software engineering and management activities into a coherent, defined software process that is tailored from the organization's standard software process and related process assets, which are described in the organization process definition. The project's defined software process is tailored from the organization's standard software process to address the specific characteristics of the project. The software development plan is based on the project's defined software process and describes how the activities of the project's defined software process will be implemented and managed. The management of the software project's size, effort, cost, schedule, staffing, and other resources is tied to the tasks of the project's defined software process.

Because the projects' defined software processes are all tailored from the organization's standard software process, the software projects can share process data and lessons learned. The basic practices for estimating, planning, and tracking a software project are described in the Software Project Planning and Software Project Tracking and Oversight key process areas. They focus on recognizing problems when they occur and adjusting the plans or performance to address the problems. The practices of this key process area build on, and are in addition to, the practices of those two key process areas. The emphasis of Integrated Software Management shifts to anticipating problems and acting to prevent or minimize the effects of these problems.

Software Product Engineering should consistently execute a well-defined engineering process that integrates all the software engineering activities to produce correct, consistent software products effectively and efficiently. Software Product Engineering involves performing the engineering tasks to build and maintain the software using the project-defined software processes, methods, and tools.

The software engineering tasks include

- Analyzing the system requirements allocated to software
- Developing the software requirements
- Developing the software architecture
- Designing the software
- Implementing the software in the code
- Integrating the software components
- Testing the software to verify that it satisfies the specified requirements

Documentation needed to perform the software engineering tasks include the software requirements document, software design document, test plan, and test procedures. They are developed and reviewed to ensure that each task addresses the results of predecessor tasks, and that the results produced are appropriate for the subsequent tasks [Paulk93a].

Intergroup Coordination

Intergroup coordination establishes a means for the software engineering group to participate actively with the other engineering groups, so that the project is better able to satisfy the customer's needs effectively and efficiently. It involves the software engineering group's participation with other project engineering groups to address system-level requirements, objectives, and issues. Representatives of the project's engineering groups participate in establishing the system-level requirements, objectives, and plans by working with the customer and end users, as appropriate. These requirements, objectives, and plans become the basis for all engineering activities.

The technical working interfaces and interactions between groups are planned and managed to ensure the quality and integrity of the entire system. Technical reviews and interchanges are regularly conducted with representatives of the project's engineering groups to ensure that all engineering groups are aware of the status and plans of all the groups, and that system and intergroup issues receive appropriate attention.

Peer Reviews

Peer reviews are designed to remove defects from the software work products early and efficiently. An important corollary effect is to develop a better understanding of the software work products and of defects that might be prevented.

Peer reviews involve a methodical examination of software work products by the producers' peers to identify defects and areas where changes are needed. The specific products that will undergo a peer review are identified in the project's defined software process and scheduled as part of the software project planning activities, as described in the Integrated Software Management key process area. This key process area covers the practices for performing peer reviews. The practices identifying the specific software work products that undergo peer review are contained in the key process areas that describe the development and maintenance of each software work product.

CMM Level 4

CMM Level 4 processes must be managed. This level includes all the attributes of Level 2 and 3 and also includes quantitative process management and software quality management.

Quantitative Process Management controls the process performance of the software project quantitatively. Software process performance represents the actual results achieved from following a software process. Quantitative Process Management involves establishing goals for the performance of the project's defined software process, which is described in the Integrated Software Management key process area; taking measurements of the process performance; analyzing these measurements; and making adjustments to maintain process performance within acceptable limits. When the process performance is stabilized within acceptable limits, the project's defined software process, the associated measurements, and the acceptable limits for the measurements are established as a baseline and used to control process performance quantitatively.

The organization collects process performance data from the software projects and uses these data to characterize the process capability (i.e., the process performance a new project can expect to attain) of the organization's standard software process, which is described in the Organization Process Definition key process area. Process capability describes the range of expected results from following a software process (i.e., the most likely outcomes that are expected from the next software project the organization undertakes). This process capability data is, in turn, used by the software projects to establish and revise their process performance goals and to analyze the performance of the projects' defined software processes.

Software Quality Management involves defining quality goals for the software products, establishing plans to achieve these goals, and monitoring and adjusting the software plans, software work products, activities, and quality goals to satisfy the needs and desires of the customer and end user for high-quality products.

This practice builds on the Integrated Software Management and Software Product Engineering key process areas, which establish and implement the project's defined software process, and the Quantitative Process Management key process area. It establishes a quantitative understanding of the ability of the project's defined software process to achieve the desired results. The goals are to establish software products based on the needs of the organization, the customer, and the end users. They are achieved by developing strategies and plans that address these goals.

CMM Level 5

CMM Level 5 processes must optimize all of the Level 2 through 4 attributes as well as identifying the cause of defects and preventing them from occurring. The purpose of Technology Change Management is to identify new technologies (i.e., tools, methods, and processes) and track them into the organization in an orderly manner. It involves identifying, selecting, and evaluating new technologies, and incorporating effective technologies into the organization. The objective is to improve software quality, increase productivity, and decrease the cycle time for product development.

By maintaining an awareness of software-related technology innovations and systematically evaluating and experimenting with them, the organization selects appropriate technologies to improve the quality of its software and the productivity of its software activities. With appropriate sponsorship by the organization's management, the selected technologies are incorporated into the organization's standard software process and current projects, as appropriate, using pilot programs to assess new technologies. Other Level 5 activities include imparting Process Change Management and training to the organization's standard software process (as described in the Organization Process Definition key process area); the projects' defined software processes (as described in the Integrated Software Management key process area) resulting from these technology changes are handled as described in the Process Change Management key process area [Paulk93a].

Process Change Management involves defining process improvement goals and, with senior management sponsorship, proactively and systematically identifying, evaluating, and implementing improvements to the organization's standard software process and the projects' defined software processes on a continuous basis. Training and incentive programs are established to enable and encourage everyone in the organization to participate in process improvement activities. Improvement opportunities are identified and evaluated for potential payback to the organization. Pilot efforts are performed to assess process changes before they are incorporated into normal practice.

ISO 7498

The purpose of this reference model of Open Systems Interconnection is to provide a common basis for the coordination of standards development for the purpose of systems interconnection, while allowing existing standards to be placed into perspective within the overall reference model. The term *Open Systems Interconnection* (OSI) qualifies standards for the exchange of information among systems that are "open" to one another for this purpose by virtue of their mutual use of the applicable standards.

This ISO standard does not specifically address requirements analysis, but the ISSAP should be familiar with its content when architecting information systems. The fact that a system is open does not imply any particular systems implementation, technology, or means of interconnection, but refers to the mutual recognition and support of the applicable standards.

It is also the purpose of this reference model to identify areas for developing or improving standards, and to provide a common reference for maintaining consistency of all related standards. It is not the intent of this reference model to serve as an implementation specification. Nor is it a basis for appraising the conformance of actual implementations, or to provide a sufficient level of detail to precisely define the services and protocols of the interconnection architecture. Rather, this reference model provides a conceptual and functional framework that allows international teams of experts to work productively and independently on the development of standards for each layer of the OSI reference model.

The reference model has sufficient flexibility to accommodate advances in technology and expansion in user demands. This flexibility is also intended to allow the phased transition from existing implementations to OSI standards.

While the scope of the general architectural principles required for OSI is very broad, the reference model is primarily concerned with systems comprising terminals, computers, and associated devices and the means for transferring information between such devices. Other aspects of OSI requiring attention are described briefly.

The description of the Basic Reference Model of OSI is developed in the following stages:

- Clause 4 establishes the reasons for Open Systems Interconnection, defines what is being connected, the scope of the interconnection, and describes the modeling principles used in OSI.
- Clause 5 describes the general nature of the architecture of the reference model; namely, that it is layered, what layering means, and the principles used to describe layers.
- Clause 6 names and introduces the specific layers of the architecture.
- Clause 7 provides the description of the specific layers.
- Clause 8 provides the description of management aspects of OSI.
- Clause 9 specifies compliance and consistency with the OSI reference model.

An indication of how the layers were chosen is given in Annex A to the Basic Reference Model. Additional aspects of this reference model beyond the basic aspects are described in several parts. The first part describes the Basic Reference Model. The second part describes the architecture for OSI Security. The third part describes OSI Naming and Addressing. The fourth describes OSI System Management.

The Basic Reference Model serves as a framework for the definition of services and protocols that fit within the boundaries established by the reference model. In those few cases where a feature is explicitly marked (optional) in the Basic Reference Model, it should remain optional in the corresponding service or protocol (even if at a given instant the two cases of the option are not yet documented).

The reference model does not specify services or protocols for OSI. It is neither implementation specific for systems nor a basis for appraising the conformance of implementations. For standards that meet the OSI requirements, a small number of practical subsets are defined from optional functions to facilitate implementation and compatibility.

Concepts of a Layered Architecture

Clause 5 sets forth the architectural concepts that are applied in the development of the reference model of OSI. First, the concept of a layered architecture (with layers, entities, service access points, protocols, connections, etc.) is described. Second, identifiers are introduced for entities, service access points, and connections. Third, service access points and data units are described. Fourth, elements of layer operation are described, including connections, transmission of data, and error functions. Then, routing aspects are introduced and, finally, management aspects are discussed.

The concepts described in clause 5 are those required to describe the reference model of Open Systems Interconnection. However, not all of the concepts described are employed in each layer of the reference model. There are four basic elements to the reference model:

- Open systems
- The application entities that exist within the OSI environment

- The associations that join the application entities and permit them to exchange information
- The physical media for OSI

Clause 6 states that when referring to these layers by name, the (N)-, (N + 1)-, and (N − 1)-prefixes are replaced by the names of the layers, for example, transport protocol, session entity, and network service.

Payment Card Industry Data Security Standard (PCI-DSS)

Payment Card Industry Data Security Standard (PCI-DSS) was developed by the major credit card companies as a guideline to help organizations that process card payments prevent credit card fraud, cracking, and various other security vulnerabilities and threats. A company processing, storing, or transmitting payment card data must be PCI-DSS compliant or risk losing their ability to process credit card payments and being audited or fined. Merchants and payment card service providers must validate their compliance periodically. This validation gets conducted by auditors (i.e., persons who are the PCI-DSS Qualified Security Assessor [QSAs]). Although individuals receive QSA status reports, compliance can only be signed off by an individual QSA on behalf of a PCI council-approved consultancy. Smaller companies, processing *fewer* than about 80,000 transactions a year, are allowed to perform a self-assessment questionnaire. The current version of the standard (1.2) specifies 12 requirements for compliance, organized into six logically related groups, which are called "Control Objectives."

The control objectives and their requirements are the following:

- Build and Maintain a Secure Network
    - Requirement 1: Install and maintain a firewall configuration to protect cardholder data.
    - Requirement 2: Do not use vendor-supplied defaults for system password and other security parameters.
- Protect Cardholder Data
    - Requirement 3: Protect stored cardholder data.
    - Requirement 4: Encrypt transmission of cardholder data across open, public networks.
- Maintain a Vulnerability Management Program
    - Requirement 5: Use and regularly update antivirus software.
    - Requirement 6: Develop and maintain secure systems and applications.
- Implement Strong Access Control Measures
    - Requirement 7: Restrict access to cardholder data by business need to know.
    - Requirement 8: Assign a unique ID to each person with computer access.
    - Requirement 9: Restrict physical access to cardholder data.

■ Regularly Monitor and Test Networks
  – Requirement 10: Track and monitor all access to network resources and cardholder data.
  – Requirement 11: Regularly test security systems and processes.
■ Maintain an Information Security Policy
  – Requirement 12: Maintain a policy that addresses information security.

PCI-DSS originally began as five different programs: Visa Information Security Program, MasterCard Site Data Protection, American Express Data Security Operating Policy, Discover Information and Compliance, and the JCB Data Security Program. Each company's intentions were roughly the same: to create an additional level of protection for customers by ensuring that merchants meet minimum levels of security when they store, process, and transmit cardholder data. The Payment Card Industry Security Standards Council (PCI-SSC) was formed and, on December 15, 2004, these companies aligned their individual policies and released the PCI-DSS.

In September 2006, the PCI standard was updated to version 1.1 to provide clarification and minor revisions to version 1.0. PCI is one of multiple data security standards that have emerged over the past decade: Basel II, Gramm–Leach–Bliley Act (GLBA), Health Insurance Portability and Accountability Act (HIPAA), Sarbanes–Oxley Act of 2002, and California Senate Bill 1386. The current version 1.2 was released in October 2008. Standards derived from the PCI-DSS include Payment Application Best Practices (PABP), which was renamed Payment Application Data Security Standards (PA-DSS).

Architectural Solutions

The ISSAP should be familiar with current architectures such as Service Oriented Architecture (SOA), Client Server Architecture, distributed centralized architectures, or database architectures. The functional architectures describe the types of data that need to be processed and transmitted as well as the bandwidth needed and whether or not the topology is hub and spoke, Ethernet, Star, Token Ring, and so on. The ISSAP will need to develop a security architecture that complements and supports the functional architecture. The architecture must provide security mechanisms that implement the appropriate levels of security to ensure the confidentiality, integrity, availability, and accountability of the system.

The security architecture hardware and software may require an evaluation under the Common Criteria. A discussion on this type of evaluation is included in the next section. Security architectures include hardware and software people processes and environment as part of the overall information systems and security.

Best security practices should include an architecture that provides defense in depth where layers of technology are designed and implemented to provide data protection. These layers include people, technology, and operations (including processes and procedures). Defense in depth includes

- Protect—preventative controls and mechanisms
- Detect—identify attacks, expect attacks
- React—respond to attacks, recover

Three primary elements of defense in depth include

- People—They can defeat the most complex security at times due to a lack of knowledge of the policies. By nature, we would rather trust than distrust others, but when a lot of regulations are in place, it looks as if we do not trust them. People are considered part of the defense-in-depth strategy because they are users of the system and must be able to use it safely and securely. People must be aware of policies, procedures, and safe security practices. Training the users in these aspects of the system can prevent inadvertent compromise of data and potential harm to the operational systems. Security awareness training can help prevent users from attempting to circumvent security on the system for convenience. Users should be part of the systems design and development team to give input and feedback on decisions that affect their access, operation, and use.
- Technology—Evaluation of products, IA architecture and standards, validation by a reputable third party, as well as configuration standards and guidance are all elements of implementing IT security technology. The ISSAP must be abreast of current technology, and its capabilities to ensure the right security services and protections are included in the design. Within the defense-in-depth (DiD) technology framework, layered protection should be considered. The ISSAP can work from the desktop to the security perimeter or from the perimeter to the desktop. Security mechanisms such as access controls (i.e., userID and password, authentication mechanisms, virus protection, operating systems lockdown or systems hardening, intrusion detection systems, firewall, and various types of encryption mechanisms) are technologies to be considered.
- Operations—Security Policy, Certificate Authority (CA), Security Management, Key Management, Respond quickly, and restore critical services. The systems should be under configuration management controls to ensure that changes made to the operational system are authorized. Other considerations for operations are backup and recovery as well as incident response, awareness training, and management of encryption mechanisms and keys.

The effectiveness of information protection is based on the value of the information. In that way, decisions are based on risk analysis and aligned with the operational objectives of the organization. Key elements of the people side of the defense-in-depth equation are

- Awareness training—ongoing
- Clearly written policy—that users can understand

- Consequences to the organization and individual—liability for management
- Incentive/reward

Table 4.4 illustrates the types of mechanisms that are required to defend the computing environment.

There are as many architectures as there are ways to configure information systems. For example, let us begin by looking at the outer perimeter of the network where security mechanisms, such as firewalls and intrusion detection systems, are in place to provide filtering and monitoring to defend the network perimeter. Firewall devices filter incoming and outgoing IP traffic to permit or deny access based on a rule set or policy settings that are enabled or disabled within the device. These settings should be documented and protected to ensure that they can be duplicated should the need arise.

Encryption such as Secure Socket Layer (SSL) may be used to protect the confidentiality of data being transmitted over the Internet. If the network is physically connected with dedicated leased lines, then other encryption appliances will be used to encrypt the point-to-point connections. These types of connections require network encryption devices as opposed to IP encryption devices.

The security architecture process depicted in Figure 4.3 shows the steps that should be taken to develop the systems and security architecture. The security architecture is closely integrated with the system functional architecture and supports those functional mechanisms based on a set of defined threats, vulnerabilities, customer and regulatory requirements, and best practices.

During the design process, countermeasure selections are made based on the results of a thorough functional and security analysis of the baseline requirements established during the early phases of the design. Countermeasure selection is a collaborative activity between the security architect and the security engineer. The architect defines the security features and conducts the analysis review. The security engineer develops and applies the detailed analysis to support the countermeasures selected. If an architecture framework was used to develop the architecture, such as U.S. Department of Defense (DoD) Architecture Framework (DoDAF), then a

Table 4.4 Computer Security Services and Mechanisms

Defend	Mechanism or Process
Defend the computing environment	Access control
Defend the enclave boundaries	Firewalls and IDS
Defend the network and infrastructure	Protection from denial of service (DOS), inbound and outbound traffic protection
Defend the supporting infrastructures	Key management and other infrastructures

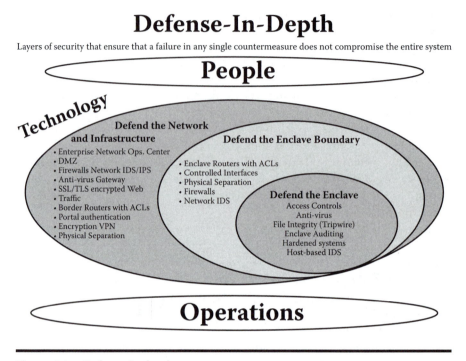

Defense-In-Depth

Layers of security that ensure that a failure in any single countermeasure does not compromise the entire system

People

Technology

Defend the Network and Infrastructure
- Enterprise Network Ops. Center
- DMZ
- Firewalls Network IDS/IPS
- Anti-virus Gateway
- SSL/TLS encrypted Web
- Traffic
- Border Routers with ACLs
- Portal authentication
- Encryption VPN
- Physical Separation

Defend the Enclave Boundary
- Enclave Routers with ACLs
- Controlled Interfaces
- Physical Separation
- Firewalls
- Network IDS

Defend the Enclave
Access Controls
Anti-virus
File Integrity (Tripwire)
Enclave Auditing
Hardened systems
Host-based IDS

Operations

Figure 4.2   Defense in depth.

systems view Level 5A SV-5a might be used to show what services are being provided and how they are being secured. If the architects and engineers are not using a framework or model, then a matrix can be developed to serve the same purpose.

Determining whether the systems require redundant architecture elements depends on the data requirement, performance, and criticality of the data where the single points of failure in the architecture are located. For instance, if all the data is stored in a single database and this data is the lifeblood of the organization, it would be wise to have backups and perhaps an alternate database that is updated frequently with the date. If the architecture calls for heavy use of the Internet or transmission of data to other sites, then redundant communications equipment and transmission paths might be necessary.

Enterprise Information Security architecture is a key component of the information security technology governance process at any organization of significant size. More and more companies are implementing a formal enterprise security architecture process to support the governance and management of IT. However, as noted in the opening paragraph of this article, it ideally relates more broadly to the practice of business optimization in that it addresses business security architecture, performance management, and process security architecture as well. Enterprise Information Security architecture is also related to IT security portfolio management and Metadata in the enterprise IT sense.

Figure 4.3   Security architecture process. (From Hansche, S. *The Official Guide to the CISSP-ISSEP CBK*, New York: Auerbach Publications, 2005.)

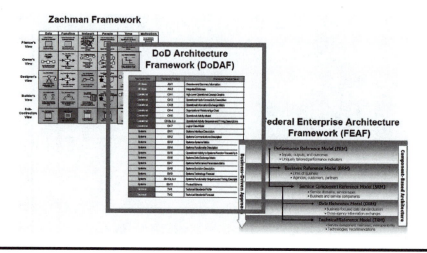

Figure 4.4   Enterprise architecture frameworks.

Architecture Frameworks

The enterprise architecture frameworks shown in Figure 4.4 are high-level depictions of the frameworks. There are numerous architecture frameworks, and the lists continue to grow. They include architectural frameworks such as those listed in the following text as well as a number of reference architectures designed to provide fast development of typical network architectures for specific projects. The list provides a general idea of the type of architecture frameworks you may want to become more familiar with as you engage in various projects based on your customer needs and requirements. The frameworks include the following:

- The U.S. Department of Defense (DoD) Architecture Framework (DoDAF)
- Zachman Framework
- U.S. Government Federal Enterprise Architecture Framework (FEAF)
- The Open Group Architecture Framework (TOGAF)
- Capgemini's Integrated Architecture Framework
- The U.K. Ministry of Defense (MoD) Architecture Framework (MoDAF)
- National Institute of Health Enterprise Architecture Framework
- Open Security Architecture
- Sherwood Applied Business Security Architecture (SABSA) Framework and Methodology
- Service-Oriented Modeling Framework (SOMF)

Let us briefly discuss the Zachman Framework, the U.S. Department of Defense (DoD) Architecture Framework (DoDAF), and the U.S. Government Federal Enterprise Architecture Framework (FEAF). If we had to simplify the conceptual

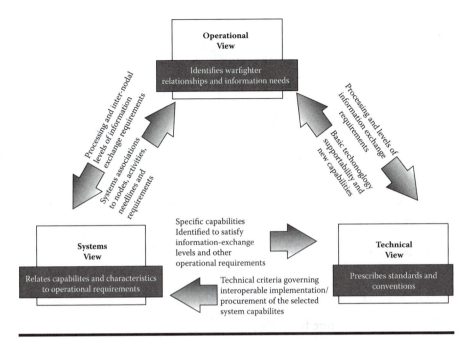

Figure 4.5   XYZ Inc. enterprise architecture.

abstraction of Enterprise Information Security Architecture within a generic framework, each would be acceptable as a high-level conceptual architecture framework.

Figure 4.5 represents the information that links the operational view, systems and services view, and technical standards view. The three views and their interrelationships are driven by common architecture data elements that provide the basis for deriving measures such as interoperability or performance and for measuring the impact of the values of these metrics on operational mission and task effectiveness.

Department of Defense Architecture Framework (DoDAF)

DoDAF is the standard framework chosen by the U.S. Department of Defense to comply with the Clinger–Cohen Act and the U.S. Office of Management and Budget based on Circulars A-11 and A-130. It is administered by the Office of the DoD Deputy CIO Enterprise Architecture and Standards Directorate. Other derivative frameworks based on DoDAF include the NATO Architecture Framework (NAF) and Ministry of Defense United Kingdom Architecture Framework (MoDAF).

Similar to other enterprise architecture approaches, The Open Group Architecture Framework (ToGAF) and DoDAF are organized around a shared repository to hold work products. The repository is defined by the Core Architecture Data Model 2.0 (CADM)—essentially a common database schema) and the DoD Architecture Repository System (DARS). A key feature of DoDAF is interoperability, which is organized as a series of levels, called Levels of Information System Interoperability (LISI). The developing system must not only meet its internal data needs but also those of the operational framework into which it is set. The current version of DoDAF 2.0 consists of 26 views organized into four basic view sets:

- All View (AV)—AV 1 and 2
- Operational View (OV)—OV-1 through OV-7
- Systems View (SV)—SV-1 through SV-11
- Technical Standards View (TV)—TV-1 and TV-2

Only a subset of the full DoDAF view set is usually created for each system development. An ISSAP who plans to use this model should plan on developing parallel views that focus specifically on developing the security architecture. For instance, the All View should best be depicted by overlaying the high-level security services, capabilities, and function over the functional architecture view. This method would apply to the Operational View as well. By taking this approach, the ISSAP establishes a link between the functional system and the security functionality.

Figure 4.6 shows XYZ Inc. (XYZnet), a small LAN in the context of an Operational View 1 (OV-1). The high-level graphic shows typical network connections over the Internet through WAN or MAN connections. These connections are to the customers, suppliers, and other stakeholders over the public switched telephone networks (PSTN).

The functional OV-1 for the XYZ Inc. shows the need to communicate with internal and external organizations. Security mechanisms typically are used to ensure that these networks operate securely, and safety would be overlaid on the functional OV-1 to show where security mechanisms and services would typically

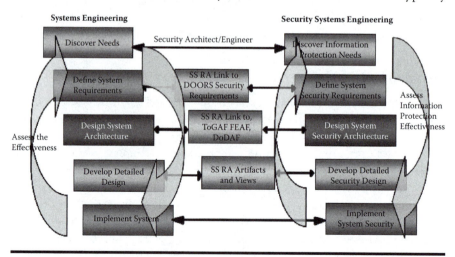

Figure 4.6 Systems engineering, architecture, and security engineering relationships.

be placed. These security mechanisms would include firewall or demilitarized zone (DMZ) to filter or proxy incoming and outgoing traffic, intrusion detection systems (IDS) to monitor and analyze both malicious and legitimate activities, and virus protection to ensure that the latest virus signatures are blocked. The OV-1 is a typical DoDAF artifact that shows the overall connections to various networks.

The Zachman Framework

The Zachman Framework is a logical structure for identifying and organizing the descriptive representations that are important in the management of enterprises and to the development of the system, both automated and manual, that comprise them. It is a schema that represents the intersection between two classifications. The first is the fundamentals of communication found in the interrogatives: *what, how, when, who, where, and why*. It is the integration of answers to these questions that enables the comprehensive, composite description of complex ideas. The second is derived from reification, the transformation of an abstract idea into an instantiation, that was initially postulated by ancient Greek philosophers and is labeled in the Framework: Identification, Definition, Representation, Specification, Configuration, and Instantiation.

More specifically, the Zachman Framework is an ontology—a theory of the existence of a structured set of essential components of an object for which explicit expressions is necessary and perhaps even mandatory for creating, operating, and changing the object (the object being an enterprise, a department, a value chain, a "sliver," a solution, a project, an airplane, a building, a product, and a profession of whatever).

According to Zachman, this ontology was derived from analogous structures that are found in the older disciplines of architecture, construction, engineering, and manufacturing that classify and organize the design artifacts created in the process of designing and producing complex physical products (e.g., buildings or airplanes). It uses a two-dimensional classification model based on the six basic interrogatives (*what, how, where, who, when, and why*) intersecting six distinct perspectives, which relate to stakeholder groups (Planner, Owner, Designer, Builder, Implementer, and Worker). The intersecting cells of the framework correspond to models that, if documented, can provide a holistic view of the enterprise.

Design Process

The design process follows the systems engineering and architecture framework. These steps are discussed in the following section.

System Security Engineering Methodologies

Information System Security Engineering (ISSE) is the art and science of discovering users' information protection needs and the designing and making of information systems, with economy and elegance, so that they can safely resist attacks, malicious activities, or other threats to which they may be subjected [IATF v3.0].

There must be an alignment of the SE and the ISSE. The Security Engineering and System Engineering steps take place at the same time. While the Systems Engineers are discovering the system needs, the system requirements the Systems Security Engineers are discovering the security needs and security requirements and so on. The System Engineering Process consists of the following six steps:

1. *Discover information protection needs.* Ascertain why the system needs to be built and what information needs to be protected.
2. *Define system security requirements.* Define the system in terms of what security is needed.
3. *Define system security architecture.* Define the security functions needed to meet the specific security requirements. This process is the core of designing the security architecture.
4. *Develop detailed security design.* Based on the security architecture, design the security functions and features for the system.
5. *Implement system security.* Following the documented security design, build and implement the security functions and features for the system.
6. *Assess security effectiveness.* Assess the degree to which the system, as it is defined, designed, and implemented, meets the security needs. This assessment activity occurs during and with all the other activities in the ISSE process.

Let us look at the details of the ISSE process, systems engineering, and architecture process. Discovering the information protection needs includes developing an understanding of the customer's mission or business needs. The ISSAP should work with the customer to determine what information management is needed to support the mission or business, and draft the Information Management Model (IMM) (shown in Table 4.5) and conduct a threat analysis. This will be the basis for creating an Information Protection Plan (IPP) that describes how this information will be protected. The results of these two activities should be documented in the Information Management Plan (IMP).

These results should support Certification and Accreditation by identifying the Accreditation Authority and any security oversight bodies and identify the classes of threats, security services, and design constraints.

Some common pitfalls of not adequately determining the information protection needs are

■ Poor working relationships with stakeholders
■ Inadequate coordination/support
■ Business understanding
■ Excessive categorization

Table 4.5   Information Management Tool

Information Domain	User	Rules/ Privileges	Process	Information
Data entry	Data entry personnel	Read/write	Entry	Raw
Accept	Course coordinator/ manager	Read/write	Accept	Analyzed
Distribute materials	Course coordinator	Read/write	Distribute	Releasable/ processed
Review data	Manager	Read	Review/print reports	Processed

- Failure to document critical information
- Excessive documentation

The next step is to understand the Systems Security Requirements. These requirements will drive the system development and include functional, contractual, or regulatory requirements. These requirements are most often found in statements of work (SOW), statement of requirements (SOR), statements of objectives (SOO), or service level agreements (SLAs). A key of this model is a feedback loop, and the key stakeholders are involved in each process.

Design Validation

Design validation is done during phase 2 of the systems development life cycle. It ensures that the design meets the security requirements that were allocated to the original baseline for the development. Validation is often done in accordance with an established design specification, functional capability, security policy, customer requirements, or any combination of these.

Design validation requires the development of a test and evaluation plan. These plans are often called Security Tests and Evaluation Plans or Certification Tests and Evaluation Plans. They include test methods that identify how the test is conducted, the criteria for testing, and how the requirement is met. The test and evaluation methods include functional demonstration of the security feature, documentation that includes policies, and procedures that describe how the system, feature or capability is operated. Other methods may include electronic instrumented tests and interviews with employees, managers, and users of the system.

Step 3 activities define the system's security architecture. This design is based on a thorough understanding of the system's Security Concept of Operations (SECONOP), which discusses how the system's security mechanisms will be implemented. The security functions needed to meet the specific security requirements called for in the specifications should also include the system security modes of operation. Will the system be a stand-alone, closed LAN not connected to the Internet or will it have Internet access with a variety of users with different types of need to know and user roles. Once this is established, trade-off studies should be conducted to ensure that the appropriate hardware and software are selected. Some products may require CC-evaluated products, as discussed earlier. Finally, the ISSAP should be involved in assessing the information protection effectiveness. These are the core processes involved in designing the security architecture.

Step 4 involves developing the detailed architecture so that security services can be allocated to architecture by selecting the appropriate security mechanisms. The architecture is then submitted for evaluation by the test and evaluation team. The architecture is revised to accommodate mission capabilities and requirements that may need adjusting in order to function properly. A risk analysis is conducted to evaluate all potential vulnerabilities that may be caused by relaxing or restraining the configuration settings. The results are provided to customers to obtain concurrence that the architecture meets their needs.

The ISSAP also participates in the various decisions that are taken at particular development milestone Preliminary Design Reviews, Critical Design Reviews, Systems Readiness Reviews, and Technical Interchange meetings. A variety of working groups may also be established to resolve design or program management issues that occur throughout the design process. These working group meetings and the like should include the oversight committees, accreditors, and systems certifiers in support of the Certification and Accreditation process if one is required.

Certification

Certification has been defined as the comprehensive evaluation of the security features and functions of an information system. It provides evidence that the system is configured to provide the most effective security protection based on specific security policies, standards, or industry best practices. Certification can be done based on a variety of public security policies or standards. A list of some of the certification policies include but are not limited to the following:

- Health Insurance Portability and Accountability Act (HIPAA)
- NIST Certification and Accreditation Process (NIST SP 800-37)
- ISO/IEC 27002, Certification for commercial information systems
- Sarbanes–Oxley Act of 2002
- Payment Card Industry Data Security Standard (PCI-DSS)

Peer Reviews

Peer review processes exist in many companies, particularly those with CMM Level 3 or higher. They may be automated or manually implemented. If they are

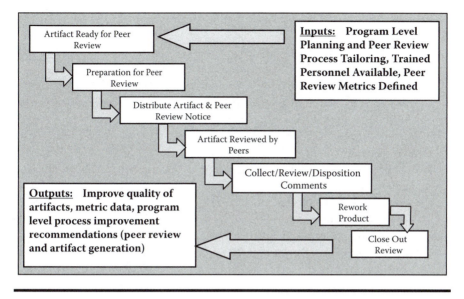

Figure 4.7   Peer review process.

automated, they contain processes and procedures for inviting peers to the review, prework such as reviewing the document or code prior to meeting, recording the defects, or problems with the article under review. The chair of the peer review should assign roles to individuals supporting the review.

Peer review is a methodical examination of a work product by the author's peers to provide comments and to identify and categorize defects in the work product as efficiently and as early in the life cycle as possible (see Figure 4.7). The peer review process requires planning, advanced preparation, discussion, recording, measurement, rework, and follow-up. It typically reviews contract deliverable documentation for internal and external customers based primarily on materials (PDR and CDR charts). Program Planning Documents (e.g., SEP, HDP, Tailoring Matrix) include the requirements for a peer review process. Design and Development of work products (Requirements, Design description, Module Design Specifications, Board layout, S/W Code, Trade Studies, Plans and Procedures) should all be peer-reviewed.

There are several types of peer reviews:

- **Formal inspection**—Typically used for initial deliveries of contractually required products
- **Structured walkthrough**—Typically used for complex products, where an off-line review may not be efficient. Product is reviewed in real time during a meeting
- **Critique**—Used for simple products, small changes, or use of the product limited to internal customers

Peer review teams can be composed of the following types of personnel:

- **Manager/team lead**—Ultimately responsible for the product; ensures that the product is ready for PR; assists author in identifying reviewers.
- **Moderator**—In a formal or walkthrough review, conducts the PR meeting; is responsible for identifying predicted defects using the Inspection Calculator and for determining if a reinspection is required.
- **Author**—Generates the product, schedules the PR, and incorporates comments.
- **Recorder**—In a formal or walkthrough review, records defect data during the meeting.
- **Reviewers**—Relevant stakeholders review the work product to identify defects and potential issues.
- **Reader**—In a walkthrough review, presents the item under review.
- **Quality engineer**—Ensures the PR process is followed, and ensures compliance with standards and conventions.

The benefit of having a peer review process is to ensure that a quality product is delivered to the customer without any defects. This reduces rework and shows the customer that you are conducting due diligence in product delivery.

Audit reports are sometimes referred to as Security Test and Evaluation Reports or certification reports. They are assessments of the system's security mechanisms and services based on the predefined requirements that were implemented in the system during the development process. They can range from running simple risk assessment tools to full-blown penetration testing and reporting the findings or results back to the system owners or regulators. The level of the evaluations is dependent on the sensitivity of the information being processed or stored on the system.

Audit reports provide evidence to the system owners and regulators that the system has met the prescribed specifications for security assurance. The reports point out the strengths and weaknesses of the system and provide recommendations to correct any deficiencies. Sometimes, the deficiencies are so severe that the recommendation is not to allow the system to proceed to operation. When this happens, it is often because of a failure to implement a countermeasure to provide adequate protection to the system. Deficiencies are often ranked as to the severity of the vulnerability. For instance, when a technical protection mechanism does not work, a procedural one might do the trick in the short term. When deficiencies are less severe, the system may be allowed to operate as long as those deficiencies are corrected within a prescribed timeline. The ultimate goal of the audit report is to determine if the system meets an acceptable level of risk for secure operation.

Following the documented security design, build, and implementation of the security functions and features of the system, the ISSAP works with the systems engineer and security engineer to ensure that all the requirements of the system have been satisfied. They support the system certification and assist in verifying the

Figure 4.8   XYZ Enterprise architecture.

interoperability of security tools and mechanisms against the security design and evaluate security components against the evaluation criteria as well as the integration and configuration of components.

Finally, the ISSAP supports the build, test, and evaluation strategy for the system. This may include developing test plans and procedures using the demonstration, observation, analysis, and testing methods. The ISSAP assesses available test and evaluation data for applicability, supports development of test and evaluation procedures and evaluation activities to ensure that the security design is implemented correctly, and conducts or updates a final risk analysis. If certification and accreditation is required, the ISSAP ensures the completeness required for C&A documentation with the customer and the customer's certifiers and accreditors or regulators. Security training on the system may also be required, and the ISSAP may be called upon to support development of security training material.

Documentation

A variety of documents is usually required as part of the program administration. The ISSAP will have input into these documents and may be directly responsible for developing program documents or providing input to the list of documents being developed. Document development may be required by policy or regulation as part of the contract. The documents list includes but is not limited to the following:

- IMM—Information Management Model
- MNS—Mission Needs Statement (what is the overall mission and need for this product)

- IPP—Information Protection Policy
- PNE—Protection Needs Elicitation (appendix H of the IATF)
- CONOPS—Concept of Operations (user perspective and functional/technical—sometimes on large projects the security is removed and made a different document)
- SSP—System Security Plans
- Security Architecture—Discusses the security functions, safeguards, and configurations

Some common pitfalls of this security architecture and design:

- The security architecture is not compatible with system architecture, which means the wrong mechanisms may have been selected for a particular function or provide inadequate security protections.
- The security is not integrated with nonsecurity functionality or use of modified COTS/GOTS products.
- Occasionally, a poorly documented architecture, meant to clearly describe the costs/benefits of the security design elements or provide adequate design context or rationale, may leave the customer in doubt as to whether the system meets their specification, so it is important to ensure that the documentation is complete and is written to address the appropriate audience.

Summary

This domain covers the information essential to understanding requirements analysis and security standards/guidelines criteria and their elements. We discussed requirement analysis, current architectures and solutions, systems engineering methodologies, methods of attack vectors, design validation, and legal and regulatory requirements.

Requirements analysis is one of the most important activities of systems security architecture and systems development. Security requirements are based on industry best practices, regulatory statutes, customer needs, and contractual obligations. Proper analysis of the requirements can prove to be critical to developing and delivering a secure system that is usable and provides customer satisfaction. The ISSAP begins by gathering requirements from customers who submit statements of work (SOW), contract documents, system specifications, service level agreements (SLAs), requests for proposals (RFPs), legal and regulatory documents from federal, state, local, or international policy, or other documents such as security best practices and industry standards for safety and security. The ISSAP should be able to gather the relevant requirements and determine at a high level the best solutions to satisfy those requirements and the impact they may have on the system as the system development life cycle progresses.

The ISSAP should be intimately familiar with the most common types of attacks in order to select countermeasures that will combat these attacks. An attack vector is a path or means by which a hacker or cracker can gain access to a computer or network server in order to deliver a payload or malicious outcome. Attack vectors enable hackers to exploit system vulnerabilities, including the human element. This includes viruses, e-mail attachments, Web pages, pop-up windows, instant messages, chat rooms, and deception. All of these methods involve programming or, in a few cases, hardware, except deception, in which a human operator is fooled into removing or weakening system defenses. It is unrealistic to think that 100% protection against all possible threats, at all times, is attainable or desirable. The objective is to develop a system that allows the customer to conduct their business or mission at an acceptable level of residual risk.

There are a number of methods and techniques used by the ISSAP to ensure that the requirements are satisfied. These include using CC-evaluated products when required for security relevant applications and services, engaging architecture processes such as DoDAF, MoDAF, FEAF, or Zachman, and supporting the Systems Security Engineering process. The ISO/IECs and RFCs can also be helpful in providing best practice guidance. A secure information system is best achieved when the ISSAP practices due diligence and pays attention to details of standards, threats awareness, risks identification, and the value of the data. In all cases, the ISSAP should be aware of the relevant policies, procedures, and techniques needed to architect an information system using defense in depth.

References

Bradley, M., Data valuation: rethinking "one size fits all" data protection—Storage Networking, *Computer Technology Review*, Jan., 2003.

Capability Maturity Model (CMM) Key Practices Version 1.1

Common Criteria (CC) for Information Technology Security Evaluation Part 1: Introduction and general model September 2006 Version 3.1, Revision 1.

Common Criteria (CC) for Information Technology Security Evaluation Part 2: Security Functional Component, September 2006 Version 3.1, Revision 1.

Common Criteria (CC) for Information Technology Security Evaluation Part 3: Security Assurance Component, September 2006 Version 3.1 Revision 1.

Hansche, S., *The Official Guide to the CISSP-ISSEP CBK*™, Auerbach Publications, Boca Raton, FL, 2005

Happy Trails Computer Club, http://cybercoyote.org/index.shtml)

Information Assurance Technical Framework IATF V.3.0

IT Law Group, http://www.itlawgroup.com/Resources/Archives.html, Accessed Nov. 2009.

Paulk, M. C., Weber, C. V., Garcia, S. M., Chrissis M. B., and Bush, M. (1993a) *Key Practices of the Capability Maturity Model*SM*, Version 1.1,* Software Engineering Institute Carnegie Mellon University Pittsburgh, Pennsylvania 15213 CMU/SEI-93-TR-25 ESC-TR-93-178.

Paulk, M. C., Curtis, B., Chrissis M. B., Weber, C. V. (1993b), *Capability Maturity Model for Software, Version 1.1, Technical Report,* CMU/SEI-93-TR-024, ESC-TR-93-177, February 1993.

Sample Questions

1. The approach in which policies, procedures, technology, and personnel are considered in the system security development process is called
   a. Defense in depth
   b. Requirements analysis
   c. Risk assessment
   d. Attack vectors

2. Software that adds hidden components to your system without your knowledge is
   a. Virus
   b. Spyware
   c. Adware
   d. Malware

3. Risk is assessed by which of the following formulas?
   a. Risk = Vulnerability × Threat × Impact Divided by Countermeasure
   b. Risk = Annual Loss Opportunity × Single Loss Expectancy
   c. Risk = Exposure Facture divided by Asset Value
   d. Risk = Vulnerability × Annual Loss Expectancy

4. Requirements definition is a process that should be completed in the following order:
   a. Document, identify, verify, and validate
   b. Identify, verify, validate, and document
   c. Characterize, analyze, validate, and verify
   d. Analyze, verify, validate, and characterize

5. A path by which a malicious actor gains access to a computer or network in order to deliver a malicious payload is
   a. Penetration test
   b. Attack vector
   c. Vulnerability assessment
   d. Risk assessment

6. Which of the following is useful as a guide for the development, evaluation, and/or procurement of IT products with security functionality?
   a. ISO/IEC 27001
   b. FIPS 140-2
   c. Common Criteria
   d. SEI-CMM

7. Which of the following defines evaluation criteria for Protection Profile (PP) and Security Target (ST) and presents evaluation assurance levels rating assurance for the TOE?
   a. Part 3—Security assurance requirements
   b. Part 2—Security functional requirements
   c. Part 1—Introduction and general model
   d. Part 4—History and previous versions

8. The National Voluntary Laboratory Accreditation Program (NVLAP) must be in full conformance with which of the following standards?
   a. ISO/IEC 27001 and 27002
   b. ISO/IEC 17025 and Guide 58
   c. NIST SP 800-53A
   d. ANSI/ISO/IEC Standard 17024

9. A software application in combination with an operating system, a workstation, smart card integrated circuit, or cryptographic processor would be considered examples of a
   a. Functional Communications (FCO)
   b. Functional Trusted Path (FTP)
   c. Target of Evaluation (TOE)
   d. Security Target (ST)

10. An ISSAP requires a device with a moderate level of independently assured security, and a thorough investigation of the TOE and its development without substantial reengineering. It should be evaluated at which CC EAL?
    a. EAL6
    b. EAL5
    c. EAL4
    d. EAL3

11. At which CC EAL would an ISSAP select a device appropriate for application in extremely high-risk situations or where the high value of the assets justifies the higher costs?
    a. EAL4
    b. EAL5
    c. EAL6
    d. EAL7

12. A list of Common Criteria–evaluated products can be found on the Internet on the site at the
    a. NIAP
    b. CCEVS
    c. IASE
    d. CERIS

13. Which of the following describes the purpose of the Capability Maturity Model?
    a. Determine business practices to ensure creditability for the company's commitment to quality and excellence.
    b. Provide assurance through active investigation and evaluation of the IT product in order to determine its security properties.
    c. Establish a metric to judge in a repeatable way the maturity of an organization's software process as compared to the state of the industry practice.
    d. Provide an overview of standards related to the Information Security Management family for uniformity and consistency of fundamental terms and definitions.

14. Which one of the following describes the key practices that correspond to a range of maturity levels 1–5?
    a. Common Criteria
    b. SEI-CMM
    c. ISO/IEC 27002
    d. IATF v3

15. Which of the following CMMI levels include quantitative process management and software quality management as the capstone activity?
    a. CMMI Level 5
    b. CMMI Level 4
    c. CMMI Level 3
    d. CMMI Level 2

16. Where can the general principles of the OSI Reference Model architecture be found that describes the OSI layers and what layering means?
    a. Clause 3
    b. Clause 5
    c. Clause 7
    d. Clause 9

17. A company processing, storing, or transmitting payment card data must be compliant with which of the following?
    a. Gramm–Leach–Bliley Act (GLBA)
    b. Health Insurance Portability and Accountability Act (HIPAA)
    c. Sarbanes–Oxley Act of 2002
    d. PCI-DSS

18. In which phase of the IATF does formal risk assessment begin?
    a. Assess effectiveness
    b. Design system security architecture
    c. Define system security requirements
    d. Discover information protection needs

19. Which of the following describes a methodical examination of a work product by the author's coworkers to comment, identify, and categorize defects in the work product?
    a. Formal inspection
    b. Structured walkthrough
    c. Critique
    d. Peer review
20. Which of the following is a critical element in the design validation phase?
    a. Develop security test and evaluation plan
    b. Develop protection needs elicitation
    c. Develop the concept of operation
    d. Requirements analysis

Chapter 5

Technology-Related Business Continuity Planning (BCP) and Disaster Recovery Planning (DRP)

Kelley Okolia

Contents

Business continuity planning (BCP) and disaster recovery planning (DRP) involve the identification of adverse events that could threaten the ability of the organization to continue normal operations. Once these events are identified, the security professional will implement counter-measures to reduce the risk of such incidents occurring. Furthermore, the security professional will play a key role in designing and develop-ing business continuity plans that will meet the operational business requirements of the organization through planning for the provisioning of appropriate solutions. Key areas of knowledge include

- Evaluating recovery requirements and strategy
- Designing and developing business continuity plans
- Assessing the business continuity plan and disaster recovery plan

This chapter is written to help security professionals understand the business con-tinuity and disaster recovery domain and to prepare them to develop plans for the protection and recovery of the critical IT infrastructure. The chapter focuses on the technology recovery strategies in support of the overall business continuity program.

BCP is defined as preparation that facilitates the rapid recovery of mission-critical business operations, the reduction of the impact of a disaster, and the continuation of critical business functions. DRP is a subset of BCP that emphasizes the procedures for emergency response relating to the information infrastructure of the organization. This includes extended backup operations and postdisaster recovery for data center, network, and computer resources. A business continuity plan is the tool that results from the planning and is the basis for continued life-cycle development [Waxvik 2007]. Continuity planning is a significant corporate issue and should include all parts or functions of the company. Together, BCP and DRP ensure adequate prepa-rations and procedures for the continuation of all business functions.

Planning Phases and Deliverables

When developing a new plan or updating a significantly old plan, the following phases are recommended:

1. Identify the planning team and critical staff.
2. Validate vital records.

3. Conduct risk and business impact analyses.
4. Develop recovery strategy.
5. Select alternate sites.
6. Document the plan.
7. Test, maintain, and update the plan.

Planning team and critical staff—You need to identify and build contact lists for the planning team, leadership, and critical staff. The deliverable from this phase is the Emergency Notification List (ENL).

Vital records—Validating that all the records needed to rebuild the business are stored off-site in a secure location that will be accessible following a disaster. This includes backups of your technology as well as paper records. The deliverable from this phase is a list of your vital records, where they are stored off-site, how to retrieve them, and who is authorized to retrieve them.

Risk analysis and business impact analysis—This is where you make decisions about what risks you will mitigate and which processes you will recover and when. The deliverable from this phase of the planning is a list of risks by site and recommendations to be implemented to reduce the impact of the risk. You cannot mitigate against every possible risk because of the costs involved.

Strategy development—In this phase, you review the different types of strategies for the recovery of business areas and technology based on the recovery time frame you have identified for each, do a cost–benefit analysis on the viable strategies to be selected, and make a proposal to leadership to implement the selected strategies. The deliverable from this phase is the recommended strategies for recovery.

Alternate site selection and implementation—In this phase, you select and build out the alternate sites you will used to recover. The deliverable from this phase is a functional alternate site.

Documenting the plan—This phase is where all the information collected up to this point is combined into a plan document. The deliverable from this phase is the documented plan for recovery for each site.

Testing, maintenance, and update—This final phase is where you validate the recovery strategies you have implemented through testing, establish a maintenance schedule for the plan, and an update schedule for the plan documentation. The deliverable from this phase is ongoing results from validating the plan.

Risk Analysis

As part of the planning process, you will need to perform a risk analysis or assessment to determine the threats to which your organization is vulnerable and where you should spend mitigating dollars to attempt to reduce the impact of a threat.

To do this, you need to determine the risks your particular organization faces. This includes risk from natural hazards, industry risks, and environmental risks.

You need to look at natural hazard risks based on the location of the business; industry risks based on your company's type of business; crime risks based on the location of your business; man-made hazards such as transportation accidents based on proximity to highways, train lines, airports, etc.; proximity risks based on other industries near where you conduct business such as chemical plants, and natural gas storage facilities; and recommend mitigating strategies to protect your business where appropriate.

Natural Hazard Risks

You can check with the U.S. Geological Survey (USGS) for a natural hazards map of your area. Some common natural hazards include

- Earthquake
- Tornado
- Floods
- Hurricane
- Ice storms
- Blizzards
- Tsunami

Industry Risks

Some risks are associated with the business you are in. Convenience stores face a threat of robbery. Banks may not only face robbery but also need to be concerned about money laundering. Department stores are frequent victims of shoplifting and also need to worry about identity theft. Insurance companies sometime face threats of workplace violence from claimants who are dissatisfied with the handling or a claim. Some common industry risks are as follows:

- Robbery and theft
- Workplace violence
- Money laundering
- Identity theft
- Theft of trade secrets
- Fraud
- Loan defaults
- Market risk
- Credit risk
- Labor disputes

Do Not Forget the Neighbors!

Some neighbors you may want to evaluate are

- Nuclear power plants
- FBI/CIA
- Oil storage facilities
- Hazard waste producers
- Chemical factories
- Biomedical research

As you go through the list of threats, you will notice that some of them are events that are fairly localized, such as a facility fire, and others, such as a hurricane, have a more regional impact. These are important factors in the risk consideration. A regional risk can impact not just your business but the homes and families of your employees, and can cause competition for the availability of contracted alternate sites.

When you identify a risk, you need to make choices about how to respond to that risk: accept it, transfer it, or reduce it.

Risk acceptance. If the risk of occurrence is so small or the impact so minimal or the cost to mitigate it so substantial, you can simply choose to accept the risk.

Risk transfer. This is where insurance comes into play. If a risk is too costly to mitigate, but too big to just accept, you can choose to transfer the risk by purchasing an insurance policy. Similar to car insurance, business interruption insurance is often used to transfer the risk of an event that cannot be mitigated either because of cost or some other factor.

Risk reduction. If you can put controls in place to prevent the most likely of risks from having an impact on your ability to do business, you will have fewer actual events from which to recover. The ones you address are the ones most likely to occur. A business continuity plan is one type of mitigation. In fact, a business continuity plan is what we implement when all other mitigating factors fail.

Business Impact Analysis

The business impact analysis (BIA) attempts to determine the consequences of disruptions that could result from a disaster and guides the organization's decision regarding what needs to be recovered and how quickly it needs to be recovered. The BIA is the foundation of the plans that will be built for the business.

While performing the BIA, avoid using the term *critical* or *essential* in defining the processes or people during this phase of the planning. Instead, use the term *time sensitive*. Generally speaking, organizations do not hire staff to perform nonessential tasks. Every function has a purpose, but some are more time sensitive than others when there is limited time or resources available to perform them.

A bank that has suffered a building fire could easily stop its marketing campaign but would not be able to stop processing deposits and checks written by its customers. The bank's marketing campaign is very essential to the bank's growing its business in the long term but in the middle of a disaster, marketing will take a backseat, not because it is not critical but because it is not time sensitive.

All business functions and the technology that supports them need to be classified based on their recovery priority. Recovery time frames for business operations are driven by the consequences of not performing the function. The consequences may be the result of business lost during the down period; contractual commitments not met, resulting in fines or lawsuits; lost goodwill with customers, etc. Impacts generally fall into one or more of these categories: financial, regulatory, or customer.

All applications, such as all business functions, need to be classified as to their time sensitivity for recovery even if they do not support business functions that are time sensitive. For applications, this is commonly referred to as recovery time objective (RTO). This is the amount of time the business can function without that application before significant business impact occurs.

Once the business has determined the time frame for recovery of the different business operations and identified the applications that are essential to perform those functions, we can establish RTOs for each of the applications to be recovered by the technology plan. The RTO will define for the technology recovery team how much time can elapse between the time the disaster occurs and the time the application is recovered and available to the business.

The business also needs to determine the amount of work in process that can be at risk in an event. The data that is on an employee's desk when a fire occurs would be lost forever if that information was not backed up somewhere else. The information stored in file cabinets, incoming mail in the mailroom, and the backup tapes that have not yet left the building are all at risk.

Decisions need to be made about all types of data because data is what is needed to run the business. How much data is it acceptable to lose? A minute's worth? An hour's worth? A whole business day's worth? This is commonly used to determine the recovery point objective (RPO). This is the point in time that the planner will recover to. The vital records program, backup policies, and procedures for electronic data and hard copy data need to comply with the RPO established by the business.

Data Stored in Electronic Form

Backup strategies for data used to restore technology are varied and are driven by the RTO and the RPO needed to support the business requirements. Some organizations have begun tiering data based on its importance to the business and frequency of use. The more time-sensitive data is replicated off-site either synchronously or asynchronously to ensure its availability and its currency. Other data is backed up to tape and sent off-site once or a day or oftener.

If the data needed to rebuild the technology environment is stored somewhere else besides your alternate site, then the time it takes to pack and transport that data must be included in the RTO. Factors such as how the data is stored, how far away it is, and how it will be delivered to the recovery facility will determine how much the recovery time could be increased. Delivery of off-site data to the recovery facility could delay the recovery by hours or even days. To reduce the recovery time, the data that will be used to recover your systems and applications should be stored in the recovery site whenever possible.

It is vital that the data that is stored off-site include not only the application data but also the application source code, hardware and software images for the servers and end user desktops, utility software, license keys, etc. Application data alone cannot rebuild an application.

Remote Replication and Off-Site Journaling

Remote replication involves moving data over a network to secondary storage devices in another location. It is an expensive solution, but the one that will meet the needs of an application RPO that is immediate or near immediate. It can be done either synchronously or asynchronously.

Synchronous replication is when the data is written to the production environment disk and to the remote disk at the same time. Until both "writes" occur, the next process cannot begin. There are distance limitations on performing synchronous remote replication as well as network bandwidth requirements that can be extremely expensive. Synchronous replication has the potential to impact production, but is the best solution when time to recovery and data loss matter. This type of replication is commonly deployed in dual data center environments where applications are load-balanced between the two or more sites but can be used for other strategies when the currency of the data, not the actual time of the recovery is key.

Asynchronous replication occurs when the data is written to the production environment and then is queued to write to the backup environment at scheduled intervals depending on the RPO for the data. This can occur several times a day, several times an hour, or several times a minute, depending again on the need for data currency.

Asynchronous data replication's advantage is that it does not impact production performance as it occurs offline to the production environment and provides long-distance, remote data replication while still providing disaster recovery data protection.

Remote replication does not eliminate the need for point-in-time copies of the data. If data in your production environment becomes corrupt, your replicated data will also be corrupt. A point-in-time copy of your data is still required for restoration from this type of event.

Backup Strategies

Most companies, no matter what strategy they employ for storing data off-site, start by performing full backups of all their data followed by periodic incremental backups. Incremental backups take copies of only the files that are new or have changed since the last full or incremental backup was taken, and then set the archive bit to "0." The other common option is to take a differential backup. Differential backups copy only the files that are new or have changed since the last full backup and do not change the archive bit value.

If a company wants the backup and recovery strategy to be as simple as possible, then they should only use full backups. They take more time and hard drive space to perform, but they are the most efficient in recovery. If that option is not viable, a differential backup can be restored in just two steps. The full backup of the data is restored first, then the differential backup on top of it. Remember, the differential backs up every piece of data in file that has changed since the last full backup was taken.

An incremental backup takes the most time to restore because you must lay down the full backup first and then every incremental backup taken since the last full backup. If you take daily incremental backups but only monthly full backups, and you are recovering on the 26th day of the month, you will have to perform your full backup restore first and then 26 incremental backups must be laid on top in the same order that they were taken in. You can see how the backup method you use could have a significant impact on your recovery timeline.

The RTO for a business process or for an application is going to determine the recovery strategy for the process or application. The more time that can elapse before the recovery needs to occur, the more recovery options are available. The more time sensitive an application or function is, the fewer options you will have in selecting a recovery strategy. Also, the plan will be more detailed and require more testing and training.

Selecting a Recovery Strategy for Technology

Depending on how much downtime you can accept before the technology recovery must be complete, recovery strategies selected for the technology environment could be one of the following:

- Dual data center—This strategy is employed for applications that cannot accept any downtime without unacceptably impacting business. The applications are split between two geographically dispersed data centers and either load-balanced between the two centers or hot-swapped between them. The surviving data center must have enough capacity to carry the full production load in either case.

- Internal hot site—An internal hot site is standby ready with all necessary technology and equipment necessary to run the applications recovered there. The planner will be able to effectively restart an application in hot site recovery without having to perform any bare metal recovery of servers. Because this is an internal solution, often the business will run non-time-sensitive processes there, such as development or test environments that will be pushed aside for recovery of production when needed. When employing this strategy, it is important that the two environments be kept as close to identical as possible to avoid problems with OS levels, hardware differences, capacity differences, etc., from preventing or delaying recovery.

- External hot site—This strategy has equipment on the floor waiting for recovery, but the environment must be rebuilt for the recovery. These are services contracted through a recovery service provider. Again, it is important that the two environments be kept as close to identical as possible to avoid problems with OS levels, hardware differences, capacity differences, etc., from preventing or delaying recovery. Hot site vendors tend to have the most commonly used hardware and software products to attract the largest number of customers to utilize the site. Unique equipment or software would generally need to be provided by the organization either at the time of disaster or stored there.

- Warm site—A warm site is a leased or rented facility that is usually partially configured with some equipment, but not the actual computers. It will generally have all the cooling, cabling, and networks in place to accommodate the recovery, but the actual servers, mainframe, and other equipment are delivered to the site at the time of disaster.

- Cold site—A cold site is a shell or empty data center space with no technology on the floor. All technology must be purchased or acquired at the time of disaster.

- Reciprocal agreement—In this strategy, the organization signs an agreement with a similar business operation to provide backup capabilities to each other in the event either experiences a disaster.

- Mobile unit—A mobile unit is typically a contract with a vendor to provide a mobile trailer at time of disaster, which contains equipment necessary to support recovery.

- Outsourcing—The technology environment is outsourced to a vendor who provides the disaster recovery plan for the applications.

Each of these recovery strategies has advantages and disadvantages.

Dual Data Center

Advantages	Disadvantages
Little or no downtime	Most expensive option
Ease of maintenance	Requires redundant hardware, networks, staffing
No recovery required	Distance limitations

Internal or External Hot Site

Advantages	Disadvantages
Allows recovery to be tested	Expensive; an internal solution more expensive than external
Highly available	Hardware and software compatibility issues in external sites
Site can be operational within hours	

Advantages of Warm and Cold Site

Advantages	Disadvantages
Less expensive	Not immediately available
Available for longer recoveries	Not testable

Reciprocal Agreement

Advantages	Disadvantages
No cost	Technology upgrades, obsolescence, or business growth
Viable for small business operations with limited technology	Security and access by partner users

Mobile Unit

Advantages	Disadvantages
Self-contained unit with technology and network	Difficult and expensive to test unless you own it
Transportable to any site	Travel time to bring unit where it is needed

Outsourcing

Advantages	Disadvantages
Transfer the ownership of recovery to vendor	Cost
May provide same recovery as dual data center but at less cost	No ownership or control over recovery program except contractually
No recovery plan to maintain or test	

Cost–Benefit Analysis

Each of the foregoing strategies can be considered for the business and technology recovery. Those that are recommended need to have a cost–benefit analysis (CBA) performed to determine if the costs of the strategy being recommended fits within the amount of risk or business loss the business is trying to avoid. The company would not spend $1,000,000 a year on a recovery strategy to protect $100,000 of profit. Every business does not need a dual data center recovery strategy. The strategy selected must fit the business need.

The cost of implementing the recovery strategy recommended needs to include the initial costs associated with building out the strategy as well as ongoing costs to maintain the recovery solution, and where applicable, the cost of periodic testing of the solution to ensure it remains viable.

Implementing Recovery Strategies

Once the strategy has been agreed to and funded, the next step is to implement the various strategies approved. This may involve negotiating with vendors to provide recovery services for business or technology, doing site surveys of existing sites to determine excess capacity, wiring conference rooms or cafeterias to support business functions, buying recovery technology, installing remote replication software, installing networks for voice and data recovery, assigning alternate site seats to the various business areas, and the like.

The implementation phase is a project unto itself, perhaps multiple projects, depending on the complexity of your environment and the recovery strategies selected.

Documenting the Plan

Once recovery strategies have been developed and implemented for each area, the next step is to document the plan itself. The plan includes plan activation procedures, the recovery strategies to be used, how recovery efforts will be managed, how human resource issues will be handled, how recovery costs will be documented and paid for, how recovery communications to internal and external stakeholders will be handled, and detailed action plans for each team and each team member. The plan then needs to be distributed to everyone who has a role.

The documentation for recovery of the technology environment needs to be detailed enough that a person with a similar skill set who has never executed the procedures before could use them to perform the recovery. Documentation tends to be a task that no one really likes to do; however, there is no guarantee that the people who perform this function in the production environment or the person who restored the infrastructure and application at the last test is going to be available at the time of disaster. In addition, disasters tend to be chaotic times where many things are happening at once. Without the proper documentation, a practiced recovery strategy can fall apart and add to the chaos. Restoring an application can be challenging, and restoring an entire data center just destroyed by a tornado can be overwhelming, if not impossible, without good documentation.

The documentation needs to be stored at the recovery facility, and every time the recovery is tested, the documentation should be used by the recovery participants and updated as needed. Once the level of confidence in the documentation is high, have someone who has never performed the procedure attempt it with an expert looking over their shoulder. It may slightly delay the recovery time at that particular test, but once complete, confidence in the documentation will be strong.

The Human Factor

One common factor left out of many plans is human resource issues. Disasters are human events, and it is important that the plan document the responsibility of the firm to the employees participating in the recovery. Companies need to recognize that to respond to the company's needs in a disaster situation, it must also recognize the hardships placed on the families of its response teams. To be able to give the best to the company at the time when it is needed most, employees need to have a level of comfort that their family members are safe and the employee's absence during the recovery effort will not place undue hardship on them.

Logistics

The plan needs to document the logistics of the recovery, not just the technical documentation for recovery of the hardware and applications. The plan needs to contain the following:

- How the disaster will be declared and who has the authority to declare it
- How recovery team members will be contacted and who will contact them

- How recovery team members are to travel to the alternate site, and who will make any required reservations and pay for those costs
- Where documentation is stored and how to get it
- How off-site backups will be retrieved, who will do it, and how long it will take
- Address, phone number, and directions to the alternate site
- How necessary supplies will be provided and how more can be requested
- Command center location and phone number
- How problems will be reported and managed

Plan Maintenance Strategies

As with any documentation, version control is important, particularly with detailed technical procedures. The use of version control numbers on the plan helps to ensure that everyone is using the current version of the plan documentation. The plan needs to be published to everyone who has a role and also needs to be stored in a secure off-site location that not only survives the disaster but is accessible immediately following it.

It is important that the plan be kept up to date as the business and technology environments of your company continue to change and adapt. Tying plan updates to your change management process is critical to keeping pace with significant changes in technology. The BCP must be reviewed and updated at least annually, and more often if significant business changes occur. Plan updates also frequently occur following tests of the plan, if issues or action items from the test require plan documentation changes.

Once the plan has been completed and the recovery strategies are fully implemented, it is important to test all parts of the plan to validate that it would work in a real event. The purpose of testing is to validate the readiness to recover from a real event. If we knew that it all worked, we would not need to test it in the first place. Test to find out what does not work, so that it can be fixed before it happens for real. No test is a failure as long as it provides opportunities to better the recovery process, so that if it happened for real, the organization is more likely to recover.

The first rule of conducting tests of the recovery plans is that no matter what type of test you are conducting, it is important to protect the production environment.

There are many different types of exercises that the planner can conduct. Some will take minutes, and others hours or days. The amount of exercise planning needed is entirely dependent on the type of exercise, length of the exercise, and the scope of the exercise planned to be conducted. The most common types of exercises for technology recovery are walkthrough exercises, simulated or actual exercises, and compact exercises.

In a walkthrough or tabletop exercise, the team that would need to execute the plan holds a meeting to review the plan. When the organization has a new plan, the best type of tabletop exercise to do is a walkthrough of the actual plan document with everyone who has a role in the plan. Even the planning team is unlikely to read the entire document, and walking through the plan helps to ensure that everyone knows the whole story and everyone's role. Walking through the plan with the team will help identify gaps in the plan so that they can be addressed.

Once the planner has conducted that type of walkthrough, the scenario-based tabletop exercises can begin. In these exercises, the planner will gather the team in a meeting and pretend that something has happened, and the team members are supposed to respond as if it is a real event. The planner could pretend that there is a power outage, and, based on what is backed up by alternate power sources such as UPS and generators and what is not, the team would discuss how the technology or business would be impacted and how they would exercise the portions of the plan to address that scenario.

Tabletop exercises are used to validate the plan within an actual scenario without having to actually execute the recovery procedures. The planner will "talk through" what the team would do; they will not actually do it. These types of exercises are especially helpful in working through the decision processes that will have to be tackled by the leadership team when faced with an event and by other teams to talk through recovery options based on the scenario being presented for the exercise.

A simulated or actual exercise tests the actual recovery in the alternate site. The difference between a simulated and an actual exercise is that a simulated exercise operates completely independently of the production environment, whereas in an actual exercise the production environment is "moved" to the alternate site as is done with a dual data center strategy.

The purpose of this type of exercise is to validate alternate site readiness. The planner should run this exercise as closely as possible to how it would happen if it happened for real. Clearly, because exercises are planned events, the planner will have an opportunity to reduce the actual timeline by prestaging certain things that the planner could not do if this were an unplanned event, such as pulling backup tapes from off-site storage and having it delivered to the alternate site for use on the day of the exercise. What the planner should not do as part of the planning is plan for success. Remember, the reason to test is to find out what does not work so that it can be fixed before it happens for real.

The final exercise is a compact exercise. This is where the planner will begin with a call to the recovery team, assuming a scenario, and have them respond as if this were a real event and continue right through an actual exercise in the alternate site. These are sometimes done as surprise exercises, with very few people knowing in advance when they are going to happen.

After every exercise the planner conducts, the exercise results need to be published and action items developed to address the issues uncovered by the exercise. Action items should be tracked until they have been resolved and, where appropriate, the plan updated. It is very unfortunate when an organization faces the same issue in subsequent tests simply because someone did not update the plan.

Summary

In summary, the security professional should have an understanding of the business continuity and disaster recovery domain to assist the business in being prepared to recover in the event of a disaster.

Business continuity and disaster recovery continue to evolve, but the basic principles remain the same. We have changed the way we recover through the years. The world had changed its expectations of how available a business should be.

Expectations have changed, and the business of recovery will continue to change and evolve in time, but the reasons for businesses to develop recovery capabilities remain the same: to continue the business. The more competitive an industry, the more important recoverability may be. More companies have built recovery programs because their customers required it, not because the regulators did. Having a plan versus not having one is a competitive advantage. As the demand for availability grows, as customers demand proof of recovery capabilities before signing the contract, the more the demand for qualified, experienced planners will grow.

The way we recover will continue to evolve. Technology recovery is moving from a recovery strategy to a restart strategy where you never really recover but instead have backup technology in place that simply picks up from where the primary center stopped.

The introduction of "cloud computing," where we have technology on demand the same as we have utilities on demand, if it ever comes to full maturity, will change the face of the technology environment and the recovery environment.

The goal—to continue the business—remains the same.

Reference

1. Eric Waxvik, Risk, response, and recovery, in *Official (ISC)2 Guide to the SSCP CBK*, New York: Auerbach Publications, 2007, p. 212.

Sample Questions

1. Which phrase best defines a business continuity/disaster recovery plan?
   a. A set of plans for preventing a disaster
   b. An approved set of preparations and sufficient procedures for responding to a disaster
   c. A set of preparations and procedures for responding to a disaster without management approval
   d. The adequate preparations and procedures for the continuation of all business functions

2. Which of the following statements best describes the extent to which an organization should address business continuity or disaster recovery planning?
   a. Continuity planning is a significant corporate issue and should include all parts or functions of the company.
   b. Continuity planning is a significant technology issue, and the recovery of technology should be its primary focus.
   c. Continuity planning is required only where there is complexity in voice and data communications.
   d. Continuity planning is a significant management issue and should include the primary functions specified by management.

3. Risk analysis is performed to identify
   a. The impacts of a threat to the business operations
   b. The exposures to loss of the organization
   c. The impacts of a risk on the company
   d. The way to eliminate threats

4. During the risk analysis phase of the planning, which of the following actions could manage threats or mitigate the effects of an event?
   a. Modifying the exercise scenario
   b. Developing recovery procedures
   c. Increasing reliance on key individuals
   d. Implementing procedural controls

5. The reason to implement additional controls or safeguards is to
   a. Deter or remove the risk.
   b. Remove the risk and eliminate the threat.
   c. Reduce the impact of the threat.
   d. Identify the risk and the threat.

6. Which of the following statements most accurately describe business impact analysis?
   a. Risk analysis and business impact analysis are two different terms describing the same project effort.
   b. A business impact analysis calculates the probability of disruptions to the organization.
   c. A business impact analysis is critical to development of a business continuity plan.
   d. A business impact analysis establishes the effect of disruptions on the organization.

7. The term *disaster recovery* commonly refers to:
   a. The recovery of the business operations
   b. The recovery of the technology environment
   c. The recovery of the manufacturing environment
   d. The recovery of the business and technology environments

8. Which of the following terms best describe the effort to determine the consequences of disruptions that could result from a disaster?
   a. Business impact analysis
   b. Risk analysis
   c. Risk assessment
   d. Project problem definition
9. A key advantage of using a cold site as a recovery option is that it
   a. Is a less expensive recovery option
   b. Can be configured and operationalized for any business function
   c. Is preconfigured for communications and can be customized for business functions
   d. Is the most available option for testing server recovery and communications restorations
10. The term RTO means
    a. Recovery time for operations
    b. Return to order
    c. Resumption time order
    d. Recovery time objective
11. If a company wants the fastest time to restore from tape backup, it should perform backup using the following method:
    a. Full backup
    b. Incremental backup
    c. Partial backup
    d. Differential backup
12. One of the advantages of a hot site recovery solution is
    a. Lowered expense
    b. High availability
    c. No downtime
    d. No maintenance required
13. Which of the following methods is not acceptable for exercising the business continuity plan?
    a. Tabletop exercise
    b. Call exercise
    c. Simulated exercise
    d. Halting a production application or function
14. Which of the following is the primary desired result of any well-planned business continuity exercise?
    a. Identification of plan strengths and weaknesses
    b. Satisfaction of management requirements
    c. Compliance with auditor's requirements
    d. Maintenance of shareholder confidence

15. A business continuity plan should be updated and maintained
    a. Immediately following an exercise
    b. Following a major change in personnel
    c. After installing new software
    d. On an ongoing basis

16. The primary reason to build a business continuity and disaster recovery plan is
    a. To continue the business
    b. To restore the data center
    c. To meet regulatory environments
    d. Because the customers expect it

17. A company would chose to use synchronous remote replication for its data recovery strategy if
    a. It wanted to replace point-in-time backups.
    b. It wanted to minimize the amount of time taken to recover.
    c. Time to recovery and data loss are important to the business.
    d. Distance limitations existed.

18. One of the reasons asynchronous replication differs from synchronous replication is
    a. Because it can impact production
    b. Because it can be done over greater distances
    c. Because it involves less loss of data
    d. Because it improves recovery time

19. The purpose of doing a cost–benefit analysis on the different recovery strategies is
    a. To make certain the cost of protection does not exceed the cost of the risk it is protecting
    b. To determine the cost of implementing the recovery strategy
    c. To determine that the strategy will be effective
    d. To analyze the cost of the different strategies

20. Which of the following should a planner *never* do during the planning stages of a test or exercise?
    a. Let test participants know what the scenario for the test will be.
    b. Use prestage tapes for the recovery exercise at the alternate site.
    c. Plan for the test to be successful.
    d. Document a test timeline.

Chapter 6

Telecommunications and Network Security

Gilbert Held

Contents

The telecommunications and network security domain addresses the security concerns related to the critical role of telecommunications and networks in today's distributed computing environments. The security professional understands the risks to communications networks, whether they be data, voice, or multimedia networks. This includes understanding of communications processes and protocols, threats and countermeasures, support for organizational growth and operations, and the ability to design, implement, and monitor secure network architectures.

The security professional must be vigilant to recognize the threats and available countermeasures in order to ensure the provisioning of secure communications. Key areas of knowledge include

- Secure voice and fax communications
- Data communications architecture
  - Network topologies
  - Network protocols
  - Network security devices
  - Accountability and monitoring
- Data and network protection
- Telecommunications security management and techniques
- Remote access protocols
- Network design validation

This chapter focuses on the interrelationship between telecommunications and network security. The term *telecommunications* can have several meanings based on the period in which the term was used. This chapter uses the most modern definition of the term telecommunications, which describes the transmission of voice and facsimile information over both circuit-switched and packet-switched networks.

After discussing voice and facsimile communications and the convergence of packet- and circuit-switched networks, we will turn our attention to obtaining a solid overview of voice security, voice protocols, and the various hardware and software that contribute to protecting networks. In concluding this chapter, we will focus on a series of network design issues related to enhancing security and how we can configure and validate our efforts. So, with this in mind, grab your favorite beverage and a few munchies while we increase our knowledge of telecommunications and network security.

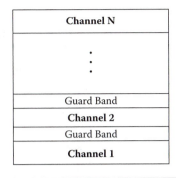

Figure 6.1   Frequency division multiplexer (FDM).

Voice and Facsimile Communications

Both voice and facsimile communications were originally developed to be transported via analog transmission. Although a typical person's voice has a range of 20 kHz, the frequency range of a communications channel was limited by the use of low-pass and high-pass filters to an approximate 3 kHz passband, with multiple conversations between two locations carried by analog multiplexing, which shifts conversations onto predefined channels of frequency division multiplexers (FDMs). The use of FDM was prone to frequency shifting, which required the use of guard bands, limiting the number of channels that could be transported by the technology. Figure 6.1 illustrates a frequency division multiplexer, where multiple voice conversations are shifted up in frequency, with guard bands of a set frequency to minimize the effect of voice drift. The entire bandwidth is then output onto a trunk circuit, which enables multiple voice conversations to be carried on a common line between cities. The Y-axis of Figure 6.1 is deliberately omitted as its values depend on the type of voice channel multiplexed. For example, a 3000 Hz voice channel typically has a 75 Hz guard band, while a 48 kHz wideband voice channel uses a much wider guard band of approximately 1 kHz. Although once commonly used in North America, due to the conversion of communications carriers to digital technology, FDMs are now obsolete.

Similar to voice communications, facsimile transmission was initially an analog system. Due to the use of low-pass and high-pass filters by communications carriers, facsimile transmission was restricted to the use of an approximate 3 kHz channel, which represented the standard telephone analog bandwidth.

Pulse Code Modulation (PCM)

With the development of the computer during World War II, technology started to became focused on the design of digital products. Within a short period of time, pulse code modulation (PCM) was used to encrypt voice by the Allies. PCM

C1	C2	C3 ...		C24	Framing bit
8-bits	8-bits	8-bits		8-bits	F

Figure 6.2   Forming a channelized T1 frame.

represents one of the earliest methods developed to digitize an analog signal, such as human voice or facsimile transmission. First, the analog signal is sampled at predefined time intervals. Next, each sample, which can have an infinite number of heights, is quantized into a predefined value that is closest to the height of the signal. Then, the resulting height is encoded into a series of bits. Early PCM systems used 7 bits per quantized value, with more modern systems using 8 bits. Using a sample rate of 8000 samples per second with 8 bits per sample, a voice conversation that is digitized using PCM results in a data rate of 64 kbps.

PCM was used by AT&T and other communications carriers to develop a digital highway for transportation calls between telephone company offices. First, 24 voice calls were sampled and encoded into 8 bits, and a framing bit was added to provide a pattern used for synchronization. This was the well-known T1 frame, which comprises 193 bits ($8 \times 24 + 1$). Because sampling occurs 8000 times per second, the data rate of the now ubiquitous T1 line became 193 bits/frame × 8000 frames/second, or 1.544 Mbps. Figure 6.2 illustrates the format of a T1 line. Note that when structured to hold 24 voice conversations, the T1 line is referred to as a "channelized" T1, while when used to transport data such as for Internet access, the T1 is referred to as a "nonchannelized" T1 line.

Moving up the initial digital highway are the T2 and T3 lines. A T2 consists of four T1 lines multiplexed with additional framing that is used between telephone company offices and operates at 6.312 Mbps, while a T3 consists of 28 T1 lines multiplexed with framing that is used for high-capacity communications and operates at 44.736 Mbps. Table 6.1 provides a summary of the initially developed digital highway in North America. Note that the DS0 (pronounced digital signal level zero) signal level references the basic voice bandwidth data channel encoded via PCM.

Circuit-Switched versus Packet-Switched Networks

Due to the relative high cost of long-distance communications prior to the 1980s, it was expensive to access remote computers. Both dial-up and leased lines were expensive, with dial-up long distance based on the time of day a call occurred, its duration, and the distance between the caller and called telephone numbers. Using dial-up resulted in the telephone company network establishing a series of switched network segments within their network infrastructure to connect the caller to the called party. Thus, the term switched or circuit-switched network resulted as a reference to a dialed call. Initially, frequency division multiplexing (FDM) was

Table 6.1 The Initial North American Digital Highway

Digital Signal Level/Transmission Facility	Data Rate	Number of DS0s
DS0	64 kbps	1
T1	1.544 Mbps	24
T2	6.312 Mbps	96
T3	44.736 Mbps	672

used to enable multiple calls to flow between telephone company offices. With the development of digital technology, time division multiplexing (TDM) replaced FDM, with signaling software allocating the routing of DS0s as 64 kbps PCM data streams onto and off various TDMs on a path that was established to link the caller to the called party. Once the circuit-switched path is set up, the digitized voice conversation flows over that path with no loss or interruptions.

The high cost associated with the use of the public switched telephone network resulted in the development of a new type of communications that was at first designed to transport data. Referred to as packet switching, vendors such as Telenet and Tymnet established networks consisting of modems that customers would dial in various cities, minicomputers located in those cities, and high-speed communications lines that connected the minicomputers to form a mesh-structured network. A customer would dial a Telenet or Tymnet telephone number to connect his terminal device to the network. He would then enter an authorization code, which the service provider would use to allow the customer the use of the network as well as for billing him or her. This would then be followed by an access code that would identify the resource connected to the network the customer wished to access. The minicomputer would packetize the data received from each customer in a particular city, placing a series of identifiers in each packet that indicated the source and destination address of the packet and its sequence number. This enabled packets from different customers to flow over the circuits that formed the backbone of the packet network.

Figure 6.3 illustrates a packet-switched network consisting of many nodes, shown as circles, where initially minicomputers were used for examining packet information and forwarding packets based on the contents of certain packet fields. Later, routers replaced the use of minicomputers in most packet networks.

In examining Figure 6.3, note that a client is shown dialing into the network. After the client obtains authorization to use the network, packets are examined and a path is established through the packet network, which is indicated by heavy lines, to a destination computer located in Chicago and connected to the network via a leased line. Although the connection shown would be "taken down" once the client or computer completes the session, which is referred to as an "on demand" session, a

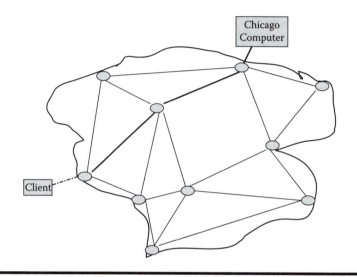

Figure 6.3 Using a packet network.

connection can also be "permanent"; however, other users can have their data transmitted over most or all of the same connection paths as the permanent connection.

The use of packet-switched networks offered certain advantages over the use of the telephone network for transporting data. First, numerous data sources could be routed over common high-speed circuits to either different or the same destination based on the connection desired by users. Second, each packet had its integrity checked via the use of a cyclic redundancy check (CRC) character that was appended to each packet. The CRC was computed by treating the data in the packet as a long binary number, dividing that number by a fixed polynomial, discarding the integer, and keeping the remainder as the CRC. This CRC was referred to as the local CRC because it was computed locally. At the next minicomputer or router, the received packet was buffered and another CRC was computed, which was compared to the CRC in the packet. If they matched, the packet was forwarded toward its destination. If the two CRCs did not match, the packet was rejected, and the sender was requested to send another copy of the packet.

The use of CRCs for error checking on packet networks provides a higher level of data integrity than when asynchronous data is transmitted via the telephone network. This is because most asynchronous communications used parity checking, which cannot detect multiple bit errors commonly caused by machinery turning on or off, electric ballasts, and even sunspots. In comparison, the use of CRC checking reduces the probability of an undetected error to one in tens of millions of bits. Thus, packet networks offer a higher level of data integrity than the telephone network.

Other features common to early packet networks included reverse charges, which was similar to a collect call and alternate routing. Concerning the latter, if a packet network node that was typically a minicomputer failed or a circuit linking two nodes became inoperative, the network would use a series of predefined algorithms to route around the impediments. Once the problem was fixed, the alternate routing would terminate. Today, alternate routing is built into most of the routers on the Internet, enabling traffic to be moved around bottlenecks due to both line outages and high occupancy without the user being able to tell they are on an alternate route unless they use a traffic routing display program, such as traceroute, to determine the path from source to destination.

Although packet networks have significant advantages over circuit-switched networks, they also have many disadvantages. Foremost among the disadvantages was the delay resulting from the need to retransmit packets because of CRC mismatches caused by spurious hits on circuits resulting primarily from machinery and weather conditions. Fortunately, most impairments were due to the use of high-speed analog circuits by packet network operators during the 1970s. As fiber-optic cables began to interconnect cities, their use significantly reduced the error rate associated with older analog connections. Another problem associated with packet networks is data loss. Unlike circuit switching, which results in a dedicated connection between source and destination that prevents data loss, packet networks will drop data packets as they become overloaded. This is because network engineers size the transmission facilities to maximize revenues with minimum cost, knowing that dropped packets will result in the retransmission of the packet by the originator if a response (negative or positive acknowledgement) from the next node is not received within a predefined period of time.

The development of packet networks was based primarily on economics. In their prime, they could transport data from New York to San Francisco for the equivalent of 30 cents per minute while a long-distance call might cost well over $1 per minute. However, as the cost of telephone calls decreased, their reduction had a significant effect on the initial series of packet networks, with most of those networks shutting down in the late 1980s.

The packet networks previously described were based on the X.25 protocol, and were often referred to as X.25 networks. Their development paved the way for the growth of a new type of packet network based on the TCP/IP protocol suite, which is now commonly referred to as the Internet protocol. Although originally developed to convey data between computers, advances in a series of technologies resulted in the transmission of digitized voice along with data, resulting in the convergence of voice and data on a common network.

VoIP Architecture Concerns

There are several key areas of concern in the development of a network architecture designed to move digitized voice over a packet network originally developed to transport data. Those concerns include the end-to-end delay associated with packets carrying digitized voice, jitter, the method of voice digitization used, the packet loss rate, and security.

Table 6.2 Comparing Circuit-Switched and Packet-Switched Network Characteristics

Characteristic	Circuit-Switched	Packet-Switched
Bandwidth allocation	Fixed slots	Variable
Traffic delay (jitter)	Minimal fixed	Variable, can be lengthy
Traffic support	Voice/video	Designed for data
Traffic type	Designed for constant	Designed for traffic bursts
Data loss	Not by design	Routers drop packets during periods of high traffic

End-to-End Delay

The end-to-end delay affects the ability of a user to know when the person at the other end of the connection has completed saying something. When the end-to-end delay is too long, a common conversational pause becomes so noticeable that the other party may begin to speak when the talker has merely paused in his or her conversation, resulting in a disjointed conversation. Table 6.2 compares five important characteristics of circuit- switched and packet-switched networks.

Jitter

Jitter represents the variation in packet transit caused by queuing, contention, and the propagation of data through a network. In general, the telephone network provides a fixed path for the transmission of data on an end-to-end basis, resulting in a near-uniform amount of jitter resulting primarily from transmission propagation. In comparison, on a packet network where multiple data sources can contend for transmission on a common backbone circuit, heavily congested links can result in variable jitter. This in turn can result in the reconstructed voice sounding awkward. To compensate for jitter, most VoIP devices employ a jitter buffer, allowing data arriving with different delays to be extracted uniformly with respect to time.

Method of Voice Digitization Used

Currently over ten voice digitization methods are used to encode a voice conversation. While it is fairly obvious that the decoding method must match the encoding method, less obvious but very important is the encoding method used. Currently, voice-encoding methods range in scope from the generation of a 64 kbps data stream developed via PCM encoding to more modern encoding methods that require as little as 2400 bps for the encoding of voice. While in general a lower encoding rate enables more voice conversations to be transported over a packet network, there is usually a reduction in the quality of a reconstructed voice conversation when an encoding method generates a lower digitization rate, especially when the digitization rate falls below 8000 bps.

Packet Loss Rate

A packet network experiences peaks and valleys with respect to packet flow, similar to a highway. However, instead of a traffic backup occurring on a highway when too many vehicles are entering the facility, on a modern packet network routers will drop packets. Although significant improvements have occurred in the type of packets dropped due to various expedited traffic flow methods, packets transporting voice will periodically be dropped along with data packets. While data packets can be retransmitted without adversely affecting data integrity, packets transporting digitized voice cannot be retransmitted if a real-time conversation is in effect. Thus, dropping too many packets transporting digitized voice will adversely affect a conversation.

Security

Perhaps an often-overlooked voice architecture concern is security. After all, many persons feel that if their voice conversation is somehow known to others, minimal harm will result. While this may be true, it may be possible for an unauthorized party to take control of a data PBX, router, or voice server; the unauthorized party can then take over a company's hardware, dial persons in Bangladesh, China, South America, or other locations and run up an expensive communications bill that could endanger the organization's financial health. While the preceding just touches the surface of voice security concerns, let us probe a bit deeper and discuss some applicable policies and procedures.

Voice Security Policies and Procedures

There are several areas associated with voice that security managers must consider. Those areas include encryption, administrative change control, authentication, integrity, and availability. Let us discuss each as a separate entity.

Encryption

The use of encryption is significantly different when voice is transmitted via packets instead of being digitized and sent on a circuit-switched network. When voice is encrypted on a circuit-switched telephone network, the encryption and decryption process occurs on an analog waveform. Although the voice conversation is digitized, digitization occurs at the telephone company central office, and the subscriber line to the central office transports voice in analog form. To accomplish encryption,

Encryption

Data to be encrypted	11100100
Pseudo random key	10010101
Transmitted data	01110001

Decryption

Received data	01110001
Pseudo random key	10010101
Reconstructed data	11100100

Figure 6.4   Encryption and decryption.

portions of the frequency spectrum are moved through the use of expensive filters. In comparison, when voice is transmitted over a packet network, there are two significant differences. First, each packet represents a digitized bit stream, so digital encryptors can be used. Second, encryption cannot occur on the full packet as each packet header contains one or more fields of routing information as well as other data that routers within the network must be able to examine and take action depending on their contents. Thus, this limits the type of encryption to hardware and software products specifically developed to operate with packet data.

Figure 6.4 illustrates the ease with which digital data, to include digitized voice, can be encrypted via simple modulo 2 addition and modulo 2 subtraction. At the top of the referenced figure, the encryption process is shown. Here, the data to be encrypted is modulo 2 added with a pseudo-random key, resulting in the encrypted data being transmitted. In the lower portion of Figure 6.4, the decryption process is shown. Here, the same pseudo-random key is used; however, this time it is modulo 2 subtracted from the received encrypted data to produce the decrypted or reconstructed original data.

Through the use of encryption, it becomes very difficult for an unauthorized third party to hear different voice conversations. (Thus, if someone was able to tap into a circuit connecting a business office to a packet network, the unauthorized party, for example, would normally not be able to ascertain that the company was able to bid up to $4 million on a project, fly executives to a merger meeting in Ohio, or ascertain other valuable information. However, if one had the resources of NSA, it might be possible to decrypt the voice conversation and determine what was said, which explains why between the two Gulf wars, Iraq transferred most of its military communications onto fiber-optic lines, which were used in place of microwave towers that were relatively easy to monitor.

Authentication

Authentication represents the process of determining whether someone or something is, in fact, who or what it is declared to be. In voice communications, you can use Caller ID to authenticate the calling number and if known, the person's voice to authenticate the calling party. In the data world, authentication is commonly implemented through the use of logon passwords. Knowledge of the password is assumed to guarantee that the user is authentic. Within the past few years, two-factor authentication has gained prominence. In this technique, a user has a key fob or similar display device which changes its numeric display every minute or so. The user must enter both the numeric displayed on the device and their "secret" password to gain access to the computer or network; hence, the term two-factor authentication.

Administrative Change Control

The process of administrative change control in a voice security environment refers to examining hardware and software to locate and modify default settings that control access to the product's administrative controls. Most readers probably have used Wi-Fi in the home, office, or as a "road warrior." The transmission between the user's portable device and the Internet via an Internet Service Provider (ISP) occurs via a wireless router. That wireless router has a set of administrative controls that govern the type of data traffic permitted, hours when such traffic can flow to the Internet, and the WEP key that governs encryption and other settings. All too often, routers have a default administrative password that is in the manual and never changed by the administrator. This allows a third party to simply gather a list of default passwords from different vendor manuals located on the Internet and try one after another to gain control of the router. Once control is achieved, the unauthorized person, depending on the router's capability, may be able to transfer a duplicate data stream of traffic flowing through the router to another location for analysis that is totally transparent to the users of the router. Similarly, in a voice environment and even for large Web servers and other types of computer and communications hardware, many products are shipped with default passwords that should be the first item changed when configuring such equipment.

Integrity

In a communications environment, it is important that what you say is received correctly. Integrity refers to the ability of communications being received as sent. In a voice environment, there are several mechanisms that can result in a loss of integrity, including the recording and selective replay of a conversation, spoofing or someone pretending to be the person he or she claims to be, and the injection of speech into an existing conversation to distort the meaning of the conversation. Although integrity is rarely compromised, it represents a threat that must be considered.

Availability

In the field of communications, the term *availability* refers to the period of time that a system, subsystem, or circuit is operable and can function to perform its mission. As an example of availability, consider a voice answering system that is operational 8750 hours in a year. Then, its availability becomes

$$A = \frac{\text{Uptime}}{\text{Uptime} + \text{Downtime}} = \frac{8750}{8750 + 10}$$

Now that we have a general appreciation for some of the factors associated with network security, including encryption, administrative change control, and availability, let us turn our attention to three voice protocols.

Voice Protocols

While there are numerous voice protocols that have attained a degree of prominence, we will concentrate our attention on an umbrella protocol and two signaling protocols in this section. The umbrella protocol is referred to as the H.323 Recommendation, which defines a series of protocols to support audiovisual communications on packet networks. SIP, which is an acronym for Session Initiation Protocol, defines the signaling required to establish and tear down communications, including voice and video calls flowing over a packet network. The third voice protocol we will discuss is Signaling System 7 (SS7), which represents a signaling system protocol originally used for establishing and tearing down calls made over the world's series of public switched telephone networks. However, to make a call over a packet network such as the Internet, SS7 information must be conveyed. This occurs by transporting SS7 over the Internet Protocol (IP). Now that we have a basic understanding of the use of the three protocols, let us probe deeper into each.

The H.323 Protocol

The H.323 standard can be considered to represent an umbrella recommendation from the International Telecommunications Union (ITU) that covers a variety of standards for audio, video, and data communications across packet-based networks and, more specifically, IP-based networks, such as the Internet and corporate intranets. The H.323 standard was specified within the ITU-Telecommunications organization by Study Group 16. The original standard was promulgated in 1996, and further enhancements have been developed in the intervening years.

One of the functions of H.323 is to define standards for multimedia communications over local area networks (LANs) that do not provide a guaranteed quality of service (QoS). Such networks represent a vast majority of connectivity for corporate desktops and include packet-switched TCP/IP and Novell's NetWare IPX over Ethernet, Fast Ethernet, Gigabit Ethernet, and the now-obsolete Token Ring network technologies. Thus, the H.323 standards represent important building blocks for a broad range of collaborative, LAN-based applications for multimedia communications. This umbrella standard includes parts of H.225.0—RAS (Registration and Administration Status), Q.931, H.245, and the RTP/RTCP (Real Time Transport Protocol/Real Time Control Protocol).

H.225 is a call signaling protocol for packet-based multimedia communication systems. RAS, as its name implies, is concerned with registration, admission, and status. Q.931 is ISDN's connection control protocol, which is roughly comparable to TCP in the Internet protocol stack. Q.931 does not provide flow control or perform retransmission, because the underlying layers are assumed to be reliable and the circuit-oriented nature of ISDN allocates bandwidth in fixed increments of 64 kbps. However, Q.931 manages the connection setup and breakdown process.

H.245 represents a control signaling protocol in the H.323 multimedia communication architecture that is used for the exchange of end-to-end H.245 messages between communicating H.323 endpoints/terminals. H.245 control messages are carried over an H.245 control channel with logical channel 0 permanently open, unlike media channels. Messages carried include exchanging the capabilities of terminals as well as opening and closing logical channels. After a connection has been set up via the call signaling procedure, the H.245 call control protocol is used to resolve the call media type and establish the media flow.

RTP defines a standardized packet format for delivering audio and video over the Internet, while RTCP provides out-of-band control information for an RTP flow. The RTP includes fields for carrying a sequence number, time stamp (which is useful in ensuring that playback at a receiver occurs correctly), a synchronization source field that identifies the synchronization source, and a field that can define up to 15 contributing sources, which enables a conference with many participants to be held. RTCP partners with RTP in the delivery and packaging of multimedia data, but does not transport any data itself. RTCP is used periodically to transmit control packets to participants in a streaming multimedia session. Thus, the primary function of RTCP is to provide feedback on the QoS provided by RTP. One of the key features of RTCP is its statistics-gathering capability. RTCP gathers statistics such as bytes sent, packets sent, lost packets, packet jitter, and round trip delay, which an application can use to perform different functions, such as increasing QoS by limiting data flow or selecting the use of a different codec. As previously mentioned, media streams are transported on RTP/RTCP. RTP carries the actual media, and RTCP carries status and control information. Signaling is transported reliably over TCP.

The H.323 standard defines the following components:

Terminal
Gateway
Gatekeeper
MCU (multipoint control unit)
Multipoint controller
Multipoint processor
H.323 proxy

Terminal

An H.323 terminal (client) represents an endpoint in a LAN that participates in real-time, two-way communications with another H.323 terminal, gateway, or multipoint control unit (MCU). Under the H.323 standard, a terminal must support audio communication and can also support audio with video, audio with data, or a combination of all three.

Gateway

An H.323 gateway (GW) provides the physical and logical connections from a packet-switched network to and from circuit-switched networks. The gateway can perform a variety of functions, such as translation between H.323 conferencing endpoints on a LAN and other compliant terminals on other ITU-compliant circuit-switched and packet-switched networks. Such services include a translation between transmission formats and communications procedures. A gateway may also be required to perform the translation between audio and video CODECs as well as perform call setup and call clearing operations.

Gatekeeper

Gatekeepers are optional devices within an H.323 network. When present they perform three important call control housekeeping functions, which assist in the preservation of the integrity of the packet network. Those functions are admission control, address translation, and bandwidth management. Address translation is used to associate LAN aliases with terminals and gateways and IP or IPX addresses. Under bandwidth management, the gatekeeper can be configured to enable a maximum number of simultaneous conferences on a LAN. Once that limit is reached, the gatekeeper would refuse additional connection requests. The result of this action limits the bandwidth of voice or video to a predefined fraction of the total bandwidth available, with the rest left for Web surfing, file transfers, e-mail and other data applications.

MCU

A multipoint control unit (MCU) represents an endpoint on a LAN that provides the capability for three or more terminals and gateways to participate in a multipoint conference. It controls and mixes video, audio, and data from terminal devices to create a video conference. An MCU can also connect two terminals in a point-to-point conference that can later develop into a multipoint conference. The collection of all terminals, gateways, and multipoint control units managed by a single gatekeeper is known as an H.323 Zone.

Figure 6.5   An H.323 zone communicating with other devices.

Multipoint Controller

A multipoint controller that is H.323 compliant provides negotiation capacity with terminals to carry out different communications. The multipoint controller can also control conference resources, such as video multicasting.

Figure 6.5 illustrates an H.323 zone that is connected via a gateway to other LANs or terminal devices via the public switched telephone network.

Network Calling

The various H.323 components illustrated in Figure 6.5 show three PCs with voice cards as H.323 terminal devices. All three are connected to a common Ethernet LAN. The LAN is in turn connected to the switched public telephone network, which enables call originating on the top network to be routed over the public switched telephone network to the client's other LANs or to other voice and video terminal devices.

SIP

The Session Initiation Protocol (SIP) represents an application layer signaling protocol that enables telephony and VoIP services to be delivered over a packet network. This protocol is used for establishing, manipulating, and tearing down sessions in an IP network. A session can vary from a simple two-way telephone call to a collaborative multimedia conference. The ability to establish a variety of calls allows a number of innovative services to be developed, such as Web page click-to-dial, most prominently offered to eBay customers via Skype, instant messaging with buddy lists, and IP Centrex services. The major goal of SIP is to assist session originators to deliver invitations to potential session participants wherever they may be. SIP was modeled after the HyperText Transport Protocol (HTTP), using Uniform Resource Locators (URLs) for addressing and the Session Description Protocol (SDP) to convey session information.

SIP is a text-based protocol that uses UTF-8 encoding, transmitting on port 5060 both for UDP and TCP. SIP supports such common Internet Telephony features as calling, media transfer, multiuser conference calling, call holding, call transfer, and call end tasks.

SIP uses an "invite" message to create sessions that transport descriptions which allow participants to agree on a set of compatible media types. During the negotiation process, SIP recognizes that not all parties support the same features; thus, SIP negotiates a common set of features that all of the parties can support. In addition, SIP can issue a "reinvite" message to change an established session and a "cancel" message to cancel an invite.

SIP makes use of proxy servers to help route requests to a user's current location, authenticate and authorize users for services, implement provider call-routing policies, and provide numerous other features to users. SIP also provides a registration function that allows users to upload their current locations for use by proxy servers. This enables a call to reach a called party wherever he or she is located. Once a session is established, SIP can be used to terminate the session through the use of a "bye" message, which hangs up the session.

Comparing H.323 with SIP

A comparison of the H.323 protocol to SIP underscores the considerable difference between the two protocols. The H.323 protocol defines a unified system to support multimedia communications over IP networks, providing support for audio, video, and even data conferencing. Within the umbrella protocol, H.323 defines methods for handling device failures, such as using alternative gatekeepers and endpoints, and messages are encoded in binary. In comparison, SIP was developed to initiate a call, referred to as a *session*, between two devices and has no support for multimedia conferencing. In addition, SIP does not define procedures for handling device failures, and messages are encoded in ASCII text. The latter results in larger messages that are less suitable for use on low-bandwidth circuits, but are easier to interpret than the binary messages associated with the H.323 protocol.

SS7

SS7, a mnemonic for Signaling System No. 7, represents a global telecommunications standard defined by the ITU. This standard defines the manner in which public switched telephone networks (PSTNs) perform call setup and breakdown, routing, and control by exchange signaling information over a digital signaling network that is separate from the network which actually transports calls. SS7 supports both landline or hardwired calls as well as cellular or mobile calls, with the latter including subscriber authentication and wireless roaming. Through the use of SS7, such enhanced features as call forwarding, caller identification, and three-way calling become possible. In addition, such products as toll-free calling via an 800, 888, or 878 and other prefixes, as well as toll services via the well-known 900 prefix, becomes possible.

Although the PSTN was at one time restricted to circuit-switched technology, over the past decade telephone companies have moved a considerable amount of traffic to their Internet, referred to as a corporate intranet. Using VoIP, telephone companies have saved considerable funds because the use of packet-switched technology and better voice digitization techniques permit more conversations to be transported per unit of bandwidth.

Because calls originated over the PSTN can be transported over IP, a method was required to transport signaling information over an IP network. That method is referred to as SS7-over-IP and employs protocols defined by the Signaling Transport (sigtran) working group of the Internet Engineering Task Force (IETF), the international organization responsible for recommending Internet standards. The actual conversion of SS7 signals to packets transported via IP is performed by a signaling gateway. The signaling gateway can perform such functions as terminating SS7 signaling or translating and relaying messages over the IP network to a media gateway, media gateway controller, or another signaling gateway. Due to its critical role in integrated voice networks, signaling gateways are often deployed in groups of two or more to ensure high availability.

The function of the media gateway is to terminate voice calls originating on interswitch trunks from the public switched telephone network, compress and packetize the voice data, and deliver compressed voice packets to the IP network. For voice calls originating in an IP network, the media gateway performs these functions in reverse order. For ISDN calls from the PSTN, Q.931 signaling information is transported from the media gateway to the media gateway controller for call processing. In comparison, the media gateway controller handles registration and management of resources at the media gateways. A media gateway controller exchanges messages with the PSTN central office switches via a signaling gateway. Because media gateway controllers are often created on a computer platform through the use of off-the-shelf software, a media gateway controller is sometimes referred to as a softswitch.

Facsimile Security

When we discuss modern facsimile transmission, we are actually referencing the use of what is referred to as the Group 3 Facsimile Protocol (G3). G3 dates to 1980, when the International Telecommunications Union published its initial set of standards. Those standards included T.4, which specifies the image transfer protocol, and T.30, which specifies session management procedures that support the establishment of a fax transmission.

Because there are over 100 million facsimile G3-compatible devices in use around the world, the ability of one device to communicate with another is provided by the G3 protocol. While this provides worldwide compatibility, it also results in a number of security-related problems. Those can range from the lack of a policy defining the use of facsimile devices to the failure to use a coversheet that specifies who the sender and recipient are and the number of pages "faxed." Two of the major facsimile security-related problems are verifying the facsimile number dialed so the fax is not misdirected and the failure to enable the local facsimile device to print a confirmation of the delivery of the fax, which will include the number of pages transmitted and the receiving telephone number. Other facsimile security-related issues include having a secure location for a fax device and ensuring that incoming faxes are delivered to the correct recipient.

By itself, the G3 standard does not directly deal with security. Although a modified Huffman coding is employed to reduce transmission time of each scanned line, anyone who has the knowledge to tap a transmission can more than likely decode the transmission. Because the transmission of a fax is not secure, there are military standards that govern the encryption of fax transmission. In addition, because a fax machine radiates energy at certain frequencies that could be "read" by an unauthorized party, most military facsimile devices are "Tempest"-hardened by placing them in a secure area that is shielded from emitting frequencies that an uninvited third party sitting in a van in a parking lot might "read."

Network Architecture

In this section, we will turn our attention to an examination of network architecture and terminology. Doing so will provide us with the ability to better understand methods we can use to control and secure our network facilities.

Redundancy and Availability

From a network engineering perspective, redundancy represents the duplication of circuits and equipments, with the goal of the additional components resulting in an increase in network availability. For example, an Internet service provider might connect its hub in one city to peering points at two different locations. Thus, if the connection to one peering point should become inoperative, data flow to and from the Internet could continue via the second peering point.

Internet versus Intranet

Most end users have little control over the network architecture of the Internet, with the exception of their access method. Concerning the latter, it is common for

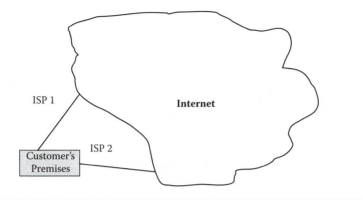

Figure 6.6   Using two ISPs for redundant access to the Internet.

organizations to have multiple ISPs, because the failure of one vendor's network would usually not affect the second vendor. To take full advantage of redundant vendors, you would ensure that the connection from your organization to each vendor occurs over different communication facilities. Figure 6.6 illustrates the use of two ISPs to provide redundant communications to the Internet from a customer premises.

Extranet

An extranet is a private network that while resembling an intranet extends the internal IP-based network of an organization to suppliers, vendors, and other types of business partners. Because an extranet is created by one or more organizations for their exclusive use, those vendors can control the network architecture of the extranet. Thus, they can order network circuits as well as equipment such as routers, DNS servers, and other devices to match the level of reliability and availability they both desire and can afford.

Perimeter Controls

In this section, we will turn our attention to products that can be used to control the flow of data at the entryway to the network. Referred to as perimeter control, devices that can be used include routers, firewalls, and special types of modems. As we will shortly note, the place at the network perimeter where such equipment is commonly installed is referred to as the network demilitarized zone (DMZ).

Figure 6.7 illustrates a common architecture for a corporate DMZ. In this example, a router provides a connection to the Internet while the firewall, which is sometimes referred to as a corporate gateway, resides between two LANs, one of which has a router as its only device while the second LAN is populated by terminals, routers, various types of servers such as e-mail servers or gateways, Web

Figure 6.7   Creating a DMZ.

servers and VPN servers, and other networking devices protected by the firewall. This architecture ensures that all data flow to and from the corporate network and Internet are examined by the firewall. Although the devices behind the firewall are protected from many types of attacks, this architecture does not protect devices from persons bringing disks to work that could be infected, nor does it protect against persons using USB memory devices to off-load corporate data from computers and servers. This is why many organizations prohibit the use of diskettes, purchase computers without such drives, and use special software to deactivate USB ports.

In Figure 6.8, a revised corporate DMZ is shown. In this example, a bank of security modems were added to the upper LAN, between the firewall and the corporate terminals, servers, and other devices on the protected network. To better understand how each device operates, let us turn our attention to the operation of each of the three communications devices, with particular emphasis on their security role.

Figure 6.8   Boundary router.

Figure 6.9   The delivery of TCP/IP application data onto a LAN.

In addition to providing a communications capability that takes LAN frames and strips the header and trailer to convert them to IP datagrams for transport on the Internet, routers have a key role as the first line of defense in many organizations. Through the use of rule-based access lists, it becomes possible to filter packets based on a variety of data carried in the packet. Although most packet filtering occurs on the fields within a packet header, some boundary routers extend filtering into the packet, making it difficult to functionally separate the security features of a router from a firewall.

Figure 6.9 illustrates the delivery of TCP/IP application data onto a LAN. Note that as data delivery occurs, a string of headers is appended to the application data. Each header has a number of fields that can be examined by a router or firewall that can allow or deny the flow of data based on predefined criteria.

Figure 6.10 illustrates the composition of the IPv4 header, which is appended to either a TCP header or UDP header to form an IP datagram. By looking into the IP header, the router can perform many security-related operations, such as accepting or rejecting datagrams based on the source or destination IP address within the IP header. Unfortunately, source addresses are not checked by devices on the Internet, so filtering on a source address can be problematic. For example, you can program your computer to send constant pings to www.whitehouse.gov and use the source address for the FBI gateway. Although not recommended, this would result in a stream of pings to the White House server that appeared to originate from the FBI.

As previously mentioned, filtering based on the contents of packet headers, such as the headers in IP, TCP, and UDP, are commonly incorporated into firewalls. With applicable programming, the network manager can configure the router to reject packets either inbound, outbound, or both, based on source or destination

0	4	8	16	31
Vers	Hlen	Type of Service	Total Length	
Identification			Flags	Fragment Offset
Time to Live		Protocol	Header Checksum	
Source IP Address				
Destination IP Address				
Options + Padding				

Figure 6.10   The IPv4 header.

address or type of packet or both. Concerning filtering based on packet type, this is accomplished by using port numbers to filter TCP or UDP packets.

Figure 6.11 illustrates the fields within the TCP header. Of particular importance—and used by both router access lists and firewalls for filtering purposes—are the source and destination port field values. TCP is used to transport connection-oriented, reliable data, such as control information. In comparison, UDP is used to transport connectionless data and reliability if an issue is provided by higher layers in the protocol stack. For example, setting up a VoIP call would require TCP data to convey the dialed number and other control information, while UDP would be used to transport digitized voice. By default, most router and firewall vendors disable the flow of data on all ports to each interface. Thus, because many applications use both TCP and UDP, it is quite common for routers and firewalls to be programmed to enable ports on both devices to allow corporate users to use certain types of Internet applications. In addition, many security devices can be programmed to support time-of-day functions, allowing the router and firewall administrators to open "holes" through their devices by equating data flow through

Source Port		Destination Port	
Sequence Number			
Acknowledgement Number			
Hlen	Reserved	Code bits	Window
Checksum		Urgent Pointer	
Options		Padding	
Data			

Figure 6.11   The Transport Control Protocol.

certain ports on specific interfaces to the time of day. For example, a corporation could allow employees access to Amazon and eBay during lunch hour while blocking such access during the rest of the workday.

In addition to the previously mentioned types of filtering, many routers can be programmed to block all or certain types of Internet Control Message Protocol (ICMP) packets as well as some widely employed hacker attacks, such as the well-known SYN attack. Thus, many routers when programmed correctly can become an organization's first line of network defense.

Security Modems

A security modem represents a special type of modem that allows remote access from trusted locations, may encrypt data, and may support Caller ID to verify the calling telephone number. When security modems first appeared on the market, they were configured with a list of allowable callback numbers and passwords. A remote user who wished to gain access to the corporate LAN would first dial the telephone number associated with the dial-in security modem. Upon establishing a connection, the person would be prompted to enter his or her callback number and a password associated with the callback phone number. If the password is correct, the security modem would disconnect the connection and dial back the callback number.

Modern security modems have considerably evolved from a simple list of authorized locations that would be dialed back upon the entry of an applicable password. Today, in addition to a callback feature, security modems may be capable of using Caller ID and passwords to authenticate a user and encrypt data based on the key entered by a verified user. In addition, some security modems provide the authenticated user with the ability to select an encryption algorithm from a series of supported algorithms, such as 3DES and various versions of the Advanced Encryption Standard (AES).

The rationale behind the use of a security modem is the fact that the PSTN assigns telephone numbers to fixed locations and cell phone numbers are assigned to known persons, with the exception of prepaid cell phones. Thus, an organization can decide the telephone numbers that can receive connections to the corporate network and then associate passwords with those numbers. This means that not only will the security modem call predefined numbers but, in addition, to do so the person at that number must first call the security modem and enter an applicable password. This duality of events can be considered as the beginning of what is now referred to as two-factor authentication. Through the addition of encryption to security modems, it becomes possible to minimize potential threats while transmitting data over the public switched telephone network. Although the use of security modems as well as modems in general has to a large degree been replaced by the use of VPNs communicating over the Internet, certain applications continue to use security modems. For example, sales personnel, government investigators, and other travelers who must communicate securely and cannot use the Internet due to lack of availability or cost considerations frequently dial security modems at a corporate location. While mobility can adversely affect the use of callback, the use of cell phones provides a fixed telephone number that avoids the problem of coordination and the reconfiguring of callback numbers as sales personnel move from motel to vendor location and need to quickly check the status of an order or the latest price of a product.

One of the major problems associated with the callback feature of security modems results from the use of Local Area Signaling Service (LASS) codes. LASS codes are numbers entered on a telephone touchpad to access special features of the telephone system. Two well-known LASS codes are 67, which toggles Caller-ID blocking, and 69 for Call Return. By knowing how to use LASS codes, a hacker may be able to exploit the configuration of the callback feature of a security modem.

Firewall

The major difference between a router and firewall lies in three areas: the transfer of packets based on routing tables; the degree of packet inspection; and acting as an intermediate device by hiding the address of clients from users on the Internet, a technique referred to as acting as a proxy.

A router has routing tables that associate IP addresses with ports on the device. When a packet arrives at a router port, the device examines the destination address in the IP header. Then, through a table lookup process that associates IP addresses with router ports, the router forwards the packet onto and through the port listed in the routing table, with the packet then flowing onto a communications connection with the port. That communications connect depends on the type of router port, ranging from an Ethernet or Token Ring LAN to a serial port connected to a 56 kbps, T1, or even a T3 connection. In comparison, a firewall only performs one type of basic packet processing. That is, if a packet fails a test, it is discarded or more fondly referred to as being sent to "the great big bucket in the sky." Otherwise, the packet is forwarded through the firewall to its destination.

A second significant difference between a router and a firewall governs the degree of packet inspection. A router typically examines the headers in IP, TCP, and UDP. In comparison, a firewall looks deeper into packets, in some cases, examining the contents of the data transported within the packet, looking for repetitive potentially dangerous operations, such as attempted sign-ons to different IP addresses that might represent different corporate servers. The ability of a firewall to keep track of the content of packets over a period of time is referred to as stateful inspection. Stateful inspection was developed by Checkpoint Software Technologies during the 1990s and has supplemented and, in many cases, replaced static packet filtering. Under stateful inspection, both inbound and outbound packets can be monitored. Outbound packets that request specific types of services are tracked, with inbound packet responses allowed through the firewall. Because inbound ports are only opened in response to a specific outbound packet flow, this nullifies the ability of hackers to scan a site for open ports, a common hacker practice.

Figure 6.12 Computer acting on behalf of another provides a proxy service.

A third difference between a router and a firewall may result in the firewall performing proxy services. In doing so, the firewall services the requests of its clients by forwarding requests onto the Internet. In this situation, a client connects to the proxy service of the firewall, requesting some type of service, such as a file transfer (File Transfer Protocol (FTP)) operation or Web page access. The proxy service of the firewall provides the resource by connecting to the specified IP address requesting the service on behalf of the client. In doing so, the proxy service of the firewall may use a single source IP address for all clients, keeping track of client sessions by using different port numbers to associate the client's real IP address with the common IP address used for all clients. Hiding the IP addresses of clients makes them more difficult to attack. If the proxy service passes all requests and replies in their original form, the service is usually referred to as a tunneling proxy service.

There are two basic types of firewall proxy services: circuit level and application. Previously, we discussed what is referred to as an application proxy service. In comparison, a circuit-level proxy is limited to a controlled network connection between internal and external systems. A circuit-level proxy results in a virtual "circuit" being established between the internal client and the proxy server. Internet requests are then routed through the circuit to the proxy server, and the proxy server forwards those requests to the Internet after changing the IP address of the internal client. Thus, external users are limited to denoting the IP address of the proxy server. In the reverse direction, responses are received by the proxy server and sent back through the circuit to the client. Although traffic is allowed to flow through the proxy, external systems never see the internal systems. This type of connection is often used to connect "trusted" internal users to the Internet.

Figure 6.12 illustrates an example of a proxy service. In this example, the highlighted middle computer acts as the proxy server between the other two devices.

Demilitarized Zone's Perimeter Controls

In concluding our discussion of perimeter controls, we will turn our attention to demilitarized zones. In some of the literature, you will see the term *perimeter network* used to reference the manner by which a DMZ is employed by a firewall.

The perimeter network represents an additional network between the protected network and the unprotected network, which, as we previously noted provides an additional layer of security. By controlling access from the "untrusted" network through the perimeter network to a "trusted" network, security is enhanced. However, it is important to realize that the perimeter network also represents a vulnerability. Thus it is extremely important to ensure that equipment is correctly configured and that software operates at the latest release to provide an effective level of protection.

IDS/IPS

In this section, we will turn our attention to types of security systems commonly marketed as Intrusion Detection Systems (IDSs) and Intrusion Prevention Systems (IPSs).

An IDS represents hardware or software that is specifically designed to detect unwanted attempts at accessing, manipulating, and even disabling networking hardware and computers connected to a network. Such attempts can be made by hackers or even disgruntled existing or former employees. Here, the key to an IDS system is its ability to detect attacks. It is important to note however, that unless an IDS system has access to keys used for encryption, the IDS cannot directly detect attacks within properly encrypted traffic.

The capabilities of an IDS can significantly vary from vendor to vendor. Because the goal of an IDS is to detect malicious behavior that can adversely effect computer or communications hardware, at a minimum it should detect a troika of malware directed at computers, such as viruses, Trojans, and worms as well as denial of service (DoS) attacks, logon attempts that cycle through passwords and IDs against a host or set of computers, as well as attempts to use guest or other accounts to gain access to sensitive files, such as the corporate payroll.

Architecture

A typical IDS consists of a console that monitors events reported by sensors, controls such sensors, and generates alerts. Concerning the latter, alerts can range from simple messages displayed on a console to the transmission of an e-mail or pager message and prerecorded telephone or cell phone calls.

Figure 6.13 illustrates a distributed IDS system with a centralized monitoring facility. In this example, agents designated by the letter A in boxes are placed at the entry point to remotely located subnets. Of course, one or more agents may also be located on the monitoring network, but they are not shown, because we want to focus on how remote intrusion detection can occur. This type of IDS represents a network IDS (NIDS). Sensors or agents can be physical hardware or software that is designed to operate promiscuously and examine all traffic flowing on a network

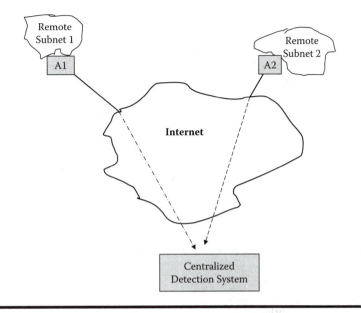

Figure 6.13   A centralized detection architecture.

segment. If you think of your home alarm system, you can note the similarities with a centralized monitoring approach to intrusion detection. Your windows and doors have sensors that can be considered to represent agents. Those agents are wired to a central panel in your home that broadcasts messages to your control panels, typically located in a master bedroom and home entryways. When a door or window is open, a signal flows to the control panel. The control panel examines the state of the alarm (off, at home, etc.) and generates a preplanned action, such as dialing a monitoring company. Similarly, when an intrusion is detected, the IDS will perform some predefined action based on its configuration. Most NIDS implementations use sensors located at choke points in the network to be monitored, such as the DMZ or at network borders. The sensors capture all network traffic, analyzing the contents of those packets for malicious traffic. Although many vendors market distributed NIDS systems, in less complex IDS implementations, all components are combined in a single device or network appliance.

There are numerous types of IDS systems that are designed to perform specific functions. For example, one common type of IDS is a protocol-based intrusion detection system that commonly is implemented in software and resides on servers, examining, for example, the HTTP data stream on a Web server. Another common type of IDS is a host-based IDS (HIDS) that represents software tailored to operate on different types of computers, ranging from small Web servers to large IBM mainframes. A typical HIDS consists of an agent on a host that identifies intrusions by analyzing system calls, application logs, file-system modifications (such as password and access threshold files), and other host activities and state.

Intrusion Prevention System

Intrusion prevention systems (IPSs) can be considered to represent an evolution in security progress from IDS technology. Whereas an IDS represents a passive system, an IPS represents an active system that detects and responds to predefined events. Thus, the IPS represents technology built on an IDS system. This means that the ability of the IPS to prevent intrusions from occurring is highly dependent on the underlying IDS.

An IPS represents a software or a hardware appliance that monitors a network or system activities for malicious or unwanted behavior, such as repeated attempts to log onto a computer or gain access to a router's command interface and will in real time react to either block or prevent those activities. Of course, it will also issue one or more alarms via a console, e-mail, or dialing a predefined telephone number to alert applicable persons of the event. A network-based IPS, for example, will operate in-line to monitor all network traffic for malicious code or attacks. When an attack on a router's command port is detected, it can drop the offending packets while still allowing all other traffic to pass.

As one might expect, to operate effectively, an IPS must have an excellent intrusion detection capability. This also means that the software or hardware appliance itself should not become a liability by becoming subject to one or more types of network or computer attacks. Thus, some IPS products are designed to be installed without an IP network address. Instead, they operate promiscuously, examining each packet flowing on the network and responding to predefined attacks by dropping packets, changing equipment settings, and generating a variety of alerts. Thus, unlike a firewall that has an IP address, resides at the perimeter of a network, and will usually filter packets based on predefined packet addresses and packet content, the IPS can reside behind the firewall, has no IP address, and operates invisibly on the network.

Wireless Considerations

No discussion of network security would be complete without discussing wireless networks. Thus, let us turn our attention to this topic.

Wireless LANS consist of computers with wireless adapters either built in or inserted into card slots, which collectively are referred to as stations, and one or more access points. An access point normally functions as a multiport bridge, with a wireless port and one or more wired ports. As data flows between wireless stations, from one wireless station to the Internet or from a wireless station onto the corporate LAN to a server, the access point operates as a bridge and broadcasts data onto all other ports, which makes it relatively easy for a person with a laptop with a promiscuous adapter to read traffic from or to other stations to include those stations residing on the LAN as they communicate with wireless stations.

Figure 6.14   The Independent Basic Service Set.

Architectures

One or more stations and an access point are referred to as a Basic Service Set (BSS). To differentiate one BSS from another, each access point is assigned a service set identifier (SSID). The SSID is periodically broadcast by the access point, which enables a station to examine the names of networks within range and connect to the most appropriate one. One popular method to increase wireless security, which is not particularly practical when facing network-savvy hackers, is to turn off SSID broadcasting. While the network name is not shown, you can easily connect to the network by configuring your station to select the "unknown" network or configuring your station to use the network name "any." In addition, others can also capture the SSID in cleartext by observing association frames from legitimate clients.

Figure 6.14 illustrates the formation of an independent BSS. Wireless LANs can communicate is two different ways referred to as peer-to-peer and infrastructure. In peer-to-peer mode, stations communicate directly with one another. In the infrastructure mode of operation, stations communicate via the use of an access point. Thus, Figure 6.14 shows how three stations can communicate with one another without an access point.

The wireless access point, which is more popularly referred to as a wireless router when used in a home or small business, is the most common communications product used to connect wireless stations to a corporate LAN. In actuality, the basic access point is a two-port bridge, with one port representing the wireless interface while the second port is the wired interface. When functioning as a bridge, the access point operates according to the three-F rule, flooding, filtering, and forwarding, as it builds a table of MAC addresses associated with each port. As the access point evolved, many manufacturers added a routing capability to the device as well as several Ethernet switch ports, referring to the device as a wireless router. In actuality, most wireless routers perform limited routing capability at layer 3 and primarily operate at layer 2 to perform bridging among its wired and wireless ports. Unfortunately, this device is similar to other networking hardware with respect to a security loophole many people fail to close. That is, it is configured at the factory with a default setting, such as "admin" or the name of the manufacturer for the password needed to access its configuration settings. Thus, the first thing a

Figure 6.15   The Infrastructure Basic Service Set.

user should consider after the device is set up is to change the administrative password from its default setting.

Figure 6.15 illustrates an Infrastructure BSS, which is the most common type of BSS used. In this example two wireless stations are shown communicating via a common access point which is in turn cabled to a wired hub or switch, which provides connectivity to the corporate network. If default settings are not changed on the access point, not only can a hacker easily access the administrative functions of the access point, but, in addition, he or she can change the settings to either cause havoc to the organization or silently transmit a stream of data flowing through the device to a third party address for analysis.

When two BSSs are connected via a repeater or wired connection, they form an Extended Service Set (ESS). The ESS has an identifier or network name referred to as an Extended Service Set Identifier (ESSID). The ESSID can be considered as the network identifier for the wireless network. Devices may be set to "any" or to a specific ESSID. When set, they will only communicate with other devices using the same ESSID. Figure 6.16 illustrates the relationship between the BSS and ESS for two BSSs linked via a wired LAN. In this example, each BSS could be located

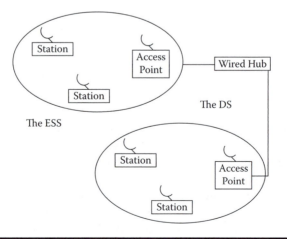

Figure 6.16   The Extended Service Set and the distribution system.

in different buildings on a campus, and the movement of a notebook user from one building to another would occur similar to cell phone roaming. The connection between the two BSSs is referred to as a distribution system (DS). The DS can be a wired LAN, a leased line, or even a wireless LAN repeater to extend the range between the two service sets.

Security Issues

The original security for wireless LANs, referred to as Wired Equivalent Privacy (WEP), as its name implies, permits the equivalent of wired network privacy and nothing more. WEP was broken by several persons many years ago, and many improvements were made to the security technology to include rotating WEP keys and the use of RADIUS servers to strengthen wireless security. Other security enhancements include permitting only predefined MAC addresses via filtering, the use of better encryption beyond WEP, and level-3 security measures associated with Web browsing. While these security techniques made it a bit more difficult for hackers to recover the WEP key in use, they still represented security vulnerabilities.

In an attempt to minimize the vulnerability of wireless transmissions, several additional security-related techniques were developed. These techniques included two versions of Wi-Fi Protected Access (WPA and WPA2), and two new wireless-security-related standards from the IEEE referred to as the 802.11i and 802.1X. Concerning the latter, this standard includes a security protocol referred to as the Temporal Key Integrity Protocol (TKIP). Let us now familiarize ourselves with WPA and WPA2.

WPA and WPA2

Both WPA and WPA2 represent security protocols created by the Wi-Fi Alliance to secure wireless transmission, and resulted from the security weakness of WEP. The protocols implement a large portion of the IEEE wireless security standard referred to as 802.11i, and WPA included the use of TKIP to enhance data encryption. TKIP was designed to add a level of security beyond that provided by WEP. To do so, TKIP added a key mixing function, a sequence counter that protects against replay attacks, and a 64-bit message integrity check to eliminate the potential of a man-in-the-middle attack. TKIP was launched during 2002 and has been superseded by more robust encryption methods, such as AES and CCMP, which will shortly be described.

Because WPA2 replaced WPA, we will focus on the latter. Under WPA2, two modes of operation are supported: Personal mode and Enterprise mode. Personal mode was developed to support wireless security in the home and small office environment that lacked access to an authentication server. This mode of operation is referred to as Pre-shared key (PSK), and its use requires wireless network devices to encrypt traffic using a 256-bit key. That key can be entered as a passphrase of 8 to 63 printable ASCII characters or as a string of 64 hex digits. Because WPA-PSK automatically changes encryption keys, a technique referred to as rekeying, it provides a level of security significantly beyond that of WEP.

Its important to note that although WPA and WPA2 are not IEEE standards, they implement the majority of the IEEE 802.11i standard, with WPA2 supporting the relatively recent Advanced Encryption Standard (AES). AES supports three block ciphers; AES-128, AES-192, and AES-256. While each block size is 128 bits, the keys can be 128, 192, or 256 bits, resulting in the terms used to reference each portion of the standard. Today, most wireless products sold for use in the home or small office support WPA2. Because setup involves a few clicks within the operating system to enter a passphrase or string of hex digits, the major difficulty reported by users typically involves the failure to use the same passphrase or hex code on each wireless device.

IEEE 802.11i and 802.1X

While WPA and WPA2 represent a majority of the 802.11i standard, they are not fully compatible with it. While 802.11i makes use of the AES block cipher, both the original WEP and WPA use the RC4 stream cipher. Another difference is the fact that the 802.11i architecture includes support for the 802.1X standard as an authentication mechanism based on the use of the Extensible Authentication Protocol (EAP) and an authentication server as well as the use of AES-based Counter Mode with Cipher Block Chaining Message Authentication Code Protocol (CCMP), the latter an encryption protocol based on AES that provides confidentiality, integrity, and origin authentication. These additions in the 802.11i standard are well suited for the enterprise. To obtain a better understanding of the suitability of 802.1X for the enterprise, let us discuss some of its features.

802.1X

The IEEE 802.1X standard provides port-based authentication, requiring a wireless device to be authenticated prior to it's gaining access to a LAN and its resources. Under this standard, the client node is referred to as a supplicant, while the authenticator is usually an access point or a wired Ethernet switch. By default, the authenticator bars the supplicant's access to the network. The authenticator passes the supplicant's request to access the network to an authentication server. Assuming the authentication server accepts the supplicant's request, the authenticator opens the port to the supplicant's traffic, otherwise it is blocked. Messages from the supplicant authenticator and server are transported via EAP.

In addition to the previously mentioned wireless enhancements, another technique commonly used to provide a high level of security is the use of a layer 3 VPN. Because we will describe the use of VPNs later in this chapter, we will just mention at this time that they provide an alternative security mechanism that can be

Figure 6.17   VLAN switch partitioned by ports.

valuable when users are traveling or their organization does not fully support the 802.1X standard.

Zones of Control

Through the use of virtual LANs, it becomes possible to partition switch-based networks into zones of control. Not only does this restrict who can access devices attached to specific switch ports, but in addition, this can enhance throughput by limiting broadcast traffic.

Figure 6.17 illustrates an 8-port LAN switch subdivided into two networks based on port associations. In this example, ports 1, 2, 3, and 4 are assigned as VLAN 1, while the other ports are assigned to VLAN2. Note that traffic in VLAN1 is never seen by users in VLAN2 and vice versa, which provides a degree of both administrative control and security. Concerning the former, all accounting personnel could be assigned to VLAN1, while all engineering personnel could be assigned to VLAN2. Concerning security, the partition of the switch into two VLANs would then preclude accountants from accessing the engineering server, and vice versa. Also note that the segmentation of a switch into two or more VLANs can enhance performance. This results from the fact that broadcasts are restricted to each VLAN.

Network Security

In this section, let us turn our attention to some specific network security measures. In doing so, we will describe and discuss the use of generic products at different layers in the ISO reference model as well as different types of tunneling and endpoint security measures.

Content Filtering

Content filtering represents a technique whereby the contents of packets are either blocked or allowed based on an analysis of its content, rather than its IP address or other criteria. The most prominent use of content filtering is in programs that operate as add-ons to Web browsers or at a corporate gateway, blocking unacceptable messages that might be pornographic or racist. In an e-mail environment, the use of content filtering is designed to place e-mail advertisements and similar types of junk mail based on subject, content, or both in a spam folder that most persons ignore.

Antimalware

Antimalware software can be considered as a special type of content filter. However, instead of examining the content of packets for pornography, racist remarks, and similar content, this software is focused on detecting viruses, worms, Trojans, and other potentially harmful software. Once detected, the antimalware software will, based on its configuration, either block the packets or quarantine them. Often, antimalware is sold as a virus-checking system that operates on a separate e-mail server in a corporate environment and checks for a variety of potentially malicious software.

One special type of software product that is incorporated into many routers is designed to block DoS attacks. One type of DoS attack occurs due to the manner in which TCP operates, which results in a three-way handshake. Figure 6.18 illustrates an example of the TCP three-way handshake process, which results in

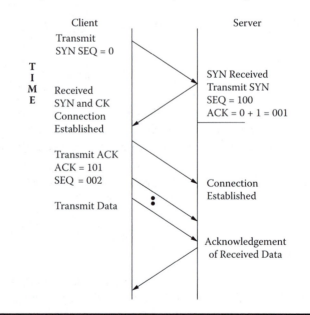

Figure 6.18   The three-way handshake.

the exchange of SYN, SYN/ACK, and ACK messages. First, a client accessing a server transmits a SYN message to the server. The server responds with a SYN/ACK message, to which the client would normally respond with an ACK. However, if a hacker spoofs the IP source address, the SYN/ACK message will not receive an ACK. Although the server will eventually time out the connection, during the period it remains open it takes resources away from the server. When a hacker floods the server with spoofed IP addresses in a series of connection requests, the result is a DoS attack, which limits the ability of real clients to access the server.

Through the use of DoS prevention, most routers can be configured to restrict the number of open connections at a specific time or from a specific address.

Antispam

As previously discussed in this section, content filtering is the building block upon which antispam products operate. For example, an e-mail spam filter could examine the originator, subject, or content of e-mails to decide whether to pass the mail to the recipient or place it in his or her spam folder. Figure 6.19 illustrates a portion of a spam folder on Yahoo mail. Note that the "From" column has names instead of e-mail addresses, which makes it easy to differentiate span from genuine e-mail. Turning your attention to the date column, note that at the time this author's spam file was captured, spam e-mailers were using improper dates, which represents another way to filter their junk mail. Between the two columns is the column labeled Subject, which can also be used to filter junk mail. Here, such keywords as *lenders*, *free*, and *medication* can be used to place e-mail in the spam filter.

| Spam | | | Upgrade to the all-new Yahoo! Mail |

SpamGuard is ON: [Edit Settings]
SpamGuard ensures that suspected spam is delivered to the **Spam** folder, and is deleted after one month.

View: All | Unread | Flagged | From Connections   Messages 1-25 of 1179 First | Previous | Next | Last

| Delete | Mark ▼ | Move... ▼ | | | |

☐	✉	From	⬦ Subject	Date ⬔	Size
☐	·	Cash Locator	Lenders waiting to loan you money !	Mon, 1/18/38	4KB
☐	·	The Fun Cards	Send Christmas eCards to Family and Friends for Free ...	Mon, 1/18/38	3KB
☐	·	Josefina	Hurry...High-quality Medications! Don't miss the chance !	Mon, 1/18/38	2KB
☐	·	Need Cash Quick	Get up to $1500 in 1 hour- Fast Approval for !	Mon, 1/18/38	4KB
☐	·	eBay Profit Machine	Retire Early: Ebay Needs New Workers Gilbert Held	Mon, 1/18/38	4KB
☐	·	Real Visa	Get A REAL Visa. Right Away Gilbert Held today!	Mon, 1/18/38	4KB
☐	·	Jesus Kennedy	Can't find high-quality medications?	Mon, 1/18/38	2KB
☐	·	Henry Otto	Quality medications all over the world	Mon, 1/18/38	2KB
☐	·	Henry Otto	Quality medications all over the world	Mon, 1/18/38	2KB
☐	·	Dillard Rocky	Find the Huge Selection of Replicas	Mon, 1/18/38	2KB
☐	·	Mary johnson	Hurry.. CHEAP CIALIS,Viagra ONLINE - LOWEST NET P...	Mon, 1/18/38	2KB
☐	·	Google Business	Let Google Make You Money While You Sleep Gilbert ...	Mon, 1/18/38	4KB

Figure 6.19   Examining a Yahoo spam folder.

Outbound Traffic Filtering

There are several types of communications devices that can be used to perform outbound traffic filtering. Such devices are primarily used to control the use of e-mail and Web access.

When filtering outbound e-mail, some organizations use a special server to encrypt messages to certain third parties, forcing the recipient to register to receive mail as well as to either set up a user ID and password to access the mail server or to use a private key to decrypt the message encrypted with a public key. In other situations, an organization may configure a mail server to block mail sent to certain addresses, such as those with the domain .xxx.

The filtering of outbound Web traffic is commonly employed by several well-known security programs. Although the primary goal of Web outbound traffic filtering is to block users from accessing predefined URLs, such as phishing sites or sites considered racist, sites offering gambling or pornography, a secondary goal is to enhance employee productivity by limiting the time that workers can access the Internet.

The ability to restrict outbound Web traffic to certain periods of time is commonly incorporated into routers, firewalls, and certain network appliances. For example, an organization might restrict outbound Web traffic to all locations other than servers at different organizational locations, with the exception of lunch hour, when employees are allowed to pay bills, shop, or perform other Internet-related chores.

Mobile Code

Another type of outbound traffic filtering involves blocking mobile code. This type of code is software obtained from remote system or systems, transmitted over a network, and then downloaded and executed on a local system, all without the computer operator being aware of the activity taking place. Some common examples of mobile code include code developed using script languages such as JavaScript and VBScript, Java applets, ActiveX controls, Flash animations, and even macros embedded within Microsoft Office documents such as Excel and Word documents. Mobile code can occur by a hacker scanning a network for holes in the perimeter and sending mobile code to specific addresses or through the use of e-mail attachments that when activated by clicking execute the code.

Some mobile code can be harmful, consisting of Distributed Denial of Service (DDoS) agents designed to attack a target or list of targets at specific times, viruses, worms, and other harmful software. By examining the content of outbound packets, the spread of malware may be contained; however, it does not rid the computer of the problematic software. To do so, a virus checker or the alert message of the device performing the outbound traffic filtering must be examined.

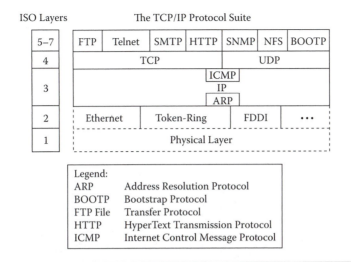

ISO Layers   The TCP/IP Protocol Suite

Legend:
ARP   Address Resolution Protocol
BOOTP   Bootstrap Protocol
FTP File   Transfer Protocol
HTTP   HyperText Transmission Protocol
ICMP   Internet Control Message Protocol

Figure 6.20   Comparing the TCP/IP protocol suite to the ISO reference model.

Application and Transport Layer Security

If you compare the well-known seven-layer International Organization for Standardization (ISO) Open System Interconnection (OSI) reference model to the TCP/IP protocol suite, you will note that the latter in effect combines the upper three layers of the ISO model (application, presentation, and session), as shown in Figure 6.20, into a single layer that is commonly referenced as a TCP/IP application. Over the past two decades, several application protocols were developed to support secure e-commerce and in turn safe browsing and purchasing from different Web sites. In this section, we will describe and discuss some of those security-related protocols that enable safe credit card transactions and deposits and withdrawals from checking accounts.

Secure E-Commerce Protocols

A protocol represents a set of rules that govern communication between two network entities. Some of the most widely used protocols are members of the TCP/IP family, such as the Internet Protocol (IP), the Transmission Control Protocol (TCP), the User Datagram Protocol (UDP), and the Internet Control Message Protocol (ICMP). A security protocol is a communication protocol that is specifically designed to provide secure communications. Several security protocols are either in use or being developed for use on the Internet. Such security protocols are designed for different applications ranging from the use of credit cards to spending micro dollars, which add up cumulatively to a large amount spread over hundreds

Application Layer (HTTP)
SSL
TCP
IP

Figure 6.21　SSL and the TCP/IP protocol stack.

to thousands of Web sites. In addition, each security protocol may provide different benefits, depending on where it is positioned in the TCP/IP protocol suite.

The most widely used security protocol is the Secure Socket Layer (SSL) because it is built into every popular Web server and browser. As its name implies, SSL does not secure a transaction directly; instead, it provides a secure connection for any information flowing between a browser and server via the HyperText Transmission Protocol (HTTP). SSL has been used over the past few years to migrate to a derivative IETF standard referred to as Transport Layer Security (TLS) that is very similar to SSL Version 3.0; we will refer to these standards interchangeably in this chapter. SSL resides just above TCP but below the application it protects and is transported by underlying protocols, so it does not require modification to the operating system's networking software and does not affect data or document structures. Figure 6.21 illustrates the relationship of SSL to other layers in the TCP protocol stack.

SSL/TSL and the TCP/IP Protocol Stack

As the name Secure Sockets Layer indicates, SSL connections act like sockets connected by TCP. Therefore, you can think of SSL connections as secure TCP connections because the place for SSL in the protocol stack is right above TCP. It is important to note, however, that SSL does not support some TCP features, such as out-of-band data.

The SSL protocol was developed by Netscape Communications Corporation in 1994. SSL allows clients, such as Web browsers and HTTP servers, to communicate over a secure communications connection. To accomplish this, SSL supports encryption, source authentication, and data integrity as key mechanisms that are used to protect information exchanged over insecure public networks such as the Internet. There are several versions of SSL, with SSL 3.0 being the latest version, which is universally supported. A newer "version" of SSL known as the Transport Layer Security (TLS) is an improvement over SSL 3.0, was promulgated as an Internet standard, and is supported by just about all recent software.

Encryption

Encryption is used to protect data from observation and potential use by converting it to an apparently meaningless form prior to transmission. The data is encrypted by one side (either the client or the server), transmitted, and then decrypted by the other side prior to being processed.

Authentication

Authentication represents a method of verifying the identity of the other party in a communications session. In e-commerce, this enables the client accessing a server to verify its identity and the server to verify the identity of the client.

There are several way of configuring authentication. First, if you do not configure or enable an authentication method, no authentication will occur. You can also enable basic server authentication, which provides authentication of the server accessed by a client. A third authentication method is referred to as mutual authentication, which results in the server authenticating the client while the client authenticates the server.

The first time a browser or other client attempts to communicate with a Web server over a secure connection, the server presents the client with a set of credentials. Those credentials are in the form of a certificate.

Certificates and Certificate Authorities

Certificates are issued and validated by trusted authorities referred to as certification authorities (CAs). A certificate represents the public-key identity of a person. It is a signed document that in effect says: "I certify that the public key in this document belongs to the entity named in this document." One of the most widely used CAs are certificates issued by VeriSign.

Data Integrity

The function of data integrity is to ensure that data has not been modified. Implementing data integrity can include monitoring and modification detection of key files, regardless of whether the modification was malicious, or accidental. In a Windows environment, this can include looking for changes to the registry, changes to files' security access permissions, changes to services, as well as changes to the contents of files.

SSL/TLS Features

The original design of SSL and its subsequent reincarnation as TLS were well thought out and resulted in the two protocols being used for secure e-commerce transactions. SSL represents a de facto standard, while TLS represents a formal standard

Figure 6.22   Accessing a secure Web site.

promulgated by the IETF. At the very beginning, the designers of SSL were aware of the fact that not all parties would use the same client software. In addition, due to different hardware platform processing, clients would not embrace a single encryption algorithm. This is because an encryption algorithm suitable for one hardware platform might be unsuitable for another. The same was true for servers. Thus, under SSL and TLS, the client and server at the two ends of a connection negotiate the encryption and decryption algorithms (cipher suites) during their initial handshake.

Although SSL permits both the client and the server to authenticate each other, typically only the server is authenticated in the SSL layer. Clients are primarily authenticated in the application layer, through passwords sent over an SSL-protected communications link between client and server

Figure 6.22 illustrates the beginning of an SSL session when this author used a browser to access the Smith Barney Web site. In the background, note the lock in the upper right that is used to indicate a secure connection. Depending on the browser and version used, the lock can be at different locations on the Web page. In general, SSL- or TLS-enabled Web sites are recognizable by the lock or key icon displayed at the top or bottom of a browser window when visiting a site that supports transmission security.

Limitations of SSL/TLS

A key limitation of SSL/TLS is the fact that information passed over a secure connection becomes nonsecure when the server being accessed stores the received data on a hard drive. In fact, this major limitation allowed hackers to obtain millions of credit card numbers and other information by hacking into an organization's server and downloading the contents of various server files. Unfortunately, that server held account information for several brands, resulting in the credit card information of over a million persons who purchased items at over a thousand stores being compromised. Thus, for additional safety, SSL should be supplemented by the encryption of data stored on e-commerce servers.

In addition to its use for securing access to Web servers, SSL can be used to secure communications with mail servers via POP3 (Post Office Protocol Version 3), IMAP (Internet Message Access Protocol), and SMTP (Simple Mail Transfer Protocol), directory servers via LDAP (Lightweight Directory Assistance Protocol), CA servers, FTP servers, and many custom applications.

Other Security Protocols

Some additional security-related protocols include Secure Multimedia Internet Mail Extensions (S/MIME), used for securing e-mail; iKP, which represents a family of protocols that provides a model for secure credit card transactions; Millicent, which was developed as a method for micropayments; and Netcash and Digicash, the latter two developed for anonymous transactions.

S/MIME is an application-layer protocol that was developed to provide security for e-mail documents. It accomplishes this by securing the transmission of e-mail through store-and-forward processing and even during storage on a destination hard drive. S/MIME can be used to create signed orders and other types of e-commerce records. Currently, several popular e-mail programs support S/MIME; however, the requirement for a full Public Key Infrastructure (PKI) to deploy digital identities to users has hindered its widespread adoption

The iKP family of protocols was designed at IBM-Zürich to provide secure credit card payments over an insecure network, such as the Internet. Millicent was designed by Digital Equipment's Systems Research Center at Palo Alto, California, to enable secure micropayments, enabling transactions that cost a fraction of a cent to occur on the Internet. Because the cost associated with a typical security protocol can exceed a micropayment, Millicent addresses this economic problem by providing lightweight secure transactions more suitable for micropayment transactions. Another series of security-related protocols such as IPSec, L2TP, and SOCKS are used for constructing virtual private networks (VPNs) and will be shortly described. However, prior to doing so, we need to discuss the security-related aspects of remote procedure calls.

Secure Remote Procedure Calls

Prior to discussing the securing of remote procedure calls (RPCs), it is important to understand what it is and how it is used. An RPC represents a technique for building client–server-based applications. An RPC can be considered to be similar to a function call, with calling arguments passed to the remote procedure while the calling software waits for a response from the remote procedure operating on a server. At the client, the software thread that initiated the RPC is blocked from further processing until either a response is received from the server or a timeout occurs. At the server, a routine is initiated that performs the requested service and transmits a response to the client.

To secure RPCs, several steps are required. First, the client software must create an association with a server. The client then invokes appropriate security services to compute a checksum of the previously created checksum. Finally, the client initializes two 32-bit sequence numbers that are used to establish pairwise credentials between the client and server. At the server, upon receipt of an association request, the computer stores the association checksum. Next, the server creates two 32-bit sequence numbers. Although client and server sequence numbers are not transmitted, they are used to compute a variety of security checks, such as ensuring that data is transmitted and received in the same order.

The programming of the RPS permits various security options, such as defining a desired protection level and the algorithm used to protect data via an authentication service. Because some options are more CPU intensive than others, a distinction can be made between intranet and Internet RPCs. That is, in an intranet environment where the threat is substantially reduced, processing may be enhanced by reducing security. In comparison, when used over the Internet, RPCs should be configured for maximum security.

Network Layer Security and VPNs

VPN technology is based on a technique referred to as tunneling. Under VPN tunneling, a logical connection is established and maintained between two locations connected via a packet network. Over this connection, packets are formed and transmitted via a client according to a specific VPN protocol being used. The client typically places a header and possibly a trailer around each packet, which encapsulates each packet and, depending on the protocol used, may encrypt and add authentication to the packet. At its destination, the packet is stripped of its header and optional trailer, and may be authenticated and decrypted based on the protocol in use.

The primary purpose of a VPN is to enable clients to access servers via a public packet network such as the Internet in a secure manner. Another reason for the use of VPNs is economics. That is, a VPN enables two or more locations to use the Internet as a transmission facility, enabling companies to avoid the cost of expensive leased lines or dial charges. One key application of VPNs is to link or interconnect networks in two or more distributed locations to one another via the Internet. In fact, over the years, VPNs have progressed from being client–server tunneling protocols to developing network-to-network protocol capability; the introduction of network appliances that support VPNs enables network operators to purchase

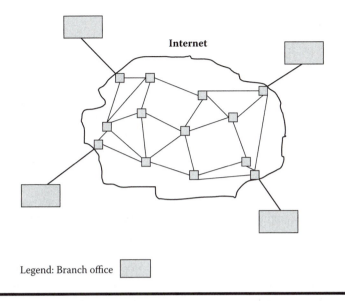

Figure 6.23 Using the Internet to connect four distributed locations to one another.

off-the-shelf hardware that facilitates interconnecting networks at multiple locations via the Internet in a secure manner.

Other reasons for the use of VPNs include securing wireless transmission from hot spots in airports and coffee shops back to a corporate server, perhaps reducing the need for third-party support, network scalability and, sometimes, ease of use. Concerning network scalability, while the cost associated with constructing a network using dial-up and leased lines may appear reasonable at first, as the need to add more branch offices expands, so does the cost. By using a VPN, all that is required to add additional locations is a line connecting the office to the Internet, making the Internet's vast collection of interconnected lines and routers available to an organization both domestically and overseas.

Figure 6.23 illustrates the use of the Internet to interconnect four geographically distributed branch offices. Note that only four connections to the Internet are required, one from each location. In comparison, 6 leased lines would be required to interconnect the offices without the use of the Internet. If the organization expanded its branches by two, it would need six Internet connections; however, the number of leased lines would increase to 15 to provide a similar interconnectivity capability. In addition, the mesh structure of the Internet provides a high degree of alternate routing capability, which routes data around impairments such as network outages or traffic bottlenecks; this capability would be very costly to duplicate on an individual organizational basis. Thus, for some organizations, the ability to add branch connections at a nominal cost makes economics and scalability an important driver for the use of VPNs.

Types of VPN Tunneling

VPN interconnects two or more locations via tunneling. There are two basic types of VPN tunneling: voluntary and compulsory. Both types of tunneling are commonly used in different VPN protocols. In addition, while we will first examine the basic differences between these two tunneling techniques, we need to note that, depending on the VPN protocol used, additional differences may exist.

Under voluntary tunneling, the VPN client manages the connection setup process. The client first initiates a connection to the communications carrier, which is an Internet service provider (ISP), when establishing an Internet VPN. Then, the VPN client application creates the tunnel to a VPN server over the connection.

Under compulsory tunneling, the communications carrier network provider is responsible for managing the VPN connection setup process. Thus, when the client initiates a connection to the carrier, the carrier in turn immediately initiates a VPN connection between that client and a designated VPN server. As viewed by the client, the VPN connection is set up in just one step compared to the two-step procedure required for voluntary tunnels. Compulsory VPN tunneling automatically authenticates clients and associates them with specific VPN servers by using predefined programming in the carrier network. The predefined programming is commonly referred to as a VPN Front End Processor (FEP), Network Access Server (NAS), or Point of Presence Server. Note that compulsory tunneling hides the details of VPN server connectivity from VPN clients and transfers management control over the tunnels from clients to the ISP. In return, service providers become responsible for the installation and maintenance of VPN hardware and software in their network. However, as you might expect, there is literally no free lunch, and the communications carrier charges a variety of fees for compulsory tunneling.

VPN Tunneling Protocols

Since the early 1980s, several computer network protocols were developed to support VPN tunnels. Some of the more popular VPN tunneling protocols include the Point-to-Point Tunneling Protocol (PPTP), Layer 2 Tunneling Protocol (L2TP), IP Security (IPSec), a combination of L2TP and IPSec referred to as L2TP/IPSec, and TCP Wrappers.

Point-to-Point Tunneling Protocol (PPTP)

Although PPTP is bundled with most versions of Windows beginning with Windows 95, its actual development resulted from a joint effort between Microsoft Corporation and several other vendors, including Ascend Communications, a router manufacturer. The initial version of PPTP for Windows was for dial-up access, with later versions supporting tunneling via the Internet. Encryption is based on the RC4 algorithm, which Microsoft refers to as Microsoft Point-to-Point Encryption

(MPPE) and is not part of the PPTP specification. Instead, it is performed by the RAS server and is not supported by all vendors.

Operation

PPTP is built on top of the Point-to-Point Protocol (PPP), which is commonly used as the login protocol for dial-up Internet access. PPTP stores data within PPP packets, then encapsulates the PPP packets within IP datagrams for transmission through an Internet-based VPN tunnel. PPTP supports data encryption and compression and uses a form of General Routing Encapsulation (GRE) to get data to and from its final destination. PPTP VPN tunnels are created via the following two-step process. First, the PPTP clients connect to their ISP using PPP dial-up networking, typically via a modem or ISDN connection. Next, PPTP creates a TCP control connection between the VPN client and the destination VPN server to establish a tunnel. PPTP uses TCP port 1723 for these connections. PPTP also supports VPN connectivity via a LAN. If the VPN is localized to the LAN, then ISP connections are not required, allowing PPTP tunnels to be created directly, because PPTP will create a TCP control connection between the VPN client and the destination VPN server.

A common security method implemented in routers is to employ access lists to allow IP datagrams containing a specified source and destination address that transports TCP with a destination port of 1723. In effect, this action creates a PPTP tunnel. Figure 6.24 illustrates the use of the Internet to create a tunnel between locations A and B. Assuming for simplicity that the IP address of the client at location A is 1.2.3.4 and the IP address of the VPN server at location B is 4.3.2.1, then

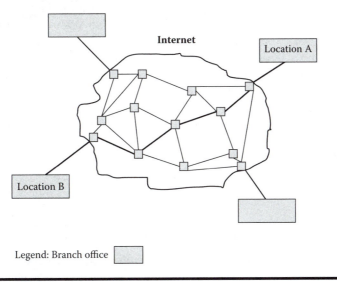

Figure 6.24   Using the Internet to create a PPTP tunnel from one location to another.

the generic statements in an access list for the router at location B to allow PPTP datagrams from the VPN tunnel established by a client at location A becomes

```
Allow IP 1.2.3.4 4.3.2.1 TCP any 1723
```

Here we assume that the access list format requires specifying a protocol (IP) followed by source and destination IP addresses followed by another protocol (TCP) and source and destination ports.

PPTP Security

PPTP supports authentication, encryption, and packet filtering. PPTP authentication uses PPP-based protocols such as the Password Authentication Protocol (PAP), the Challenge-Handshake Authentication Protocol (CHAP), and the Extensible Authentication Protocol EAP. PPTP supports packet filtering on VPN servers. Intermediate routers and other firewalls can also be configured to selectively filter PPTP traffic.

PPTP Advantages and Disadvantages

A key advantage of PPTP is its inclusion in just about every version of Windows. Thus, Windows servers also can function as PPTP-based VPN servers without having an organization bear any additional cost.

Unfortunately, PPTP has several vulnerabilities. First, it is vulnerable to man-in-the-middle attacks. Second, and perhaps most important, PPTP supports only single-factor, password-based authentication. As a result, if a hacker steals or guesses an employee's password, that intruder can access the company's network. It is quite common to walk through a floor in an organization and see sticky messages with passwords posted on cubicle walls or monitors; obviously, any simple password-based system represents a risk.

Another disadvantage of PPTP is its failure to embrace a single standard for authentication and encryption. Thus, two products that both fully comply with the PPTP specification can be totally incompatible with each other if they encrypt data differently. In addition, numerous concerns have arisen over the level of security PPTP provides compared to alternative VPN protocols. As a result of questions regarding its security, PPTP has been made obsolete by Layer 2 Tunneling Protocol and IPSec.

Layer 2 Tunneling Protocol (L2TP)

When PPTP was being developed for VPN tunneling by Microsoft and Ascend Communication, Cisco Corporation was supporting the development of an alternative VPN, referred to as Layer 2 Forwarding (L2F). L2F was primarily used in Cisco products and did not provide either encryption or authentication, relying on the protocol being tunneled to provide either or both. While L2F was specifically designed to tunnel PPP traffic, it was capable of carrying many other protocols. In an attempt to improve on L2F, the best features of it and PPTP were combined to create new standard called the Layer 2 Tunneling Protocol (L2TP).

Similar to PPTP, L2TP exists at the data link layer (Layer 2) in the OSI reference model; hence, the origin of its name. However, in actuality, L2TP is a Layer 5 protocol and operates at the session layer of the OSI model using UDP Port 1701.

L2TP does not actually provide encryption or authentication, relying on the protocol that passes within the tunnel it provides for this capability. The protocol was originally published in 1999 as proposed standard RFC 2661. A more recent version of L2TPv3 was published as proposed standard RFC 3931 in 2005. The key difference between the latter and earlier version is the fact that L2TPv3 provides additional security features, improved encapsulation, and the ability to transport data links such as Frame Relay, Ethernet, and ATM over an IP network, whereas the original L2TP was restricted to supporting PPP.

Operation

L2TP uses the User Datagram Protocol (UDP). In doing so, the entire L2TP packet, including payload and L2TP header, is sent within a UDP datagram. Although PPP sessions are commonly transported within an L2TP tunnel, as previously mentioned, Ethernet, Frame Relay, and other types of data can be transported under L2TPv3.

The two endpoints of an L2TP tunnel are called the LAC (L2TP Access Concentrator) and the LNS (L2TP Network Server). The LAC is the initiator of the tunnel, while the LNS is the server, which waits for new tunnels to be established. Once a tunnel is established, network traffic is bidirectional. When higher-level protocols are then run through an L2TP tunnel, an L2TP session is established within the tunnel for each higher-level protocol, such as PPP, Frame Relay, or Ethernet. Either the LAC or LNS may initiate sessions. The traffic for each session is isolated by L2TP, so it becomes possible to set up multiple virtual networks across a single tunnel.

The packets exchanged within an L2TP tunnel can be categorized as either control packets or data packets. L2TP provides reliability features for the control packets, but no reliability for data packets. If reliability is required for data packets, it must be provided by protocols running within each session of the L2TP tunnel.

Figure 6.25 illustrates the equipment required to provide multiple tunnels from one location to another via the Internet. In the lower-left corner, a modem bank terminates calls from the PSTN and passes them to a network access server (NAS), which is normally combined with an L2TP Access Concentrator (LAC). The L2TP Access Concentrator encapsulates PPP frames with L2TP headers and transmits them over the Internet as UDP packets. Or, as previously mentioned, the LAC can transmit over an ATM, Frame Relay, or X.25 network. At the destination, the

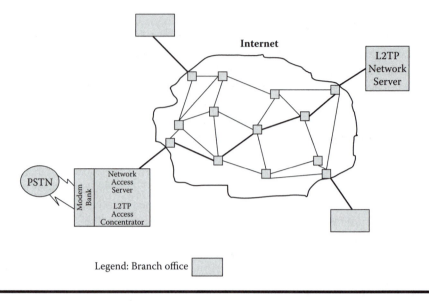

Figure 6.25 Using the Internet to create a L2TP tunnel from one location to another.

L2TP Network Server (LNS) terminates the PPP session and passes the IP packets to the LAN. Because L2TP software can execute in a PC, the tunnel can extend from a remote user dialing the modem bank through the NAS and LAC to the LNS and destination LAN.

Today, most L2TP deployments are used to support the creation of VPNs via LAN connections over the Internet. Because such use is primarily by businesses, such PPP authentication protocols as CHAP, PAP, and EAP are employed for corporate access authentication. To support such authentication methods, L2TP creates a tunnel between the client and the corporate network. Then, the users' identification is verified, and they can proceed as if they were directly connected to the distant network.

As we mentioned earlier in our discussion of VPNs, there are two basic types of tunneling: compulsory and voluntary. Under L2TP, compulsory tunneling is ideal for a business environment. This is because the tunnel is created from the LAC via the Internet to the LNS on a distant corporate network, and neither remote client has knowledge of the tunnel nor needs L2TP client software. Instead, each remote client creates a PPP connection to the LAC and is then tunneled to the LNS. Another advantage of compulsory L2TP tunneling is the fact that remote clients need to access the LAC to gain access to the distant corporate network. Thus, network managers can configure a single point, the LAC, to control permissions to include the authentication of remote clients.

The major problem associated with compulsory L2TP tunneling is its difficulty to support mobility away from a remote LAN. Thus, in an L2TP environment, an individual client to LNS tunneling method is required to support mobility. This method of tunneling is referred to as voluntary L2TP tunneling.

As briefly mentioned earlier, L2TP does not provide any encryption. In addition, by itself, it lacks authentication and data integrity methods because it was designed primarily as a mechanism to extend a PPP tunnel. To overcome the previously mentioned security deficiencies, it is common to combine IPSec with L2TP. Using IPSec, the L2TP tunnel can be secured, either from the LAC to LNS under compulsory tunneling or from a remote client to the LNS under voluntary tunneling.

Under L2TP, authentication occurs via PPP at the LAC or the LNS. Authentication can occur using PPP authentication protocols such as CHAP, PAP, or EAP. When the PPP connection process is encrypted by IPSec, any PPP authentication method can be used, with mutual authentication occurring if EAP or CHAPv2 is used.

The type of encryption used is determined during the establishment of the IPSec security association. Available encryption algorithms include the original 56-bit Digital Encryption Standard (DES), 3DES, and certain versions of Advanced Encryption Standard (AES). Data authentication and integrity are accomplished by the use of a hash message authentication code, such as Message Digest 5 (MD5), which is a hash algorithm that generates a 128-bit hash of the authenticated payload or the Secure Hash Algorithm (SHA), which produces a 160-bit hash of the authenticated payload. Thus, the use of IPSec with L2TP can considerably strengthen the tunneling protocol.

L2TP Packet Exchange

The setup of an L2TP connection results in the exchange of a series of control packets between clients and servers to establish tunnels and sessions in each direction. During the setup process, a specific tunnel and session ID is assigned. Through the use of the assigned tunnel and session ID numbers, multiple tunnels can be established on the same path with data packets exchanged using compressed PPP frames as the payload. Because L2TP does not include encryption (as does PPTP), it is often used in combination with IPSec to provide VPN connections from remote users to the corporate LAN. Thus, let us turn our attention to IPSec.

IPSec

IP Security (IPSec) represents a family of security protocols promulgated as RFCs from the IETF that provides both authentication and encryption over the Internet. Unlike SSL, which provides services at Layer 4 and secures two applications, IPSec operates at Layer 3 and secures everything in the network. Also, unlike SSL, which is typically built into every Web browser, IPSec requires a client installation. IPSec can provide security for both Web and non-Web applications, whereas SSL is primarily used for Web access, but with additional effort can be used to secure such applications as file sharing and e-mail.

The primary use of IPSec is for building VPNs. IPSec secures individual packets flowing between any two computers connected to an IP network. IPSec includes the ability to establish mutual authentication between computers at the beginning of the session and supports the negotiation of encryption keys to be used during the session. In addition to securing data flows between a pair of computers, IPSec can be used to secure communications to routers, firewalls, and other devices that are IPSec compliant.

Operation

IPSec operates at the IP layer (Layer 3) of the Internet Protocol Suite. The operation of IPSec at Layer 3 makes this security protocol more flexible than SSL/TLS and higher-layer protocols. This results from the fact that IPSec can be used for protecting all the higher-level protocols. This enables applications to avoid having to be designed to use IPSec, whereas the use of TLS/SSL or other higher-layer protocols must be incorporated into the design of an application.

As previously mentioned, IPSec represents a family of security-related protocols. Each protocol was designed to perform different security-related functions. Those protocols and their functions include

Authentication Header (AH): Provides authentication for IP datagrams as well as protection against replay attacks.

Encapsulating Security Payload (ESP): Provides authentication, data integrity, and confidentiality of packets transmitted. While ESP supports encryption-only and authentication-only modes of operation, note that using encryption without authentication is strongly discouraged because it is insecure.

Internet Key Exchange (IKE): It is an IPSec protocol that is used to set up a security association (SA) by handling negotiation of the encryption and authentication keys to be used by IPSec.

Security Association

The IP security architecture uses the concept of a security association as the basis for building security functions into IP. A security association represents the bundling of algorithms and parameters that are used to encrypt and authenticate a particular flow in one direction. Because data traffic is normal bidirectional traffic, the flows are secured by a pair of security associations. The actual choice of encryption and authentication algorithms can be selected from a predefined list by the IPSec administrator.

IPSec uses a Security Parameter Index (SPI), which points to a location in a security association database (SADB), along with the destination address in a packet header, which together uniquely identify a security association for that packet. A similar procedure is performed for an outgoing packet, where IPSec gathers decryption and verification keys from the security association database.

Authentication Header (AH)

AH operates directly above IP, using IP protocol number of 51. AH is employed to authenticate the origin of data as well as provide for the data integrity of IP datagrams. In addition, it can optionally protect against replay attacks through the use of a sliding window technique and discarding old packets. AH protects the IP payload and all header fields of an IP datagram except for fields that might be altered in routing, such as router fields that are changed when data flows through the device.

Figure 6.26 illustrates where an AH packet resides within an IP datagram and the fields within the header.

The Next Header is an 8-bit field that identifies the type of the next payload after the Authentication Header. The value of this field is chosen from the set of IP Protocol Numbers defined in the most recent "Assigned Numbers" RFC from the Internet Assigned Numbers Authority (IANA). For example, hex 6 is used for TCP, whereas hex 11 designates UDP. The following field, Length, defines the size of the AH packet. The third field, shown padded to zero, represents a "Reserved" field that is currently not used. The fourth field, Security parameters index (SPI), identifies the security parameters, which, in combination with the IP address, identifies the security association (SA). The SA represents a simplex or one-way channel and logical connection that provides a secure data connection between network devices implemented with this packet. The fifth field, Sequence number, represents

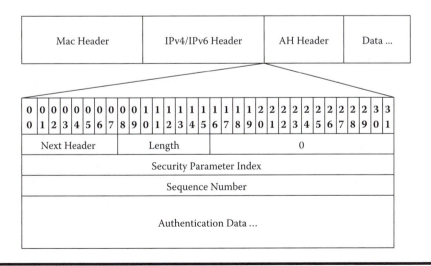

Figure 6.26   The AH header provides authentication and data integrity.

an increasing number that is used to prevent replay attacks. The sixth field is the Authentication Data field. This field contains the integrity check value (ICV) necessary to authenticate the packet.

Modes of Operation

There are two "modes" of operation that are supported by AH and ESP: tunnel mode and transport mode. Transport mode provides a secure connection between two endpoints as it encapsulates IP's payload, while tunnel mode encapsulates the *entire* IP packet to provide a virtual "secure hop" between two gateways. Tunnel mode is used to form a traditional VPN, where the tunnel generally creates a secure "tunneled" path across a packet network, such as the Internet or extranet.

Transport Mode

Transport mode is used to protect end-to-end communications between two hosts. This protection can be either authentication or encryption or both, but it is not a tunneling protocol. Thus, it has nothing to do with a traditional VPN as it simply represents a secured IP connection. In AH transport mode, the IP packet is modified only slightly to include the new AH header placed between the IP header and the protocol payload, such as TCP, UDP, or another payload. In addition, there is a shuffling of the protocol code that links the various headers together, which allows the original IP packet to be reconstituted at the other end. At the destination, assuming the packet passes the authentication check, the AH header is removed and once again some protocol field values are shuffled, which results in the IP datagram reverting to its original state.

Tunnel Mode

Tunnel mode provides a more familiar VPN type of functionality, where entire IP packets are encapsulated inside another and delivered to their destination. Similar to transport mode, each packet is sealed with a hash message authentication code (HMAC) that is usually created via the use of Message Digest 5 (MD5) or SHA1 (Secure Hash Algorithm 1). The HMAC is used to both authenticate the sender as well as to prevent the modification of data from occurring as it flows between source and destination. Under AH tunnel mode, the full IP header as well as payload data is encapsulated, which enables source and destination addresses to be different from those of the original packet. This encapsulation permits the packet to flow between two intermediary devices that form the tunnel, such as IPSec-compatible routers. At the destination router, an authentication check is performed, and packets that pass the check have their entire IP and AH readers removed, resulting in the recreation of the original datagram. That datagram is then routed to its original source IP address.

Figure 6.27   IPSec in an AH tunnel mode.

Figure 6.27 illustrates the manner by which an IP datagram is encapsulated within another IP header when AH is used in tunnel mode. Note that the wrapped or new header usually had the destination IP address of a network appliance representing a hardware box. That box is typically a computer with multiple fast processors that can rapidly compute integrity check values and different types of encryption and thus support AH, ESP, and iKey.

Encapsulating Security Payload (ESP)

ESP represents the portion of IPSec that provides origin authentication, data integrity, and confidentiality of packets. ESP also supports encryption-only and authentication-only configurations, but using encryption without authentication is strongly discouraged because it is insecure.

Unlike AH, ESP does not protect the IP packet header. However, in tunnel mode, where the entire original IP packet is encapsulated with a new packet header added, ESP protection is afforded to the whole inner IP packet to include the inner header, while the outer header remains unprotected because it provides the unencrypted address information necessary for routing. ESP operates directly on top of IP, using IP protocol number 50.

Similar to AH, ESP can operate in transport or tunnel mode. In transport mode, the datagram's payload is encrypted and transported via a new IPv4 header, which is essentially the same as the old header but has a few field values shifted while source and destination IP addresses are unchanged. Thus, similar to AH, ESP in transport mode is designed for host-to-host communications. In tunnel mode, ESP is similar to AH, where the encapsulation covers the original datagram, enabling the original IP header, TCP header, and payload to be encrypted. Thus, ESP in tunnel mode would be similar to Figure 6.27, with the AH replaced by an ESP header. Concerning that header, it is much simpler having just two fields: a security parameters index (SPI) and a sequence number. The SPI identifies the security parameters in combination with an IP address, while the sequence number represents a monotonically increasing number that is used to prevent replay attacks. Although replacing the AH with an ESP header shown in Figure 6.27 represents a majority of ESP tunnel mode connections, it should be mentioned that we can construct a real VPN supporting both encryption and authentication by adding authentication data to ESP in tunnel mode. This option is frequently used, with authentication data being added to a tunneled packet after the encryption of the IP header, TCP header, and payload. Another method is to use ESP+AH instead of AH+ESP. The reason ESP is not wrapped inside of AH is that most networks have routers that perform Network Address Translation (NAT), and by using AH+ESP, this tunnel becomes incapable of traversing a NAT device. Thus, ESP+AH is primarily used in tunnel mode to completely encapsulate and encrypt datagrams, adding authentication to protect the data and ensure its integrity as it flows across an untrusted network.

Cryptographic Algorithms

There are several cryptographic algorithms presently defined for use with IPSec. Some of the more popular algorithms include the Hash Message Authentication Code Secure Hash Algorithm (HMAC-SHA1) for data integrity protection and 3DES and AES for confidentiality. A list of algorithms is included in RFC 4835.

L2TP/IPSec

Due to the lack of encryption and authentication in the L2TP protocol, it is often implemented along with IPSec; the result is referred to as L2TP/IPSec, and is standardized as RFC 3193. The process of setting up an L2TP/IPSec VPN is a three-step process. First, a negotiation of the IPSec Security Association (SA) occurs, typically performed through the use of the Internet Key Exchange (IKE). This exchange occurs over UDP port 500, and commonly uses either a shared password (so-called "pre-shared keys"), public keys, or X.509 certificates on both ends, although other keying methods exist. Next, the establishment of an ESP transport mode occurs with the IP Protocol number for ESP inserted as 50. Once this occurs, a secure channel has been established, but no tunneling is taking place. Thus, the third step involves the negotiation and establishment of an L2TP tunnel between the SA endpoints. The actual negotiation of parameters takes place over the SA's secure channel, within the IPSec encryption, with L2TP using UDP port 1701. This action results in L2TP packets between the endpoints being encapsulated by IPSec. Because the L2TP packet is both wrapped and hidden within the IPSec packet, no information about the content of the packet can be obtained from the encrypted packet. In addition, a side benefit is the fact that it is not necessary to open UDP port 1701 on firewalls between the endpoints, because the inner packets are not acted upon until after IPSec data has been decrypted, which only occurs at the endpoints of the connections.

Authentication Using EAP

An additional benefit from the use of IPSec with L2TP is the ability to enhance authentication via the use of EAP. Created as an extension of PPP, EAP is used when

Figure 6.28   Selecting the use of EAP.

PPP peers negotiate to perform this authentication method during the connection authentication process. Technically, the negotiation of EAP is referred to as an EAP method, resulting in an exchange of messages between the client (referred to as the supplicant) and the authentication server, which is commonly a RADIUS server. Once an EAP method is agreed upon, an exchange of messages will occur between the supplicant and authentication server based on requests for authentication information.

Figure 6.28 illustrates the selection and operation of EAP. In this example, a client is shown using PPP initially to communicate with an access point or network access server (NAS) to obtain EAP authentication prior to obtaining access to a network. Both wired and wireless devices can operate as the EAP authenticator, with the IEEE 802.1X standard defining how EAP operates when used for authentication by 802 devices, such as wireless access points and wired Ethernet switches. In this example, the NAS is shown communicating with a Remote Authentication Dial-In User Service (RADIUS) authentication server to negotiate the specific EAP method to use, with EAP messages flowing between the client and server.

Now that we have developed an appreciation for IPSec and L2TP/IPSec, we will conclude our examination of VPNs by briefly turning our attention to a useful but not popularly used method known as SOCKS. However, before that, we will briefly examine a packet filtering method referred to as TCP wrappers.

TCP Wrapper

TCP wrappers represent a host-based networking access control list (ACL) system that can also be considered as a filtering method. Through the use of ACLs, network access to Internet Protocol servers on (UNIX-like) operating systems such as Linux or BSD can be controlled. By filtering on destination or source IP address, one can control access to hosts, subnets, and query replies.

The original code was written by Wietse Venema at the Eindhoven University of Technology, The Netherlands, between 1990 and 1995. As of June 1, 2001, the program was released under its own BSD-style license.

SOCKS

SOCKS represents an abbreviation for "sockets," which provides a reference to the Berkeley socket interface used in UNBIX. The protocol was originally developed by David Koblas, a system administrator at MIPS Computer Systems. The latest version of SOCKS is version 4.

The SOCKS protocol is designed to route packets between client-server applications via a proxy server. The protocol operates at Layer 5, the Session Layer of the OSI reference model, between the presentation layer and the transport layer. Clients behind a firewall have to connect to a SOCKS proxy server to access external services provided by the server. The proxy server controls the ability of the client to access the external server in the client-server access attempt. If the client is approved by the proxy server, the latter will then pass the request on to the destination server. SOCKS is bidirectional; thus, it can also be used in the opposite way, allowing the clients outside the firewall to connect to servers inside the firewall.

Currently, the latest version of SOCKS is V.5. Under V.5, SOCKS supports several authentication methods to include EAP, one-time passwords, MD5-challenge, and token cards. Through additions to SOCKS V.5, several vendors now offer modules that work with Windows, intercepting WinSock communications requests issued by application programs and processing those requests based on a previous set of configurations. This enables network managers to specify the use of different types of authentication and encryption for different applications or the use of fixed methods.

Comparing SOCKS and HTTP Proxies

SOCKS employs a handshake protocol to inform the proxy software about the connection that a client initiated. The SOCKS protocol supports any form of TCP or UDP socket connection. In comparison, an HTTP proxy will analyze HTTP headers to determine the address of the destination server, which restricts its support to HTTP traffic.

VPN Selection

The selection of an appropriate VPN can include a variety of factors ranging from technical issues to cost, with the latter including personnel and maintenance.

Table 6.3   VPN Technical Considerations

Topology supported
Authentication support
Encryption supported
Scalability
Management
VPN client software
Operating system and browser support
Performance

Table 6.3 lists eight technical features readers should examine when considering the selection of a VPN.

Topology Supported

Many businesses that need to interconnect sites via a site-to-site topology will opt for a VPN that supports compulsory tunneling. In comparison, the need to support mobile workers in a secure environment will result in a requirement for voluntary tunneling. Fortunately, most, but not all VPN methods support both; however, the personnel cost associated with voluntary tunneling will increase as the number of remote users increases.

Authentication Supported

There are numerous authentication methods supported by different types of VPNs. Those methods can range from the simple use of passwords to digital certificates and two-factor authentication employing key fobs with numeric displays that change the digits periodically. While the latter two methods, for example, are considerably more viable than a simple password, you need to consider the cost of certificates and key fobs as well as maintenance issues.

Encryption Supported

As previously mentioned, some VPNs by themselves do not perform encryption, which results in the ability of a third party to easily observe the contents of tunneled packets. If your organization requires encryption, you then need to consider either the use of a VPN protocol that natively supports encryption or a protocol that can be added to a VPN to provide encryption, such as adding IPSec to L2TP.

Scalability

Although most countries are currently in a recession, you can expect that at some point in time growth will commence anew. As organizations add staff at different locations, the need for a VPN that provides scalability assumes importance. Thus, most organizations need to consider the scalability of different types of VPNs under consideration.

Management

The ease of configuration as well as the ability to generate reports are two key areas that should be examined. In addition, the type of reports provided by a VPN management system can enhance the ability of the network manager to denote potential bottlenecks and take action before users complain about a sluggish network.

VPN Client Software

Certain types of VPNs, such as L2TP used in compulsory tunneling, do not require any additional client software. In addition to obvious cost saving, this also simplifies the configuration of the VPN in a site-to-site environment. Thus, you need to consider the role of client software when selecting a VPN.

Operating System and Browser Support

Often easily overlooked, both operating system and browser support are important criteria for the selection of a VPN. While there are many VPNs that support Windows, this is a generic term and does not mean that support for a specific version of Windows is available. Similarly, if your organization has a large base of Firefox users or uses Opera or another browser, you need to carefully check the support of the VPN for the type and versions of the browsers used or anticipated to be used.

Performance

As features are added to a VPN, additional processing can be expected. While the additional processing may not be noticeable on a new computer, users with legacy platforms may receive sluggish responses. Thus, a benchmark on various types of computers may provide important information concerning the ability of VPNs to appropriately operate on different hardware platforms used by the organization.

Endpoint Security

One of the more modern security problems networking personnel face is controlling the termination of endpoint locations within a network. If you examine a modern computer, you will note that the floppy drive has been replaced by a variety of USB and sometimes even FireWire ports. Thus, instead of having to contend with deactivating floppy drives with limited storage, managers now have to consider disabling USB ports as well as preventing Zipped files being transferred via e-mail. Concerning USB ports, with 4 GB USB adapters now costing under $20, it becomes possible for an employee to make off with a significant amount of corporate data at an insignificant cost. In fact, because most smart phones include an SD or micro SD slot, even an employee who wants to set up his computer–phone relationship at work can now copy documents onto the memory card in his or her smart phone. Along with the previously mentioned threats, the availability of WinZip and similar programs makes it very easy for an employee to "zip" a number of documents and mail the zipped file as an attachment addressed to themselves at an alternate e-mail address or to the address of a third party. Due to these potential security breaches, many organizations use software to block the use of USB ports and automatically drop zip files from outbound e-mail.

Encryption

One of the chief means of enhancing endpoint security is encrypting traffic. Depending on the manner in which are transmitting data from an endpoint, encryption may be built into the transmission method, such as with the use of several types of VPNs, or you can add encryption to enhance security. With the latter, you can select an encryption method from a variety of sources as long as the recipient uses the same encryption method and, when required, has the same key so that decryption occurs correctly. Encryption sources vary widely, from the addition of hardware-based datacryptors that can be used with both dial-up and dedicated circuits to various software add-ons, such as Pretty Good Privacy (PGP). PGP encryption uses public-key cryptography and includes a system that binds the public keys to a user name or an e-mail address, which results in both encryption and authentication being performed.

Network Security Design Considerations

In this section, we will focus on a series of network security design considerations, including cross-domain attacks and methods to minimize such attacks, device and data flow interoperability, audits, monitoring, and remote network access.

Interoperability and Associated Risks

Interoperability in a networking environment references the ability of diverse systems to work together or interoperate. In a modern network environment where routers, firewalls, virus checkers, and other devices are employed, it becomes a relatively easy process to overlook one or more coding or configuration settings. In doing so, you can open a hole in your network defense or close a legitimate opening necessary for an approved application. Thus, the use of security audits and monitoring can be an effective tool to determine risks associated with the configurations and parameter settings of various devices that need to interoperate with one another.

Cross-Domain Risks and Solutions

There are a variety of cross-domain attacks that can adversely affect the user and his or her organization. Some of the more popular attack methods include cross-site request forgery, cross-site scripting, DNS rebinding, time of check/time of use, and wildcarding attack methods. In this section, we will focus on each attack method as well as potential solutions to mitigate their effect.

A cross-site request forgery (CSRF) represents an attack method developed to fool a victim into loading a Web page that contains a malicious request. The page to be loaded is malicious because it inherits the identity and privileges of the victim, enabling the attacker to assume the victim's identity. Examples of malicious actions can include changing the victim's e-mail address, home page address, or even purchasing something. Most popular virus-checking software recognizes the potential of a CSRF attack and warns before they arrive at a site where CSRF software is known to exist.

A second type of popular Web-based attack is referred to as a cross-site scripting attack. This type of attack exploits the trust most users place in accessing a Website. Cross-site scripting attacks commonly occur in two basic forms, such as when an attacker embeds a script in data pushed to the user as a result of a GET or POST request (first order) or when the script is retained in long-term storage before being activated (second order). Similar to CSRF prevention, most modern comprehensive virus-checking software provides protection against cross-scripting attacks. In addition, under Windows Vista, the operating system will prompt users to allow or deny the operation of programs, providing a mechanism to disable the program.

DNS rebinding represents an attack on the insecure binding between DNS host names and network addresses. During a DNS rebinding attack, the attacker manipulates DNS records for a Web site he or she controls. The attack can at times use the host name at a server under his or her control, while at other times the host name can be used to point to a victim server or device, such as a router. Through a DNS rebinding attack, the attacker is able to bypass a same-origin-policy restriction because both the victim and attacker have the same host name, albeit at different points in time. This attack technique can also result in the circumvention of a firewall, as a victim server behind an organizational firewall is normally reachable by a browser operated by an employee of the organization. One solution to nullify the potential effect of DNS rebinding is to strengthen the client's binding between a DNS host name and the network address. In addition, the use of HTTPS and verification of the host header on inbound requests can also be used to minimize the threat of DNS rebinding.

The time of check/time of use (TOC/TOU) represents two types of attacks that are based on changes in principals or permissions. Such attacks occur in requests where principals or permissions have changed between the time of permission checking and the time of actual use of the permissions. Most such attacks result from the failure of server software to remove cached permissions after a reconfiguration that changes client permissions. Over the years, both SUN Microsystems and Microsoft have issued several patches to their server software designed to block such attacks. However, an organization either has to enable automatic software updates or manually apply such software patches to close such security-related holes.

Another attack that warrants attention is the wildcarding attack. This attack occurs when access controls are set in error and open a security hole for unintended access. For example, if access control rules are set to *.edu, any .edu site can access your resource. Wildcard mistakes can occur due to typographical errors, when organizations merge, when contractors or employees make simple mistakes, and for numerous other reasons. As access-control rules become more complex, the likelihood of configuration errors increases. Thus, the use of configuration checking of software products may be justified for some organizations that operate a variety of communications equipment that perform access control.

Audits and Assessments

It is important to understand that routers, firewalls, and virus checkers as well as IDS and intrusion protection systems can together have hundreds to thousands of possible settings. Due to this diversity of potential settings, it is highly recommended that you periodically audit your network to include your device configuration settings. While it is possible to perform a manual audit of equipment used within a small organization, as the organization expands and its network complexity increases, it becomes much harder to perform auditing without the use of software. Today, several vendors provide software designed to do the following: perform auditing as well as reporting, enable the changing of equipment configurations from a central management platform, employ a third-party database management system to track both hardware and software, etc. Such software typically includes a Simple Network Management Protocol (SNMP) and Remote MONitoring (RMON) capability, enabling the software to collect information on up to tens of thousands of assets, security, and configuration settings into a configuration database for reporting, auditing, baselining, and change tracking.

Monitoring

An SNMP-compatible system consists of one or more central monitoring systems and distributed agents operating on various types of hardware and even embedded into software. Today, most hardware and software products include a built-in RMON-compatible agent, allowing a central site SNMP system to monitor network activity, change device permissions and configurations as well as to gather statistics. For example, in a Cisco router environment, each router port can be enabled for SNMP monitoring, providing the network manager with detailed information about the use of router ports as well as denoting potential or actual bottlenecks. Through the use of SNMP systems available from many vendors, software overlaying the SNMP capability can even issue projections as to when, for example, a router port can be expected to operate at 75% of utilization or drop a certain percentage of packets.

Operating Environment

In an operational environment, it is quite common for network managers to create a "protected bench network" of equipment prior to its actual use. Here, the term *protected bench network* references a network of devices to be used that are not connected to an operational network. This then provides you with the luxury of performing penetration testing to uncover any inadvertent holes in your security defense without compromising actual live data. Here, the term *penetration test* represents a method of evaluating the security of the network—and if desired the computers attached to the network—by simulating different types of attacks and observing the ability of the network and computers to fight those attacks. Of course, if you do not have the luxury of creating a protected bench network, you could still employ penetration testing against your network and newly installed hardware or software to determine vulnerabilities before those vulnerabilities being discovered by a third party and exploited to attack your organization. The penetration test is one of several components that make up a security audit. The other major components include monitoring traffic and certain logs available on both network hardware products and computers.

Remote Access

Before setting up a new application for remote access, you should consider testing it with respect to various network security issues. Such testing can include configuring authentication and encryption methods as well as planning for the establishment of firewall and router configuration changes to enable the application to take effect. For example, this author was in charge of establishing a secure network dial-in facility that supported 850 investigators. The investigators typically spent their day contacting various personnel references for persons applying for federal jobs. In the evening, they would type up reports and transmit them from the hotel room they were staying at to a central location. By first acquiring the laptop investigators would use and configuring the hardware and operating software to work in an authenticated and encrypted manner with devices at the central site, the rollout of new equipment to investigators and its use was performed without problems.

Monitoring

You can monitor both network traffic as well as logs maintained by communications devices and computers to validate the architectural design of your network as well as to ensure that any potential holes that could present a security risk are closed. For example, most modern computer operating systems, including Microsoft Windows, SUN's Solaris, and various versions of Linux, support audit event logging, which provides a variety of valuable information. In the area of network equipment, routers, firewalls, virus checkers, IDS, and intrusion protection systems have a similar logging capability. In addition, you can usually program such devices to generate alerts upon the occurrence of predefined conditions. Thus, like the Boy Scouts, proper planning will prevent inadvertent security holes from becoming a danger to your organization.

Design Validation

When designing or modifying a network, it is extremely important to ensure that the design will work as expected. The process used to verify that the network will operate correctly is referred to as design validation. In a security environment, there are several methods that can be employed to ensure that your network design will perform correctly. Those methods include penetration testing, vulnerability assessments, and network monitoring.

Penetration Testing

Penetration testing is a critical method used to validate the security associated with a network. This type of testing literally can involve throwing the preverbal kitchen sink at a network, trying every known type of malicious software in an attempt to break into a system. Because most network managers do not have the resources to assemble a collection of such software, third-party products are commonly used. Such products perform an analysis of the network, including checking for the latest software releases designed to plug security holes as well as examining router, firewall, and even DNS configurations. Any security issues are reported usually with an assessment of the criticality of each issue.

Vulnerability Assessment

Penetration testing can be considered as the predecessor to a vulnerability assessment. That is, until you determine what weaknesses exist in your network, you cannot determine the vulnerability due to those weaknesses. For example, penetration testing could result in a report showing that a firewall was misconfigured, allowing all employees instead of just engineers to access the Internet at lunch time and that a server operating system does not have a patch to negate a well-known vulnerability. Here, the second vulnerability would be more critical to fix for most organizations, and they would prioritize their efforts by placing the server patch at the top of their list of fixes.

Monitoring and Network Attacks

Because nothing is static in the wonderful world of communications, network managers need to continuously monitor network traffic. Doing so may provide you with the ability to recognize that your network is being scanned for open ports, a hacker is attempting to run a password checker against a server, or some other security-related issue. Sometimes, a reconfiguration of a firewall to block a hacker from further attacks may suffice, while the apparent recognition of a new type of attack may require you to contact a security organization for assistance.

Risk-Based Architecture

In concluding our examination of telecommunications and network security, we will discuss the network as an enterprise where data flows on an end-to-end basis. In attempting to minimize network attacks, we need to minimize the risk of an attack.

We can minimize the risk of an attack by identifying risk elements, risk metrics, and network controls and assessing the vulnerability level of the network. Each organization more than likely has a different network configuration. However, by developing a risk-based architecture, we can minimize its vulnerability. That is, we need to ensure that we create a DMZ to protect our network structure. In addition, we need to verify that equipment such as routers and firewalls are correctly configured and both clients and servers are operating with the latest patches. By performing these functions as well as staying abreast of the latest security vulnerabilities and corrections, we can develop and maintain a network architecture that minimizes the threat to the enterprise.

Sample Questions

1. Compare the frequency range of a person's voice to the size of the passband in a voice communications channel obtained over the telephone. How do you account for the difference between the two?
   a. The telephone company uses Gaussian filters to remove frequencies below 300 Hz and above 3300 Hz because the primary information of a voice conversation occurs in the passband.
   b. The telephone company uses low-pass and high-pass filters to remove frequencies below 300 Hz and above 3300 Hz because the primary information of a voice conversation occurs in the passband.
   c. The telephone company uses packet filters to remove frequencies below 500 Hz and above 4400 Hz because the primary information of a voice conversation occurs in the passband.
   d. The telephone company uses low-pass and high-pass filters to remove frequencies below 500 Hz and above 4400 Hz because the primary information of a voice conversation occurs in the passband.

2. What is the data rate of a PCM-encoded voice conversation?
   a. 128 kbps
   b. 64 kbps
   c. 256 kbps
   d. 512 kbps

3. How many digitized voice channels can be transported on a T1 line?
   a. Up to 48
   b. Up to 12
   c. Up to 60
   d. Up to 24

4. How many T1 lines can be transported on a T3 circuit?
   a. 12
   b. 18
   c. 24
   d. 36

5. The three advantages accruing from the use of a packet network in comparison to the use of the switched telephone network are a potential lower cost of use, a lower error rate as packet network nodes perform error checking and correction, and
   a. The ability of packet networks to automatically reserve resources
   b. The greater security of packet networks
   c. The ability of packet networks to automatically reroute data calls
   d. Packet networks establish a direct link between sender and receiver

6. Five VoIP architecture concerns include
   a. The end-to-end delay associated with packets carrying digitized voice, jitter, the method of voice digitization used, the packet loss rate, and security
   b. The end-to-end delay associated with packets carrying digitized voice, jitter, attenuation, the packet loss rate, and security
   c. The end-to-end delay associated with packets carrying digitized voice, jitter, the amount of fiber in the network, the packet loss rate, and security
   d. The end-to-end delay associated with packets carrying digitized voice, jitter, the method of voice digitization used, attenuation, and security

7. What is the major difference between encrypting analog and digitized voice conversations?
   a. Analog voice is encrypted by shifting portions of frequency, making the conversation unintelligible.
   b. Digitized voice is generated by the matrix addition of a fixed key to each digitized bit of the voice conversation.
   c. Analog voice is encrypted by shifting portions of amplitude to make the conversation unintelligible.
   d. Digitized voice is encrypted by the modulo-2 addition of a fixed key to each digitized bit of the voice conversation.

8. In communications, what is the purpose of authentication?
   a. Establishing a link between parties in a conversation or transaction
   b. Ensuring that data received has not been altered
   c. Securing wireless transmission
   d. Verifying the other party in a conversation or transaction

9. What is the purpose of integrity?
   a. Integrity is a process that ensures data received has not been altered.
   b. Integrity is a process that ensures a person stands by his beliefs.
   c. Integrity is a process that ensures that the amount of data sent equals the amount of data received.
   d. Integrity is a process that ensures data received has been encrypted.

10. The key purpose of the Session Initiation Protocol (SIP) is to
    a. Define the protocol required to establish and tear down communications, including voice and video calls flowing over a packet network.
    b. Define the signaling required to establish and tear down communications, including voice and video calls flowing over a PSTN.
    c. Define the protocol required to establish and tear down communications, including voice and video calls flowing over a circuit-switched network.
    d. Define the signaling required to establish and tear down communications, including voice and video calls flowing over a packet network.

11. Briefly describe the H.323 protocol.
    a. It represents an umbrella recommendation from the ITU that covers a variety of standards for audio, video, and data communications across circuit-switched networks.
    b. It provides port-based authentication, requiring a wireless device to be authenticated prior to its gaining access to a LAN and its resources.
    c. It defines the protocol required to establish and tear down communications, including voice and video calls flowing over a packet network.
    d. It represents an umbrella recommendation from the ITU that covers a variety of standards for audio, video, and data communications across packet-based networks and, more specifically, IP-based networks.
12. What is the difference between RTP and RTCP?
    a. RTP defines a standardized port for delivering audio and video over the Internet, while the RTCP provides out-of-band control information for an RTP port.
    b. RTP defines the protocol required to establish and tear down communications, including voice and video calls flowing over a packet network, while the RTCP provides out-of-band control information for an RTP port.
    c. RTP defines a standardized packet format for delivering audio and video over the Internet, while the RTCP provides out-of-band control information for an RTP flow.
    d. RTP defines a standardized port for delivering audio and video over the Internet, while the RTCP defines the protocol required to establish and tear down communications, including voice and video calls flowing over a packet network.
13. List the components defined by the H.323 standard.
    a. Terminal, gateway, gatekeeper, multipoint control unit (MCU), multipoint controller, multipoint processor, and H.323 proxy
    b. Path, gateway, gatekeeper, multipoint control unit (MCU), multipoint controller, multipoint processor, and H.323 proxy
    c. Terminal, gateway, gatekeeper, multipoint control unit (MCU), multipoint transmitter, multipoint receiver, and H.323 proxy
    d. Protocol, terminal, gatekeeper, multipoint control unit (MCU), multipoint controller, multipoint processor, and H.323 proxy
14. What are some of the major functions performed by a security modem?
    a. Allows remote access to occur from trusted locations, may encrypt data, and may support Caller ID to verify the calling telephone number
    b. Allows remote access to occur from any location, may encrypt data, and may support Caller ID to verify the calling telephone number
    c. Allows remote access to occur from a mobile location, may encrypt data, and may support Caller ID to verify the calling telephone number
    d. Allows remote access to occur from trusted locations, may encrypt data, and may identify the calling telephone number

15. The major difference between a router and firewall lies in three areas:
    a. The transfer of packets based on routing tables, the degree of packet inspection, and ensuring that the header data is correct
    b. The transfer of packets based on absolute addresses, the degree of packet inspection, and acting as an intermediate device by hiding the address of clients from users on the Internet
    c. The transfer of packets based on routing tables, the degree of packet inspection, and acting as an intermediate device by hiding the address of clients from users on the Internet
    d. The transfer of packets based on routing tables, the degree of packet inspection, and creating a DMZ behind Internet-facing applications

16. What is the purpose of an intrusion detection system (IDS)?
    a. To hide the address of clients from users on the Internet
    b. To detect unwanted attempts to access, manipulate, and even disable networking hardware and computers connected to a network
    c. To detect and respond to predefined events
    d. To prevent unauthorized access to controlled areas within a site or a building

17. What are the two methods that can be used for wireless LAN communications?
    a. Peer-to-peer and infrastructure
    b. Peer-to-peer and cloud
    c. Cloud and infrastructure
    d. Peer-to-peer and remote

18. What is the benefit of WPA over WEP for enhancing wireless LAN security?
    a. WPA permits the equivalent of wired network privacy and includes the use of TKIP to enhance data encryption.
    b. WPA implements a large portion of the IEEE 802.11i and includes the use of TKIP to enhance data encryption.
    c. WPA implements a large portion of the IEEE 802.11i and includes the use of IKE to enhance data encryption.
    d. WPA implements IEEE 802.11a and g and includes the use of IKE to enhance data encryption.

19. What is the purpose of the IEEE 802.1X standard?
    a. To provide port-based authentication
    b. To provide port-based authorization
    c. To detect and respond to predefined events
    d. To secure wireless transmission

Questions and Answers

Chapter 1: Access Control Systems and Methodologies

1. Which of the following represents the type of access given to a user?
   a. Permissions
   b. Subjects
   c. Objects
   d. Rights

   The correct option is *a*. Permissions regulate the type of access a subject is given to an object. Common permissions include: read, write, delete, and execute.

2. Select the most widely adopted access control method:
   a. Discretionary access control
   b. Mandatory access control
   c. Rule-based access control
   d. Role-based access control

   The correct option is *a*. Discretionary Access Control is the predominant access control technique in use today. Most commodity systems implement some form of DAC.

3. No read up and no write down are properties of
   a. Discretionary access control
   b. Mandatory access control
   c. Rule-based access control
   d. Role-based access control

   The correct option is *b*. This is the basic functionality of Mandatory Access Control. The fundamental principles of MAC prevent a subject from reading up and writing down between classifications.

4. Access control for proprietary distributable content is best protected using
   a. Discretionary access control
   b. Digital rights management

c. Distributed access control

d. Originator controlled

The correct option is *b*. Among the options given, only DRM provides a means to control proprietary content.

5. When designing least privilege in a system, a security architect should consider least

a. Business requirements

b. Organizational mission

c. Affected usability

d. Disaster recovery

The correct option is *d*. Disasters are unlikely; therefore, least privilege should not be designed with limitations.

6. Separation of duties are ideally implemented using

a. Roles

b. Permissions

c. Rights

d. Workflows

The correct option is *a*. Separation of duties is best implemented with roles composed of granular rights and permissions.

7. A good supplemental control for weak separation of duties is

a. Intrusion detection

b. Biometrics

c. Auditing

d. Training

The correct option is *c*. Accountability becomes more important when separation of duties is weak or unachievable. Auditing is paramount. Consider implementing object-level auditing for individuals with multiple roles. Identify key areas where abuse might occur, and implement multiple methods to monitor for violations.

8. Centralized access control

a. Is only implemented in network equipment

b. Implements authentication, authorization, and accounting

c. Is implemented closest to the resources it is designed to protect

d. Is designed to consider and accept business partner authentication tokens

The correct option is *b*. Authentication, authorization, and accounting are important aspects of centralized access control.

9. Firewalls typically employ

a. Centralized access control

b. Decentralized access control

c. Federated access control

d. Role-based access control

The correct option is *a*. A firewall with an integrated authentication mechanism is an example of a centralized access control device using the gatekeeper approach. This type of approach is primarily used to control access to resources and services at particular locations within the protected network.

10. A feature that distinguishes decentralized from centralized access control is its
    a. Audit logging
    b. Proxy capability
    c. Security kernel
    d. Shared database

    The correct option is *d*. Decentralized access control relies on shared databases.

11. Federated access control
    a. Is implemented with RADIUS
    b. Is designed to be mutually exclusive with single sign-on
    c. Is implemented closest to the resources it is designed to protect
    d. Is designed to consider and accept business partner authentication tokens

    The correct option is *d*. Federated Access Control enables a business partner type of single sign-on.

12. Lightweight Directory Access Control is specified in
    a. X.509
    b. X.500
    c. RFC 4510
    d. RFC 4422

    The correct option is *c*. RFC 4510 describes a simplified X.500 Directory Access Control protocol.

13. Auditing seeks to record all of the following except
    a. Who
    b. Why
    c. When
    d. What

    The correct option is *b*. "Why" is the subject's motivation and cannot be measured by the system.

14. This technique is commonly used to collect audit logs:
    a. Polling
    b. Triggers
    c. Workflows
    d. Aggregation

    The correct option is *a*. Polling by a centralized server is commonly used to query other servers to periodically collect events.

15. A word processing application, governed by DAC, executes in the security context of the
    a. End user
    b. Process itself

    c. Administrator

    d. System kernel

The correct option is *a*. In DAC, nonsystem processes run in the memory space owned by the end user.

16. Peer-to-peer applications are problematic primarily because they

    a. Are prohibited by policy

    b. May be able to access all the user's files

    c. Are a new technology that is difficult to evaluate

    d. May be derived from untrustworthy open source projects

The correct option is *b*. Vulnerabilities in the design or implementation could enable network penetration.

17. Business rules can be enforced within a database through the use of

    a. Proxy

    b. Redundancy

    c. Views

    d. Authentication

The correct option is *c*. Views can be used as a type of access control for designated users or database requests.

18. A well-designed demilitarized zone (DMZ) prevents

    a. Direct access to the DMZ from the protected network

    b. Access to assets within the DMZ to unauthenticated users

    c. Insiders on the protected network from conducting attacks

    d. Uncontrolled access to the protected network from the DMZ

The correct option is *d*. The goal of a DMZ is to prevent or control information flow from outside to inside.

19. Dual control is primarily implemented to

    a. Complement resource-constrained separation of duties

    b. Distribute trust using a rigid protocol

    c. Support internal workflows

    d. Supplement least privilege

The correct option is *b*. Dual control requires explicit separation of duties and protocols.

20. A well-designed security test

    a. Requires penetration testing

    b. Is documented and repeatable

    c. Relies exclusively on automated tools

    d. Foregoes the need for analysis of the results

The correct option is *b*. The results of a test that is not documented or repeatable are questionable.

Chapter 2: Cryptography

1. What cryptographic hash function would be the acceptable replacement for MD4?
   a. MD5
   b. RIPEMD
   c. RIPEMD-160
   d. SHA-1

   The correct option is *c*. This strengthened version of RIPEMD was successfully developed as a collision-resistant replacement for other hash functions including MD4, MD5 (Option *a*), and RIPEMD (Option *b*) [Collisions]. Because collisions were also announced in SHA-1 (Option *d*) [SHA-1 Collisions], RIPEMD-160 would be the acceptable replacement [RIPEMD-160].

2. An IPSec Security Association (SA) is a relationship between two or more entities that describes how they will use security services to communicate. Which values can be used in an SA to provide greater security through confidentiality protection of the data payload?
   a. Use of AES within AH
   b. SHA-1 combined with HMAC
   c. Using ESP
   d. AH and ESP together

   The correct option is *c*. Encapsulating Security Protocol (ESP) also provides data origin authentication and data integrity, and also offers confidentiality for the IP payload it protects.

3. Suppose a secure extranet connection is required to allow an application in an external trusted entity's network to securely access server resources in a corporate DMZ. Assuming IPSec is being configured to use ESP in tunnel mode, which of the following is the most accurate?
   a. Encryption of data packets and data origin authentication for the packets sent over the tunnel can both be provided.
   b. ESP must be used in transport mode in order to encrypt both the packets sent as well as encrypt source and destination IP Addresses of the external entity's network and of the corporate DMZ network.
   c. Use of AH is necessary in order to provide data origin authentication for the packets sent over the tunnel.
   d. Source and destination IP Addresses of the external entity's network and of the corporate DMZ network are not encrypted.

   The correct option is *a*. ESP optionally provides a means of data origin authentication, and while it can be nested within AH, ESP does not require AH for this (Option *c*) [RFC 2406]. With ESP operating in transport mode (Option *b*), the original IP headers are not encapsulated within the ESP header, and the original IP addresses (source and destination IP addresses of the external entity's network and of the corporate DMZ network) are in fact not encrypted. With ESP operating in tunnel mode, the original IP addresses are actually encrypted (Option *d*).

[*ESP*: Encapsulating Security Protocol provides data origin authentication and data integrity, and also offers confidentiality for the IP payload it protects.] .

4. What is the best reason a network device manufacturer might include the RC4 encryption algorithm within an IEEE 802.11 wireless component?

   a. They would like to use AES, but they require compatibility with IEEE 802.11i.

   b. Their product must support the encryption algorithm WPA2 uses.

   c. RC4 is a stream cipher with an improved key-scheduling algorithm that provides stronger protection than other ciphers.

   d. Their release strategy planning includes maintaining some degree of backward compatibility with earlier protocols.

   The correct option is *d*. RC4 is widely used, and the manufacturer wants to make its product compatible with WPA or even WEP, which use RC4. This does not mean they do not include AES; in fact, they would likely do so in the case of a new product, because IEEE 802.11i does in fact use AES for encryption (Option *a*). Option *b* is incorrect because WPA2, which is based on IEEE 802.11i, uses AES. Option *c* is incorrect because while RC4 is a stream cipher, it has a weak key-scheduling algorithm and offers less protection than other ciphers such as AES [WPA].

5. What is true about the Diffie–Hellman (DH) key agreement protocol?

   a. The protocol requires initial exchange of a shared secret.

   b. The protocol depends on a secure communication channel for key exchange.

   c. The protocol needs other mechanisms such as digital signatures to provide authentication of the communicating parties.

   d. The protocol is based on a symmetric cryptosystem.

   The correct option is *c*. It is true that the original Diffie–Hellman key exchange protocol does not provide authentication of the sender and receiver. Other protocols such as digital signatures or HMAC must be used for this [RFC4650]. The Diffie–Hellman (DH) protocol involves computing a shared secret based on exchange of a public key (Option *a*), and is intended to be performed over insecure channels (Option *b*). DH is based on public-key cryptography because it involves deriving a shared secret based on the sender and receiver each having private keys and sharing public keys, and the property of the discrete logarithm problem, which makes it computationally infeasible to derive the private key from the public key [SCHNEIER].

6. What is the main security service a cryptographic hash function provides, and what is the main security property a cryptographic hash function must exhibit?

   a. Integrity and ease of computation

   b. Integrity and collision resistance

c. Message authenticity and collision resistance

d. Integrity and computational infeasibility

The correct option is *b*. Message authentication codes and digital signatures provide message authenticity (Option *c*). While ease of computation is important (Option *a*), cryptographic hash algorithms are build on one-way functions, and their primary function is to produce a unique message digest. Computational infeasibility may be important in general, but collision resistance is the more specific property of hash algorithms, thus excluding Option *d*.

7. What is necessary on the receiving side in order to verify a digital signature?

a. The message, message digest, and the sender's private key

b. The message, message digest, and the sender's public key

c. The message, the MAC, and the sender's public key

d. The message, the MAC, and the sender's private key

The correct option is *b*. Verifying a digital signature is performed by decrypting the message digest using the sender's public key. Exposing the private key would mean that anyone with the private key could now forge the signature (Option *a*). Message authentication codes (MACs) do not use public key encryption, but produce a hash of the combined message input and a secret key (Options *c* and *d*).

8. What is a known plaintext attack used against DES to show that encrypting plaintext with one DES key followed by encrypting it with a second DES key is no more secure than using a single DES key?

a. Meet-in-the-middle attack

b. Man-in-the-middle attack

c. Replay attack

d. Related-key attack

The correct option is *a*. This attack applies to double encryption schemes such as 2DES by encrypting known plaintext using each possible key and comparing results obtained "in the middle" from decrypting the corresponding ciphertext using each possible key. Option *b* is a network-based cryptanalytic attack involving intercepting and forwarding a modified version of a transmission between two parties. Option *c* is also a network-based attack involving capturing and retransmitting a legitimate transmission between two parties. Option *d*, a related-keys attack, is often employed against stream ciphers and involves the relationships between keys that become known or are chosen while observing differences in plaintext and ciphertext when a different key is used.

9. What is among the most important factors in validating the cryptographic key design in a public key cryptosystem?

a. Ability of a random number generator to introduce entropy during key generation

b. Preimage resistance

c. Confidentiality of key exchange protocol

d. Crypto period

The correct option is *a*. The purpose of randomness in the key or keystream is to make it less likely that cryptanalysts will be able to guess or deduce the key. A random number generator that does not exhibit the property of randomness or entropy in its output will produce weak keys. Option *b* applies to cryptographic hash functions and is known as the "one-way" property of hash functions. Because the question asks about public-key cryptosystems, Option *c* is less valid because public keys can be exchanged without loss of the private key. Option *d* applies more to the operation and management of keys, because the crypto period is the time span during which an actual key can remain valid for use.

10. What factor would be most important in the design of a solution that is required to provide at-rest encryption in order to protect financial data in a restricted-access file sharing server?

a. Encryption algorithm used

b. Cryptographic key length

c. Ability to encrypt the entire storage array or file system versus ability to encrypt individual files

d. Individual user access and file-level authorization controls

The correct option is *d*. The encryption algorithm, key length, and scope of encryption provided (Options *a*, *b*, and *c*) are generally less important than the access controls that the at-rest encryption solution will require. Storage encryption is typically performed in order to ensure confidentiality, and is tied to an access control mechanism because those individuals or entities who must be able to decrypt the data will need authorized access to do so.

11. A large bank with a more than one million customer base implements PKI to support authentication and encryption for online Internet transactions. What is the best method to validate certificates in a timely manner?

a. CRL over LDAP

b. CRLDP over LDAP

c. OCSP

d. CRLDP over ODBC

The correct option is *c*. Options *a*, *b*, and *d* are CRL-based methods that require significant network traffic between the verifying party and the LDAP or DB server where the CRL is published. It is most significant with a large base of subscribers whose certificates may point to different CRLDP and require pulling many different CRL fragments from the points of publication.

12. A car rental company is planning to implement wireless communication between the cars and rental support centers. Customers will be able to use these centers as concierge services, and rental centers will be able to check the car's status if necessary. PKI certificates will be used to support authentication,

non-repudiation, and confidentiality of transactions. Which asymmetric cryptography is a better fit?

a. RSA 1024

b. AES 256

c. RSA 4096

d. ECC 160

The correct option is *d*. Option *b* refers to a symmetric algorithm that does not support non-repudiation. The algorithms in Options *a* and *c* have significantly longer keys than the algorithm in Option d, which has equivalent strength. For wireless communication, a smaller key length is an important factor.

13. A key management system of a government agency's PKI includes a backup and recovery (BR) module. PKI issues and manages separate certificates for encryption and verification. What is the right BR strategy?

a. Back up all certificates and private keys

b. Back up all private keys and verification certificates

c. Back up decryption keys and all certificates

d. Back up signing keys and all certificates

The correct option is *c*. Options *a* and *b* assume backing up signing keys, which is wrong. Option *d* assumes signing keys, which is wrong, and does not include decryption keys, which is wrong, too.

14. A company needs to comply with FIPS 140-2 level 3, and decided to use split knowledge for managing storage encryption keys. What is the right method for storing and using the key?

a. Store the key components on the encrypted media.

b. Create a master key and store it on external media owned by the first security officer.

c. Store key components on separate external media owned by a different security officer.

d. Publish key components on an LDAP server and protect them by officers' asymmetric keys encryption.

The correct option is *c*. Storing key components on the same media (Option *a*) will expose them to one administrator or officer. One officer is in possession of all components (Option *b*) and can recreate the whole key. Storing secret keys on intermediate storage (Option *d*) is not acceptable.

15. An agency is using symmetric AES 128 cryptography for distributing confidential data. Because of its growth and key distribution problems, the agency decided to move to asymmetric cryptography and X.509 certificates. What is the optimal strength asymmetric cryptography to match the strength of the current symmetric cryptography?

a. RSA 2048

b. ECC 160

c. ECC 256

d. RSA 7680

The correct option is *c*. According to NISTSP800-57, ECC 256 cryptographic strength is equivalent to AES 128. Options *a* and *b* are wrong because they are weaker than AES 128; Option *d* is stronger than required and comes with impractically long keys.

16. One very large company created a business partnership with another, much smaller company. Both companies have their own PKI in-house. Employees need to use secure messaging and secure file transfer for their business transactions. What is the best strategy to implement this?

    a. The larger company creates a PKI hierarchical branch for the smaller company, so all parties have a common root of trust.

    b. The larger company enrolls all employees of the smaller company and issues their certificates, so all parties have a common root of trust.

    c. Companies should review each other's CP and CPS, cross-certify each other, and let each other access each other's search database.

    d. Employ an external third-party CA and have both company's employees register and use their new certificates for secure transactions.

    The correct option is *c*. Options *a*, *b*, and *d* either partially or completely disregard existing PKI infrastructure and require significant expenses for restructuring PKI or hiring an outside service.

17. When applications of cross-certified PKI subscribers validate each other's digitally signed messages, they have to perform the following steps:

    a. The signature is cryptographically correct, and sender's validation certificate and sender's CA cross-certificate are valid.

    b. Validate CRL and ARL.

    c. Validate sender's encryption certificate, ARL, and CRL.

    d. The signature is cryptographically correct, and sender's CA certificate is valid.

    The correct option is *a*. Option *b* is incorrect because CRL and ARL just verify revocation status without crypto and validity period validation; Option *c* is incorrect because signature verification requires verification certificate validation rather than encryption; Option *d* is incorrect because verification of signature verification certificate is missing.

18. A company implements three-tier PKI, which will include a root CA, several sub-CAs, and a number of regional issuing CAs under each sub-CA. How should the life span of the CA's certificates be related?

    a. Root CA = 10 years; sub-CA = 5 years; issuing CA = 1 year

    b. Root CA = sub-CA = issuing CAs = 5 years

    c. Root CA = 1 year; sub-CA = 5 years; issuing CA = 10 years

    d. Root CA = 5 years; sub-CA = 10 years; issuing CA = 1 year

    The correct option is *a*. In a hierarchical PKI, the upper CA should issue certificates to the subordinate CAs with a longer life span than those subordinates issue certificates to their subordinates. Otherwise, the chain will be expiring before the intermediate CA and entity certificates expire.

19. Management and storage of symmetric data encryption keys most importantly must provide
    a. Integrity, confidentiality, and archiving for the time period from key generation through the life span of the data they protect or the duration of the crypto period, whichever is longer
    b. Confidentiality for the time period from key generation through the life span of the data they protect or duration of crypto period, whichever is longer
    c. Integrity, confidentiality, and archiving for the duration of the key's crypto period
    d. Integrity, confidentiality, non-repudiation and archiving for the time period from key generation through the life span of the data they protect or duration of crypto period, whichever is longer

    The correct option is *a*. Option *b* is incorrect because without an integrity requirement a key may be tampered with. Option *c* is incorrect because if an encryption key crypto period expires before the encrypted data life span, the key destruction may leave data that is never possible to decrypt. Option *d* is incorrect because non-repudiation is not relevant to symmetric cryptography.

20. Management and storage of public signature verification keys most importantly must provide
    a. Integrity, confidentiality, and archiving for the time period from key generation until no protected data needs to be verified
    b. Integrity and archiving for the time period from key generation until no protected data needs to be verified
    c. Integrity, confidentiality and archiving for the time period from key generation through the life span of the data they protect or the duration of crypto period, whichever is longer
    d. All of the above

    The correct option is *b*. Options *a*, *c*, and *d* are incorrect because confidentiality is not required for public keys.

Chapter 3: Physical Security Integration

1. The primary function of a physical protection system is
   a. Determine, direct, and dispatch
   b. Deter, detection, delay, and response
   c. Display, develop, initiate, and apprehend
   d. Evaluate, dispatch, and detain

   The correct option is *b*. A physical protection system typically has a number of elements that fall into the pattern of deter–detect–delay–respond.

2. The single most important goal in planning a site is
   a. Protection of life, property, and operations

  b. Threat definition, conflict control, and facility characterization

  c. Risk assessment, threat identification, and incident review

  d. Threat identification, vulnerability appraisal, and access review

 The correct option is *a*. The single most important goal in planning a site is the protection of life, property, and operations.

3. Intrusion sensor performance is described by three fundamental characteristics:

  a. Balanced magnetic switches (BMSs), passive infrared sensors (PIRs), and video motion detectors (VMDs)

  b. Interior boundary penetration, critical infrastructure facility, and proximity sensors

  c. Probability of detection, nuisance alarm rate (NAR), and vulnerability to defeat

  d. Capacitance proximity, intrusion detection rate (IDR), and boundary penetration frequency

 The correct option is *c*. Intrusion sensor performance is described by three fundamental characteristics: probability of detection, nuisance alarm rate (NAR), and vulnerability to defeat.

4. The strategy of forming layers of protection around an asset or facility is known as

  a. Secured perimeter

  b. Defense in depth

  c. Reinforced barrier deterrent

  d. Reasonable asset protection

 The correct option is *b*. With defense in depth, barriers are arranged in layers with the level of security growing progressively higher as one comes closer to the center or the highest protective area.

5. The regulation of movement into, from, and within a designated building or area is called

  a. Restricted access

  b. Access control

  c. Security access

  d. Security control

 The correct option is *b*. Access control is the regulation of movement into, from, and within a designated building or area. The primary objective of controlling entry into a facility or area is to ensure that only authorized persons are allowed to enter.

6. The key to a successful physical protection system is the integration of

  a. People, process, and technology

  b. Technology, risk assessment, and human interaction

  c. Protecting, offsetting, and transferring risk

  d. Detection, deterrence, and response

The correct option is *a*. The key to a successful physical protection system is the integration of people, process, and technology.

7. What is the primary objective of controlling entry into a facility or area?
   a. Provide time management controls for all employees.
   b. Ensure that only authorized persons are allowed to enter.
   c. Keep out potential hazards and dangerous material that could be used to commit sabotage.
   d. Identification purposes

   The correct option is *b*. The primary objective of controlling entry into a facility or area is to ensure that only authorized persons are allowed to enter.

8. The best way to test your security operation is by
   a. Observation
   b. Penetration test
   c. Security survey
   d. Risk assessment

   The correct option is *b*. A penetration test is the best way to test your security operation.

9. CCTV technologies make possible three distinct yet complementary functions. The first is visual assessment of an alarm or other event. This permits the operator to assess the nature of the alarm before initiating a response. What are the other two functions of CCTV?
   a. Surveillance and deterrence
   b. Intrusion detection and response
   c. Optical and lighting
   d. Monitoring and inspection

   The correct option is *a*. CCTV provides a highly flexible method of monitoring surveillance and deterrence.

10. High-tech integrated technologies not only offer greater protection opportunities but also help minimize cost by
    a. Reducing electrical costs
    b. Reducing reliance on multiple operators and guard force
    c. Providing government tax incentives for increased physical protection systems
    d. Increasing capital value of property

11. A vulnerability assessment tour of a facility is designed to gather information regarding the general layout of the facility, the location of key assets, and information about facility operations, production capabilities, and locations and types of physical protection systems. During this tour—and subsequent tours—the vulnerability assessment member or team should be looking to
    a. Determine where all the fire exits are located.
    b. Examine the locations of physical protection system components.
    c. Count the number of employees within the facility.
    d. Determine the structural strength of the perimeter walls.

The correct option is *b*. A vulnerability assessment tour of a facility is designed to gather information regarding the general layout of the facility, the location of key assets, information about facility operations and production capabilities, and locations and types of physical protection systems.

12. Designing a new building to mitigate threats is simpler and more cost-effective than retrofitting an existing building. Important security benefits are achieved not by hardware and electronic devices but by shrewd site selections, proper placement of the building on the site, and careful location of building occupants and functions to minimize exposure to threat. These factors also have the benefit of reducing operating expenses over the lifetime of the building. An obvious example of this is planning for
    a. Limiting the number of entrances to the site that must be monitored, staffed, and protected
    b. Reducing the cost associated with energy needs in providing the physical protection system
    c. Giving employees easy access to the facility without their knowledge of the security components used in monitoring their activities
    d. Blast reinforcement film on all perimeter windows
    The correct option is *a*.

13. How must classified material and sensitive information be disposed of?
    a. Torn in half and thrown in the trash can
    b. Shredded
    c. Removed to a decontamination room
    d. Marked declassified and thrown in a trash can
    The correct option is *b*. There are several methods for proper destruction of information. An organization can contract with a licensed and bonded shredding company, which will come to the site with a mobile shredding truck and dispose of classified material and sensitive information. One can watch the process and verify the destruction, or the documents can be shredded on site, depending on the volume of information that needs to be destroyed. Shredding services can also destroy hard drives and physical components.

14. Building security involves more than bars on windows, a guard in a booth, a camera on the ceiling, or locked doors and gates. Effective security solutions call for systematic integration of
    a. Design, technology, and facility operations and management
    b. Reducing vulnerability by protecting, offsetting, or transferring the risk
    c. Operational readiness, physical protection systems, standard operating processes
    d. Increase awareness, environmental design, and physical security
    The correct option is *a*. Effective building security requires careful planning, design, and management of the physical protection system, integrat-

ing people, procedures, and equipment; the foundation of all facility security operations.

15. In which order should the designing of a security plan for a new complex progress?
    a. Outer perimeter, interior, exterior
    b. Interior, outer perimeter, exterior
    c. Interior, exterior, outer perimeter
    d. Exterior, interior, outer perimeter

    The correct option is *c*. The design process of a security plan for a new facility should begin with the interior, then the exterior, and finally the outer perimeter.

16. Physical security is applied by using _____ of physical protective measures to prevent or minimize theft, unauthorized access, or destruction of property.
    a. Layers
    b. Methods
    c. Varieties
    d. Types

    The correct option is *a*. In the concept of defense in depth, barriers are arraigned in layers, with the level of security growing progressively higher as one comes closer to the center or the highest protective area. Defending an asset with a multiple posture can reduce the likelihood of a successful attack; if one layer of defense fails, another layer of defense will hopefully prevent the attack, and so on. This design requires the attacker to circumvent multiple defensive mechanisms to gain access to the targeted asset.

17. Employee badges are an excellent method of control. Two functions they serve are
    a. Identify and credit
    b. Payroll and identification
    c. Identification and access
    d. Access and personal information

    The correct option is *c*. Employee badges are an excellent method of control for both identification and access.

18. Which security control is most effective in curtailing and preventing "piggybacking" or "tailgating" as a means of unauthorized access?
    a. Cameras
    b. Turnstiles
    c. Security guards
    d. Mantraps

    The correct option is *d*. A common and frustrating loophole in an otherwise secure access control system can be the ability of an unauthorized person to follow through a checkpoint behind an authorized person; this is called "piggybacking" or "tailgating." The traditional solution is an airlock-style arrangement called a mantrap.

Chapter 4: Requirements Analysis and Security Standards and Guidelines Criteria

1. The approach in which policies, procedures, technology, and personnel are considered in the system security development process is called
   a. Defense in depth
   b. Requirements analysis
   c. Risk assessment
   d. Attack vectors

   The correct option is *a*. Best security practices should include an architecture that provides defense in depth where layers of technology are designed and implemented to provide data protection. These layers include people, technology, and operations (including processes and procedures). Defense in depth includes

   > Protect—preventative controls and mechanisms
   > Detect—identify attacks, expect attacks
   > React—respond to attacks, recover

2. Software that adds hidden components to your system without your knowledge is
   a. Virus
   b. Spyware
   c. Adware
   d. Malware

   The correct option is *b*. Spyware is software that adds hidden components to your system on the sly.

3. Risk is assessed by which of the following formulas?
   a. Risk = Vulnerability × Threat × Impact Divided by Countermeasure
   b. Risk = Annual Loss Opportunity ÷ Single Loss Expectancy
   c. Risk = Exposure Facture divided by Asset Value
   d. Risk = Vulnerability × Annual Loss Expectancy

   The correct option is *a*. Option *a* is correct the others are mixed-up derivatives of risk management.

4. Requirements definition is a process that should be completed in the following order:
   a. Document, identify, verify, and validate
   b. Identify, verify, validate, and document
   c. Characterize, analyze, validate, and verify
   d. Analyze, verify, validate, and characterize

The correct option is *b*. The proper order for completing the Requirements Definition phase is Option *b*. Documentation would not be done first, thus eliminating Option *a*. "Characterize" in Options *c* or *d* is not correct.

5. A path by which a malicious actor gains access to a computer or network in order to deliver a malicious payload is
   a. Penetration test
   b. Attack vector
   c. Vulnerability assessment
   d. Risk assessment

   The correct option is *b*. Option *b* is the definition of an attack vector. Risk and vulnerability assessments and penetration testing deal with ways of analyzing and protecting the system.

6. Which of the following is useful as a guide for the development, evaluation, and/or procurement of IT products with security functionality?
   a. ISO/IEC 27001
   b. FIPS 140-2
   c. Common Criteria
   d. SEI-CMM

   The correct option is *c*. FIPS 140-2 deals with assessing type 2 encryption, SEI-CMM is the capability maturity model, and ISO/IEC 27001 deals with the overall system security posture based on best practice implementation.

7. Which of the following defines evaluation criteria for Protection Profile (PP) and Security Target (ST) and presents evaluation assurance levels rating assurance for the TOE?
   a. Part 3—Security assurance requirements
   b. Part 2—Security functional requirements
   c. Part 1—Introduction and general model
   d. Part 4—History and previous versions

   The correct option is *a*. Parts 2 and 1 deal with other security requirements and general CC model and part 4 does not exist.

8. The National Voluntary Laboratory Accreditation Program (NVLAP) must be in full conformance with which of the following standards?
   a. ISO/IEC 27001 and 27002
   b. ISO/IEC 17025 and Guide 58
   c. NIST SP 800-53A
   d. ANSI/ISO/IEC Standard 17024

   The correct option is *b*. Option *a* deals with best practice implementation on the system. Option *c* provides IA controls for federal government systems, and Option *d* is the standard for certifications such as the CISSP®.

9. A software application in combination with an operating system, a workstation, smart card integrated circuit, or cryptographic processor would be considered examples of a
   a. Functional Communications (FCO)

    b. Functional Trusted Path (FTP)

    c. Target of Evaluation (TOE)

    d. Security Target (ST)

The correct option is *c*. Options *a* and *b* refer to families of security functions, and Option *d* refers to the evaluation criteria that TOE (Option *c*) will be assessed by.

10. An ISSAP® requires a device with a moderate level of independently assured security, and a thorough investigation of the TOE and its development without substantial reengineering. It should be evaluated at which CC EAL?

    a. EAL6

    b. EAL5

    c. EAL4

    d. EAL3

The correct option is *d*. Option *d* refers to the criteria for EAL3 evaluation by definition. EAL6 is semiformally verified design and tested, EAL5 is semiformally designed but not verified, and EAL4 is methodically designed, tested, and reviewed.

11. At which CC EAL would an ISSAP® select a device appropriate for application in extremely high-risk situations or where the high value of the assets justifies the higher costs?

    a. EAL4

    b. EAL5

    c. EAL6

    d. EAL7

The correct option is *d*. Again, Option *d* refers to the criteria for EAL 7 evaluation by definition. EAL6 is semiformally verified design and tested, EAL 5 is semiformally designed but not verified, and EAL 4 is methodically designed, tested, and reviewed. Options *a*, *b*, or *c* would not be appropriate for extremely high-risk situations.

12. A list of Common Criteria–evaluated products can be found on the Internet on the site at the

    a. NIAP

    b. CCEVS

    c. IASE

    d. CERIS

The correct option is *b*. NIAP is the partnership between NIST and NSA for the evaluation of products, and IASE is the site run by DISA to promote best security practices. CERIS is a consortium run by the University of Notre Dame Computer Science and Information Security department. CCEVS is the site that lists all evaluated products, those in the evaluation process, and those that have been removed or superseded.

13. Which of the following describes the purpose of the Capability Maturity Model?

a. Determine business practices to ensure creditability for the company's commitment to quality and excellence.

b. Provide assurance through active investigation and evaluation of the IT product in order to determine its security properties.

c. Establish a metric to judge in a repeatable way the maturity of an organization's software process as compared to the state of the industry practice.

d. Provide an overview of standards related to the Information Security Management family for uniformity and consistency of fundamental terms and definitions.

The correct option is *c*. Options *a* and *d* are from ISO/IEC 27001, and Option *b* is from the Common Criteria.

14. Which one of the following describes the key practices that correspond to a range of maturity levels 1–5?

a. Common Criteria

b. SEI-CMM

c. ISO/IEC 27002

d. IATF v3

The correct option is *b*. It is the only option that discusses maturity levels. Options *a*, *c*, and *d* are standards and processes.

15. Which of the following CMMI levels include quantitative process management and software quality management as the capstone activity?

a. CMMI Level 5

b. CMMI Level 4

c. CMMI Level 3

d. CMMI Level 2

The correct option is *b*. CMMI Level 4 includes quantitative process management and software quality management as the capstone activity.

16. Where can the general principles of the OSI Reference Model architecture be found that describes the OSI layers and what layering means?

a. Clause 3

b. Clause 5

c. Clause 7

d. Clause 9

The correct option is *b*. ISO 7498 discusses the OSI model. Within the model are clauses that describe the basis reference model. Clause 7 provides the description of the specific layers, and Clause 9 specifies compliance and consistency with the OSI reference model. Clause 3 does not exist.

17. A company processing, storing, or transmitting payment card data must be compliant with which of the following?

a. Gramm–Leach–Bliley Act (GLBA)

b. Health Insurance Portability and Accountability Act (HIPAA)

c. Sarbanes–Oxley Act of 2002

d. PCI-DSS

The correct option is *d*. Options *a*, *b* and *c* do not have anything to do with card payment or credit card data.

18. In which phase of the IATF does formal risk assessment begin?
    a. Assess effectiveness
    b. Design system security architecture
    c. Define system security requirements
    d. Discover information protection needs

    The correct option is *b*. Although risk assessment occurs during the assess effectiveness process after each stage, a formal risk assessment is conducted at the end of the Design System Security Architecture phase.

19. Which of the following describes a methodical examination of a work product by the author's coworkers to comment, identify, and categorize defects in the work product?
    a. Formal inspection
    b. Structured walkthrough
    c. Critique
    d. Peer review

    The correct option is *d*. The overall methodical examination of the work is called the peer review. The others are specific types of peer review.

20. Which of the following is a critical element in the design validation phase?
    a. Develop security test and evaluation plan
    b. Develop protection needs elicitation
    c. Develop the concept of operation
    d. Requirements analysis

    The correct option is *a*. Design validation culminates with the development of test and evaluation plans. It requires elicitation, requirements analysis, and concept of operations to be done in the early stages before the design is developed.

Chapter 5: Technology-Related Business Continuity Planning and Disaster Recovery Planning

1. Which phrase best defines a business continuity/disaster recovery plan?
   a. A set of plans for preventing a disaster
   b. An approved set of preparations and sufficient procedures for responding to a disaster
   c. A set of preparations and procedures for responding to a disaster without management approval
   d. The adequate preparations and procedures for the continuation of all business functions

   The correct option is *d*. The plan needs to be written for the recovery of all business operations and the technology that supports them.

2. Which of the following statements best describes the extent to which an organization should address business continuity or disaster recovery planning?
   a. Continuity planning is a significant corporate issue and should include all parts or functions of the company.
   b. Continuity planning is a significant technology issue, and the recovery of technology should be its primary focus.
   c. Continuity planning is required only where there is complexity in voice and data communications.
   d. Continuity planning is a significant management issue and should include the primary functions specified by management.

   The correct option is *a*. Recovering from an expected disruption to normal operations requires a plan addressing all parts of the organization.

3. Risk analysis is performed to identify
   a. The impacts of a threat to the business operations
   b. The exposures to loss of the organization
   c. The impacts of a risk on the company
   d. The way to eliminate threats

   The correct option is *b*. Risk Analysis identifies the different risk exposures a company has so that mitigation plans can be identified and agreed on, including a Business Continuity Plan.

4. During the risk analysis phase of the planning, which of the following actions could manage threats or mitigate the effects of an event?
   a. Modifying the exercise scenario
   b. Developing recovery procedures
   c. Increasing reliance on key individuals
   d. Implementing procedural controls

   The correct option is *d*. Implementing procedural controls is one method of managing an identified risk.

5. The reason to implement additional controls or safeguards is to
   a. Deter or remove the risk.
   b. Remove the risk and eliminate the threat.
   c. Reduce the impact of the threat.
   d. Identify the risk and the threat.

   The correct option is *c*. You cannot eliminate a threat; you can only reduce the impact a threat can have on your organization.

6. Which of the following statements most accurately describe business impact analysis?
   a. Risk analysis and business impact analysis are two different terms describing the same project effort.
   b. A business impact analysis calculates the probability of disruptions to the organization.
   c. A business impact analysis is critical to development of a business continuity plan.

d. A business impact analysis establishes the effect of disruptions on the organization.

The correct option is *d*. A business impact analysis identifies what would happen to the organization if a risk occurred, despite whatever controls were in place.

7. The term *disaster recovery* commonly refers to:
   a. The recovery of the business operations
   b. The recovery of the technology environment
   c. The recovery of the manufacturing environment
   d. The recovery of the business and technology environments

The correct option is *b*. Disaster recovery has been commonly used to define the process and procedures used to recover the technology supporting the business operations.

8. Which of the following terms best describe the effort to determine the consequences of disruptions that could result from a disaster?
   a. Business impact analysis
   b. Risk analysis
   c. Risk assessment
   d. Project problem definition

The correct option is *a*. A business impact analysis identifies what would happen to the organization if a risk occurred, despite whatever controls were in place.

9. A key advantage of using a cold site as a recovery option is that it
   a. Is a less expensive recovery option
   b. Can be configured and operationalized for any business function
   c. Is preconfigured for communications and can be customized for business functions
   d. Is the most available option for testing server recovery and communications restorations

The correct option is *a*. A cold site is less expensive because it is commonly a space to house recovery but without any infrastructure in place. Everything is recovered at the time of disaster.

10. The term RTO means
    a. Recovery time for operations
    b. Return to order
    c. Resumption time order
    d. Recovery time objective

The correct option is *d*. RTO refers to the time the technology or business operation is planned to be operational following a disruption.

11. If a company wants the fastest time to restore from tape backup, it should perform backup using the following method:
    a. Full backup
    b. Incremental backup

c. Partial backup

d. Differential backup

The correct option is *a*. A full backup copies all of the data each time it is run. When you recover from a full backup, no other backups are needed. In contrast, when an incremental backup is used in recovery, the full backup must be restored first, and then each incremental backup since the last full backup was made of the data must be sequentially restored before the data can be used.

12. One of the advantages of a hot site recovery solution is

a. Lowered expense

b. High availability

c. No downtime

d. No maintenance required

The correct option is *b*. A hot site has all the technology in place for recovery, so the time from the point where the disaster is declared and the time when the recovery is complete is much shorter.

13. Which of the following methods is not acceptable for exercising the business continuity plan?

a. Tabletop exercise

b. Call exercise

c. Simulated exercise

d. Halting a production application or function

The correct option is *d*. It is important not to create a disaster in the business when testing for the recovery from one.

14. Which of the following is the primary desired result of any well-planned business continuity exercise?

a. Identification of plan strengths and weaknesses

b. Satisfaction of management requirements

c. Compliance with auditor's requirements

d. Maintenance of shareholder confidence

The correct option is *a*. The purpose of conducting any exercise is to find out what works and what does not so that any weaknesses can be addressed before an actual event.

15. A business continuity plan should be updated and maintained

a. Immediately following an exercise

b. Following a major change in personnel

c. After installing new software

d. On an ongoing basis

The correct option is *d*. The plan needs to be updated regularly in order to maintain its viability to recover the business in a real event.

16. The primary reason to build a business continuity and disaster recovery plan is

a. To continue the business

b. To restore the data center

c. To meet regulatory environments

d. Because the customers expect it

The correct option is *a*. The primary purpose of business continuity and disaster recovery is to make sure the business survives.

17. A company would chose to use synchronous remote replication for its data recovery strategy if

a. It wanted to replace point-in-time backups.

b. It wanted to minimize the amount of time taken to recover.

c. Time to recovery and data loss are important to the business.

d. Distance limitations existed.

The correct option is *c*. Synchronous remote replication is used to support business operations when the loss incurred by downtime is so substantial that it justifies the expense of implementing this solution.

18. One of the reasons asynchronous replication differs from synchronous replication is

a. Because it can impact production

b. Because it can be done over greater distances

c. Because it involves less loss of data

d. Because it improves recovery time

The correct option is *b*. Because asynchronous replication does not require that the data be written at the remote site at the same time as the production site, network latency is not as critical as it is in synchronous replication. It can therefore occur over greater distances.

19. The purpose of doing a cost–benefit analysis on the different recovery strategies is

a. To make certain the cost of protection does not exceed the cost of the risk it is protecting

b. To determine the cost of implementing the recovery strategy

c. To determine that the strategy will be effective

d. To analyze the cost of the different strategies

The correct option is *a*. The recovery strategies implemented should match the business being protected.

20. Which of the following should a planner *never* do during the planning stages of a test or exercise?

a. Let test participants know what the scenario for the test will be.

b. Use prestage tapes for the recovery exercise at the alternate site.

c. Plan for the test to be successful.

d. Document a test timeline.

The correct option is *c*. The reason for testing is to find out what does not work so that changes can be made in the recovery strategies to improve the recovery capabilities. If we knew it all worked, we would not bother to test at all.

Chapter 6: Telecommunications and Network Security

1. Compare the frequency range of a person's voice to the size of the passband in a voice communications channel obtained over the telephone. How do you account for the difference between the two?

   a. The telephone company uses Gaussian filters to remove frequencies below 300 Hz and above 3300 Hz because the primary information of a voice conversation occurs in the passband.

   b. The telephone company uses low-pass and high-pass filters to remove frequencies below 300 Hz and above 3300 Hz because the primary information of a voice conversation occurs in the passband.

   c. The telephone company uses packet filters to remove frequencies below 500 Hz and above 4400 Hz because the primary information of a voice conversation occurs in the passband.

   d. The telephone company uses low-pass and high-pass filters to remove frequencies below 500 Hz and above 4400 Hz because the primary information of a voice conversation occurs in the passband.

   The correct option is *b*. The frequency range of a person's voice typically varies between 0 and 20 kHz, while a telephone channel has a passband of 3 kHz. The telephone company uses low-pass and high-pass filters to remove frequencies below 300 Hz and above 3300 Hz because the primary information of a voice conversation occurs in the passband. This allows more channels to be multiplexed onto a wideband circuit.

2. What is the data rate of a PCM-encoded voice conversation?

   a. 128 kbps

   b. 64 kbps

   c. 256 kbps

   d. 512 kbps

   The correct option is *b*. The data rate of PCM-encoded voice conversation is 64 kbps.

3. How many digitized voice channels can be transported on a T1 line?

   a. Up to 48

   b. Up to 12

   c. Up to 60

   d. Up to 24

   The correct option is *d*. There can be up to 24 digitized voice channels on a T1 line.

4. How many T1 lines can be transported on a T3 circuit?

   a. 12

   b. 18

   c. 24

   d. 36

The correct option is *c*. Up to 24 T1 lines can be transported on a T3 circuit.

5. The three advantages accruing from the use of a packet network in comparison to the use of the switched telephone network are a potential lower cost of use, a lower error rate as packet network nodes perform error checking and correction, and

   a. The ability of packet networks to automatically reserve resources
   b. The greater security of packet networks
   c. The ability of packet networks to automatically reroute data calls
   d. Packet networks establish a direct link between sender and receiver

   The correct option is *c*. Three advantages associated with the use of packet networks in comparison to the use of the public switched telephone network include a potential lower cost of use, a lower error rate as packet network nodes perform error checking and correction, and the ability of packet networks to automatically reroute data calls.

6. Five VoIP architecture concerns include

   a. The end-to-end delay associated with packets carrying digitized voice, jitter, the method of voice digitization used, the packet loss rate, and security
   b. The end-to-end delay associated with packets carrying digitized voice, jitter, attenuation, the packet loss rate, and security
   c. The end-to-end delay associated with packets carrying digitized voice, jitter, the amount of fiber in the network, the packet loss rate, and security
   d. The end-to-end delay associated with packets carrying digitized voice, jitter, the method of voice digitization used, attenuation, and security

   The correct option is *a*. Five VoIP architecture concerns include the end-to-end delay associated with packets carrying digitized voice, jitter, the method of voice digitization used, the packet loss rate, and security.

7. What is the major difference between encrypting analog and digitized voice conversations?

   a. Analog voice is encrypted by shifting portions of frequency, making the conversation unintelligible.
   b. Digitized voice is generated by the matrix addition of a fixed key to each digitized bit of the voice conversation.
   c. Analog voice is encrypted by shifting portions of amplitude to make the conversation unintelligible.
   d. Digitized voice is encrypted by the modulo-2 addition of a fixed key to each digitized bit of the voice conversation.

   The correct option is *a*. Analog voice is encrypted by shifting portions of frequency to make the conversation unintelligible. In comparison, the encryption of digitized voice occurs by the modulo-2 addition of a random key to each digitized bit of the voice conversation.

8. In communications, what is the purpose of authentication?

   a. Establishing a link between parties in a conversation or transaction

b. Ensuring that data received has not been altered

c. Securing wireless transmission

d. Verifying the other party in a conversation or transaction

The correct option is *d*. Authentication is the process of verifying the other party in a conversation or transaction.

9. What is the purpose of integrity?

   a. Integrity is a process that ensures data received has not been altered.

   b. Integrity is a process that ensures a person stands by his beliefs.

   c. Integrity is a process that ensures that the amount of data sent equals the amount of data received.

   d. Integrity is a process that ensures data received has been encrypted.

The correct option is *a*. Integrity is a process that ensures data received has not been altered.

10. The key purpose of the Session Initiation Protocol (SIP) is to

   a. Define the protocol required to establish and tear down communications, including voice and video calls flowing over a packet network.

   b. Define the signaling required to establish and tear down communications, including voice and video calls flowing over a PSTN.

   c. Define the protocol required to establish and tear down communications, including voice and video calls flowing over a circuit-switched network.

   d. Define the signaling required to establish and tear down communications, including voice and video calls flowing over a packet network.

The correct option is *d*. SIP defines the signaling required to establish and tear down communications to include voice and video calls flowing over a packet network.

11. Briefly describe the H.323 protocol.

   a. It represents an umbrella recommendation from the ITU that covers a variety of standards for audio, video, and data communications across circuit-switched networks.

   b. It provides port-based authentication, requiring a wireless device to be authenticated prior to its gaining access to a LAN and its resources.

   c. It defines the protocol required to establish and tear down communications, including voice and video calls flowing over a packet network.

   d. It represents an umbrella recommendation from the ITU that covers a variety of standards for audio, video, and data communications across packet-based networks and, more specifically, IP-based networks.

The correct option is *d*. The H.323 standard can be considered to represent an umbrella recommendation from the International Telecommunications Union (ITU) that covers a variety of standards for audio, video, and data communications across packet-based networks and, more specifically, IP-based networks such as the Internet and corporate Intranets.

12. What is the difference between RTP and RTCP?
    a. RTP defines a standardized port for delivering audio and video over the Internet, while the RTCP provides out-of-band control information for an RTP port.
    b. RTP defines the protocol required to establish and tear down communications, including voice and video calls flowing over a packet network, while the RTCP provides out-of-band control information for an RTP port.
    c. RTP defines a standardized packet format for delivering audio and video over the Internet, while the RTCP provides out-of-band control information for an RTP flow.
    d. RTP defines a standardized port for delivering audio and video over the Internet, while the RTCP defines the protocol required to establish and tear down communications, including voice and video calls flowing over a packet network.

    The correct option is *c*. The Real Time Protocol (RTP) defines a standardized packet format for delivering audio and video over the Internet, while the Real Time Control Protocol (RTCP) provides out-of-band control information for an RTP flow.

13. List the components defined by the H.323 standard.
    a. Terminal, gateway, gatekeeper, multipoint control unit (MCU), multipoint controller, multipoint processor, and H.323 proxy
    b. Path, gateway, gatekeeper, multipoint control unit (MCU), multipoint controller, multipoint processor, and H.323 proxy
    c. Terminal, gateway, gatekeeper, multipoint control unit (MCU), multipoint transmitter, multipoint receiver, and H.323 proxy
    d. Protocol, terminal, gatekeeper, multipoint control unit (MCU), multipoint controller, multipoint processor, and H.323 proxy

    The correct option is *a*. The H.323 standard defines the following components: Terminal, Gateway, Gatekeeper, MCU (Multipoint Control Unit), Multipoint Controller, Multipoint Processor, and H.323 Proxy.

14. What are some of the major functions performed by a security modem?
    a. Allows remote access to occur from trusted locations, may encrypt data, and may support Caller ID to verify the calling telephone number
    b. Allows remote access to occur from any location, may encrypt data, and may support Caller ID to verify the calling telephone number
    c. Allows remote access to occur from a mobile location, may encrypt data, and may support Caller ID to verify the calling telephone number
    d. Allows remote access to occur from trusted locations, may encrypt data, and may identify the calling telephone number

    The correct option is *a*. A security modem represents a special type of modem that allows remote access to occur from trusted locations, may encrypt data, and may support caller ID to verify the calling telephone number.

15. The major difference between a router and firewall lies in three areas:
    a. The transfer of packets based on routing tables, the degree of packet inspection, and ensuring that the header data is correct
    b. The transfer of packets based on absolute addresses, the degree of packet inspection, and acting as an intermediate device by hiding the address of clients from users on the Internet
    c. The transfer of packets based on routing tables, the degree of packet inspection, and acting as an intermediate device by hiding the address of clients from users on the Internet
    d. The transfer of packets based on routing tables, the degree of packet inspection, and creating a DMZ behind Internet-facing applications

    The correct option is *c*. The major difference between a router and firewall lies in three areas: the transfer of packets based on routing tables, the degree of packet inspection, and acting as an intermediate device by hiding the address of clients from users on the Internet, a technique referred to as acting as a proxy.

16. What is the purpose of an intrusion detection system (IDS)?
    a. To hide the address of clients from users on the Internet
    b. To detect unwanted attempts to access, manipulate, and even disable networking hardware and computers connected to a network
    c. To detect and respond to predefined events
    d. To prevent unauthorized access to controlled areas within a site or a building

    The correct option is *b*. An IDS represents hardware or software that is specifically designed to detect unwanted attempts at accessing, manipulating, and even disabling networking hardware and computers connected to a network. In comparison, an IPS represents an active system that detects and responds to predefined events. Thus, the IPS represents technology built on an IDS system. This means that the ability of the IPS to prevent intrusions from occurring is highly dependent on the underlying IDS.

17. What are the two methods that can be used for wireless LAN communications?
    a. Peer-to-peer and infrastructure
    b. Peer-to-peer and cloud
    c. Cloud and infrastructure
    d. Peer-to-peer and remote

    The correct option is *a*. Wireless LANs can communicate is two different ways referred to as peer-to-peer and infrastructure.

18. What is the benefit of WPA over WEP for enhancing wireless LAN security?
    a. WPA permits the equivalent of wired network privacy and includes the use of TKIP to enhance data encryption.

b. WPA implements a large portion of the IEEE 802.11i and includes the use of TKIP to enhance data encryption.

c. WPA implements a large portion of the IEEE 802.11i and includes the use of IKE to enhance data encryption.

d. WPA implements IEEE 802.11a and g and includes the use of IKE to enhance data encryption.

The correct option is *b*. The original security for wireless LANs, referred to as Wired Equivalent Privacy (WEP), permits the equivalent of wired network privacy and nothing more. WEP was broken by several persons many years ago. WPA represents a security protocol created by the Wi-Fi Alliance to secure wireless transmission and was created in response to the security weakness of WEP. This protocol implements a large portion of the IEEE wireless security standard referred to as 802.11i and WPA included the use of the Temporal Key Integrity Protocol (TKIP) to enhance data encryption.

19. What is the purpose of the IEEE 802.1X standard?

a. To provide port-based authentication

b. To provide port-based authorization

c. To detect and respond to predefined events

d. To secure wireless transmission

The correct option is *a*. The IEEE 802.1X standard provides port-based authentication, requiring a wireless device to be authenticated prior to its gaining access to a LAN and its resources. Under this standard, the client node is referred to as a supplicant while the authenticator is usually an access point or a wired Ethernet switch.

Index